TODAY WHEN YOU HEAR HIS VOICE

Today When You Hear His Voice

Scripture, the Covenants, and the People of God

Gregory W. Lee

WILLIAM B. EERDMANS PUBLISHING COMPANY
GRAND RAPIDS, MICHIGAN

© 2016 Gregory W. Lee
All rights reserved

Published 2016 by
Wm. B. Eerdmans Publishing Co.
2140 Oak Industrial Drive N.E., Grand Rapids, Michigan 49505

Library of Congress Cataloging-in-Publication Data

Names: Lee, Gregory W., 1978- author.
Title: Today when you hear His voice: scripture, the covenants, and the people of God / Gregory W. Lee.
Description: Grand Rapids, Michigan: Eerdmans Publishing Company, 2016. | Includes bibliographical references and index.
Identifiers: LCCN 2016002488 | ISBN 9780802873279 (pbk.: alk. paper)
Subjects: LCSH: Bible. Hebrews — Criticism, interpretation, etc. |
Bible. Hebrews — Relation to the Old Testament. |
Bible — Hermeneutics. | Bible — Canon. |
Bible — Criticism, interpretation, etc.
Classification: LCC BS2775.52 .L44 2016 | DDC 220.6 — dc23
LC record available at http://lccn.loc.gov/2016002488

www.eerdmans.com

For Jeanette, Remy, and Audrey

Contents

	Abbreviations	viii
	Acknowledgments	ix
	Introduction	1
1.	Augustine of Hippo: Signs and Realities	17
2.	John Calvin: The Unitary Covenant of Christ	58
3.	The Epistle to the Hebrews: God's New Covenant with Israel	114
4.	The Epistle to the Hebrews: Approaching the Psalms	143
5.	Hearing the Living Word: Scripture and the Divine Address	179
6.	Witnessing the Living Word: Scripture and Tradition	218
	Conclusion	265
	Bibliography	270
	Author Index	304
	Subject Index	307
	Scripture Index	311

Abbreviations

All abbreviations not included here follow
The SBL Handbook of Style (2nd edition).

CO   *Ioannis Calvini opera quae supersunt omnia,* ed. G. Baum, E. Cunitz, and E. Reuss, *Corpus Reformatorum,* vols. 29-87 (Brunswick and Berlin, 1863-1900)

CTS Calvin Translation Society (Edinburgh, 1844-56; reprinted in 22 vols., Grand Rapids: Baker, 2003)

OE   *Ioannis Calvini opera omnia, Series 2: Opera exegetica veteris et novi testamenti* (Geneva, 1992-)

OS   *Johannis Calvini opera selecta,* ed. P. Barth, W. Niesel, and D. Scheuner, 5 vols. (Munich, 1926-62)

PLS *Patrologiae Cursus Completus, Series Latina, Supplementum,* ed. A. Hamman, 3 vols. (Paris, 1958-63)

ST   *Summa Theologiae*

WSA The Works of St. Augustine: A Translation for the 21st Century, ed. J. Rotelle (New York, 1990-)

Acknowledgments

This work represents an expansion and complete revision of a dissertation I completed through the Duke Graduate Program in Religion. My first thanks are therefore to my advisor, Geoffrey Wainwright, for his sage, careful, and evenhanded guidance throughout this project. I am also thankful to my dissertation committee for constructive feedback during the writing process and beyond: Paul Griffiths, Stanley Hauerwas, Richard Hays, Reinhard Hütter, and Kavin Rowe. Other Duke faculty members who have taught me much include Elizabeth Clark, Hans Hillerbrand, Joel Marcus, Ed Sanders, Warren Smith, and David Steinmetz. I will always be grateful to David Aers for introducing me to *City of God*. Lawrence Richardson and Reginald Foster not only taught me Latin but also assisted with various translation issues.

A vibrant graduate student community at Duke enlivened and enriched my studies: in theology, Natalie Carnes and Matthew Whelan, Ben Dillon, Keith E. Johnson, Sean Larsen, and Sheryl Overmyer; in New Testament, Hans Arneson, Nathan Eubank, T. J. Lang, and Matthew Thiessen; in early Christianity, Maria Doerfler and Tom McGlothlin; in Reformation, David Fink. Much of what I know about Hebrews may be attributed to David Moffitt.

Wheaton College has provided a stimulating new venue to pursue theology for the church. I am especially grateful to Dan Treier for extensive feedback on the entirety of the manuscript in addition to close direction throughout the publishing process. Amy Peeler offered helpful comments on the third and fourth chapters. Kevin Vanhoozer, my teacher at Trinity Evangelical Divinity School, laid the intellectual foundations for my doctoral studies and provided useful feedback in the later stages of this project. I have felt strongly supported by two Associate Deans, Jeff Greenman and

ACKNOWLEDGMENTS

his successor, Jeff Bingham, as well Dean of Humanities and Theological Studies, Jill Baumgaertner. George Kalantzis deserves special mention as both mentor and friend through The Wheaton Center for Early Christian Studies. Other colleagues who have contributed richly to my academic efforts include Keith L. Johnson, Beth Jones, Tim Larsen, David Lauber, and Matt Milliner.

Janet Xiao and Ashish Varma provided valuable assistance on bibliographic matters, and Darren Yau helped prepare the indexes. I am deeply indebted to Jon Hoglund for editing the entirety of the manuscript. I could not have completed this project without Scrivener.

I am thankful to Michael Thomson, Andrew Knapp, and the team at Eerdmans for their willingness to take a chance on a new author and their work in bringing this project to fruition. David Chao coached me through the world of academic publishing.

Three worshiping communities played an important role in the completion of this project. From Manna Christian Fellowship, David H. Kim led the senior small group on Hebrews that initiated my interest in this topic. Our alumni community supported me through the most challenging phase of my studies. For vocational encouragement, special thanks go to Risa Toha and Dave Fernandez, Bo Karen Lee, and Paul Lim. I could not have imagined a better church for my doctoral studies than Blacknall Memorial Presbyterian Church and I am especially appreciative of Allan Poole for supporting so many of us during our training to serve academy and church. Though my wife and I discovered Lawndale Christian Community Church toward the end of this project, no church has displayed more for me what I came to argue in this book. Special thanks to Wayne "Coach" Gordon, Joseph Atkins, Darryl Saffore, Kingdom Men, Hope House, and so many others who have welcomed us into the neighborhood and taught us what it means to love God and neighbor.

Finally, my greatest debts are to my family. I am thoroughly thankful for years of patient support, personal and financial, from my parents, Yoon Joo and Sook Ja, as well as my sister, Christine, and her husband, Ryan. Few will be gladder to see this work come to fruition. My nephew and niece, WonGi and EunHae, have made most delightful companions along the ride.

Everything changed when I met Jeanette, my long-awaited match. Her companionship is a daily reminder of God's grace to me, and the arrival of our children, Jeremy and Audrey, has only amplified the richness of our life together. I have never felt more undeservedly blessed. This book is for my best friend and the children we hold so dear.

Introduction

The most obvious and perplexing feature of Christian Scripture is that it consists of two parts. The early Christian movement did not arise out of whole cloth but as a historical continuation of the Jewish people, and its first authors perceived their developing community as the fulfillment of God's promises to Israel. This meant reading Israel's Scriptures in fresh ways, not least as testimony to a crucified messiah and a pneumatic new fellowship that hoped for the culmination of God's purposes in history. As what came to be called the "New Testament" took form, Christians would adopt as canon a composite, bipartite Scripture consisting of both earlier authoritative writings and a second collection of texts that, it was claimed, provided authoritative guidance on how that first set of texts should be received.

The appropriation of one community's sacred writings by another group does not go down easily and, it may be stated without exaggeration, the proper interpretation of the Old Testament constituted the central question of early Christian self-definition. This challenge first emerges in the New Testament, where Paul's ministry to the Gentiles prompts a series of difficulties about the nature and purpose of the Mosaic law, the calling of the Gentiles, and God's faithfulness to the Jewish people. The earliest recorded council in Christian history preeminently concerns the proper understanding of Israel's Scriptures in light of the new reality that God has extended his mercy to the Gentiles (Acts 15). Later writers like Justin, Irenaeus, Tertullian, and Origen continue this debate with a variety of opponents — Jews, Gnostics, Marcionites, and pagans, interlocutors both fictitious and real — with all asserting in one way or another a unity between the testaments, the legitimacy of Christian nonobservance of

Jewish practices, and the necessity of reading the Old Testament in light of Christ.[1]

At least two perplexities arise from this history, demanding theological reflection. First, there was no general consensus on the precise shape of this unity or the preparatory character of the Old Testament, and post-apostolic writers arguably departed from the New Testament's own manner of appropriating the Old.[2] Paul's key concern in Romans and Galatians

---

1. Justin Martyr, *Dialogue with Trypho;* Irenaeus, *Adversus Haereses;* Tertullian, *Adversus Marcionem;* Origen, *De Principiis* and *Contra Celsum.*

2. For studies and proposals on this matter, see Wilhelm Vischer, *The Witness of the Old Testament to Christ,* vol. 1: *The Pentateuch,* trans. A. B. Crabtree (orig. 1936; London: Lutterworth, 1949); Leonhard Goppelt, *Typos: The Typological Interpretation of the Old Testament in the New,* trans. Donald H. Madvig (orig. 1939; Grand Rapids: Eerdmans, 1982; Eugene, OR: Wipf and Stock, 2002); Erich Auerbach, "Figura," in his *Scenes from the Drama of European Literature,* trans. Ralph Manheim, Theory and History of European Literature 9 (orig. 1944; Minneapolis: University of Minnesota Press, 1984), 11-76; idem, *Mimesis: The Representation of Reality in Western Literature,* trans. Willard R. Trask (orig. 1953; Princeton: Princeton University Press, 2003); R. P. C. Hanson, *Allegory and Event: A Study of the Sources and the Significance of Origen's Interpretation of Scripture* (1959; Louisville: Westminster John Knox, 2002); Jean Daniélou, *From Shadows to Reality: Studies in the Biblical Typology of the Fathers,* trans. Don Wulstan Hibberd (Westminster, MD: Newman, 1960); Beryl Smalley, *The Study of the Bible in the Middle Ages* (Notre Dame, IN: University of Notre Dame Press, 1964); James Samuel Preus, *From Shadow to Promise: Old Testament Interpretation from Augustine to the Young Luther* (Cambridge, MA: Belknap, 1969); Hans W. Frei, *The Eclipse of Biblical Narrative: A Study in Eighteenth and Nineteenth Century Hermeneutics* (New Haven: Yale University Press, 1974); Brevard S. Childs, *Biblical Theology in Crisis* (Philadelphia: Westminster, 1970); idem, *Biblical Theology of the Old and New Testaments* (Minneapolis: Fortress, 1992), 3-51; idem, "Old Testament in Germany 1920-1940: The Search for a New Paradigm," in *Altes Testament: Forschung und Wirkung: Festschrift für Henning Graf Reventlow,* ed. Peter Mommer and Winfried Thiel (Frankfurt am Main: Peter Lang, 1994), 233-46; John David Dawson, *Allegorical Readers and Cultural Revision in Ancient Alexandria* (Berkeley: University of California Press, 1992); idem, *Christian Figural Reading and the Fashioning of Identity* (Berkeley: University of California Press, 2002); Frances M. Young, *Biblical Exegesis and the Formation of Christian Culture* (Peabody, MA: Hendrickson, 1997); Geoffrey Wainwright, "Psalm 33 Interpreted of the Triune God," *ExAud* 16 (2000): 101-20; Matthew Levering, *Christ's Fulfillment of Torah and Temple: Salvation according to Thomas Aquinas* (Notre Dame, IN: University of Notre Dame Press, 2002); The Pontifical Biblical Commission, *The Jewish People and Their Sacred Scriptures in the Christian Bible* (Vatican City: Libreria Editrice Vaticana, 2002); John J. O'Keefe and R. R. Reno, *Sanctified Vision: An Introduction to Early Christian Interpretation of the Bible* (Baltimore: Johns Hopkins University Press, 2005); Peter W. Martens, "Revisiting the Allegory/Typology Distinction: The Case of Origen," *JECS* 16 (2008): 283-317; idem, *Origen and Scripture: The Contours of the Exegetical Life,* OECS (Oxford: Oxford University Press, 2012); David L. Baker, *Two*

Introduction

is whether circumcision is necessary for justification — whether, to put it crudely, Gentiles have to become Jews to become Christians. Yet (on one reading, at least) his treatment of these issues presupposes the legitimacy of Jewish institutions and God's ongoing faithfulness to the Jewish people, appealing for this latter point to Old Testament promises that assure him of Israel's eventual restoration to Christ. Only a century later, Justin presents circumcision as a mark of opprobrium that prepared the Jews to be identified more easily for destruction in the Bar Kochba revolt, as divine punishment for having killed their own messiah. In a remarkable transformation, the sign of the covenant has become a proleptic form of judgment, and the prophets' proclamation of Israel's restoration has become a denunciation of the Jewish covenant, now superseded by God's new covenant with (primarily Gentile) Christians.

Second, those who accused Christians of innovation had a point. Against both Jewish and pagan criticism, early Christian writers had to explain how Christians could profess allegiance to the Old Testament when they did not follow its ceremonies. The most common interpretive strategies — treating the practices as prefigurements of Christ, highlighting prophetic declarations of a new covenant with the nations — presumed the legitimacy of receiving the text in ways that were at least functionally unavailable before the incarnation. On the one hand, these authors claimed, Christian contentions about the new covenant do enjoy Scriptural warrant; the righteousness of God has been revealed according to the law and the prophets. On the other hand, something new has indeed been made manifest, yielding interpretive possibilities Jews could not formerly perceive. Implicit in this argument is a particular affirmation of progressive revelation: not only has a new testament been revealed, but the original witness to God's redemptive work is more fully understood than before.

This work responds to these observations by considering theologically the relation between salvation history and Scriptural interpretation. Given the relative interpretive license New Testament and early Christian writers employed with the Old Testament, what openness remains for Christians today as they continue to receive God's Word? I argue that the appropriation of the Old Testament trades essentially on decisions about the shape of

---

Testaments, One Bible: The Theological Relationship between the Old and New Testaments, 3rd ed. (Downers Grove, IL: InterVarsity, 2010); Christopher R. Seitz, *The Character of Christian Scripture: The Significance of a Two-Testament Bible*, STI (Grand Rapids: Baker Academic, 2011).

redemption, and that the relation between the testaments legitimates qualified hermeneutical novelty. If the New Testament authors do not identify canonical fixity with exegetical rigidity, the closing of the canon after the apostolic age does not discontinue but focuses this dynamic through the Spirit's ongoing testimony to Christ.

This study takes as its starting point the Epistle to the Hebrews. A neglected text, Hebrews has for much of its history been categorized with the writings of Paul. In recent years, it has been dismissed as a paradigmatic example of supersessionism.[3] But this epistle is a far more fruitful source of reflection on the relation between the testaments than has often been appreciated. Of all the New Testament witnesses, Hebrews provides the fullest discussion of the Levitical priesthood, the most sustained narrative of the Old Testament (except perhaps Acts 7), and the richest examples of Scripture being used as a word of direct address (Paul may be a competitor). Hebrews inspires the longstanding Christian distinction between shadow and reality, and its developed high priestly Christology earns the author a place alongside the Johannine material and the Pauline correspondence as one of the most developed theological voices in the New Testament.

The last several decades of scholarship have witnessed a resurgence of interest in the complexities of early Jewish–Christian relations,[4] prompt-

---

3. For a history of the interpretation of Hebrews, see Craig R. Koester, *Hebrews: A New Translation with Introduction and Commentary*, AB 36 (New York: Doubleday, 2001), 19-63; for early Christian interpretations of the text, see Rowan A. Greer, *The Captain of Our Salvation: A Study of the Patristic Exegesis of Hebrews*, BGBE 15 (Tübingen: Mohr [Siebeck], 1973); David M. Hay, *Glory at the Right Hand: Psalm 110 in Early Christianity*, SBLMS 18 (Atlanta: Society of Biblical Literature, 1973); Fred L. Horton, *The Melchizedek Tradition: A Critical Examination of the Sources to the Fifth Century A.D. and in the Epistle to the Hebrews* (Cambridge: Cambridge University Press, 1976); Erik M. Heen and Philip D. Krey, eds., *Hebrews*, ACCS 10 (Downers Grove, IL: InterVarsity, 2005). Much of the latter volume is organized around the commentary of Chrysostom, whom Calvin engages throughout his own commentary. See Chrysostom, *Homilies on The Epistle to the Hebrews*, NPNF[2] 14. See also Bruce Demarest, *A History of Interpretation of Hebrews 7, 1-10 from the Reformation to the Present*, BGBE 19 (Tübingen: Mohr [Siebeck], 1976).

4. Recent studies include Markus Bockmuehl, *Jewish Law in Gentile Churches: Halakhah and the Beginning of Christian Public Ethics* (Grand Rapids: Baker Academic, 2000); Judith Lieu, *Neither Jew nor Greek? Constructing Early Christianity* (London: T&T Clark, 2002); Daniel Boyarin, *Border Lines: The Partition of Judaeo-Christianity*, Divinations: Rereading Late Ancient Religion (Philadelphia: University of Pennsylvania Press, 2004); Adam H. Becker and Annette Yoshiko Reed, eds., *The Ways That Never Parted: Jews and Christians in Late Antiquity and the Early Middle Ages* (Minneapolis: Fortress, 2007).

Introduction

ing a movement to read the New Testament documents according to their Second Temple Jewish context, and to reconstrue the "parting of the ways" according to a far more variegated series of developments than has formerly been recognized. While Paul has received significant attention on these issues,[5] recent work reveals burgeoning curiosity in Hebrews for an alternative perspective on the same concerns.[6] Special attention has been drawn to the particularly Jewish character of the theology of Hebrews, which is free from Pauline concerns about Gentile Christianity, the redefinition of "Israel," and God's ongoing faithfulness to the Jews. There is in Hebrews no reference to the Gentile mission, no polemic against Jewish practices (besides the sacrificial system), and no ambivalence about Jewish distinctiveness. Hebrews thus provides an especially intriguing locus for theological reflection upon the relation between the covenants and the interpretation of the Old Testament.

---

5. Krister Stendahl, *Paul among Jews and Gentiles* (Philadelphia: Fortress, 1976); E. P. Sanders, *Paul and Palestinian Judaism: A Comparison of Patterns of Religion* (Minneapolis: Fortress, 1977); idem, *Paul, the Law, and the Jewish People* (Minneapolis: Fortress, 1983); idem, *Paul: A Very Short Introduction* (Oxford: Oxford University Press, 1991); James D. G. Dunn, *Romans 1–8* and *Romans 9–16*, 2 vols., WBC 38a-b (Dallas: Word, 1988); idem, *Jesus, Paul, and the Law* (Louisville: Westminster/John Knox, 1990); idem, *The Theology of Paul the Apostle* (Grand Rapids: Eerdmans, 1998); James D. G. Dunn, ed., *Paul and the Mosaic Law* (Grand Rapids: Eerdmans, 2001); N. T. Wright, *The Climax of the Covenant: Christ and the Law in Pauline Theology* (Minneapolis: Fortress, 1991); idem, *What Saint Paul Really Said: Was Paul of Tarsus the Real Founder of Christianity?* (Grand Rapids: Eerdmans, 1997); Daniel Boyarin, *A Radical Jew: Paul and the Politics of Identity* (Berkeley: University of California Press, 1994); D. A. Carson, Peter T. O'Brien, and Mark A. Seifrid, eds., *Justification and Variegated Nomism*, 2 vols. (Grand Rapids: Baker Academic, 2001-4); Seyoon Kim, *Paul and the New Perspective: Second Thoughts on the Origin of Paul's Gospel* (Grand Rapids: Eerdmans, 2002); Douglas Harink, *Paul among the Postliberals: Pauline Theology beyond Christendom and Modernity* (Grand Rapids: Brazos, 2003); Francis Watson, *Paul, Judaism, and the Gentiles: Beyond the New Perspective*, rev. and exp. ed. (Grand Rapids: Eerdmans, 2007). Also worth mentioning are E. P. Sanders, *Jesus and Judaism* (Minneapolis: Fortress, 1985); idem, *The Historical Figure of Jesus* (London: Penguin, 1993); Fabian E. Udoh et al., eds., *Redefining First-Century Jewish and Christian Identities: Essays in Honor of Ed Parish Sanders,* Christianity and Judaism in Antiquity 16 (Notre Dame, IN: University of Notre Dame Press, 2008); and an earlier article that helped animate Sanders's work, George Foot Moore, "Christian Writers on Judaism," *HTR* 14 (1921): 197-254.

6. Note this theme in three recent collections of essays: Gabriella Gelardini, ed., *Hebrews: Contemporary Methods — New Insights* (Leiden: Brill, 2005); Richard Bauckham et al., eds., *A Cloud of Witnesses: The Theology of Hebrews in Its Ancient Contexts,* LNTS 387 (London: T&T Clark, 2008); idem, *The Epistle to the Hebrews and Christian Theology* (Grand Rapids: Eerdmans, 2009). For more bibliography on Hebrews, see chapters 3-4.

I have chosen to treat Hebrews in dialogue with two crucial figures in Western Christian thought: Augustine and Calvin. This decision is of a piece with recent scholarly interest in the history of biblical interpretation,[7] and its particular value here lies in bringing the understanding of the covenants in Hebrews into distinct relief and highlighting the richness and implications of the epistle's theological vision. Comparison is perhaps the most effective means of drawing out individual particularity, and Augustine, Calvin, and Hebrews present Scripture and redemptive history very differently indeed. Calvin considers Augustine his chief theological influence, and those in the Reformed tradition trace a strong line of continuity between the two on issues such as predestination, grace, and free will. Yet this doctrinal convergence masks a striking contrast between the figures on biblical interpretation. While Augustine engages in the kind of spiritual interpretation that characterizes much of the early and medieval church, Calvin decries allegory and insists on the primacy and sufficiency of the literal sense. As we shall see, Hebrews offers still another approach to Israel's Scriptures, which does not match either Augustine's or Calvin's paradigms.

Consider for a moment one of Augustine's most daring (yet not atypical) displays of exegetical creativity, concerning David and Bath-

---

7. For general works on the history of biblical interpretation, see Robert M. Grant, with David Tracy, *A Short History of Biblical Interpretation*, 2nd ed. (Minneapolis: Fortress, 1984); P. R. Ackroyd and C. F. Evans, eds., *The Cambridge History of the Bible*, vol. 1: *From the Beginnings to Jerome* (Cambridge: Cambridge University Press, 1970); G. W. H. Lampe, ed., *The Cambridge History of the Bible*, vol. 2: *The West from the Fathers to the Reformation* (Cambridge: Cambridge University Press, 1969); S. L. Greenslade, ed., *The Cambridge History of the Bible*, vol. 3: *The West from the Reformation to the Present Day* (Cambridge: Cambridge University Press, 1963); Roy A. Harrisville and Walter Sundberg, *The Bible in Modern Culture: Baruch Spinoza to Brevard Childs*, 2nd ed. (Grand Rapids: Eerdmans, 2002); Michael Dauphinais and Matthew Levering, eds., *Reading John with St. Thomas Aquinas: Theological Exegesis and Speculative Theology* (Washington, DC: Catholic University of America Press, 2005); Thomas G. Weinandy, Daniel A. Keating, and John P. Yocum, eds., *Aquinas on Scripture: An Introduction to His Biblical Commentaries* (London: T&T Clark, 2005); Charles Kannengiesser, with special contributions by various scholars, *Handbook of Patristic Exegesis: The Bible in Ancient Christianity* (Leiden: Brill, 2006); Donald K. McKim, ed., *Dictionary of Major Biblical Interpreters* (Downers Grove, IL: InterVarsity, 2007); John L. Thompson, *Reading the Bible with the Dead: What You Can Learn from the History of Exegesis That You Can't Learn from Exegesis Alone* (Grand Rapids: Eerdmans, 2007); Alan J. Hauser and Duane F. Watson, *A History of Biblical Interpretation*, 2 vols. (Grand Rapids: Eerdmans, 2003-9). Note also the seminal David C. Steinmetz, "The Superiority of Pre-Critical Exegesis," *ThTo* 37 (1980): 27-38.

sheba.[8] "David" means "strong-handed" or "desirable," which correspond to passages that depict Jesus as the (strong) lion of Judah (Rev. 5:5) or the desire of the nations (Hag. 2:7). "Bathsheba" means "well of satiety" or "seventh well." She must represent the church, elsewhere called a well (Song of Sol. 4:15), since the Holy Spirit corresponds to the number seven — for seven times seven plus one (for unity) equals fifty, the day of Pentecost — and Jesus describes the Spirit as a well of living water that provides ultimate satisfaction (John 4:13-14). "Uriah" means "my light of God," while "Hittite" means "cut off." He, then, symbolizes the devil, who was cut off for taking pride in the light he received from God, yet continues to disguise himself as an angel of light (2 Cor. 11:14). Yes, Augustine says, David committed a grave crime with Bathsheba. But "that one desired by all the nations, nonetheless, loved the Church, who was bathing on the rooftop, that is, cleansing herself from the filth of the world and rising above and trampling upon its house of clay by spiritual contemplation. And, after having come to know her through his first encounter with her, he afterward completely removed the devil from her, killed him, and united her to himself in perpetual marriage. Let us hate the sin but not destroy the prophecy."[9] On Augustine's extraordinary reading, David's worst sins have become a picture of Jesus "committing adultery" with the church and then "murdering" Satan.

Calvin could not countenance such a reading, and his commentary on Galatians seizes Paul's discussion of Sarah and Hagar as an opportunity to castigate medieval allegory.[10] While Paul's particular illustration is entirely consistent with the literal sense, Origen and his followers exploited the apostle's use of the term "allegory" as an occasion for "torturing Scripture, in every possible manner, away from the true sense." Since the world will always prefer speculation to solid doctrine, Calvin laments,

> the licentious system gradually attained such a height, that he who handled Scripture for his own amusement not only was suffered to pass unpunished, but even obtained the highest applause. For many centuries no man was considered ingenious, who had not the skill and daring necessary for changing into a variety of curious shapes the sacred word of God. This was undoubtedly a contrivance of Satan to undermine

---

8. *C. Faust.* 22.87.
9. Ibid.
10. *Comm. Gal.* 4.22.

the authority of Scripture, and to take away from the reading of it the true advantage. God visited this profanation by a just judgment, when he suffered the pure meaning of the Scripture to be buried under false interpretations.

Calvin's Genesis commentary presents the following judgments on Augustine's exegetical suggestions: the Trinitarian treatment of the image of God is an "excessive refinement" that rests upon "subtleties";[11] one finds "scarcely anything solid" in the allegorical application of Noah's ark to the body of Christ;[12] the relation between the eighth day of circumcision and the resurrection rests on nothing "certain and solid";[13] the suggestion that "Jacob" refers to the patriarch's present life and "Israel" to his future life is "specious rather than solid."[14] Calvin does not reject all speculation: he is, for instance, "not dissatisfied" with Augustine's suggestion that the tree of life is a figure of Christ,[15] and he acknowledges "something in man which refers to the Father, and the Son, and the Holy Spirit."[16] It is nevertheless remarkable how freely Calvin dismisses a thinker he holds in the highest regard.

My project begins by identifying the conceptual structures that animate these differences and thus producing a theological rubric for delineating the distinctions of Hebrews's approach. The first two chapters establish a typological comparison between Augustine and Calvin that locates their divergence on allegory in their differences on the unity of the testaments. In short, the argument of these two chapters is that Augustine defines the continuity between the testaments according to a unity of reference whereby the Old Testament signifies the New. Calvin defines this relation according to a unity of identity according to which the one covenant of grace mediates Christ across both testaments. This divergence gives rise to another significant difference concerning Old Testament Israel, which Augustine substantially defines as a sign of the church, and Calvin simply identifies as the church during Old Testament times. Augustine's understanding of redemptive history funds his allegorical practices, since the literal sense is a sign of the spiritual, while Calvin's insistence on the unity of the covenant eliminates the need for a spiritual sense in favor of a literal

11. *Comm. Genesis* 1.26.
12. Ibid., 6.14.
13. Ibid., 17.12.
14. Ibid., 35.10.
15. Ibid., 2.9.
16. Ibid., 1.26.

Introduction

sense that can encompass different instantiations of the single covenant of grace. The purpose of these chapters is not to produce a full study of either figure, nor to trace Augustine's historical influence on Calvin, nor to explain their differences according to their sociocultural contexts.[17] The goal is simply to take theological soundings that prove conceptually illuminating for questions Hebrews helps address. The end of the second chapter provides a summary discussion of the issues that distinguish Augustine's positions from Calvin's.

The next two chapters consider the Epistle to the Hebrews and function as a hinge for the book. These chapters engage in detail with contemporary New Testament scholarship while continuing the dialogue with Augustine and Calvin. The first of these, chapter three, considers the vision of redemptive history in Hebrews, which I argue differs significantly from either Augustine's unity of reference or Calvin's unity of identity. Hebrews locates the discontinuity between the covenants in the establishment of Christ as high priest, and the continuity across the testaments in God's ongoing faithfulness to Israel and a common hope for an eternal inheritance. Against Calvin, there are two covenants and not one; against Augustine, there is one people and not two. Following this, chapter four explores Hebrews's appropriation of the Old Testament by attending to three critical texts: Ps. 95, Ps. 110, and Ps. 8. As I will argue, the epistle's use of these Psalms reflects neither Augustine's appeal to the literal and spiritual senses, nor Calvin's expansive understanding of the literal sense, but a dynamic identification between Old Testament locutions and God's present address to his people. The author is thus far less interested in what the human authors meant to communicate in the original context than in what God is saying to the covenant community now ("today"), in the contemporary moment.

---

17. For historical studies on Calvin's engagement with Augustine and other early Christian thinkers, see Luchesius Smits, *Saint Augustin dans l'œuvre de Jean Calvin*, 2 vols. (Assen: van Gorcum, 1957-58); J. Marius J. Lange van Ravenswaay, *Augustinus totus noster: Das Augustinverständnis bei Johannes Calvin* (Göttingen: Vandenhoeck & Ruprecht, 1990); David Steinmetz, "Calvin and Patristic Exegesis," in his *Calvin in Context*, 2nd ed. (Oxford: Oxford University Press, 1995), 122-40; Johannes van Oort, "John Calvin and the Church Fathers," in *The Reception of the Church Fathers: From the Carolingians to the Maurists*, ed. Irena Backus, vol. 2 (Leiden: Brill, 1997), 661-700; Anthony N. S. Lane, *John Calvin: Student of the Church Fathers* (Grand Rapids: Baker, 1999); R. Ward Holder, *John Calvin and the Grounding of Interpretation: Calvin's First Commentaries*, Studies in the History of Christian Traditions 127 (Leiden: Brill, 2006).

The final two chapters are the most constructive. The fifth considers the possibility of generalizing the interpretive practices in Hebrews into a theology of Scripture that locates Scriptural authority in the divine address. I also explore how such a model might bear upon questions of interpretive freedom, figural reading, authorial intent, and historical inquiry. The sixth chapter moves forward in redemptive history to the Spirit's ongoing testimony to Christ, which I take to legitimate continued reception of the divine address. I conceive tradition as a witness to this address, using Nicea as a test case, and I consider the implications of this proposal for the literal sense, the importance of virtue, and the ecclesial dimensions of Scriptural interpretation. I engage throughout this chapter with issues that continue to divide Catholics and Protestants.

A few methodological remarks are in order. First, the dialogue between Hebrews, Augustine, and Calvin is not meant as a straightforward comparison between three equally matched conversation partners. Hebrews is canonical, of course, while the other two figures are not. On the other hand, both Augustine and Calvin seek to engage the entirety of Scripture — including Hebrews — while Hebrews is but one voice in the New Testament. The purpose of setting these authors next to each other is thus not to present the epistle as one reader of Israel's Scriptures alongside the others, nor to use it as a corrective of Augustine and Calvin, but to draw out the distinct theological vision in Hebrews, using Augustine and Calvin as aids, and indeed considering their own treatments of Hebrews when possible. (This option is more readily available with Calvin, who wrote a commentary on Hebrews, than with Augustine, who does not provide a sustained direct treatment of the epistle.) This orientation circumscribes the implications of my project, particularly since many points of difference between Hebrews and the other interlocutors arise from Paul's influence upon the latter. A more holistic study would ask whether Hebrews advances a better understanding of these matters than Paul, whether Augustine and Calvin read Paul appropriately, how to synthesize the diverse witnesses of the New Testament, and so forth. My aim, more simply, is to present one New Testament locus as an instance of Christian hermeneutical innovation and to interrogate the implications of its theology and interpretive practices for contemporary reception of Scripture. What follows, then, is less a theology of Scripture than a theology of Hebrews's theology of Scripture.

Second, this constructive end shapes the individual chapters on Augustine and Calvin. I am keenly aware that my effort to distill the thought

Introduction

of such complex and sophisticated minds fails to do them complete justice, particularly on topics as wide-ranging as the ones I consider. The reader will search in vain for a comprehensive, chronological treatment of either figure; some nuance and texture are admittedly lost. My approach is to investigate critical and representative texts that yield fundamental structures in each figure's thought. In many cases, these texts play an instrumental role in crystallizing the authors' articulation of certain issues, such that their subsequent treatments of these issues may be considered largely derivative (without, however, precluding the possibility of further development). I am convinced that Augustine and Calvin are substantially consistent thinkers who retain the basic contours of their mature theology across the vast range of their later writings. Focused attention on selected texts should thus suffice methodologically for the purposes of this study. I do seek in these chapters to provide readings faithful to Augustine's and Calvin's own thought, and I have resisted the temptation to warp and exploit them for my own purposes. That said, I intentionally flag issues that reveal differences between the authors as well as areas of difficulty where Hebrews's own approach brings particular illumination. As mentioned above, the purpose of this decision is not to present Hebrews as a "solution" to Augustine's and Calvin's problems — though both invite correction and criticism according to Scripture.[18] Still, the identification of the epistle's distinct approach to these matters may suggest creative new possibilities for addressing longstanding matters of theological controversy that have often been dominated by Pauline categories.

Third, my constructive purposes shape my chapters on Hebrews as well. I have relied heavily on New Testament scholarship for these discussions and have sought, as with Augustine and Calvin, to provide faithful readings of the primary source material. Yet I do not engage Hebrews simply to reconstruct the author's original meaning. New Testament scholarship is characterized by a salutary desire to discern the particular vision of an individual author without imposing upon him later theological categories that distort historical meaning. But this concern can result in a weakened theological imagination or even refusal to consider how texts fit into wider streams of theological reflection.[19] My study proceeds

---

18. Among various examples, see Augustine, *Trin.* 1.3.5.

19. For frustrations expressed along these lines, see Markus Bockmuehl, *Seeing the Word: Refocusing New Testament Study,* STI (Grand Rapids: Baker Academic, 2006), especially "The Troubled Fortunes of New Testament Scholarship," 13-26.

from the opposite direction: the fourth and sixteenth centuries set the terms of discussion, and the canonical text responds. This decision not only brings the particularities of the theology of Hebrews into sharper relief, it also demonstrates in practice the value of reading forward from the text (through the history of interpretation) in addition to reading behind it (through historical criticism). It thus models the hermeneutical posture this book seeks to defend.

This project interfaces with several scholarly conversations. The first concerns the doctrine of Scripture. While recent years have witnessed a number of valuable proposals in this area,[20] none to my knowledge has engaged extensively and exegetically with a single biblical corpus, and indeed, many apologize for the lacuna. Hans Frei presents *The Eclipse of Biblical Narrative* as a contribution to the "almost legendary category of analysis of analyses of the Bible in which not a single text is examined, not a single exegesis undertaken."[21] John Webster similarly introduces his dogmatic account of Scripture with the qualification that his volume can have "only a modest role, ancillary to the primary theological task, which is exegesis. . . . What [such an account] may not do is replace or eclipse the work of exegesis."[22] Although Kevin Vanhoozer's *The Drama of Doctrine* and especially Telford Work's *Living and Active* draw more intentionally upon the biblical text, neither focuses directly on one canonical voice in sustained dialogue with the latest developments in biblical studies. My project treats Scriptural interpretation formally and materially by advancing a theology of Scripture generated by the biblical text.

This work thus presents a methodological proposal for bridging the gap between theology and biblical studies. In a seminal lecture entitled "Biblical Interpretation in Crisis: On the Question of the Foundations and Approaches of Exegesis Today," then Joseph Cardinal Ratzinger said of the

---

20. David H. Kelsey, *Proving Doctrine: The Uses of Scripture in Modern Theology* (Harrisburg: Trinity, 1999; originally published as *The Uses of Scripture in Recent Theology* [Philadelphia: Fortress, 1975]); Nicholas Wolterstorff, *Divine Discourse: Philosophical Reflections on the Claim That God Speaks* (Cambridge: Cambridge University Press, 1995); Telford Work, *Living and Active: Scripture in the Economy of Salvation,* Sacra Doctrina (Grand Rapids: Eerdmans, 2002); John Webster, *Holy Scripture: A Dogmatic Sketch,* Current Issues in Theology (Cambridge: Cambridge University Press, 2003); Kevin J. Vanhoozer, *The Drama of Doctrine: A Canonical-Linguistic Approach to Christian Theology* (Louisville: Westminster John Knox, 2005). See chapter 5 for further bibliography.

21. Frei, *The Eclipse of Biblical Narrative,* vii.

22. Webster, *Holy Scripture,* 3.

Introduction

divide between historical and theological study: "Hardly anyone today would assert that a truly pervasive understanding of this whole problem has yet been found which takes into account both the undeniable insights uncovered by the historical method, while at the same time overcoming its limitations and disclosing them in a thoroughly relevant hermeneutic. At least the work of a whole generation is necessary to achieve such a thing."[23] The recent completion of his *Jesus of Nazareth* trilogy suggests that Pope (emeritus) Benedict XVI continues to affirm this judgment, as the foreword of the first volume largely reiterates the same themes of the lecture nearly twenty years before. Two intervening studies by the Pontifical Biblical Commission also reflect interest in this matter: *The Interpretation of the Bible in the Church* and *The Jewish People and Their Sacred Scriptures in the Christian Bible*.[24] Outside Catholic circles, the last several years have witnessed a dizzying multiplication of studies on the theological interpretation of Scripture, defined generally according to the desire to move past the strictures of historical criticism toward a more ecclesially centered approach. The Brazos Theological Commentaries on the Bible, the Two Horizons Commentary series, the *Dictionary for Theological Interpretation of the Bible*, and the *Journal of Theological Interpretation* constitute just some of the major initiatives.[25] While my project is not primarily

---

23. Joseph Cardinal Ratzinger, "Biblical Interpretation in Crisis: On the Question of the Foundations and Approaches of Exegesis Today," in *Biblical Interpretation in Crisis: The Ratzinger Conference on Bible and Church*, ed. Richard John Neuhaus, Encounter (Grand Rapids: Eerdmans, 1989), 5-6.

24. The Pontifical Biblical Commission, *The Interpretation of the Bible in the Church* (Vatican City: Libreria Editrice Vaticana, 1993). The other title is cited above. Ratzinger contributes the preface for both documents. See also José Granados, Carlos Granados, and Luis Sánchez-Navarro, eds., *Opening Up the Scriptures: Joseph Ratzinger and the Foundations of Biblical Interpretation*, Retrieval and Renewal: Ressourcement in Catholic Thought (Grand Rapids: Eerdmans, 2008), which reprints Ratzinger's earlier lecture.

25. See Francis Watson, *Text, Church, and World: Biblical Interpretation in Theological Perspective* (London: T&T Clark, 1994); idem, *Text and Truth: Redefining Biblical Theology* (Grand Rapids: Eerdmans, 1997); Stephen E. Fowl, ed., *The Theological Interpretation of Scripture: Classic and Contemporary Readings*, Blackwell Readings in Modern Theology (Oxford: Blackwell, 1997); Stephen E. Fowl, *Engaging Scripture: A Model for Theological Interpretation*, Challenges in Contemporary Theology (Malden, MA: Blackwell, 1998); Christopher R. Seitz, *Word without End: The Old Testament as Abiding Theological Witness* (Grand Rapids: Eerdmans, 1998); idem, *Prophecy and Hermeneutics: Toward a New Introduction to the Prophets*, STI (Grand Rapids: Baker Academic, 2007); idem, *The Character of Christian Scripture*; Christopher Seitz and Kathryn Greene-McCreight, eds., *Theological Exegesis: Essays in Honor of Brevard S. Childs* (Grand Rapids: Eerdmans, 1999); Joel B. Green and

concerned with prolegomena, I do conduct my study in conscious (if sometimes implicit) awareness of these questions as I present my own approach for integrating the disciplines.

Second, this project contributes to the study of the history of biblical interpretation.[26] While, again, the goal here is not to provide a comprehensive guide to Augustine's or Calvin's exegesis, it does seem to me that theologians can offer particular contributions to this area of inquiry. Augustine and Calvin were synthetic thinkers, intensely concerned with conceptual coherence, and as I will argue, their interpretive practices are intricately embedded in a textured network of theological decisions: the dynamics of sin, law, and grace; the relation between church and Israel; the trinitarian dynamics of divine communication. Full appreciation of this intellectual infrastructure demands interactive analysis, not disinterested description. My hope is that the systematic approach adopted here will illuminate rather than obscure the contours of Augustine's and Calvin's thought, even if individual nuances of historical detail do not receive as much attention.

Third, this project welcomes and responds to New Testament gestures toward constructive theology. I meet halfway those studies of the use of the Old Testament in the New that reflect synthetically on the legitimacy of such reading practices.[27] In this vein, Richard Hays's *Echoes of Scripture*

Max Turner, eds., *Between Two Horizons: Spanning New Testament Studies and Systematic Theology* (Grand Rapids: Eerdmans, 2000); Ellen F. Davis and Richard B. Hays, eds., *The Art of Reading Scripture* (Grand Rapids: Eerdmans, 2003); Kevin J. Vanhoozer, gen. ed., *Dictionary for Theological Interpretation of the Bible* (Grand Rapids: Baker Academic, 2005); Markus Bockmuehl and Alan J. Torrance, eds., *Scripture's Doctrine and Theology's Bible: How the New Testament Shapes Christian Dogmatics* (Grand Rapids: Baker Academic, 2008); Daniel J. Treier, *Introducing Theological Interpretation of Scripture: Recovering a Christian Practice* (Grand Rapids: Baker Academic, 2008); J. Todd Billings, *The Word of God for the People of God: An Entryway to the Theological Interpretation of Scripture* (Grand Rapids: Eerdmans, 2010).

26. See bibliography above, p. 6 n. 7.

27. C. H. Dodd, *According to the Scriptures* (London: Fontana, 1952); Richard N. Longenecker, *Biblical Exegesis in the Apostolic Period,* 2nd ed. (Grand Rapids: Eerdmans, 1999); Richard B. Hays, *The Faith of Jesus Christ: The Narrative Substructure of Galatians 3:1–4:11,* 2nd ed., Biblical Resource Series (Grand Rapids: Eerdmans, 2002); idem, *Echoes of Scripture in the Letters of Paul* (New Haven: Yale University Press, 1989); idem, *The Conversion of the Imagination: Paul as Interpreter of Israel's Scripture* (Grand Rapids: Eerdmans, 2005); Donald Juel, *Messianic Exegesis: Christological Interpretation of the Old Testament in Early Christianity* (Philadelphia: Fortress, 1988); David W. Pao, *Acts and the Isaianic New Exodus,* Biblical Studies Library (Grand Rapids: Baker Academic, 2000); John M. Court,

Introduction

in the Letters of Paul occupies a privileged place, having animated the questions behind this study even if my focus is not Paul but Hebrews. While Hays's work is primarily an exercise in biblical studies, I receive his final remarks on the normativity of Paul's reading practices as an invitation for theologians to enter the discussion. I thus engage the results of biblical studies in as much detail as can be expected of a non-specialist.

Finally, this project contributes to an active conversation concerning the relation between Scripture and tradition. If the ecumenical fervor of the previous century has waned somewhat,[28] the conversation between Catholics and Protestants remains quite alive, and recent years have witnessed surging Protestant interest in the history of biblical interpretation, the study of early Christianity, and the theological significance of the church.[29] I am sympathetic to such developments, though I am not convinced that differences between Catholics and Protestants on these matters have entirely been resolved. I thus conclude the sixth chapter with a series of areas for further dialogue and exploration.

A few technical notes before I begin. As this project is an exercise in Christian theology, I make ample use of the term "Old Testament." While I appreciate the potential offense of this claim upon Israel's Scriptures, the study simply makes no sense apart from the basic conviction that the Christian tradition was right to affirm the unity of the canon and the preparatory character of the Old Testament. One of the chief arguments of this work is that Hebrews is not simplistically supersessionist, and that new covenant language signals the renewal and not the rejection of Israel.

---

ed., *New Testament Writers and the Old Testament* (London: SPCK, 2002); Francis Watson, *Paul and the Hermeneutics of Faith* (London: T&T Clark, 2004); G. K. Beale and D. A. Carson, eds., *Commentary on the New Testament Use of the Old Testament* (Grand Rapids: Baker Academic, 2007); J. Ross Wagner, C. Kavin Rowe, and A. Katherine Grieb, eds., *The Word Leaps the Gap: Essays on Scripture and Theology in Honor of Richard B. Hays* (Grand Rapids: Eerdmans, 2008).

28. For a brief history of the ecumenical movement in the context of an important recent ecumenical statement, see Carl E. Braaten and Robert W. Jenson, eds., *In One Body through the Cross: The Princeton Proposal for Christian Unity* (Grand Rapids: Eerdmans, 2003), par. 11-18.

29. Besides many sources cited above, I might also mention the formation of The Wheaton Center for Early Christian Studies and two recent volumes focused on evangelical engagement with the early church: Mark Husbands and Jeffrey P. Greenman, eds., *Ancient Faith for the Church's Future* (Downers Grove, IL: InterVarsity, 2008); George Kalantzis and Andrew Tooley, eds., *Evangelicals and the Early Church: Recovery, Reform, Renewal* (Eugene, OR: Cascade, 2012).

But the epistle also presents Jesus Christ as the mediator of this new covenant, a point that can hardly be ignored by those who adopt a posture of Christian confession. In general, I use the term "Old Testament" somewhat flexibly to refer both to the covenant that characterized the time before Christ, and the body of literature to which that covenant corresponds. Later chapters will address this distinction in greater depth, considering, for instance, the possibility that the "New Testament" was operative during "Old Testament" times.

Second, I use the Revised Standard Version for English translations of biblical passages. Despite the compelling reasons for gender-neutral translation, the New Revised Standard Version often obscures linguistic features that bear upon issues central to this project. In particular, the translation of Heb. 2:5-9 according to the plural "human beings" and "mortals," and not the singular "man" and "son of man," forecloses the possibility of Christological readings that figure prominently in the fourth chapter.

Third, I have followed the orthography of the critical editions for Latin quotations despite resulting inconsistencies. The reader will notice both *u*'s and *v*'s, and both *i*'s and *j*'s; *deus* will sometimes be capitalized, sometimes not. I have, however, consistently capitalized the first letter of each sentence.

CHAPTER 1

Augustine of Hippo: Signs and Realities

Introduction

Augustine's understanding of the Old Testament, like the entirety of his theology, develops through a series of personal experiences and continues to evolve throughout his life. Upon his discovery of Cicero's *Hortensius,* the text that sparked his lifelong quest for wisdom, Augustine turned immediately to Scripture, only to turn just as quickly away, judging its undignified prose inferior to that of the classical writers.[1] Yet Augustine's problems with Scripture ran deeper than rhetoric. Manichean critiques of the Old Testament's "barbarities" — materialistic depictions of God, polygamy, animal sacrifices[2] — would leave a lasting impression on Augustine long after he abandoned the sect.

The key figure who helps Augustine address these challenges is Ambrose, bishop of Milan. Ambrose is not as eloquent as the Manichean teacher, Faustus, but he is more substantive,[3] and his great contribution to Augustine's life is to demonstrate the intellectual viability of the Catholic faith through the figural reading of the Old Testament. As Augustine recounts in *Confessions:*

---

1. *Conf.* 3.5.9.
2. Ibid., 3.7.12.
3. Augustine seems intentionally to contrast Faustus and Ambrose, who figure prominently in the beginning and end of Book 5, respectively. Faustus is eloquent but cannot defend Manichean doctrine. Ambrose is less rhetorically gifted but delivers better content. Augustine leaves his encounter with Faustus a Manichee only by default, awaiting some preferable option (5.7.13). Augustine's experiences with Ambrose persuade him to become a catechumen in the Catholic Church until some greater certainty illuminates his next steps (5.14.25).

This realization was particularly keen when once, and again, and indeed frequently, I heard some difficult passage of the Old Testament explained figuratively *(aenigmate soluto);* such passages had been death to me because I was taking them literally *(ad litteram)*. As I listened to many such scriptural texts being interpreted in a spiritual sense *(spiritaliter)* I confronted my own attitude, or at least that despair which had led me to believe that no resistance whatever could be offered to people who loathed and derided the law and the prophets.[4]

In future writings, Augustine will develop a variety of arguments in defense of the Old Testament, but the determinative importance of the spiritual sense will remain. In this chapter, I argue that the spiritual sense also bears significantly on Augustine's broad construal of salvation history and the people of God across the testaments. Redemption unfolds for Augustine according to a two-tier architecture of sign and referent that generates a series of ordered relationships between the Old and New Testaments, Israel and the church, and the literal and spiritual senses of Scripture. I will consider each in turn.

Covenants Concealed and Revealed

As Augustine's understanding of the relation between the testaments matures, a consistent theme emerges: the Old Testament exists to signify the New. If Augustine originally develops this argument with reference to the promises and practices of the Old Testament, the eventual result is a more fully orbed account of the fear and bondage of the old covenant and the love and freedom of the new. In this part, I will consider this dynamic first in Augustine's anti-Manichean writings and then in his anti-Pelagian *The Spirit and the Letter.* In the last section of this part, and the entirety of the next, I will turn to a challenge for Augustine's theology of the covenants that emerges directly from his sign–referent framework: the question of the Old Testament saints.

Against the Manichees

Augustine's most substantive treatment on the relation between the testaments is *Answer to Faustus, a Manichean* (late 390s–early 400s), writ-

---

4. Ibid., 5.14.24.

ten against the bishop Augustine once hoped would resolve his questions about Manichean doctrine.⁵ This text is by far the longest of Augustine's anti-Manichean works, a somewhat surprising detail given Augustine's negative depiction of Faustus in *Confessions* (397-401) and the fact that Faustus was already dead when Augustine wrote his reply. Yet a closer look at *Confessions* reveals that Augustine had enjoyed a fairly close personal relationship with Faustus and was more disappointed with Faustus's ability to defend Manichean doctrine — which was simply indefensible — than with his intellectual abilities or person.⁶ Indeed, Augustine seems to have taken Faustus's objections against the Old Testament seriously precisely because they were the issues that had vexed Augustine during his own Manichean days.⁷ *Answer to Faustus* addresses a series of objections Faustus had raised in a now-lost book called *The Chapters (Capitula)*, written between 386 and 390.⁸ For our purposes, Augustine's response may be taken as a fairly mature statement of his position on the relation between the testaments, which he substantially retains throughout his later writings.⁹

---

5. J. Kevin Coyle suggests a date of 398-400. See *"Faustum Manicheum, Contra,"* in *Augustine through the Ages: An Encyclopedia*, ed. Allan D. Fitzgerald et al. (Grand Rapids: Eerdmans, 1999), 356. Teske suggests that this text was written in 408-10, though this is not the majority opinion. See *Answer to Faustus*, trans. Roland Teske, WSA 1.20 (Hyde Park, NY: New City, 2007), 9, and Michael Cameron, *Christ Meets Me Everywhere: Augustine's Early Figurative Exegesis*, OSHT (Oxford: Oxford University Press, 2012), 349-50n1. Unless otherwise specified, all subsequent dates will be taken from *Augustine through the Ages*.

6. *Conf.* 5.7.12-13, *c. Faust.* 1.1.

7. *C. Faust.* 15.3, 15.7.

8. For a helpful summary of the Manichean position expounded in *c. Faust.*, see Michel Tardieu, "Principes de l'exégèse manichéenne du Nouveau Testament," in *Les règles de l'interprétation*, ed. Michel Tardieu (Paris: Cerf, 1987), 123-46.

9. Note, for instance, Augustine's several references in *civ. Dei* to *c. Faust.* for further discussion on the interpretation of the Old Testament (15.7, 15.26, 16.19, 16.41). Two recent studies that lay great weight on *c. Faust.* for Augustine's positions on the Jews and Judaism, and Christian appropriation of the Old Testament as Scripture, respectively, are Paula Fredriksen, *Augustine and the Jews: A Christian Defense of Jews and Judaism* (New York: Doubleday, 2008), and Cameron, *Christ Meets Me Everywhere*. For other studies on Augustine's treatment of the issues discussed in this part and his general doctrine of Scripture, see Maurice Pontet, *L'éxegèse de S. Augustin prédicateur* (Paris: Aubier, 1944); A. D. R. Polman, *The Word of God according to St. Augustine*, trans. A. J. Pomerans (Grand Rapids: Eerdmans, 1961); James Samuel Preus, *From Shadow to Promise: Old Testament Interpretation from Augustine to the Young Luther* (Cambridge, MA: Belknap, 1969); Gerald Bonner, "Augustine as Biblical Scholar," in *The Cambridge History of the Bible*, vol. 1: *From the Beginnings to Jerome*, ed. P. R. Ackroyd and C. F. Evans (Cambridge: Cambridge University Press, 1970), 541-63; Bertrand de Margerie, *Introduction à l'histoire de l'exégèse*, vol. 3: *Saint Augustin*

Faustus forced Augustine to address a significant and (from Augustine's perspective) irritating accusation: the Catholics were hypocrites. "Semi-Christians" *(semichristiani)*[10] who failed to recognize the basic incompatibility between the two testaments, Catholics claimed to accept the authority of the Old Testament but demonstrated no inclination to observe its laws about circumcision, sacrifices, clean and unclean foods, Sabbaths, or feasts.[11] Such an awkward position could only produce mutual adulteration, like mixing vinegar and honey, or water and wine.[12] Better, Faustus charged, to be like the Manichees, who were at least consistent and honest in their rejection of the Old Testament. "Both of us reject the Old Testament. If, then, you should ask what the difference is between your faith and mine, it is that you choose to lie and to act like a slave by praising in words what you hate in your mind. I have not learned to lie; I say what I think; I admit that I hate those who command such shameful things as much as the commandments themselves."[13]

Augustine's response is to delineate the Old and New Testaments according to the distinction between sign and reality. The signs *(signa,*

(Paris: Cerf, 1983); Pamela Bright, ed. and trans., *Augustine and the Bible* (Notre Dame, IN: University of Notre Dame Press, 1999), based on *Bible de tous les temps*, vol. 3: *Saint Augustin et la Bible,* ed. Anne-Marie La Bonnardière (Paris: Beauchesne, 1986); Elizabeth A. Clark, "Contesting Abraham: The Ascetic Reader and the Politics of Intertextuality," in *The Social World of the First Christians: Essays in Honor of Wayne A. Meeks*, ed. L. Michael White and O. Larry Yarbrough (Minneapolis: Augsburg Fortress, 1995), 353-65; idem, "Interpretive Fate amid the Church Fathers," in *Hagar, Sarah, and Their Children,* ed. Phyllis Trible and Letty M. Russell (Louisville: Westminster John Knox, 2006), 127-47; Michael Cameron, "Augustine's Construction of Figurative Exegesis against the Donatists in the *Enarrationes in Psalmos*" (PhD diss., University of Chicago, 1996); K. E. Greene-McCreight, *Ad Litteram: How Augustine, Calvin, and Barth Read the "Plain Sense" of Genesis 1–3,* Issues in Systematic Theology 5 (New York: Peter Lang, 1999); Frederick Van Fleteren and Joseph C. Schnaubelt, eds., *Augustine: Biblical Exegete,* Collectanea Augustiniana (New York: Peter Lang, 2001); Isabelle Bochet, *"Le firmament de l'Écriture": L'herméneutique augustinienne,* Collection des Études Augustiniennes: Série Antiquité 172 (Paris: Institut d'Études Augustiniennes, 2004); Charles Kannengiesser, *Handbook of Patristic Exegesis: The Bible in Ancient Christianity,* with special contributions by various scholars (Leiden: Brill, 2006), 1149-1233; Jason Byassee, *Praise Seeking Understanding: Reading the Psalms with Augustine* (Grand Rapids: Eerdmans, 2007); James A. Andrews, *Hermeneutics and the Church: In Dialogue with Augustine* (Notre Dame, IN: University of Notre Dame Press, 2012).

10. *C. Faust.* 1.1.
11. Ibid., 4.1, 6.1, 10.1, *inter alia.*
12. Ibid., 15.1. See 8.1, 9.1, *inter alia.*
13. Ibid., 6.1.

sacramenta) of the Old Testament have been replaced by the signs of the New; the realities *(res)* once prefigured are now fulfilled.[14] Throughout Augustine's discussion, Paul's remarks in 1 Cor. 10 function as a virtual refrain: "'All these were symbols of us *(figurae nostrae)*'" (6); and, "'all these things happened to them as symbols *(in figura)*, but they were written down on account of us *(propter nos)*, upon whom the end of the ages has come'" (11).[15] Thus, for instance, Christians do not place their hope in Old Testament promises of reward, but in the New Testament realities signified by those promises. "None of us doubts that the Old Testament contains promises of temporal realities and is called the Old Testament for that reason, and that the promise of eternal life and of the kingdom of heaven pertains to the New Testament."[16] Since the Old Testament did not reveal, but veiled the promise of eternal life,[17] the promises of temporal reward are valuable primarily as figures of the realities to come.[18]

Similar remarks apply for the law, which may be distinguished between "commandments that regulate life" *(praecepta uitae agendae)* and "commandments that symbolize life" *(praecepta uitae significandae)*.[19] Since these rites were written "for our sake," we should recognize "the great care with which we need to read and understand them and the great authority in which we should hold them."[20] But since they were also "symbols of us," and we now experience the realities to which they pointed, "it is no longer necessary to observe the celebration of the symbols that foretold them."[21] A series of examples illustrates Augustine's point.[22] Circumcision has to do with the heart: "for in what member is the stripping away of fleshly and mortal concupiscence more aptly prefigured than in that member from which a fleshly and mortal child comes to be?"[23] The Sabbath rest

---

14. Ibid., 19.16.
15. Both in ibid., 4.2. I depart slightly from the translation by using quotation marks instead of italics for the biblical passages. I maintain this practice in subsequent instances.
16. Ibid.
17. Ibid., 22.76. See *c. adv. leg.* 1.17.35.
18. *C. Faust.* 10.2. To be precise, Augustine does acknowledge indications in the Old Testament that earthly blessing was not an end in and of itself, and the presence in the New Testament of some earthly promises. But the distinction between Old and New Testament hope remains fundamental in Augustine's thought. See *c. Adim.* 18.1–19.2.
19. *C. Faust.* 6.2. See also 10.2-3.
20. Ibid., 6.2.
21. Ibid., 6.2.
22. In addition to the examples in 6.3-9, see 19.9-10, 32.11-13.
23. Ibid., 6.3.

is "useless to observe after the hope of our eternal rest has been revealed, but not useless to read about or understand."[24] Even the command against mixing linen with purple or wool retains some significance: one ought not live in a disordered way or confuse distinct vocations in life.[25] The Old Testament saints would have been "guilty" had they not obeyed these laws during their time, but those of the New Testament would be "foolish" to follow these observances after the realities they prefigured have been revealed.[26] Christians, Augustine says, should rather "understand them and practice them in a spiritual manner *(spiritaliter).*"[27] Scripture that once served as a "commandment" *(praeceptum)* has now become a "testimony" *(testimonium).*[28]

This interpretive strategy bears striking implications for the intended addressees of the Old Testament. Augustine concludes largely on the basis of the phrase *propter nos* (1 Cor. 10:11) that the Old Testament symbols were given for the benefit of those living in New Testament times, and not primarily for the original recipients of the law. "It is indeed wrong for us not to read what was written for our sake. For it was written more for the sake of us for whom it has been revealed than for the sake of those for whom it was hidden in symbols."[29] On Augustine's account, the significance of the Old Testament symbols was hidden by intent, while the New Testament was reserved for the revelation of the realities to which the former signs referred. Indeed, only a handful of Old Testament personages were granted the meaning of the signs — compared to the "whole peoples" who have now received the preaching of the New Testament[30] — and those privileged few deliberately buried their secret. "For, just as all those lofty commandments are not lacking to those old books, so the goal toward which they are directed is truly hidden in them, although the saints who saw its future revelation lived according to that goal, and in accord with the character of those times they either concealed it in prophecies *(prophetice tegebant)* or wisely understood what was concealed in those prophecies *(prophetice tectum sapienter intellegebant).*"[31]

---

24. Ibid., 6.4.
25. Ibid., 6.9.
26. Ibid.
27. Ibid.
28. Ibid.
29. Ibid.
30. Ibid.
31. Ibid., 19.30.

Despite the disparities between the testaments, Augustine does maintain that the more fundamental aspects of God's law remain unchanged. Augustine's goal in *Answer to Faustus* is to defend and not to denigrate the Old Testament, and his response to Faustus's challenge stresses the transformation of the law into a channel of grace and truth.[32] Augustine will, moreover, affirm the consistency of God's character and commands throughout his career,[33] and in later writings especially, the appeal to spiritual reading can become superfluous.[34] In two important texts that he seems to consider a unit alongside *Answer to Faustus* — *Answer to Adimantus* (394) and *Answer to an Enemy of the Law and the Prophets* (418-23)[35] — Augustine dedicates extended attention to alleged incompatibilities between the testaments. He eventually dismisses these incompatibilities as largely a function of distorting, selective reading practices. The longstanding effort to distinguish the Old Testament God of justice and jealousy from the New Testament God of love and mercy, for instance, falters before Paul's remarks on the "jealousy of God"[36] and Ezekiel's promises that God does not want any to perish.[37] Yet perhaps the most remarkable moment arises in a climactic section of *Answer to an Enemy of the Law and the Prophets,* where Augustine attributes to Jesus himself the God of the Old Testament's most objectionable displays: the demand for sacrifice, the slaughter of whole peoples, punishment to the third and fourth generations, and the hardening of hearts.[38] Augustine has come a long way since his *Confessions:* little in this argument demands appeal to the spiritual sense and hardly a trace of his earlier qualms about the Old Testament's barbarism can be found. There is thus a curious sense in which "Christological" interpretation — in this case, the move to identify Jesus with the God of the Old Testament — helps Augustine read the text literally.[39] Even without allegory, the two testaments

---

32. This phrase is Michael Cameron's. See *Christ Meets Me Everywhere,* 260-63, for his keen discussion of Augustine's reading of John 1:17: "The Law was given through Moses; this same Law *became* grace and truth through Jesus Christ" (gloss mine).

33. In addition to the texts cited below, see *conf.* 3.7.13–3.10.18 and *doc. Chr.* 3.12.19-20, 3.18.26–3.23.33.

34. See Michael Cameron, "The Christological Substructure of Augustine's Figurative Exegesis," in Bright, *Augustine and the Bible,* 74-103, for a treatment of Augustine's move toward the literal interpretation of the Old Testament, focusing on the Genesis commentaries.

35. *C. adv. leg.* 2.12.41.

36. *C. Adim.* 7.4, citing 2 Cor. 11:2.

37. Ibid., 7.5, citing Ezek. 18:23, 33:11.

38. *C. adv. leg.* 2.11.37.

39. I am grateful to C. Kavin Rowe for this point.

"agree and are in harmony," because "they were both written by one God,"[40] and they both share in "the great unity and peace of the Holy Spirit."[41] There is diversity across the testaments, but the covenants are indeed continuous and there is no variation in God.

The Spirit and the Letter

The next question is whether this diversity suggests a divergence in salvation. Augustine's answer, developed most clearly in *The Spirit and the Letter* (412), is basically yes. As its title suggests, Augustine's text is in large measure an exposition of 2 Cor. 3:6: "The letter kills but the Spirit gives life." But the interpretation Augustine now gives this passage differs significantly from the way he understood it in *Confessions*. There, Augustine took the apostolic maxim as a reference to the hermeneutical principle he witnessed in Ambrose: whenever the literal sense contains an absurdity, some alternate meaning must be sought.[42] Here, Augustine explicitly bypasses (without completely rejecting) this reading of Paul's words for a more soteriological interpretation.[43] The old covenant brought death because it did not help us obey the law; the new covenant brings life because the love of God is poured out in our hearts through the Spirit who has been given to us (Rom. 5:5).[44]

A number of Scriptural references, largely Pauline, support this distinction between the testaments. In Rom. 7:7-11, for instance, Paul personifies sin as having deceived and killed him through the commandment not to covet.[45] This Old Testament precept contains no absurdity and is quite valuable for salvation, since the absence of such desires is tantamount to the absence of sin. Yet without the help of the Spirit, the commandment actually increases our longing to do what it forbids, demonstrating the ministration of the old covenant to bring death. Rom. 3:21-24 advances substantially the same perspective. As Augustine reads this passage, the

---

40. *C. Adim.* 7.5.
41. Ibid., 11. See also 4, 7.1, 9.2, 10, 13.4, 17.5, 19.2, 19.27.
42. *Conf.* 6.4.6.
43. *Spir. et litt.* 4.6.
44. Ibid., 3.5. The importance of Rom. 5:5 for Augustine may be seen in the number of times (at least sixteen) he quotes or alludes to this passage: 3.5, 4.6, 5.7, 14.25, 16.28, 17.29 (2×), 21.36, 25.42, 26.46, 28.49, 29.51, 32.56 (2×), 33.57, 33.59.
45. Ibid., 4.6.

revelation of the righteousness of God *(iustitia dei)* is not God's own righteousness but the righteousness God produces in those he justifies.[46] Paul says this righteousness has been made manifest apart from the law, though the law and the prophets testify to it (3:21). For Augustine, this means the following: the law commanded without justifying, thereby exposing our need for the Spirit; the prophets foretold the coming of Christ; and Christ has now brought grace to heal our wills such that we are no longer under the law.

Augustine pays special attention to Jer. 31:31-34 as the only locus in the Old Testament that refers explicitly to a new covenant: "'I will complete a New Testament with the house of Israel and with the house of Judah.'"[47] The reference in one testament to another presents an indisputable distinction between the covenants. Nevertheless, Augustine argues, Jeremiah denies any inherent defect in the law, locating the failure of the old covenant in the sinfulness of the people and not in the covenant itself. Jesus came not to destroy but to fulfill the law (Matt. 5:17), and Paul demonstrates the value of the law in guarding and enclosing us until faith was revealed (Gal. 3:21-23). "The law, then, was given that grace might be sought; grace was given that the law might be fulfilled."[48] Jeremiah's promise, "I will complete it *(consummabo),*" must therefore mean, "I will fulfill it *(inplebo).*"[49] That is, on Augustine's account, God "completes" the New Testament by writing the law on our hearts and minds so that we may obey it, a notion that relates directly to 2 Cor. 3:3, where the apostle contrasts stone tablets with the tablets of our hearts, and the writing of ink with that of the Spirit. "The former is called the Old Testament on account of the human injury which is not healed by the command and threat of the letter; the latter is called the New Testament on account of the new condition of the Spirit which heals the new human being from the wound of the old condition."[50]

These dynamics illustrate what is for Augustine the central distinction between the testaments, the contrast between fear and love, or slavery and freedom. "'You have not, after all, received the spirit of servitude so as to live in fear again; rather, you have received the Spirit of adoption as

---

46. Ibid., 9.15.
47. Ibid., 19.33.
48. Ibid., 19.34. "Lex ergo data est, ut gratia quaereretur, gratia data est, ut lex impleretur." Translation mine.
49. Ibid.
50. Ibid., 20.35.

children. In it we cry out, Abba, Father'" (Rom. 8:15).[51] There is, Augustine asserts, an essential difference between those who obey from fear of punishment and those who act from love of righteousness. The latter alone please God, while the former bear the mentality of slaves, since they do not delight in God's law and wish his commands were different than they are. Only the internalization of God's commands through the Spirit allows us to obey the law without fear or dissembling. "The difference, then, between the Old and New Testaments is seen to be this: in the former the law is written on tablets, in the latter upon hearts, so that what in the former struck fear from without might in the latter produce delight within. In the former one became a transgressor because of the letter that kills; in the latter one becomes a lover because of the Spirit that gives life."[52]

For Augustine, then, the contrast between the testaments is not just superficial, but salvific. There are two distinct covenants that may be differentiated according to the presence or absence of the Spirit, and the concomitant presence or absence of God's love in our hearts. This disparity may be delineated more precisely by contrast with two other rubrics. First, Augustine does not simplistically contrast the Old and New Testaments in terms of works versus faith.[53] Such a suggestion would fly in the face of Paul's remarks in Rom. 7 on coveting, which presume the ongoing force of the Old Testament commandment in New Testament times. The difference, Augustine writes, is simply that "what the law of works commands by its threats *(minando imperat)* the law of faith obtains by its faith *(credendo impetrat).*"[54] Or, to recall the language of *Confessions*, "By the law of works God says: Do what I command! By the law of faith we say to God: Give what you command! After all, the law commands in order to remind us of what faith should do. It commands, that is, so that, if those to whom the command is given are not as yet able to observe it, they may know what to ask for."[55]

Second, the contrast between the letter and the Spirit does not correspond to the distinction between the ceremonies and the law's more permanent commands.[56] In 2 Cor. 3:7, Paul calls the law a "ministry of death," indicating by his reference to letters carved in stone that he has the Ten Commandments in view. Yet, Augustine observes, the Decalogue does not

---

51. Ibid., 32.56.
52. Ibid., 25.42. See also 16.28, 29.51.
53. Ibid., 13.21.
54. Ibid., 13.22.
55. Ibid. Cf. *conf.* 10.29.40.
56. See especially *spir. et litt.* 14.23.

mention anything about circumcision or sacrifices, and it includes only one ceremonial commandment concerning the Sabbath. Paul must therefore mean that the whole of the law, whether ceremonial or not, brought death by increasing sin.[57] The same can also be said of the veil: "The letter of the law justifies no one, but a veil has been drawn in their reading of the Old Testament, until they pass over to Christ and the veil is removed, that is, until they pass over to grace and understand that our justification, by which we do what he commands, comes from him."[58] For Augustine, that is, the veil does not refer merely to the fulfillment of ceremonial figures, but to the entire system of grace and righteousness made manifest in the New Testament. "This grace remained veiled *(uelata)* in the Old Testament; it has been unveiled *(reuelata)* in the gospel of Christ in accord with the perfect temporal order of providence, for God knows how to arrange all things."[59]

The "New Testament" during the "Old Testament"

If the Old Testament concealed the grace of the New Testament, questions naturally arise about the salvific status of the Jews before Christ. Were the patriarchs and the prophets — Abraham, Moses, David, and the like — consigned to the fear and bondage of the law? Augustine's solution, adopted consistently throughout his writings, is to adopt a rather curious distinction between the old and new covenants, and the chronological eras of the Old and New Testaments, which correspond roughly but not exactly to the covenants themselves. The most extended explanation of this position is found in *Answer to the Two Letters of the Pelagians* (418-22), where Augustine addresses the Pelagian charge that he holds to the following position: "In the Old Testament the Holy Spirit did not come to the help of virtue."[60]

Augustine's response trades on a definitional distinction. If "Old Testament" means that particular covenant Paul associates with slavery and fear (Gal. 4:24), then yes, the Holy Spirit was unavailable to those under it. If, however, "Old Testament" refers to the time period before the coming of Christ, then it surely is the case that the Holy Spirit was available. How else could one make sense of the Psalmists' obvious devotion, or Paul's

---

57. Ibid., 14.24-25. See also 25.42 and 29.50.
58. Ibid., 17.30.
59. Ibid., 15.27. See also 11.18.
60. *C. ep. Pel.* 3.4.6.

affirmation of Abraham as the father of those who believe? "Because the Old Testament prefigured the new, the people of God in that previous era who understood it remained according to the division of the times dispensers and ministers *(dispensatores et gestatores)* of the Old Testament, but are clearly seen to be heirs *(heredes)* of the New Testament."[61]

On Augustine's account, it seems, various individuals living during Old Testament times existed in a kind of redemptive-historical time warp, belonging proleptically to the new covenant of freedom and love while knowingly mediating the old covenant of bondage and fear.[62] This is an awkward position, yet one Augustine can hardly avoid given the contrast he has drawn between the testaments and the undeniable presence of saving faith before the time of Christ. The covenant Abraham received was for Augustine none other than the New Testament itself, characterized by promises and faith, even if it was established chronologically prior to the Mosaic law and was hidden under veils until the coming of Christ.[63] Indeed, Augustine asserts, invoking Paul's language in Gal. 4, all the righteous people from Abraham and before, through Moses and the prophets until John the Baptist, were "children of the promise and of grace like Isaac, the son of the free woman, and heirs of God and coheirs with Christ, not on the basis of the law, but on the basis of the promise."[64]

The distinction between old and new covenant people is thus less chronological than soteriological, and representatives of both can be found before and after Christ. Old covenant people are those who think the letter can bring them life and so do not seek God's mercy, who seek earthly goods and obey God from fear and greed instead of love.[65] This group includes

---

61. Ibid.

62. Cameron dubs such figures "spiritually amphibious 'double agents',." citing *vera rel.* 28.51 for Augustine's position. He also notes Augustine's remark in *ex. Gal.* 43.6 that David, a representative of the Old Testament saints, was "in" the Old Testament but not "of" it *(homo in ueteri testamento sed non homo de ueteri testamento)*. See Cameron, *Christ Meets Me Everywhere*, 90-91 and 238, respectively.

63. *C. ep. Pel.* 3.4.7.

64. Ibid., 3.4.8. For other instances of this position, see *c. Adim.* 17.2; *c. Faust.* 4.2, 15.2; *c. adv. leg.* 2.7.26-27, 2.8.31. Note also *cat. rud.* 3.6 and 19.33, where Augustine presents the birth of Jacob, whose hand emerged before his head, as an image of the body of Christ's partial emergence before Christ and the rest of his body fully appear. The implication for Augustine is that the Old Testament saints were united with the rest of Christ's body though they preceded Christ in time. For discussion of this image, see Cameron, *Christ Meets Me Everywhere*, 246.

65. *C. ep. Pel.* 3.4.9.

the "Old Testament" figures who worshiped idols or fell in the desert, the "New Testament" figures who crucified Jesus, and many Jews who continue to reject Christ now. The people of the new covenant are those who live by grace, obey from love, seek spiritual goods, and above all, believe in the mediator for the forgiveness of sins and receive the Spirit for the obedience of God's commands:

> Of this sort were all the righteous of old and Moses himself, the minister *(minister)* of the Old Testament, but heir *(heres)* of the new, because they lived from the one and same faith from which we live. They believed that the incarnation, passion, and resurrection would come, just as we believe they have taken place.... The same faith, then, is found in those people who were not yet Christians in name, but were so in reality *(qui nondum nomine, sed re ipsa fuerunt antea Christiani)*, and in these people who not only are Christians, but are also called Christians *(qui non solum sunt, uerum etiam vocantur)*.[66]

Given the coexistence of Old and New Testament people during both dispensations, Augustine reasons, the use of the terms "Old" and "New" must derive not from the exclusive administration of one covenant or the other before or after the time of Christ, nor from the dates of their institution (since Abraham received the New Testament 430 years before Sinai), but from the historical revelation of each in turn.[67] The law was revealed through Moses to increase knowledge of sin, but the righteousness of God was revealed only several hundred years later with the coming of Christ. Thus, the narrative of redemptive history is the determinative reason the New Testament is "newer" than the Old Testament, but this is not to deny the presence of the new covenant before the incarnation.

Israel Between the Two Cities

Augustine's theology of the covenants thus results in a surprising conclusion. According to his sign–reality framework, the Old Testament veiled but symbolized the New Testament, concealing the grace of Christ until

---

66. Ibid., 3.4.11. See also *ex. Gal.* 23.5-7, 24.10-13; *civ. Dei* 18.47.
67. *C. ep. Pel.* 3.4.13. Augustine also considers one other explanation: Paul commands us to clothe ourselves with a "new" human being and to put the "old" to death.

its revelation in the incarnation. Yet this framework excludes the Old Testament saints from their dispensation and raises significant questions concerning Augustine's broader theology of the Jews and Judaism. For if Old Testament figures like Abraham or Moses were redemptive-historical aberrations before the incarnation, Israel as a whole would seem to remain a slave people characterized by fear, blindness, and obsession with temporal reward — a particularly biting proposal when Augustine suggests the patriarchs administered the old covenant while belonging to the new.

Contemporary scholarship has sought to rescue Augustine from such conclusions, not least because of their negative freight for present understandings of the relation between Christianity and Judaism. As I will argue, however, Augustine's position on Israel and the church resembles his position on the old and new covenants: there are two distinct entities, and the former is instrumental to the latter. Augustine's theology of Israel is not, as we shall see, wholly negative, and he does retain confidence in the massive future restoration of ethnic Jews. Nevertheless, his basic judgment on these matters substantially excludes Old Testament Israel and contemporary Jews from the salvation God has reserved for the (primarily Gentile) church, and can thus fairly, though not simplistically, be described as supersessionist.

This part will outline Augustine's theology of Israel as presented in *City of God*, first by considering the broader relation between the earthly and heavenly cities, and then by tracing Augustine's narrative depiction of Old Testament Israel in the text. In the final section, I dedicate extended attention to the most substantive recent treatment on Augustine's theology of Israel, Paula Fredriksen's *Augustine and the Jews: A Christian Defense of Jews and Judaism*.

The Earthly City

City of God (413-27) is Augustine's greatest work, a tremendously wide-ranging treatise that advances both a sweeping polemic against Roman religion, politics, and culture, and a positive presentation of Christianity canvassing the entire biblical narrative from the fall of the angels to the hope of our eschatological vision of God.[68] Despite the length of the

---

68. For general treatments of *civ. Dei*, see R. H. Barrow, *Introduction to St. Augustine, The City of God* (London: Faber and Faber, 1950); A. Lauras and H. Rondet, "Le thème des

Augustine of Hippo

text and its digressive character,⁶⁹ Augustine's basic argument is fairly straightforward and easily understood. Since the fall, humanity has been divided into two broad communities, the City of God and the city of man, which arose and oppose each other according to their contrasting objects of loves, and will continue to exist uneasily with each other until the end of time. The earthly city is characterized by pride, violence, idolatry, and overweening desire for temporal things, while the heavenly city manifests humility, peace, proper worship, and hope for eternal reward.

Contemporary discussion divides over the degree to which these two cities can be identified with actual sociopolitical entities, with many scholars suggesting they function primarily as eschatological ideals.⁷⁰ Some have

---

deux cités dans l'œuvre de saint Augustin," in *Études Augustiniennes,* ed. H. Rondet, M. Le Landais, A. Lauras, and C. Couturier (Paris: Aubier, 1953), 97-160; John O'Meara, *Charter of Christendom: The Significance of* City of God (New York: Macmillan, 1961); Johannes van Oort, *Jerusalem and Babylon: A Study into Augustine's* City of God *and the Sources of His Doctrine of the Two Cities* (Leiden: Brill, 1991); Dorothy F. Donnelly, ed., The City of God: *A Collection of Critical Essays* (New York: Peter Lang, 1995); Christoph Horn, ed., *Augustinus, De civitate dei,* Klassiker Auslegen 11 (Berlin: Akademie, 1997); Gerald O'Daly, *Augustine's* City of God: *A Reader's Guide* (Oxford: Oxford University Press, 1999); idem, "Ciuitate dei (De -)," in *Augustinus-Lexikon,* vol. 1, ed. Cornelius Mayer (Basel: Schwabe, 1986), 969-1010. See also Etienne Gilson's foreword to *Saint Augustine: The City of God: Books 1-7,* trans. Demetrius B. Zema and Gerald G. Walsh, Fathers of the Church 8 (New York: Fathers of the Church, 1950), xi-xcviii. For a survey of important studies, see Dorothy F. Donnelly and Mark A. Sherman, eds., *Augustine's* De Civitate Dei: *An Annotated Bibliography of Modern Criticism, 1960-90* (New York: Peter Lang, 1991). For decades, *La Cité de Dieu,* Œuvres de saint Augustin: Bibliothèque Augustinienne 33-37 (Paris: Desclée de Brower, 1959-60) has been the closest approximation to a modern commentary on the entirety of the text. The French translation has since been updated by Isabelle Bochet, Gustave Combès, and Goulven Madec in *La Cité de Dieu,* 3 vols., Nouvelle Bibliothèque Augustinienne 3-4 (Paris: Institut d'Études Augustiniennes, 1993-95), which includes a lengthy new introduction. At least two other efforts are under way. The first is P. G. Walsh, ed., *De Civitate Dei (The City of God)* (Oxford: Aris & Phillips Classical Texts), which has been completed through Book 10 (six volumes thus far). Another effort, currently funded by a five-year grant from the Arts and Humanities Research Board, will be published by Oxford University Press.

69. O'Donnell notes: "Civ. is the longest single work presenting a sustained argument unified around a coherent single theme to survive from Greco-Roman antiquity (apart from histories and compilations, whose bulk is inherent in the matter and whose disposition is far less than artful than that required in a work such as *ciu.*)." See "Augustine, City of God," Section IV: Contents, written on commission in 1983 but never published. As of submission of this manuscript, O'Donnell's text can be found at http://www9.georgetown.edu/faculty/jod/augustine/civ.html.

70. The classic study on this issue is R. A. Markus, *Saeculum: History and Society in the Theology of St. Augustine,* 2nd ed. (Cambridge: Cambridge University Press, 1988), originally

adduced Augustine's equivocal use of the terms "earthly city" and "City of God" as evidence for a bifurcation between the ambiguities of present-day communities and the final division between the two cities.[71] Yet the narrative contours of *City of God* suggest a tighter connection between the two cities and observable communities than has often been acknowledged.[72] The overarching structure of the text is a theological recital of the whole of the human race (the scope is formally, though not materially comprehensive), told primarily through the rise of the world empires (especially the Roman), and the story of Israel and the church, respectively. While

---

published in 1970. His *Christianity and the Secular* (Notre Dame, IN: University of Notre Dame Press, 2006) presents an updated version of the same argument. For further discussion, see John Neville Figgis, *The Political Aspects of S. Augustine's 'City of God'* (London: Longmans, Green, and Co., 1921); Norman H. Baynes, "The Political Ideas of St. Augustine's *De Civitate Dei*," in his *Byzantine Studies and Other Essays* (London: Athlone, 1955), 288-306; H. I. Marrou, "Civitas Dei, civitas terrena: num tertium quid?" in *Studia Patristica: Papers presented to the Second International Conference in Patristic Studies held at Christ Church, Oxford,* vol. 2, ed. Kurt Aland and F. L. Cross (Berlin: Akademie, 1957), 342-50; Herbert A. Deane, *The Political and Social Ideas of St. Augustine* (New York: Columbia University Press, 1963); Oliver O'Donovan, "The Political Thought of *City of God* 19," in Oliver O'Donovan and Joan Lockwood O'Donovan, *Bonds of Imperfection: Christian Politics, Past and Present* (Grand Rapids: Eerdmans, 2004), 48-72, substantially revised from his "Augustine's *City of God* XIX and Western Political Thought," *Dionysius* 11 (1987): 89-110; Rowan Williams, "Politics and the Soul: A Reading of *City of God*," *MilS* 19/20 (1987): 55-72; John Milbank, *Theology and Social Theory: Beyond Secular Reason,* 2nd ed. (Malden, MA: Blackwell, 2006); Miikka Ruokanen, *Theology of Social Life in Augustine's* De civitate Dei (Göttingen: Vandenhoeck & Ruprecht, 1993); Jean Bethke Elshtain, *Augustine and the Limits of Politics* (Notre Dame, IN: University of Notre Dame Press, 1998); Robert Dodaro, *Christ and the Just Society in the Thought of Augustine* (Cambridge: Cambridge University Press, 2004); John Doody, Kevin L. Hughes, and Kim Paffenroth, eds., *Augustine and Politics* (Lanham, MD: Lexington, 2005); Gilbert Meilaender, *The Way That Leads There: Augustinian Reflections on the Christian Life* (Grand Rapids: Eerdmans, 2006).

71. For discussions of this issue, see F. Edward Cranz, "*De Civitate Dei,* XV, 2, and Augustine's Idea of the Christian Society," originally published in *Spec* 25 (1950): 215-25, reprinted in R. A. Markus, ed., *Augustine: A Collection of Critical Essays* (Garden City, NY: Anchor, 1972), 404-21; John O'Meara, *Charter of Christendom,* 51-54; Gilbert Meilaender, *The Way That Leads There,* 82-95; David Aers, *Salvation and Sin: Augustine, Langland, and Fourteenth-Century Theology* (Notre Dame, IN: University of Notre Dame Press, 2009), 1-24. Van Oort defends a basic, though not complete equivalence between *civitas Dei* and *ecclesia,* arguing that both are primarily eschatological terms that also designate empirical realities (*Jerusalem and Babylon,* 123-29).

72. For a more substantive defense of this position, see my "Republics and Their Loves: Rereading *City of God* 19," *Modern Theology* 27 (2011): 553-81, upon which much of this section is based.

acknowledging the ambiguity of the times, Augustine does present these two narratives as histories of the two cities, whose development in these concrete communities follows their origins in the fall of the angels and humanity, and leads organically to their eternal ends, whether in judgment or blessing.[73] Israel falls awkwardly between the two cities, for reasons that will be considered in the next section.

Augustine's fullest treatment of Rome's history arises in Books 3-5, where his general objective is to demonstrate that the gods were of no benefit for earthly blessings.[74] Though Book 3 recounts the development of Rome from the fall of Troy through Augustus Caesar, Augustine's purpose is not archival. The central motif of this history is violence, both that inflicted upon the Romans and that which they inflicted upon others, and Augustine carefully designs his narrative to shape the readers' perception of Rome's moral character. Even in their early days, the Romans began "'to regard the lust for dominion *(libidem dominandi)* as an adequate cause for war, to think that the highest glory lay in the widest empire.'"[75] By the end of this history, the Romans had wreaked worse evils upon their fellow citizens than those foreign nations had brought upon them. Book 4 takes aim at Rome's other obsession, idolatry, as Augustine enumerates with fastidious scorn Rome's bewildering array of gods, each assigned to some discrete, minute, and often contradictory task supposedly necessary for the extension and care of the empire.[76] On Augustine's account, this frenetic multiplication of gods was ultimately the expression of a restless, acquisitive spirit,[77] and a betrayal of the Romans' fear that the gods could not actually deliver what they promised.[78] Rome's violence and idolatry were thus twin symptoms of the same disease: an

---

73. Technically, the heavenly city includes angels and the earthly city includes demons. Augustine's primary concern in *civ. Dei* is with those members of the heavenly city who reside on earth, but he repeatedly sets forth fellowship with the angels as the reward of those who endure this present pilgrimage. See *civ. Dei* 11.9, 14.28, *inter alia*.

74. For a slightly different spin on Books 1-5, see Robert Dodaro, "Eloquent Lies, Just Wars and the Politics of Persuasion: Reading Augustine's *City of God* in a 'Postmodern' World," *AugStud* 25 (1994): 77-137.

75. *Civ. Dei* 3.14. Augustine applies to the Romans the words of Sallust, who is actually describing the Greeks.

76. Ibid., 4.8, 4.10, 4.11, 4.16, 4.21.

77. Ibid., 4.16. The resonances with *conf.* are obvious.

78. On this point, see Augustine's discussion in 4.18ff. of Felicity, whose very presence in the Pantheon renders the entire system incoherent, since happiness just is that for the sake of which everything else is sought and all the gods were created.

inordinate desire for earthly goods coupled with a refusal to seek them from God.[79]

As Augustine proceeds in Books 4 and 5, he sets forth a theory on why God allowed the growth of the Roman Empire. Augustine traces the beginning of world empires back to Ninus, the king of Assyria, who was the first recorded ruler to seek not only to protect, but also to extend his borders.[80] Ninus eventually extended Assyria's rule over almost all the nations of the East, creating an empire that would last 1,240 years, even longer than Rome's history thus far. The Roman Empire succeeded the Assyrian, a development Augustine claims God coordinated with respect to Rome's lust for glory. As Rome's own authors acknowledged, lust for glory was the driving ambition of the Roman people, the force that prompted Rome to pursue first liberty from slavery, and later dominion over other nations.[81] In the general case, Augustine argues, lust for glory is a vice,[82] yet the Romans made glory an end in and of itself, failing (with a few exceptions) to recognize that glory should be the reward for virtue.[83] Nevertheless, lust for glory does provide one curious and non-trivial benefit: it checks other vices, as prideful people desire to be honored for appearing virtuous though they are not. "At least it is good that the desire for human praise and glory makes them, not indeed saints, but less depraved men."[84] This is the reason, according to Augustine, God saw fit to raise up the Roman Empire to replace the Eastern nations: by her national vice, Rome would suppress all manner of other evils in the peoples under her rule.[85]

---

79. Dodaro argues persuasively that this inordinate desire for earthly goods can itself be traced to fear of death. See especially *Christ and the Just Society*, 32-43. On his account, this fear explains a variety of vices that come under criticism in *civ. Dei:* indulgence in luxury and illicit pleasures is a distraction from the inevitability of death (41); fear of annihilation drives the growth of a political and military apparatus to fend off foreign threats (42); athletic contests, local religious festivals, theater arts, and literature that obscure knowledge of God were originally instituted to mitigate the same fear (48). For further reflections in this regard, see Luigi Alici, "The Violence of Idolatry and Peaceful Coexistence: The Current Relevance of *civ. Dei*," *AugStud* 41 (2010): 203-18.

80. *Civ. Dei* 4.6.

81. Ibid., 5.12.

82. Augustine nuances this matter somewhat in 5.19, where he speaks of the propriety of receiving praise for genuinely virtuous actions.

83. Ibid., 5.12.

84. Ibid., 5.13.

85. Ibid.

In other parts of *City of God,* Augustine will complete his narrative of the earthly city, extending the story from Rome back to Cain, and forward to the contemporary age. Book 18, whose argument I have treated elsewhere, is of particular significance for recounting the rise of the other world empires from Ninus to the Romans.[86] For our purposes, Augustine's aim in those sections is the same as in Books 3-5: to substantiate his identification and diagnosis of the earthly city, demonstrating through concrete examples and evidence that overweening desire for temporal goods results almost by necessity in violence and idolatry. The earthly and heavenly cities are not just eschatological types; they are empirically observable social entities whose histories reflect the character of their loves. "The two cities were created by two kinds of love: the earthly city was created by self-love reaching the point of contempt for God, the Heavenly City by the love of God carried as far as contempt of self."[87] As Augustine will repeat, the two cities are interwoven and intermixed in this temporal existence, and the members of the two cities will not finally be revealed until God sifts the wheat from the tares. Still, there are indeed two different peoples, they can substantially be identified — enough, in any case, that Augustine can narrate their development throughout human history — and they differ as much as their objects of worship.[88]

Israel's Story

Israel becomes a theological conundrum against this bifurcation, for *City of God* repeatedly criticizes her narrow concern with temporal goods (thus

---

86. Lee, "Republics and Their Loves," 563-67.

87. *Civ. Dei* 14.28: "Fecerunt itaque ciuitates duas amores duo, terrenam scilicet amor sui usque ad contemptum Dei, caelestem uero amor Dei usque ad contemptum sui." James J. O'Donnell judges rightly of this passage, "In this statement all the doctrine of *City of God* is summarized" (*Augustine* [Boston: Twayne, 1985], 51). One important precursor to *civ. Dei* 14.28 is *Gn. litt.* 11.15.20. "Hi duo amores . . . distinxerunt conditas in genere humano ciuitates duas" ("These two loves . . . distinguished the two cities founded in the human race").

88. Baynes gets the balance right in "The Political Ideas of St. Augustine's *De Civitate Dei,*" 291. "When Augustine is expounding the *theory* of his conception of history the *civitas terrena* — the society of earth — is not the State: the *civitas caelestis,* the heavenly society, is not the Church, but when he comes to consider the *representatives* of these two societies on earth — when he is treating the matter, not purely theoretically, but empirically — then the Roman State comes to be regarded as the earthly *civitas,* and the Church as the divine society."

equating her with the pagans) while also commending her rejection of idolatry (thus elevating her above the pagans). This uneasy dynamic reflects inherent ambiguities in Augustine's position on the Jews. For the bishop of Hippo, Israel was part of the earthly city, yet more honorable than the empires, and God's ongoing commitment to her will eventually result in her conversion to Christ at the end of time. In this way, Israel is neither like Rome nor like the church. She is a third thing — a sign, but a privileged one, called to the realities of the New Testament.[89]

Let us begin with Augustine's introductory remarks on this topic in *City of God* 15.2:[90]

> There was certainly a kind of shadow *(umbra . . . quaedam)* and prophetic image *(imago prophetica)* of this City which served rather to point towards it *(significandae)* than to reproduce *(praesentandae)* it on earth at the time when it was due to be displayed. This image was also called the holy city, in virtue of its pointing to that other City *(merito significantis imaginis)*, not as being the express likeness of the reality which is yet to be *(non expressae, sicut futura est, ueritatis)*. Concerning this

---

89. For recent treatments of Augustine's theology of Jews and Judaism, see Fredriksen, *Augustine and the Jews;* and idem, "*Excaecati Occulta Justitia Dei:* Augustine on Jews and Judaism," *JECS* 3 (1995): 299-324, in addition to several related articles listed in *Augustine and the Jews,* 443-44; Jeremy Cohen, *Living Letters of the Law: Ideas of the Jew in Medieval Christianity* (Berkeley: University of California Press, 1999); idem, "'Slay Them Not': Augustine and the Jews in Modern Scholarship," *ME* 4 (1998): 78-92; idem, "The Mystery of Israel's Salvation: Romans 11:25-26 in Patristic and Medieval Exegesis," *HTR* 98 (2005): 247-81. See also Marcel Dubois, "Jews, Judaism and Israel in the Theology of Saint Augustine: How He Links the Jewish People and the Land of Zion," *Imm* 22/23 (1989): 162-214; Michael Signer, "Jews and Judaism," in *Augustine through the Ages,* ed. Fitzgerald et al., 470-74; Lisa A. Unterseher: *The Mark of Cain and the Jews: Augustine's Theology of Jews and Judaism,* Gorgias Dissertations 39 (Piscataway, NJ: Gorgias, 2009); idem, "The Mark of Cain and the Jews: Augustine's Theology of Jews," *AugStud* 33 (2002): 99-121; Franklin T. Harkins, "Nuancing Augustine's Hermeneutical Jew: Allegory and Actual Jews in the Bishop's Sermons," *JSJ* 36 (2005): 41-64; C. C. Pecknold, "Theo-Semiotics and Augustine's Hermeneutical Jew: Or, 'What's a Little Supersessionism between Friends?'" *AugStud* 37 (2006): 27-42.

90. This passage comes at a critical juncture in the structure of *City of God.* For four books (11-14), Augustine has focused on the entrance of sin into the created order, both in the heavenly realms (angels) and on earth (Adam and Eve). In Books 15-18, Augustine will treat the development of the City of God from Abel to the time of Jesus, which occurs primarily within the nation of Israel. Before he begins this sequence, though, Augustine indicates the way he will read this narrative. He thus introduces Book 15 with this methodological discussion on the allegory of Hagar and Sarah.

image, in its status as a servant *(imagine seruiente)*, and that free City *(libera ciuitate)* to which it points, the Apostle says, when writing to the Galatians . . . [Augustine quotes Gal. 4:21-5:1].

This manner of interpretation, which comes down to us with apostolic authority, reveals to us how we are to understand the Scriptures of the two covenants, the old and the new. One part of the earthly city *(pars . . . quaedam terrenae ciuitatis)* has been made into an image of the Heavenly City *(imago caelestis ciuitatis)*, by symbolizing something other than itself, namely that other City *(non se significando, sed alteram)*; and for that reason it is a servant *(seruiens)*. For it was established not for its own sake but in order to symbolize another City *(non . . . propter se ipsam, sed propter aliam significandam)*.[91]

A number of points about Augustine's remarks should be noted. First, the development of the heavenly city is found within the history of Israel but does not coincide with it. Israel was not the City of God in and of herself, but a subset of the earthly city. Second, Israel serves to signify the City of God as a shadow of the heavenly city — just as, for instance, Levitical sacrifices were shadows of Christ's sacrifice. Israel's value is thus instrumental in that she was created for the sake of the true City, and her function is not to constitute but to point toward it. As a servant of the heavenly city, she can only take the name "City of God" by virtue of her dependence on the real City. Finally, Augustine understands the basic relation between Israel and the Heavenly City according to the terms set forth in Galatians 4: the allegorical relation of sign and referent.

Books 15-18 bear out this perspective, tracing sequentially the basic fault line that runs throughout humanity, first between the good and the wicked generally, then between Israel and the rest of the world, and finally within Israel herself. The story of Israel begins with Abraham, who was

---

91. *Civ. Dei* 15.2: "Vmbra sane quaedam ciuitatis huius et imago prophetica ei significandae potius quam praesentandae seruiuit in terris, quo eam tempore demonstrari oportebat, et dicta est etiam ipsa ciuitas sancta merito significantis imaginis, non expressae, sicut futura est, ueritatis. De hac imagine seruiente et de illa, quam significat, libera ciuitate sic apostolus ad Galatas loquitur . . . Haec forma intellegendi de apostolica auctoritate descendens locum nobis aperit, quem ad modum scripturas duorum testamentorum, ueteris et noui, accipere debeamus. Pars enim quaedam terrenae ciuitatis imago caelestis ciuitatis effecta est, non se significando, sed alteram, et ideo seruiens. Non enim propter se ipsam, sed propter aliam significandam est instituta."

born in the land of the Chaldeans, which was part of the Assyrian Empire. The family of Abraham's father, Terah, stood fast against surrounding idolatry to worship the one true God, thus preserving a "seedbed" *(plantatio)* for the City of God.[92] During his sojourning, Abraham received a series of promises, which Augustine understands to speak alternately of Abraham's physical and spiritual descendants, the land of Canaan and the conversion of all the nations.[93] As the story proceeds, Augustine increasingly casts the division between peoples as one between Jews and Christians. The choices of Isaac over Ishmael and Jacob over Esau, both favoring the younger son, prefigure a division between the "older" and "younger" peoples of the old and new covenants.[94] Isaac's blind blessing of Jacob signifies Christ among the nations, but also the contemporary blindness of the Jews.[95] When Jacob wrestles with his God, he is both blessed and crippled — "blessed in those who among this same people of Israel have believed in Christ, and crippled in respect of those who do not believe."[96] Joseph's reversal of blessing with his own two sons again indicates that the older Jews will serve the younger Christians.[97]

The prophetic era marks a major turning point in Old Testament history.[98] Augustine understands this dispensation to begin with Samuel, whose legacy concerns the replacement of Eli as priest and the transition of kingship to David from Saul. For Augustine, these two changes signify another, when the Old Testament priesthood and monarchy would give way to the eternal priesthood and kingship of Christ.[99] This dynamic is especially seen in Hannah's song, in which, Augustine claims, "there speaks, by the spirit of prophecy, the Christian religion itself, the City of God itself, whose king and founder is Christ; there speaks, in fact, the grace of God itself."[100] For Augustine, Samuel's appointment to the priesthood does not simply bring about

---

92. Ibid., 16.12.
93. See ibid., 16.16, 16.18, 16.21, 16.23, 16.26, 16.29. For a summary discussion of the interpretation of prophecies, see 17.2.
94. Ibid., 16.31-32, 16.35.
95. Ibid., 16.37.
96. Ibid., 16.39.
97. Ibid., 16.42.
98. Augustine's treatment of the Old Testament narrative is uneven. In 16.43, it seems, he suddenly realizes how much time he has spent on the opening book of the Bible. He thus rushes through Moses, Joshua, and the Judges in quick succession so he can begin Book 17 with a new dispensation.
99. Ibid., 17.4.
100. Ibid.

the succession of one particular priest after another; it prefigures the replacement of an entire covenant — "the death of the priesthood itself in the line of Aaron."[101] Augustine points to recent history for evidence of this reality: "No one who looks at these prophecies with the eye of faith could fail to see that they have been fulfilled. For now, to be sure, no tabernacle has been left to the Jews, no temple, no altar, no sacrifice and, it follows, no priesthood."[102]

Like Eli, Saul does not represent himself alone; he "figuratively personified Israel, the people which was to lose its kingdom when Christ Jesus our Lord should take the kingship under the new covenant, a spiritual instead of a physical kingship."[103] Nevertheless, Augustine clarifies, this prophecy does not predict the wholesale abandonment of Israel. Israel will be divided into two — "Israel the enemy of Christ *(inimicum Christo)*, and Israel which attaches itself to Christ *(adhaerentem Christo)*"[104] — the permanence of which separation may be witnessed in God's oath never to lie or change his mind (1 Sam. 15:29). Augustine writes:

> We see that by these words an utterly irrevocable sentence was divinely proclaimed concerning this division of the people of Israel, a sentence absolutely perpetual *(prorsus insolubilem uidemus per haec uerba prolatam diuinitus fuisse sententiam de ista diuisione populi Israel et omnino perpetuam)*. For all those who have passed over *(transierunt)* from that people to Christ, or who are now passing over *(transeunt)*, or who will pass over *(transibunt)*, were not of that people according to God's foreknowledge, nor by reason of the one common nature of the human race. Moreover, all those of the Israelites who attach themselves to Christ and continue steadfastly in his fellowship will never be associated with those Israelites who persist in their hostility to him to the end of this life; in fact, they will continue for ever in that state of separation which is prophesied here. For the old covenant from Mount Sinai which "has children destined for slavery" is of no value *(nihil enim prodest)* except in so far as it bears witness to the new covenant.[105]

By the time Augustine reaches the New Testament, much of his account of the Jews at the time of Jesus has already been adumbrated, except

---

101. Ibid., 17.5.
102. Ibid.
103. Ibid., 17.7.
104. Ibid.
105. Ibid.

for one innovative twist. Augustine first asserts, somewhat predictably, that the Jews failed to recognize Christ's divinity and therefore put him to death. Jerusalem would soon be destroyed and the Jews scattered throughout the world.[106] But the new element is this: "They were dispersed all over the world — for indeed there is no part of the earth where they are not to be found — and thus by the evidence of their own Scriptures they bear witness for us that we have not fabricated the prophecies about Christ."[107] According to Augustine's distinctive "witness doctrine," contemporary Jews are like blind librarians, preserving books that bring credibility to the Christian message while failing to recognize the meaning of their own Scriptures. God has thus preserved the Jews for the express purpose of building up the church. "For we recognize that it is in order to give this testimony, which, in spite of themselves, they supply for our benefit by their possession and preservation of those books, that they themselves are dispersed among all nations, in whatever direction the Christian Church spreads."[108]

In the next section, I will say more about whether the witness doctrine, which has attracted significant recent attention, constitutes a favorable element of Augustine's treatment of the Jews. For now, the final element of Augustine's narrative of Israel's history concerns her restoration at the end of time. Though Augustine's position on this issue has generated some controversy,[109] it seems clear to me and worth underscoring that Augustine believes in the massive future conversion of national Israel to Jesus, a point that receives particular emphasis when Augustine treats the latter prophets. One example concerns Hos. 3:5, where Augustine writes: "The same prophet testifies that the Israelites by physical descent *(istos autem carnaliter Israelitas)* who now refuse to believe in Christ will afterwards believe."[110] The most extended treatment arises from Mal. 4:5-6, which Augustine takes as a prediction that the "prophet Elijah will expound the Law to the Jews, and that through his activity the Jews are destined to believe in our Christ.[111] And Zech. 12:9-10 evokes Augustine's most striking explanation of this event: "For on that day even the Jews will certainly repent, even those Jews who are to receive 'the spirit of grace and mercy.'

---

106. Ibid., 18.46. See 16.37.
107. Ibid., 18.46.
108. Ibid.
109. See Fredriksen, *Augustine and the Jews,* 328, 422-23n17; Cohen, "The Mystery of Israel's Salvation," 275-76.
110. *Civ. Dei* 18.28.
111. Ibid., 20.29.

They will repent that they gloated over Christ in his suffering, when they look at him as he comes in his majesty, and recognize him as the one who formerly came in humility, whom they mocked in the persons of their parents."[112] Those Jews who turn to Jesus, Augustine clarifies, will not themselves have been responsible for killing Christ. Yet their sense of solidarity with their parents, who remain condemned, will prompt grief nevertheless — "not because they feel guilty of this crime *(non . . . reatu criminis),* but because they feel the emotions of true religion *(sed pietatis affectu).*"[113] In concluding remarks, Augustine lists the restoration of the Jews as one of the central tenets all Christians should believe concerning the last things.[114]

The consistency of these remarks leaves little doubt that, in *City of God* at least, Augustine does reserve conceptual space for some final conversion of national Israel to faith in Christ. He does not teach that each and every individual Jew will receive salvation: quite the opposite, Augustine affirms a distinction between those Jews who killed Jesus and those who will be converted at the end of time. It should also be acknowledged that Augustine does at other places define the salvation of "all Israel" in terms of the church, consisting of both Jews and Gentiles.[115] Nevertheless, Augustine does not finally eviscerate distinctive, national Jewish identity, or the ongoing validity of God's promises to this particular people. In that sense, Augustine's sign–referent framework for construing the relation between Israel and church is not simplistically supersessionist, even if it cannot completely escape the label. Augustine will not include non-Christian Jews in the heavenly city, for he cannot imagine conversion apart from Christ. Yet it remains for Augustine a matter of faith that God will remember national Israel at the end of time.[116]

---

112. Ibid., 20.30.

113. Ibid.

114. Ibid.: "In [the last judgment], or in connection with that judgement, we have learnt that those events are to come about: Elijah the Tishbite will come; Jews will accept the faith; Antichrist will persecute; Christ will judge; the dead will rise again; the good and the evil will be separated; the earth will be destroyed in the flames and then will be renewed. All those events, we must believe, will come about; but in what way, and in what order they will come, actual experience will then teach us with a finality surpassing anything our human understanding is now capable of attaining. However, I consider that these events are destined to come about in the order I have given."

115. Fredriksen, *Augustine and the Jews,* 328, citing Augustine's treatment of Rom. 11:25 in *ep.* 149.2.19.

116. Fredriksen's treatment of this issue fails to grasp some of these nuances (*Augustine and the Jews,* 422-23n17). While she is right that Augustine does not assert the salvation of

Excursus: Augustine, Defender of the Jews?

Augustine's position on the Jews and Judaism has become a topic of vibrant scholarly interest, especially through the recent contributions of Paula Fredriksen and Jeremy Cohen.[117] Despite certain points of difference, these two scholars present overlapping and complementary proposals that depict Augustine's theology of Judaism as significantly more positive than has often been recognized. Fredriksen argues that Augustine's writings on Judaism mark a dramatic shift away from early Christian anti-Jewish polemic, while Cohen finds in Augustine's doctrine the basis for a medieval policy of Jewish toleration, most prominently exemplified in Bernard of Clairvaux's warning in the Second Crusade against the eradication of the Jews. Both scholars have called particular attention to Augustine's Jewish witness doctrine, mentioned above, which explains the ongoing existence of the Jews on the basis of Ps. 59:11: "Do not slay them, lest at some time they forget your Law; scatter them by your might."[118] Given the interest this topic has generated especially with the 2008 publication of Fredriksen's *Augustine and the Jews: A Christian Defense of Jews and Judaism*, it is appropriate to consider separately how her positions correspond with Augustine's theology of Israel as I have presented it.[119]

Fredriksen locates Augustine's treatment of Judaism against the early Christian *adversus Iudaeos* tradition, especially in the writings of Justin Martyr, Melito of Sardis, and Tertullian. These authors tended to depict the Jews as a particularly recalcitrant people, the law as a form of chastisement for sin, and the ceremonies as of no ongoing value given the fulfillment of these practices in Christ. Centuries later, this stream of attack would animate the arguments of Faustus the Manichee, who criticizes the Catholics for inconsistently retaining the Old Testament instead of rejecting it altogether. On Fredriksen's account, Augustine's innovative response was to highlight the goodness of the law and the propriety of the Jews in

---

all Jews, this does not mean he denies some sort of significant conversion at the end of time for ethnic or national, and not just "spiritual" or "true" Israel. It seems indisputable to me that the passages I have cited from *civ. Dei* 18.28, 20.29, and 20.30 (2×; Fredriksen herself cites the first instance) indicate that God has reserved for the nation of Israel a particular blessing (defined as conversion to Christ) in the final days.

117. See references above.

118. Translation taken from *civ. Dei* 18.46.

119. For a fuller version of the argument that follows, see "Israel between the Two Cities: Augustine's Theology of the Jews and Judaism," *JECS* 24 (forthcoming 2016).

practicing it according to the flesh during Old Testament times. Circumcision, Sabbath, and food laws were not punishments for sin nor special measures designed for a particularly stubborn people, but God-given signs that prefigured Christ and the church. While the *adversus Iudaeos* writers considered the literal adherence of the Jews to ancestral practices a failure to understand the law spiritually, Augustine argued that the Jews "had just done what God had commanded them to do."[120]

Fredriksen lays great stress on two interpretive moves that fund Augustine's witness doctrine: the mark of Cain as considered in *Answer to Faustus*,[121] and Augustine's subsequent treatments of Ps. 59. Concerning the former, Augustine presents Cain as an image of contemporary Jews, who bemoan the loss of their kingdom and fear death at the hands of the Christians. Yet when Cain complains that his punishment is too much to bear, God graciously puts a mark on him, so that anyone who kills Cain will suffer seven punishments. For Augustine, the mark of Cain signifies the ongoing observation of the law wherever the Jews have been scattered. Augustine marvels that no emperor or king with Jews in his realm "kills them" in the sense of banning these observances and thus forcing the Jews to give up their religious identity.[122] This divine safeguard, Fredriksen argues, is a sign for Augustine that "the Jews are in a completely different category from pagans (the source of whose religion is demons) and from heretics (the source of whose error is their own pride). Jewish law together with the *catholica* share the same source, namely, God himself... Jews and catholics, [Augustine] insists, stand together in one religious community, over and against all others."[123]

The second interpretive move concerns Ps. 59, which presents for Augustine many of the same themes as God's interaction with Cain. This passage, too, refers to the punishment and protection of the Jews as they are dispersed throughout the world but retain the law and its observances for the benefit of the church. As above, the preservation of the Jews does not mean freedom from physical death, but the retention of Jewish identity through the law.[124] The "scattering" language refers to the defeat of the Jews in 70 CE.[125] And the unintentional fruit of their diaspora fidelity

---

120. Fredriksen, *Augustine and the Jews*, 244.
121. *C. Faust.* 12.11-13.
122. Fredriksen, *Augustine and the Jews*, 271.
123. Ibid., 275.
124. *En. Ps.* 58.1.21.
125. *Ep.* 149.1.3.

is to bring the messianic prophecies in their own scriptures to the whole world, such that the Gentiles may be converted.[126] As Augustine develops his theology of Israel, Fredriksen suggests, he comes to prefer Ps. 59 over the mark of Cain as his primary metaphor for the Jews. Cain's status as an exile muddies Augustine's image of the church as a sojourning people, and Cain's murderous jealousy and establishment of a city furnish too suggestive a picture for the founding of Rome. Ps. 59:11, and not Gen. 4:15, thus becomes the exegetical hook for the mature Augustine's reflections on the ongoing existence of the Jews as Jews, and will subsequently provide the basis for medieval policies of toleration for the Jews.[127]

On my reading of *City of God*, Fredriksen is basically right that the Jews constitute for Augustine a distinct category from the pagans,[128] but Augustine's sensitivity on this point should not be considered "a Christian defense of Jews and Judaism" (the subtitle of Fredriksen's book). The mark of Cain illustrates this dynamic. For Augustine, Abel's offering compares to Cain's as the grace of the New Testament compares to the earthly works of the Old.[129] Abel's death at the hands of his older brother prefigures the crucifixion of Christ, the head of a younger people, at the hands of the elder people, the Jews.[130] Cain's feigned innocence before God mirrors the Jews' supposed ignorance about their own prophecies.[131] Cain is cursed by the earth, which will not give him its strength (Gen. 4:12). Augustine reasons, "The Church recognizes that the Jewish people is cursed and reveals that, after Christ was killed, that people still carries out the works of earthly circumcision, the earthly Sabbath, the earthly unleavened bread, and the earthly Pasch. All these earthly works keep hidden the strength derived from understanding the grace of Christ, which is not given to the Jews who continue in their impiety and unbelief."[132]

In this context, Augustine's remarks on the mark of Cain can at best be taken as qualification of a basically negative judgment of the Jews, and not

---

126. Ibid., 149.1.9.

127. For Fredriksen's summary of Augustine's unique contributions on these issues, see *Augustine and the Jews*, 316-19.

128. For a series of positive reviews of Fredriksen's text, alongside her response to the reviews, see *AugStud* 40 (2009): 279-99.

129. *C. Faust.* 12.9.

130. Ibid.

131. Ibid., 12.10.

132. Ibid., 12.11.

as affirmation of their continued adherence to ancestral practices. Augustine's concern is descriptive, not prescriptive. He does not encourage an imperial policy of Jewish toleration; he simply explains why God has seen fit to preserve the Jewish people and what value this has for the church. Augustine takes as a given that the scattered Jews retain their ancestral practices — it is a datum for theological reflection — but he does not prefer that Jews remain Jewish if this means not converting to Christianity. Thus, at the end of the section in *Answer to Faustus* to which Fredriksen draws so much attention, Augustine expresses hope that Cain would cease to be "Cain." The Jews are "set apart from the community of the other nations by a certain distinct and proper sign of their own observance," but if any of them "crosses over to Christ *(ad Christum transierit)* . . . Cain may no longer be found and may not go away from the face of God nor dwell in the land of Nod, which is said to mean 'commotion.'"[133]

Methodologically, Fredriksen's problem arises, at least in part, from an overemphasis on *Answer to Faustus* and a misreading of this text as a defense of Judaism. Augustine's purpose is not to protect the Jews or Judaism per se, but to respond to Manichean attacks against the Old Testament and to defend its ongoing authority despite the fact that Catholics no longer follow its practices. This requires him to make distinctions between different kinds of laws and to affirm the value of the Old Testament ceremonies as prefigurements of Christ. But his concern is far less with Jews than with Catholics and the legitimacy of Christian non-observance of Jewish practices. *City of God,* considered above, provides a more appropriate starting point for understanding Augustine's theology of the Jews, for it is in this text that Augustine sets forth his broad categorizations of humanity and locates Israel against the backdrop of the earthly and heavenly cities. By seeking temporal reward, Israel fails to recognize in her own Scriptures prophecies about Christ and the church. Still, Israel stands apart from other nations because of her privileged status as a shadow or prophetic image of the City of God, as that unique nation set apart by God to announce the coming of Christ and to nurture members of the heavenly city before his arrival.[134]

By and large, Augustine does not characterize Israel according to the vices that define the earthly city,[135] and at one point, he elevates the Jews

---

133. Ibid., 12.13.
134. *Civ. Dei* 7.32, 10.32, 15.8, 16.3.
135. Ibid., 4.31, 4.34.

above the philosophers.¹³⁶ Indeed, he even acknowledges the propriety of Israel seeking temporal rewards in the dispensation prior to Christ, since God teaches humanity in successive stages to lift its eyes from visible things to the invisible.¹³⁷ But Israel refused to move beyond these earthly blessings, and the result was the death of her own messiah.

> The Jews put Christ to death, when the New Testament revealed what was veiled in the Old Testament, the knowledge that God, the one true God, is to be worshipped for the sake of eternal life and everlasting gifts and for participation in that City on high, and not for earthly and temporal blessings, which divine providence bestows on good and evil without discrimination. And for this the Jews were justly given over to the Romans, for the greater glory of Rome, so that those who had sought earthly glory and attained it by their virtue (of whatever kind), overcame those who in their perverse wickedness spurned and put to death the giver of true glory and of citizenship in the Eternal City.¹³⁸

This is the perspective behind both Augustine's affirmation of Israel's fidelity to the law and his harsh remarks about Jews who continue to observe their ancestral practices apart from Christ. Old Testament Israel was for Augustine a kind of *tertium quid:* part of the earthly city, yet not identical with it, possessing within herself both prophecies of Christ and the church, and individual members of the heavenly city — only a sign of reality, according to Augustine's twofold schema, but also a privileged sign. If Augustine's position on these matters seems inherently ambiguous, this is a function of the ambiguities in Scripture itself.

Old Testament Signs and the Enjoyment of God

We can now examine Augustine's theology of Scripture. If the old covenant is a sign of the new, and Israel is a sign of the church (albeit awkwardly), what implications arise concerning the spiritual interpretation of Scripture, which trades critically for Augustine on his conception of *word*-signs?

---

136. Ibid., 18.41.
137. Ibid., 10.14-15. Cf. 10.25, 18.11.
138. Ibid., 5.18.

The focus of this part will be *De doctrina Christiana,* the fullest treatment of hermeneutical theory in Augustine's corpus and the conceptual backbone for his interpretation of the Old Testament.

Scholarship has divided on *De doctrina*'s intended purpose and audience,[139] and Michael Cameron has recently presented the text as a "half-finished classic" that leaves unresolved a series of issues addressed more fully in later works, especially *Answer to Faustus.*[140] Augustine began writing *De doctrina* in 396 or 397 but only completed the work when writing *Retractationes* some thirty years later. The delimitations of Cameron's study, which ends with *Answer to Faustus* (ca. 400), prevent him from treating the later sections of *De doctrina.* While acknowledging the experimental character of the earlier sections, I nevertheless take seriously Augustine's own decision in *Retractationes* to describe the entirety of *De doctrina* as a single unit.[141] I thus read *De doctrina* in light of my earlier discussions of *Answer to Faustus,* the text Cameron considers a stabilizing point for Augustine's understanding of the relation between the testaments,[142] and still later works including *The Spirit and the Letter* and *City of God.* These texts fill in the gaps for the sign–referent framework Augustine sets forth in the earlier parts of *De doctrina,* while the later parts of *De doctrina* demonstrate a basic continuity of perspective even at the end of Augustine's career.[143]

I begin by considering broadly how Augustine locates Scripture against his understanding of salvation and the Christian life, and then zoom in on the specific interpretive rules he commends for resolving ambiguities in Scripture. As we shall see, Augustine's position on Old Testament signs resembles his position on the relation between the testaments and

---

139. For a summary of this scholarly debate as well as a defense of the text's unity and suitability as a summary of Augustine's hermeneutical program, see Andrews, *Hermeneutics and the Church,* 1-5, 13-41.

140. Cameron, *Christ Meets Me Everywhere,* 215-50.

141. *Retr.* 2.4.

142. Cameron, *Christ Meets Me Everywhere,* 19.

143. For a summary of the questions Cameron raises about *De doctrina,* see *Christ Meets Me Everywhere,* 239-40. These issues tend to revolve around the degree to which Augustine perceives signs to be instrumental (and thus dispensable) or to retain their own integrity and thus mediate the realities they signify. This question, in turn, bears on the integrity of the Old Testament narrative in its literal sense and the degree to which the Old Testament mediates the grace of the New. My earlier arguments concerning the old covenant as an instrument of fear and condemnation, and the basically carnal character of Israel qualify without rejecting Cameron's conclusion that Augustine's mature approach is to conjoin signs and realities.

the relation between Israel and the church: they bear some value in and of themselves, but should ultimately be directed to Christ, the reality upon which all signs converge.

Useful Signs

Though the primary goal of *De doctrina Christiana* is to consider the study and presentation of Scripture, Augustine dedicates the first book of his work to a curious but fundamental distinction between use *(usus)* and enjoyment *(fruitio)*, which corresponds to another important distinction between signs *(signa)* and things *(res)*. The category *res* encompasses any object in creation[144] — and God, with appropriate qualifications.[145] *Signa* are "those things which are employed to signify *(significare)* something."[146] Technically, all signs are also things, but Augustine will for the purpose of discussion use the term *res* narrowly with reference to those things that do not derive their primary identity from signification. Things can additionally be distinguished according to two basic responses. "There are some things which are to be enjoyed *(quibus fruendum est),* some which are to

---

144. *Doc. Chr.* 1.2.2.
145. Ibid., 1.5.5.
146. Ibid., 1.2.2. Two standard studies on Augustine's theory of signs are R. A. Markus, "St. Augustine on Signs," *Phronesis* 2 (1957): 60-83; and B. Darrell Jackson, "The Theory of Signs in St. Augustine's *De doctrina christiana*," *REAug* 15 (1969): 9-49. Both can be found in R. A. Markus, *Augustine: A Collection of Critical Essays*. Other studies on Augustine's hermeneutical theory in *De doctrina* include Belford Darrell Jackson, "Semantics and Hermeneutics in Saint Augustine's *De doctrina christiana*" (PhD diss., Yale University, 1967); Mark D. Jordan, "Words and Word: Incarnation and Signification in Augustine's *De doctrina Christiana*," *AugStud* 11 (1980): 177-96; Robert William Bernard, "*In Figura:* Terminology Pertaining to Figurative Exegesis in the Works of Augustine of Hippo" (PhD diss., Princeton University, 1984); idem, "The Rhetoric of God in the Figurative Exegesis of Augustine," in *Biblical Hermeneutics in Historical Perspective: Studies in Honor of Karlfried Froehlich on His Sixtieth Birthday,* ed. Mark S. Burrows and Paul Rorem (Grand Rapids: Eerdmans, 1991), 88-99; Christopher Kirwan, "The Nature of Speech," in his *Augustine* (London: Routledge, 1989), 35-59; Duane W. H. Arnold and Pamela Bright, eds., *De doctrina christiana: A Classic of Western Culture* (Notre Dame, IN: University of Notre Dame Press, 1995); Karla Pollmann, *Doctrina christiana: Untersuchungen zu den Anfängen der christlichen Hermeneutik unter besonderer Berücksichtigung von Augustinus, De doctrina christiana* (Freiburg: Universitätsverlag, 1996); Richard Leo Enos et al., eds., *The Rhetoric of St. Augustine of Hippo:* De Doctrina Christiana *and the Search for a Distinctly Christian Rhetoric* (Waco, TX: Baylor University Press, 2008); Andrews, *Hermeneutics and the Church.*

be used *(quibus utendum)*, and some whose function is both to enjoy *(fruuntur)* and use *(utuntur)*."[147] Objects of enjoyment make us happy *(beati)* and are sought for their own sake, while objects of use are sought for the sake of things that are to be enjoyed.

The rest of Book 1 draws upon these categories to present a précis of salvation and the Christian life. Humanity, Augustine suggests, is like a traveler who utilizes various vehicles to return to the homeland *(patria)*. But if she were to delight in the very act of traveling, thereby confusing use and enjoyment, she would remain alienated from the homeland and happiness. So, too, Christians should consider themselves pilgrims in this foreign land of mortality, referring temporal, corporal goods to eternal, heavenly reward such that they might one day enjoy God. God is the only proper object of enjoyment — "a kind of single, supreme thing, shared by all who enjoy it *(una quaedam summa res communisque omnibus fruentibus)*"[148] — but humans tend to enjoy the created order instead and therefore need purification.[149] Yet this purification has now been made available through Christ, the incarnate Son, who can himself be understood as a kind of word-sign:

> When we speak, the word which we hold in our mind becomes a sound in order that what we have in our mind may pass through ears of flesh into the listener's mind: this is called speech. Our thought, however, is not converted into the same sound, but remains intact in its own home, suffering no diminution from its change as it takes on the form of a word in order to make its way into our ears. In the same way the word of God became flesh in order to live in us but was unchanged.[150]

On Augustine's account, we communicate to others by forming words from our thoughts, a sort of externalization of the mind that then gets transferred to the mind of the listener. But just as our thoughts remain unchanged during this process, so also did Christ retain his divinity in the

---

147. *Doc. Chr.* 1.3.3.
148. Ibid., 1.5.5.
149. Ibid., 1.12.12. See 1.10.10 for Augustine's comparison of this process to a journey.
150. Ibid., 1.12.13. See *conf.* 1.8.13 for a similar picture of communication through word-signs. On the relation between signs and the fall, see Ulrich Duchrow, "'Signum' und 'Superbia' beim jungen Augustin (386-390)," *REAug* 7 (1961): 369-72; Bernard, "Rhetoric of God"; David Dawson, "Sign Theory, Allegorical Reading, and the Motions of the Soul in *De doctrina christiana*," in Arnold and Bright, *De doctrina christiana*, 123-41.

incarnation. And it is this union of humanity and divinity that makes our salvation possible: Christ is the means to God in his humanity, while he simply is God, coequal with the Father, in his divinity.[151] Put differently, Christ is both the road *(via)* and the destination *(patria)* of our salvation — *summa res* and ultimate sign.[152]

The end of Book 1 brings the conversation back to Scriptural interpretation, after a lengthy consideration of whether humans are to be used or enjoyed. That section, much discussed in the scholarly literature,[153] presents Augustine's conviction that the essence of Christian ethics, encapsulated in the twofold love commandment, concerns properly ordered loves indexed fittingly to different objects on the hierarchy of being. Since we must love God with all our heart, soul, and mind, the love we direct toward other things, humans included, can only be secondary, derivative, and referential toward that primary love.[154] Yet Augustine's aim in this discussion is not to commend a general moral philosophy: "The chief purpose of all that we have been saying in our discussion of things is to make it understood that the fulfillment and end of the law [cf. Rom. 13:10; 1 Tim. 1:5] and all the divine Scriptures is to love the thing which must be enjoyed and the thing which together with us can enjoy that thing (since there is no need for a commandment to love oneself)."[155] In short, the *telos* of Scripture and the *telos* of the Christian life are for Augustine the same, which is why

---

151. *Doc. Chr.* 1.34.38.

152. Ibid., 1.11.11: "Cum ergo ipsa sit patria, uiam se quoque nobis fecit ad patriam." Rowan Williams winsomely draws out this point in his "Language, Reality and Desire in Augustine's *De doctrina*," *Journal of Literature and Theology* 3 (1989): 138-50. This article will shape much of what follows.

153. Anthony Dupont, "Using or Enjoying Humans: *Uti* and *Frui* in Augustine," *Augustiniana* 54 (2004): 475-506 provides a survey that is "exhaustive to a large degree" (503). Important works on this issue include Anders Nygren, *Agape and Eros,* trans. Philip S. Watson, rev. ed. (orig. 1953; repr., New York: Harper and Rowe, 1969); John Burnaby, *Amor Dei: A Study of the Religion of St. Augustine* (orig. 1938; repr., Eugene, OR: Wipf and Stock, 2007); Oliver O'Donovan, *The Problem of Self-Love in St. Augustine* (orig. 1980; repr., Eugene, OR: Wipf and Stock, 2006); idem, "*Usus* and *Fruitio* in Augustine, *De Doctrina Christiana I*," *JTS* 33 (1982): 361-97; Raymond Canning, *The Unity of Love for God and Neighbor in St. Augustine* (Heverlee-Leuven, Belgium: Augustinian Historical Institute, 1993). See also William Riordan O'Connor, "The *Uti/Frui* Distinction in Augustine's Ethics," *AugStud* 14 (1983): 45-62. A recent discussion of this issue is found in Eric Gregory, *Politics and the Order of Love: An Augustinian Ethic of Democratic Citizenship* (Chicago: University of Chicago Press, 2008), 319-50.

154. *Doc. Chr.* 1.22.21, 1.27.28.

155. Ibid., 1.35.39.

he had to expend so much energy on the broader contours of redemption before considering biblical interpretation. Any interpretation of Scripture that does not support the twofold love commandment is ultimately a misreading, while anyone whose interpretation of Scripture builds up love for God and neighbor "has not made a fatal error"[156] even if he misses the author's intent.[157] In a moment of revealing pragmatism, Augustine even compares such a person to a walker who gets lost for a while but eventually arrives at the right destination.[158]

In Books 2-3, Augustine addresses more directly how to interpret Scripture according to the twofold love commandment. Here, the spiritual interpretation of the Old Testament becomes paramount. Augustine structures his discussion in these two books according to four categories of signs, delineated according to whether they are unknown *(ignota)* or ambiguous *(ambigua)*, literal *(propria)* or metaphorical *(translata)*.[159] The distinction between unknown and ambiguous signs is neither clearly defined nor essential to Augustine's discussion,[160] but the distinction between literal and metaphorical signs plays a crucial role in framing Augustine's theology of the Old Testament. Literal signs refer directly to the realities they name, while metaphorical signs arise "when the actual things which we signify by the particular words are used to signify something else."[161] The word "ox," for instance, literally signifies the animal that goes by that name, but metaphorically signifies a worker in the gospel (1 Cor. 9:9) in that the animal is a signified thing that itself signifies something else. Of the four kinds of signs Augustine delineates (unknown literal, unknown metaphorical, ambiguous literal, ambiguous metaphorical), it is clearly the last, ambiguous metaphorical signs, that most strongly attracts his attention.[162]

---

156. Ibid., 1.36.40.

157. For further discussion of this rule, see Roland J. Teske, "Criteria for Figurative Interpretation in St. Augustine," in Arnold and Bright, *De doctrina christiana,* 109-22.

158. *Doc. Chr.* 1.36.41.

159. Ibid., 2.10.15.

160. For comparison, see Augustine's discussion of the difference between *obscuritas* and *ambiguitas* in *dial.* 8. See also Jackson, "Semantics and Hermeneutics in Saint Augustine's *De doctrina christiana,*" 160-61.

161. *Doc. Chr.* 2.10.15.

162. Pollmann, *Doctrina christiana,* 155: "Daß die nun folgende Behandlung der *verborum translatorum ambiguitates* über 80% des dritten Buches einnimmt, zeigt den großen methodischen Aufwand, den Augustin ihnen zugesteht; er subsumiert darunter die gesamte Figuralexegese."

With the other kinds of signs, learning more about language, nature, numbers, or music may suffice for the elucidation of some otherwise perplexing locution.[163] Ambiguous metaphorical signs, on the other hand, demand "no ordinary care and attention,"[164] as they are the type that most directly demands the practice of figural exegesis. For Augustine, the primary danger with ambiguous metaphorical signs concerns interpreting them literally, or, to speak technically, receiving signs as things *(signa pro rebus accipere)*.[165] Augustine variously describes this mistake as "carnal," "death of the soul," "a miserable kind of spiritual slavery," degradation to the level of beasts, and an instance of Paul's axiom: "The letter kills but the spirit gives life" (2 Cor. 3:6).[166] As one might guess, the chief examples of this category mistake concern Old Testament practices. For Christians, the word "Sabbath" does not pertain only to a literal day, nor does the word "sacrifice" refer only to a ritual act with animals and produce. Some Jews saw this, too, and indeed, the degree to which they recognized the signs as signs would determine their response to Jesus. Since Jesus did not observe their practices, those who clung to these signs rejected him and refused to believe that he was God, or had come from God.[167] But those who held to the signs properly received Christ and founded the first church, thereby demonstrating the usefulness *(utilitas)* of the law as pedagogue. Before the coming of Christ, they were "very close to being spiritual *(proximi spiritalibus)*" even though "they did not know how to interpret the signs spiritually *(quomodo spiritaliter essent intellegenda nescirent)*."[168] After the coming of the Holy Spirit, they immediately sold their possessions and distributed them to the poor — something no Gentile church ever did, since the Gentiles had not received the benefits of spiritual preparation provided by useful, Jewish signs.

In either response to Christ, the Jews were better than the pagans. The Jews may not have understood the purpose of the ceremonies, but they did know to worship the one true God. The Gentiles, by contrast, indulged in idolatry, worshiping images of the created order. "If, then, it is a carnal form of slavery to follow a sign divinely instituted for a useful purpose instead of the thing that it was instituted to represent *(signum*

---

163. *Doc. Chr.* 2.16.23ff.
164. Ibid., 3.5.9.
165. Ibid.
166. Ibid.
167. Ibid., 3.6.10.
168. Ibid.

utiliter institutum pro ipsa re sequi), is it not far worse to accept as things the humanly instituted signs of useless things *(inutilium rerum signa instituta pro rebus accipere)*?"[169] Jewish signs were useful in the sense that they referred to the one true God, while pagan signs referred to nothing useful at all. Christ brought fulfillment to the Jewish signs, since he was the very thing to which the observances referred. Pagan signs, by contrast, were simply to be destroyed, as God called the Gentiles to turn not just to "useful signs," but to the realities those Jewish practices signified.[170]

Augustine's treatment of ambiguous metaphorical signs thus brings him full circle. In Book 1, Augustine establishes God's status as the unique object for enjoyment, and Christ as both *summa res* and pure *signum* — that which perfectly represents the reality to which it refers and whose sole function is so to refer. Two books later, Augustine construes the Old Testament signs as "useful" with respect to Christ. The Jewish ceremonies did not exist for their own sake, but only for the sake of Jesus, who directs us to the enjoyment of God, the love of whom is the purpose and summation of all Scripture. To cling to Sabbath or sacrifice is, therefore, not just a category mistake; it is to miss the one who draws us toward ultimate reality.

Tyconius's Rules

It remains for Augustine to provide specific guidelines on how to recognize and interpret particular instances of ambiguous metaphorical signs. This is a challenging task, for while there will presumably be some similitude between the sign (or primary referent) and the ultimate object of reference, there are many ways to draw analogies between different things. "We should not imagine that there is a hard and fast rule that a word will always have the meaning that it has in a particular place."[171] Nevertheless, close examination of the biblical text does reveal certain patterns, and the presentation of these recurrent themes will occupy the final section of Book 3. For our purposes, the most relevant observation concerns the centrality of the sign–referent framework.

Augustine leans heavily in this discussion on a former Donatist, Tyconius, who had written a book of rules Augustine had found extremely

---

169. Ibid., 3.7.11.
170. Ibid., 3.8.12.
171. Ibid., 3.25.35.

helpful, somewhat to his dismay. Augustine's dependence on Tyconius may explain *De doctrina*'s famously odd compositional history, mentioned briefly above. Augustine began writing the first two books and the first part of Book 3 (up to 25.35) in 396/397, but did not finish the rest of Books 3 and 4 until 426 when he was preparing his *Retractationes*. The key section that would follow was the discussion of Tyconius, and while the exact reasons for Augustine's delay cannot be known with certainty, the awkwardness of invoking a figure with such incendiary associations provides a plausible explanation.[172] Whatever the case, it is remarkable that Augustine, a North African bishop now in the twilight of his life, would dedicate the concluding section of his manual on biblical interpretation to an exegetical handbook associated with the very schismatics whose influence he had spent decades trying to destroy.

Augustine's discussion of Tyconius is full of qualification.[173] Tyconius was a "Donatist heretic,"[174] he claimed too much for his rules,[175] and he

---

172. Charles Kannengiesser, "Interrupted *De doctrina christiana*," in Arnold and Bright, *De doctrina christiana*, 3-13. Kannengiesser suggests that Augustine was not yet prepared intellectually to deal with Tyconius's work. In the introduction to his translation of *De doctrina christiana*, Hill suggests, somewhat differently, that Augustine was more concerned with the politics of invoking a Donatist (even if a rejected one) in the midst of the most significant controversy of his bishopric. Thirty years later, the Donatist controversy is basically over and Augustine's stature more established, so he can appeal to Tyconius with less hesitation. See *Teaching Christianity* (De doctrina christiana), trans. Edmund Hill, WSA 1.11 (Hyde Park, NY: New City, 1996), 96-97. For an argument that the very section where Augustine pauses reflects his concern for Tyconius's rules, particularly with regard to the ambiguity of signs, see Pamela Bright, "Biblical Ambiguity in African Exegesis," in Arnold and Bright, *De doctrina christiana*, 25-32.

173. On Tyconius's *Book of Rules* and Augustine's (mis)appropriation of this text, see Pamela Bright, *The Book of Rules of Tyconius: Its Purpose and Inner Logic* (Notre Dame, IN: University of Notre Dame Press, 1988), and a series of contributions in Pamela Bright, ed., *Augustine and the Bible*: Pamela Bright, "'The Preponderating Influence of Augustine': A Study of the Epitomes of the *Book of Rules* of the Donatist Tyconius," 109-28; Robert A. Kugler, "Tyconius's *Mystic Rules* and the Rules of Augustine," 129-48; Charles Kannengiesser, "Augustine and Tyconius: A Conflict of Christian Hermeneutics in Roman Africa," 149-77. See also Pollmann, *Doctrina christiana*. For English translation and facing Latin edition, see Tyconius, *The Book of Rules*, trans. William S. Babcock (Atlanta: Scholars, 1989). For the purposes of this discussion, Augustine's depiction of Tyconius is more relevant than what Tyconius actually presented in his *Liber regularum*. I will thus follow the terminology Augustine uses, even if it is at variance with Tyconius himself.

174. *Doc. Chr.* 3.30.43.

175. Kannengiesser and Bright argue that Augustine's criticism of Tyconius on this point is based on a misunderstanding of *regulae*, which are, in Tyconius's terms, the princi-

often made mistakes, not just as any human would but especially because of his questionable and idiosyncratic theology.[176] Tyconius rejected Donatist ecclesiology, especially in his positions that the church is universal and includes evil people, yet he was never willing to join the other side of the battle in North Africa — an inconsistency Augustine finds deeply perplexing. Nevertheless, Augustine does acknowledge the value of Tyconius's text and expresses hope that others will read it, so long as they recognize its deficiencies. Of particular note are Tyconius's seven rules, which can "be used like keys *(clauibus)* to open up the secrets *(occulta)* of the divine scriptures."[177] By secrets, Augustine seems to mean the manner in which various things in Scripture can bear multiple meanings, the topic he introduces immediately after the thirty-year delay.[178] Tyconius's work attracts Augustine's attention precisely because the Donatist heretic recognized and addressed this basic phenomenon.

Tyconius divided his text according to specific patterns whereby one can discern in Scripture shifting or multiple referents. The sections are: 1) on the Lord and his body; 2) on the Lord's twofold body; 3) on the promise and the law; 4) on species and genus; 5) on measurements of time; 6) on recapitulation; and 7) on the devil and his body.[179] Augustine does not consider the third rule a hermeneutical principle so much as a basic framework for understanding faith and works, and dismisses it with reference to the Pelagian controversy. The other rules concern ways in which one thing is understood by another, which is exactly what it means for something to be a metaphorical expression.[180] Thus, the first rule concerns the manner in which Scripture switches between head (Christ) and body (church) without warning, and the necessity of discerning which statements refer to Christ and which to the church. One detects here the roots of *totus Christus,* the chief hermeneutical principle of Augustine's expositions on the Psalms.[181]

---

ples by which God wrote Scripture and not, as Augustine understood them, hermeneutical principles by which we are to interpret Scripture. See sources cited above.

176. For an illuminating treatment on the differences between Tyconius and Augustine on ecclesiology, see Joseph Ratzinger, "Beobachtungen zum Kirchenbegriff des Tyconius im *Liber regularum,*" *REAug* 2 (1956): 173-85.

177. *Doc. Chr.* 3.30.42.

178. Ibid., 3.25.36.

179. 1) De domine et eius corpore; 2) de domini corpore bipertito; 3) de promissis et lege; 4) de specie et genere; 5) de temporibus; 6) de recapitulatione; 7) de diabolo et eius corpore.

180. *Doc. Chr.* 3.37.56.

181. Studies on this issue include Cameron, "Augustine's Construction of Figurative Exegesis"; idem, *Christ Meets Me Everywhere,* 165-212; Byassee, *Praise Seeking Understanding.*

The second rule explains why blessings and curses can be addressed to the same group at the same time. The church as it appears now is mixed, and includes both the people of God and those who are not genuinely united with Christ. Sometimes Scripture addresses one group, sometimes the other, again without obvious signals that a shift has occurred.[182]

The fourth rule receives the most extended discussion. Under this principle, one part *(species)* can represent a whole *(genus)*. A city can represent a nation, a nation can represent the world, and a figure like Solomon can represent Christ and the church.[183] As with the first two rules, Scripture can switch imperceptibly between species and genus. Ezekiel's warning of imminent judgment refers to physical Israel (36:17-19), but his subsequent words of promise refer to the church amongst all the nations (36:23-29). "'Spiritual Israel' becomes not a matter of a single race, but of all the races *(non unius gentis, sed omnium)* promised to the fathers in their seed, which is Christ [Gal. 3:16]. This spiritual Israel is distinguished from the fleshly Israel, consisting of a single people *(unius gentis)*, by the novelty of grace, not by nobility of race *(nouitate gratiae, non nobilitate patriae)*, and by mentality, not nationality *(mente, non gente)*."[184] New Testament passages confirm this reading by drawing on Ezekiel's imagery (the conjunction of water and spirit, and the contrast between stone and flesh) in their reflections upon the church. Moreover, even references to the church can be distinguished according to redemptive history. When Ezekiel mentions land *(terra)*, for instance, two options present themselves. The land could refer to the New Testament church, since the church "is itself the land *(terra)* of the blessed, 'the land *(terra)* of the living' [Ps. 26:13 (27:13)]."[185] Or the prophecy could refer to the "land *(terra)* of a future generation, since there will be 'a new heaven and a new earth *(terra)*' [Rev. 21:1], in which the unjust will not be able to live."[186]

---

182. Augustine is displeased with Tyconius's title for this section, *de domini corpore bipertito*, and would prefer something like *de domini corpore uero atque permixto*, or *uero atque simulato*, or *de permixta ecclesia*. Augustine does not think the church is "bipartite," consisting of both good and evil. False Christians only appear to be part of the church, but are not actually, even now before the final judgment. This is different from Tyconius's claim that both true and false Christians really are part of the church. See Ratzinger, "Beobachtungen zum Kirchenbegriff."

183. The logic for Solomon as an example seems to be that he is a part of the church, which is the body of Christ. According to this extended series of connections, Solomon as *species* can therefore represent Christ or the church as *genus*.

184. *Doc. Chr.* 3.24.48-49. Green does well to render Augustine's Latin rhyme.

185. Ibid., 3.24.49.

186. Ibid.

In sum, Tyconius's *Book of Rules* furnishes Augustine with a developed argument that there are in Scripture recognizable patterns of ambiguous metaphorical signification. Scripture is constituted such that individual expressions may involve multiple referents: the meaning of an Old Testament sign may simply be its primary referent; or this primary referent may function as a sign to a secondary referent; and there may be multiple options for how to understand the secondary referent itself. Thus, for instance, a sign may refer literally to Israel, or figuratively to Christ; but Christ and the church are one as head and body, so the sign could also refer to the church; and the church itself can be understood in multiple ways according to its place in redemptive history. Discerning the appropriate referents demands great care, especially since the text does not always flag when a shift of referent has occurred. Yet on Augustine's terms, it is precisely the difficulty of this challenge that exercises the mind, prompts humility, and ultimately produces delight.[187] For all the obscurities of Scripture lead us, in one way or another, back to Christ, the *patria* of our journey and the only appropriate object of enjoyment. Interpreting Scripture in light of Christ is therefore an exercise in sanctification, coextensive with the hermeneutic of love.

Discussion

The consistency of Augustine's two-tier understanding of Scripture and redemptive history, across his career and a range of theological loci, should now be clear. For Augustine, the unity of Scripture is a unity of reference, as is the unity of redemption. The Old and New Testaments mediate different covenants, but these covenants are united in the signification of the new by the old. Israel and the church are two different peoples, but they are united by the prefiguration of the heavenly city in Israel. And finally, the unity of the literal and spiritual senses derives from the reference of one *res* to another. Augustine's understanding of these ordered pairs is not purely antagonistic; in many contexts, he is defending the former instance (old covenant, Israel, literal sense) against those who would reject it entirely, affirming its ability to mediate new realities. Still, there are for Augustine two covenants, two peoples, and two levels of interpretation. As we shall see in the next chapter, for Calvin there is only one.

---

187. On this matter, note the importance of 2.6.8 and Williams's discussion of this passage in "Language, Reality and Desire in Augustine's *De doctrina*," 142.

CHAPTER 2

John Calvin: The Unitary Covenant of Christ

Introduction

The central theme in Calvin's construal of redemptive history is the unity of the covenant. The consistency of God's engagement with humanity derives from the consistency of his character, and the several covenants that structure salvation history are variant instances of a single covenant of grace, grounded on Christ before and after the incarnation. Many of the characteristic features of later, broadly Calvinist traditions — strong affirmation of the law, the practice of infant baptism, "covenant" as a structuring theological theme — derive from this basic set of convictions. The result for Calvin is a theology of Scripture where the New Testament illuminates but does not alter what came before, and Christological reading merges with literal reading to form one sense. The covenant, the people of God, and the literal sense remain the same across the testaments. In this chapter, as in the previous, I will consider these three topics in turn. I will then consider the differences between Augustine's and Calvin's construals of redemption and the implications for Scriptural interpretation.

The Covenant across the Testaments

The natural place to begin for Calvin's understanding of the covenants is his *Institutes of the Christian Religion* (1559 edition) Book 2, Chapters 10 and 11, entitled "The Similarity of the Old and New Testaments" (*De similitudine Veteris et Novi testamenti*) and "The Difference between the Two Testaments" (*De differentia unius Testamenti ab altero*), respectively. These chapters constitute, alongside Ch. 9, a kind of excursus within the broad narrative portrayal of redemptive history that structures Book 2: the fallenness of humanity (Chs. 1–5), the need for a mediator (Chs. 6–8), the relation between the testaments (Chs. 9–11), and the work of Christ (Chs. 12–15).[1] For our purposes, the opening remarks of Ch. 10 are programmatic:

> Now we can clearly see from what has already been said that all men adopted by God into the company of his people since the beginning of the world were covenanted to him by the same law and by the bond of the same doctrine as obtains among us. It is very important to make this point. Accordingly I shall add, by way of appendix, how far the condition of the patriarchs in this fellowship differed from ours, though they participated in the same inheritance and hoped for a common salvation with us by the grace of the same Mediator. The testimonies that we have gathered from the Law and the Prophets to prove this make plain that God's people have never had any other rule of reverence and piety. Nevertheless, because writers often argue at length about the difference between the Old and New Testament, thus arousing some misgiving in the simple reader's mind, we shall rightly devote a special section to a fuller and more precise discussion of this matter.[2]

Some initial points from this passage and Calvin's subsequent exposition bear emphasis. First, God's covenant extends from the beginning of the world, forming one people across the testaments. Second, all God's people participate in this one covenant by the same law and the bond of the same doctrine, sharing the same rule of reverence and piety. Third, however, there are differences between the condition of the patriarchs

---

1. For a fuller discussion of this narrative, see T. H. L. Parker, *Calvin's Old Testament Commentaries* (Louisville: Westminster/John Knox, 1986), 42-55; Stephen Edmondson, *Calvin's Christology* (Cambridge: Cambridge University Press, 2004), 44-48.

2. *Inst.* 2.10.1. "Ex superioribus liquere iam potest, quoscunque ab initio mundi homines Deus in populi sui sortem cooptavit, eadem lege atque doctrinae eiusdem quae inter nos viget vinculo fuisse ei foederatos; sed quia non parum interest caput hoc stabiliri, vice appendicis annectam, quum Patres eiusdem nobiscum haereditatis fuerint consortes, et eiusdem Mediatoris gratia communem salutem speraverint, quatenus in societate hac diversa fuerit eorum conditio. Quanquam autem quae ex Lege ac Prophetis ad eius probationem collegimus testimonia, palam faciunt non aliam unquam fuisse in Dei populo religionis pietatisque regulam: quia tamen apud scriptores multa saepe de discrimine Veteris ac novi Testamenti disputantur, quae scrupulum parum acuto lectori iniicere possint, huic rei melius atque exactius discutiendae peculiarem locum iure destinabimus."

and our own, though Calvin will treat this issue in the following chapter "by way of appendix *(vice appendicis)*" to his main point on the unity of the testaments. Finally, as Calvin proceeds in this discussion, he will explicitly resist the conclusions of those, like Servetus, who denigrate the Israelites as a carnal people — as if they were "nothing but a herd of swine . . . fattened by the Lord on earth without any hope of heavenly immortality."[3] These considerations give rise to the single most quoted summary statement of Calvin's position on the relation between the testaments: "The covenant made with all the patriarchs is so much like ours in substance and reality *(substantia et re ipsa)* that the two are actually one and the same *(unum prorsus atque idem sit)*. Yet they differ in the mode of dispensation *(administratio tamen variat).*"[4] Indeed, it is more accurate to speak of the unity *(unitate)* of the testaments rather than the similarity *(similitudine)*.[5]

Having established this basic framework, Calvin delineates three similarities between the testaments in Book 2, Ch. 10, and four (or five) differences in Book 2, Ch. 11. For reference, I list them briefly here:

Similarities
1. The Jews shared in the common hope of immortality.
2. The covenant with the Jews was founded on God's mercy and not their merits.
3. The Jews had and knew Christ as a mediator.

Differences
1. God used earthly promises to direct the Jews toward the heavenly inheritance.
2. The old covenant displayed images and shadows; the new covenant reveals truth and substance.
3. The old covenant was associated with the letter, death, and condemnation; the new covenant is associated with the Spirit, life, and righteousness.

---

3. Ibid.
4. Ibid., 2.10.2.
5. Ibid. Thus Hans Heinrich Wolf: "Die zweite Hälfte unseres zuerst zitierten Satzes sagt deutlich genug, es handelt sich nicht um zwei Bünde, sondern um einen und denselben. Zwischen dem foedus patrum und dem mit uns geschlossenen Bund besteht Identität" (*Die Einheit des Bundes: Das Verhältnis von Altem und Neuem Testament bei Calvin* [Neukirchen: Verlag der Buchhandlung des Erziehungsvereins, 1958], 19).

John Calvin

4. The old covenant was characterized by bondage and fear; the new covenant is characterized by freedom, trust, and assurance.
5. The old covenant was restricted to the Jews; the new covenant has been extended to the Gentiles. (Calvin considers this point somewhat supplemental.)

Calvin's treatment of these issues is scattered throughout Book 2, Chs. 10-11 as well as other parts of *Institutes*. In what follows, I will incorporate these discussions into a broad overview of Calvin's position on the covenants according to the following topics: the promise of immortality, the purpose of the law, the dynamics of Christ's mediation, and the question of fear and bondage under the old covenant.

The Promise of Immortality

Calvin's position on the Old Testament promises cuts directly against the kind of perspective we have witnessed in Augustine.[6] Calvin resists the

---

6. For studies on Calvin's treatment of the covenants and his general approach to the Old Testament, see Ronald S. Wallace, *Calvin's Doctrine of the Word and Sacrament* (Edinburgh: Oliver and Boyd, 1953); Wolf, *Die Einheit des Bundes*; I. John Hesselink, "Calvin and Heilsgeschichte," in *Oikonomia, Heilsgeschichte als Thema der Theologie: Oscar Cullmann zum 65. Geburtstag gewidmet*, ed. Felix Christ (Hamburg: Herbert Reich Evangelischer Verlag, 1967), 163-70; idem, "Law and Gospel or Gospel and Law? Calvin's Understanding of the Relationship," in *Calviniana: Ideas and Influences of John Calvin*, ed. Robert V. Schnucker, Sixteenth Century Essays and Studies 10 (Kirksville, MO: Sixteenth Century Journal, 1988), 13-32; idem, *Calvin's Concept of the Law* (Allison Park, PA: Pickwick, 1992); Anthony A. Hoekema, "The Covenant of Grace in Calvin's Teaching," *CTJ* 2 (1967): 133-61; Wilhelm Vischer, "Calvin, exégète de l'Ancien Testament," *RRef* 18 (1967): 1-20; Hans-Joachim Kraus, "Calvin's Exegetical Principles," *Int* 31 (1977): 8-18; idem, "Israel in the Theology of Calvin — Towards a New Approach to the Old Testament and Judaism," *Christian Jewish Relations* 22 (1989): 75-86; M. Eugene Osterhaven, "Calvin on the Covenant," in *Readings in Calvin's Theology*, ed. Donald K. McKim (Grand Rapids: Baker, 1984), 89-106; T. H. L. Parker, *Calvin's New Testament Commentaries*, 2nd ed. (Louisville: Westminster/John Knox, 1993); idem, *Calvin's Old Testament Commentaries*; Richard A. Muller, "The Hermeneutic of Promise and Fulfillment in Calvin's Exegesis of the Old Testament Prophecies of the Kingdom," in *The Bible in the Sixteenth Century*, ed. David C. Steinmetz, Duke Monographs in Medieval and Renaissance Studies 11 (Durham, NC: Duke University Press, 1990), 68-82; idem, *Post-Reformation Reformed Dogmatics: The Rise and Development of Reformed Orthodoxy, ca. 1520 to ca. 1725*, vol. 2: *Holy Scripture: The Cognitive Foundation of Theology*, 2nd ed. (Grand Rapids: Baker Academic, 2003); Peter Opitz, *Calvins theologische Hermeneutik* (Neukirchener-

suggestion of Servetus and others that the Israelites cared only about the benefits of the body; he denies that Canaan constituted the entirety of God's promises to Israel; and he refuses to instrumentalize the Israelites, in contrast to those who "unhesitatingly conclude that the Jews were set apart from all other peoples not for their own benefit but for that of others *(non sua causa, sed aliena)*, in order that the Christian church might have an outward image in which it might discern proofs of spiritual things."[7] There is no strict dichotomy between those who lived before and after the time of Christ. The Old Testament was "established upon the free mercy of God" and "confirmed by Christ's intercession. . . . Who, then, dares to separate the Jews from Christ, since with them, we hear, was made the covenant of the gospel, the sole foundation of which is Christ? Who dares to estrange from the gift of free salvation those to whom we hear the doctrine of the righteousness of faith was imparted?"[8]

As Calvin argues, the New Testament repeatedly teaches that the gospel was promised in the Old Testament (Rom. 1:2-3, 3:21), and the gospel certainly secures immortality and spiritual blessings (Eph. 1:13-14, Col. 1:4-5, 2 Thess. 2:14, and elsewhere). Such blessings, moreover, were not merely "intended for the new people"[9] if, as Paul writes, the law was given for those under the law (Rom. 3:19), and the law itself bore witness to the gospel (Rom. 3:21). Indeed, Calvin argues, the sacraments of the Old Testament were just as efficacious as those of the New.[10] Paul's warning in 1 Cor. 10 not to imitate the Israelites trades on the assumption that baptism and the Lord's Supper would no more protect the Corinthians than the spiritual food and drink of the desert did the Israelites — which food and drink was Christ.[11]

Vluyn: Neukirchener, 1994); David L. Puckett, *John Calvin's Exegesis of the Old Testament*, Columbia Series in Reformed Theology (Louisville: Westminster John Knox, 1995); Peter A. Lillback, *The Binding of God: Calvin's Role in the Development of Covenant Theology*, Texts and Studies in Reformation and Post-Reformation Thought (Grand Rapids: Baker Academic, 2001); Edmondson, *Calvin's Christology;* idem, "Christ and History: Hermeneutical Convergence in Calvin and Its Challenge to Biblical Theology," *Modern Theology* 21 (2005): 1-35; Raymond A. Blacketer, *The School of God: Pedagogy and Rhetoric in Calvin's Interpretation of Deuteronomy*, Studies in Early Modern Religious Reforms 3 (Dordrecht: Springer, 2006); G. Sujin Pak, *The Judaizing Calvin,* OSHT (Oxford: Oxford University Press, 2010).

    7. *Inst.* 2.11.1.
    8. Ibid., 2.10.4.
    9. Ibid., 2.10.3.
    10. Ibid., 2.10.5.
    11. Ibid. In 2.10.6, Calvin explicitly cites Augustine's *c. Faust.* on this point. While the footnote of the McNeill/Battles translation names *c. Faust.* 15.11 and 19.16 as the sources of

The Old Testament also provides significant warrant for the promise of immortality. First, Old Testament believers participated in God's Word, which Calvin explicitly defines as special and not just general revelation.[12] Second, the very formula of the covenant, "'I will be your God, and you shall be my people'" (Lev. 26:12), testifies to the hope of immortality, since this holistic promise of blessing, life, and salvation would make no sense if it were confined to earthly happiness.[13] Third, the Old Testament saints modeled hope for immortality, which enabled figures like Noah, Abraham, and Isaac to endure suffering on this earth. As Heb. 11 teaches, the Old Testament figures did not receive on earth what they were promised, and they hoped instead for a heavenly country.[14]

Calvin acknowledges that this promise was not as explicit in the earliest phases of redemptive history as it would be later. What was for Adam but "a feeble spark"[15] would grow until the Son finally arrived. By the time of David and especially the latter prophets, though, the promise of immortality unquestionably functioned as a source of hope for Old Testament believers. The Jews

> did not manifest in such statements any secret wisdom to which only excellent spirits might individually and privately be admitted. But, as they had been appointed the teachers of the common people by the Holy Spirit, they widely published the mysteries of God that were appointed to be learned and that ought to be the principles of the religion of the people. Therefore, when we hear the public oracles of the Holy Spirit, in which he so clearly and plainly discussed spiritual life in the church of the Jews, it would be intolerable stubbornness to relegate them solely to a carnal covenant, wherein mention is made only of the earth and of earthly riches.[16]

The one significant concession Calvin acknowledges on this matter is that God used earthly goods in the Old Testament to incite people toward

---

Calvin's remark, it is not clear to me that either passage substantiates the claims attributed to Augustine concerning the promise of immortality in the Old Testament or the efficacy of the Old Testament sacraments.

12. *Inst.* 2.10.7.
13. Ibid., 2.10.9.
14. Ibid., 2.10.13.
15. Ibid., 2.10.20.
16. Ibid., 2.10.19.

heavenly reward. The Israelites' final hope was always eternal; "yet, to nourish them better in this hope, [God] displayed it for them to see and, so to speak, to taste, under earthly benefits *(sub beneficiis terrenis)*."[17] According to a basic principle throughout his work, Calvin sees no difference in the substance of what was promised, while recognizing variations in clarity of manifestation and perception. Such gradations presuppose a narrative of maturation from the Old Testament to the New. The Jews received a "lower mode of training" as a child heir under the charge of a guardian (Gal. 4:1-2).[18] They were directed toward the same inheritance but "not yet old enough to be able to enter upon it and manage it."[19] They were members of the same church "but as yet in its childhood."[20] To keep the Israelites from coveting earthly reward, God mixed heavenly promises with earthly ones, vowing to Abraham, for instance, the blessing of physical land alongside God's protection and presence (Gen. 15:1). Yet Abraham and the patriarchs hoped primarily in the latter, receiving the promise of land only "as a symbol of [God's] benevolence and as a type of the heavenly inheritance."[21] For Calvin, the hopes of the Old and New Testaments are identical, as with the one covenant.

The Purpose of the Law

The importance of the law for Calvin is most clearly discerned in the extended discussion of *Institutes* Book 2, Ch. 8, "Explanation of the Moral Law *(legis moralis explicatio)*"[22] and the structure of his combined *Commentaries on the Four Last Books of Moses, Arranged in the Form of a Harmony* (hereafter *Mosaic Harmony;* written from about 1559-63).[23] The law is "the rule of perfect righteousness,"[24] God's appointed means of cultivating our love of righteousness,[25] and we dare not add to it by inventing new

---

17. Ibid., 2.11.1.
18. Ibid.
19. Ibid., 2.11.2.
20. Ibid.
21. Ibid.
22. Book 2, Ch. 8 is one of the longest chapters in *Inst.,* totaling 56 pp. in the *Opera Selecta*. By comparison, all the chapters on election combined (Book 3, Chs. 21–24) total only 65 pp.
23. On date of composition, see Parker, *Calvin's Old Testament Commentaries,* 31-32.
24. *Inst.* 2.8.5.
25. Ibid., 2.8.4.

works to win God's favor (Deut. 12:32).²⁶ The essence of the law must therefore remain unchanged throughout redemptive history. According to Calvin, the consequences of obedience and disobedience were always eternal life and perdition, even if the Mosaic law sometimes set forth temporal rewards and punishments,²⁷ and God's character as a "spiritual lawgiver" means that "inward and spiritual righteousness" has always been in view.²⁸ Christ, the law's "best interpreter,"²⁹ did not establish a new law, but only restored what the Pharisees had defiled. There is thus no new law of the gospel that surpasses the old law. The unity of the law rather coincides with the unity of the covenant.

Calvin presents the commandments of the Decalogue as synecdoches that stand for larger principles.³⁰ Discerning these principles requires balance: we may not manipulate the law to make it say whatever we please, yet we should also avoid restricting ourselves to the "narrowness of the words."³¹ The proper strategy is to consider the reason *(ratio)* or purpose *(finis)* of each commandment, and then to define the commandment's substance *(summa)* through a summary of what is enjoined. Understanding the purpose and substance of the commandments reveals the positive duties associated with the negative injunctions.³² The commandment not to kill, for instance, means more than not wronging another person; we must also help our neighbor as much as possible. God has taught his will "by half commandments *(dimidiis praeceptis),*"³³ setting forth in each commandment the worst example of a certain kind of transgression, such that we might naturally detest all sins associated with it. Anger and hatred may not seem like serious sins, for instance, but murder reveals the dangers of related iniquities we might otherwise treat lightly.

As Calvin proceeds through Book 2, Ch. 8, he considers each commandment according to its *finis* and *summa*.³⁴ The *finis* of the first

---

26. Ibid., 2.8.5.
27. Ibid., 2.8.4.
28. Ibid., 2.8.6.
29. Ibid., 2.8.7.
30. Ibid., 2.8.8.
31. Ibid.
32. Ibid., 2.8.9.
33. Ibid., 2.8.10.
34. The *finis* and *summa* of each commandment are found in the following places in *Inst.* First: 2.8.16; second: 2.8.17; third: 2.8.22; fourth: 2.8.28 *(finis)*; 2.8.34 *(summa)*; fifth:

commandment is for the Lord to be preeminent among his people; the *summa* is to put away all impiety and superstition. The *finis* of the second commandment is to avoid profaning the worship of God by superstitious rites; the *summa* is to abstain from petty, carnal observances. At the end of this exposition, Calvin concludes that the purpose of the whole law is the cultivation of human righteousness according to divine purity, and that the *summa* of the law, as stated in Deut. 10:12-13, is to fear God, walk in his ways, love him, serve him, and keep his commands.[35] Given these broad considerations, it would be absurd to suggest that "the law teaches nothing but some rudiments and preliminaries of righteousness by which men begin their apprenticeship, and does not also guide them to the true goal, good works."[36] The law of Moses encompasses all that is necessary for true religion — in both Old and New Testament times.

The import of this *finis/summa* structure for the relation between the testaments becomes especially apparent in Calvin's *Mosaic Harmony*. This idiosyncratic commentary begins with a relatively straightforward exposition of Exod. 1–19, which recounts the escape from Egypt and the Israelites' preparation to receive the law. Then, at the beginning of Exod. 20, Calvin shifts course into a rather remarkable treatment of the law, consisting of the following sections:

2.8.35; sixth: 2.8.39; seventh: 2.8.41; eighth: 2.8.45; ninth: 2.8.47; tenth: 2.8.49. For almost all the commandments, Calvin begins his treatment by explicitly using the words *finis* and *summa* in subsequent sentences. The two exceptions are the first and the fourth. In his description of the first commandment, he uses the term *finis* but uses the phrase *id ut fiat* instead of *summa*. This commandment is thus a formal exception to the basic pattern, but not a material one. Calvin probably varies the pattern simply because he is treating the first of the commandments and wishes to show more clearly the connection between purpose and substance. The fourth commandment is an exception because it is ceremonial. Calvin explains the *finis* at the beginning of his exposition, but must then discuss how Christians have appropriated the Sabbath before he can return to the *summa* and lay out the specific behavior now required. The *finis/summa* structure of each command is obvious — and obviously intentional — in light of Calvin's introductory remarks on *finis/summa* in 2.8.8 and his use of these terms for virtually every commandment. The English translation unfortunately obscures this structure. The term *summa* is first introduced by the word "substance" (2.8.8), but the other commandments feature the phrases "to sum up" (second, fourth, sixth, seventh, eighth, ninth, tenth) and "the sum" (fifth). Most incomprehensibly, the translator uses the phrase "in brief" to express the *summa* of the third commandment, even though the phraseology *(summa igitur erit)* is exactly identical to that found in the fifth, seventh, eighth, ninth, and tenth commandments.

35. *Inst.* 2.8.51.
36. Ibid.

John Calvin

1. The Preface to the Law *(Praefatio in legem)*[37]
2. The Law *(Lex)*[38]
3. The Sum of the Law *(Summa legis)*[39]
4. The Purpose and Use of the Law *(Finis et usus legis)*[40]
5. The Sanctions of the Law Contained in the Promises and Threats *(Sanctiones a promissionibus et minis)*[41]

In the second section, by far the longest of the five,[42] Calvin categorizes literally every prescription from Exodus to Deuteronomy under one of the Ten Commandments,[43] while further grouping each of these individual prescriptions into two major categories: 1) the Decalogue itself, and all laws that correspond closely to one of the Ten Commandments; and 2) the supplements *(appendices)*, which includes both political laws and the ceremonial practices.[44] The results are often bizarre. The first commandment, for example, encompasses requirements with regard to the celebration of Passover[45]; the sanctification of the firstborn[46]; the payment of tribute[47]; the vow of the Nazirites[48]; the offering of firstfruits[49]; the purification of

---

37. *Mos. Harm.* CTS 2.1:338-417, CO 24:209-60. I use page numbers of both English and Latin editions of *Mosaic Harmony*. Since Calvin does not follow the order of the biblical text, it would otherwise be difficult to locate where he treats individual passages.

38. Ibid., CTS 2.1:417-3.3:189, CO 24:261-720.

39. Ibid., CTS 3.3:190-96, CO 24:721-24.

40. Ibid., CTS 3.3:196-201, CO 24:725-28. I have corrected the CTS translation of the title, "The Use of the Law." Calvin's reference here to the *finis* of the law makes obvious the correspondence between *Mosaic Harmony* and *Institutes*.

41. Ibid., CTS 3.3:201-89, CO 25:5-58.

42. *Lex* comprises 460 of 1122 pages in the *Calvini Opera*, over 40 percent of the entire commentary.

43. For a discussion of Calvin's reasons for thus arranging the Mosaic commentary, see Blacketer, *The School of God*, 127-170.

44. These categories are specified in the preface to the commentary (*Mos. Harm.* CTS 2.1:xvii, CO 24:7-8). Calvin says the ceremonial supplements concern the first table and the political supplements concern the second table, but he does not actually follow this arrangement. Political supplements are found under the first four commandments, and ceremonial supplements are found under the following six commandments. See Parker, *Calvin's Old Testament Commentaries*, 122-75 for an overview of the way Calvin treats the Ten Commandments. See also Hesselink's treatment in *Calvin's Concept of the Law*, 102-38.

45. *Mos. Harm.* CTS 2.1:454-77, CO 24:283-98.

46. Ibid., CTS 2.1:477-81, CO 24:298-301.

47. Ibid., CTS 2.1:481-84, CO 24:301-2.

48. Ibid., CTS 2.1:484-92, CO 24:302-7.

49. Ibid., CTS 2.1:492-97, CO 24:307-11.

women after confinement[50]; the shutting up[51] and purification[52] of lepers; pollution from semen and menstruation[53]; defects for exclusion from the tabernacle[54]; the general purification of the people[55]; nocturnal emissions and defecation[56]; the mixing of seeds, or of wool and linen[57]; the distinction between clean and unclean animals[58]; touching things accidentally unclean[59]; marriage with unbelievers.[60] (Note that this list includes only the ceremonial, and not also the political supplements Calvin delineates.)

Still, the purpose of this organizational structure is fairly transparent. Separating the commandments and supplements enables Calvin to establish a clean distinction between the substance and the appendages of the law that corresponds precisely to the framework set forth in *Institutes*. There, Calvin located the unity of the covenant in a common *substantia* across the testaments, while addressing the differences between the testaments by way of appendix *(vice appendicis)*.[61] Here, Calvin writes, "We understand that the Ceremonies and the Judicial Ordinances neither change nor detract from the rule laid down in the Ten Commandments; but are only helps, which, as it were, lead us by the hand to the due Worship of God, and to the promotion of justice towards men."[62] The sacrifices, moreover,

> are not, to speak correctly, of the substance *(substantia)* of the Law, nor avail of themselves in the Worship of God, nor are required by the Lawgiver himself as necessary, or even as useful, unless they sink into this inferior position. In fine, they are appendages *(accessiones)*, which add not the smallest completeness to the Law, but whose object is to retain the pious in the Spiritual Worship of God . . . As to all the Political Ordinances, nothing will obviously be found in them, which at all adds to the perfection of The Second Table: therefore it follows, that

50. Ibid., CTS 2.1:498-502, CO 24:311-14.
51. Ibid., CTS 2.2:5-18, CO 24:314-22.
52. Ibid., CTS 2.2:19-28, CO 24:322-27.
53. Ibid., CTS 2.2:28-33, CO 24:327-30.
54. Ibid., CTS 2.2:33-35, CO 24:330-31.
55. Ibid., CTS 2.2:35-44, CO 24:331-37.
56. Ibid., CTS 2.2:44-47, CO 24:337-38.
57. Ibid., CTS 2.2:47-52, CO 24:339-42.
58. Ibid., CTS 2.2:53-68, CO 24:342-51.
59. Ibid., CTS 2.2:68-70, CO 24:351-52.
60. Ibid., CTS 2.2:70-72, CO 24:352-54.
61. *Inst.* 2.10.1-2.
62. *Mos. Harm.* CTS 2.1:xvii, CO 24:7-8.

nothing can be wanted as the rule of a good and perfect life beyond the Ten Commandments.[63]

The unity of the law thus mirrors that of the covenant: the *substantia* remains the same, though there are changes of form and administration in the *appendices*. And since the *substantia* of the law just is the Decalogue, there is no "substantive" sense in which the Old Testament law is abrogated with the coming of Christ. The law remains essentially the same across the testaments.

This is not to suggest that the purpose of the law experienced no modification whatsoever. In *Institutes* Book 2, Ch. 7,[64] Calvin sets forth three functions of the law and then explains two ways the law has indeed been changed with the coming of Christ. The functions are familiar enough: to reveal sin and thus direct us to Christ,[65] to restrain evil,[66] and to encourage obedience to God.[67] All three concern the moral law, and each remains important in the transition from the Old Testament to the New. But two characteristics of the old covenant law are nullified, and this dynamic requires explication. First, we are released from the bonds and curse of the law, those "harsh and dangerous requirements, which remit nothing of the extreme penalty of the law, and suffer no transgression to go unpunished."[68] Though New Testament believers continue to revere the law, our consciences are no longer troubled by the fear of death. Second, the ceremonies are abrogated in "use *(usu),*" though not in "effect *(effectu)*."[69] For Calvin, the coming of Christ marks the end of the ceremonial practices, but this development actually brings them honor by revealing their true purpose. Only with their termination can one "better recognize how useful they were before the coming of Christ, who in abrogating their use has by his death sealed their force and effect."[70]

---

63. Ibid., CTS 2.1:xvii, CO 24:7-8.
64. "The law was given, not to restrain the folk of the old covenant under itself, but to foster hope of salvation in Christ until his coming *(Legem fuisse datam, non quae populum veterem in se retineret, sed quae foveret spem salutis in Christo usque ad eius adventum)*."
65. *Inst.* 2.7.6-9. Calvin especially appeals to Augustine on this point (*spir. et litt.* in particular).
66. Ibid., 2.7.10-11.
67. Ibid., 2.7.12-13.
68. Ibid., 2.7.15.
69. Ibid., 2.7.16.
70. Ibid.

The challenge for Calvin is to reconcile the substantial unity of the law with such transitions, particularly with regard to the liberation of the New Testament from the bondage and curse of the former covenant. Did Moses not set forth a different mode of relation with God than that revealed in Christ? Do these changes not bear upon the basic character of the law? Calvin's creative solution, as presented in *Mosaic Harmony* and elsewhere, is to distinguish between the general teaching of Moses and the law in its conditional particularity. The purpose of the Mosaic law was to renew the Abrahamic covenant, which had to that point fallen into disregard.[71] Thus, the law did not replace the promises to Abraham but served as testimony and confirmation of God's everlasting grace and commitment toward his people. Yet the law of Moses would also bring about one important change from the earlier covenant:

> Although the Law is a testimony of God's gratuitous adoption, and teaches that salvation is based upon His mercy, and invites men to call upon God with sure confidence, yet it has this peculiar property *(hoc tamen habere proprium et peculiare)*, that it covenants conditionally *(sub conditione paciscitur)*. Therefore it is worth while to distinguish between the general doctrine, which was delivered by Moses *(generalem doctrinam quae tradita fuit a Mose)*, and the special command which he received *(speciale quod accepit mandatum)*.[72]

This particular and conditional office, in contrast with Moses's more general teaching, was to require perfect righteousness, and to promise reward and threaten vengeance contingent upon obedience or disobedience to God's commands. Only the law in this capacity, and not the law as a whole, advanced such demands.

Calvin admits forthrightly that this arrangement created something of an antithesis in humanity's relation with God. In the law, "God sustains no other character than that of a Judge, who, after having rigidly exacted what is due to Him, promises only a just reward, and threatens the transgressors with vengeance."[73] Still, he argues, the overarching purpose of the law remains the same: to direct us toward grace. The New Testament itself supports such a position in Paul's allusion to the superiority of our

---

71. *Mos. Harm.* CTS 2.1:313, CO 24:192.
72. Ibid., CTS 2.1:313, CO 24:192-93.
73. Ibid., CTS 2.1:315, CO 24:193.

freedom over the fathers' bondage (Rom. 8:15), and in the contrast in Hebrews between Mt. Sinai and the heavenly Mt. Zion (12:18-22). "What was entrusted to Moses is separate and distinct from the gospel; because God, who appeared as an avenger, now with fatherly kindness gently invites us unto salvation, and soothes our troubled minds by offering us the forgiveness of our sins."[74] Broadly speaking, then, the law can be located against God's eternal covenant, for the threatenings of the law draw us ultimately to Christ. So, too, Moses was primarily a minister of grace who exhorted sinners toward the mercy of reconciliation.[75] But the law he established bore the particular function of coupling perfect obedience and conditional reward, and this is a point of difference between the testaments — though not one, for Calvin, that essentially undermines the covenant or God's promises of grace.

Grace, Merit, and the Mediation of Christ

Calvin's argument that the essence of the law remains unchanged despite the transition from threats to grace may seem like special pleading, and I will suggest later in this chapter that he himself struggles to maintain this position consistently. First, though, it is worth noting just how seriously he weighs this matter. For Calvin, it is not enough simply to affirm the ongoing validity of the moral law; he believes the very dynamics of salvation remain unchanged across the testaments, and the Old Testament mediated God's grace through Christ no less than the New. Indeed, Calvin asserts that Old Testament believers consciously perceived Christ to be their mediator, even if somewhat less clearly than those living in New Testament times.

Consider, for instance, *Institutes* Book 3, Ch. 17, entitled "The Agreement of the Promises of the Law and of the Gospel *(Promissionum Legis et Evangelii conciliatio).*" Calvin begins this chapter by wrestling with the problem of Old Testament passages where blessings and curses seem contingent on obedience to God's commands. Do these passages contradict the promises of the gospel that justification is by faith and not by good works? Calvin's answer reflects his basic understanding of the law: "If we cleave to the law, we are bereft of all blessing and a curse hangs over us, one

---

74. Ibid., CTS 2.1:315, CO 24:194.
75. Ibid., CTS 2.1:313, CO 24:193.

ordained for all transgressors."[76] The promised blessings would be available only for those who keep the law perfectly, but since no such person exists, all humanity would necessarily come under God's curse and wrath. The result, Calvin writes, would be the nullification of God's promises in the law — "had God's goodness not helped us through the gospel."[77]

But this last phrase is a counterfactual, and this is a crucial point, for according to Calvin, such a condition does not obtain precisely because Christ has fulfilled all righteousness. When one considers the promises only "so long as they have reference to the merit of works . . . they are in a sense abolished."[78] But "when the promises of the gospel are substituted . . . these not only make us acceptable to God, but also render our works pleasing to him."[79] Calvin explains, in a striking remark that deserves to be quoted in full:

> And not only does the Lord adjudge them pleasing; he also extends to them the blessings which under the covenant were owed to the observance of his law. I therefore admit that what the Lord has promised in his law to the keepers of righteousness and holiness is paid to the works of believers, but in this repayment we must always consider the reason that wins favor for these works.
>
> Now we see that there are three reasons. The first is: God, having turned his gaze from his servants' works, which always deserve reproof rather than praise, embraces his servants in Christ, and with faith alone intervening, reconciles them to himself without the help of works. The second is: of his own fatherly generosity and loving-kindness, and without considering their worth, he raises works to this place of honor, so that he attributes some value to them. The third is: He receives these very works with pardon, not imputing the imperfection with which they are all so corrupted that they would otherwise be reckoned as sins rather than virtues.[80]

In short, there are two ways to understand the law and its promises of reward. When the promises are read with reference to the merit of works, they have no value for us, for no one can fulfill the law perfectly. But when

---

76. *Inst.* 3.17.1.
77. Ibid., 3.17.2.
78. Ibid., 3.17.3.
79. Ibid.
80. Ibid.

treated with regard to the gospel, the promises confer benefit, for God receives us in Christ and judges our works more valuable and less imperfect than they actually are. The "New Testament" dynamics of grace and merit are actually operative under the "Old Testament" law.[81]

Yet Calvin's position goes even further than this. Not only does Christ act as mediator between God and humanity in both testaments, but Christ was actually known as such before the incarnation, and not just (as for Augustine) by an exceptional few.[82] This is the basic argument of *Institutes* Book 2, Ch. 9, "Christ, although he was known to the Jews under the law, was at length clearly revealed only in the gospel *(Christum, quanvis sub Lege Iudaeis cognitus fuerit, tamen Evangelio demum exhibitum fuisse),*" where Calvin labors to balance two apparently obverse claims: that Christ was indeed revealed to Old Testament believers, and that he was also revealed more clearly in the New Testament. Thus, Abraham saw Christ's day and rejoiced (John 8:56), but his vision of Christ remained "rather indistinct *(obscurior)*."[83] Moses bore witness to Jesus (John 5:46), though he did not see what we see now (Matt. 13:16-17; Luke 10:23-24). Even John 1:18 supports Calvin's point, with the right interpretation. There we read, "'No one has ever seen God; the only Son, who is in the bosom of the Father, he has made him known.'" Calvin writes that John "does not exclude the pious who died before Christ from the fellowship of the understanding and light that shine in the person of Christ. But, by comparing their lot with ours, he teaches that those mysteries which they but glimpsed in shadow outline are manifest to us."[84] All these examples show that the

---

81. For further discussion of how Calvin understands God to embrace works in a covenant of grace, see Hoekema, "Covenant of Grace," especially pp. 159-61.

82. Edward A. Dowey remarks, "Calvin maintains stoutly the identity of the object of the knowledge of faith throughout the changing forms in the history of revelation. The object has always been Christ. . . . [The variations] represent a change, not in the object of faith, but in the degree of clarity with which God makes it known. . . . The relation is not that of simple promise and fulfillment, but promises of different degrees of clarity" (*The Knowledge of God in Calvin's Theology,* exp. ed. [Grand Rapids: Eerdmans, 1994], 164-65). So also Parker: "Christians are, therefore, so far as promise and fulfilment go, in the same experimental position as the Old Testament believers. The difference between the Testaments lies, not in the two stages of the Church, but in the clarity of Christ's revelation and therefore the assurance of the Church's knowledge" (*Calvin's Old Testament Commentaries,* 46). See also Hesselink, *Calvin's Concept of the Law,* 165-70; Randall C. Zachman, *Image and Word in the Theology of John Calvin* (Notre Dame, IN: University of Notre Dame Press, 2007), 107-32.

83. *Inst.* 2.9.1.

84. Ibid.

gospel was manifest throughout redemptive history. As God's general remission of sins, the gospel was widely recognized during Old Testament times. Yet the "gospel" in its technical sense, namely, that uniquely clear manifestation of Christ in the incarnation, did constitute a new moment in redemptive history.[85] "The gospel did not so supplant the entire law as to bring forward a different way of salvation. Rather, it confirmed and gave substance to the shadows."[86]

Fear and Bondage

Of the five differences of administration Calvin lists between the Old and New Testaments, the third and fourth are clearly the most significant and seem basically to concern the same issue: the bondage and fear of the old covenant as compared with the freedom and assurance of the new.[87] Indeed, this distinction does not seem like a difference of administration at all. The contrast between an old covenant of death and condemnation, and a new covenant of life and righteousness would appear rather more fundamental than, for instance, differences concerning the earthly promises or ceremonial practices of Old Testament times.

Calvin wrestles with this objection several times, largely, it seems, because he recognizes the challenge Paul poses for his position. Among other passages, 2 Cor. 3 and Gal. 4 especially cause Calvin problems, as does Jer. 31. In *Institutes* Book 2, Ch. 11, Calvin enumerates four ways Paul contrasts the law and the gospel. First, the Old Testament presents the letter "published without the working of the Spirit,"[88] while the New Testament is engraved spiritually upon human hearts. Second, the Old Testament brings death and curse, while the New Testament frees people from the curse and restores them to God's favor. Third, the Old Testament brings condemnation by accusing all humanity of wickedness, while the New Testament brings righteousness by revealing God's mercy. Finally, the ceremonies of the Old Testament were tem-

---

85. Ibid., 2.9.2.
86. Ibid., 2.9.4.
87. Hesselink flags these two differences as a matter of "antithesis," in contrast to the other, "evolutionary" differences of administration, which merely chart a development from grace to grace (*Calvin's Concept of the Law*, 171). Note also the attention Opitz draws to the third and fourth differences in *Calvins theologische Hermeneutik*, 222-25.
88. *Inst.* 2.11.8.

John Calvin

porary while the gospel is eternal. Calvin even writes, "For because the Old bore the image of things absent, it had to die and vanish with time. The gospel, because it reveals the very substance, stands fast forever [II Cor. 3:10-11]."[89]

Still, these considerations do not entail for Calvin an outright contradiction between the law and the gospel. Calvin enlists at least three lines of defense for his position. First, Paul's negative remarks about the law should be understood as a polemical response against false teachers whose zeal for the ceremonies obscured the gospel. Second, Paul depicts the law only in its particularity, for the purpose of contrasting the testaments. This suggestion resembles what we have considered above concerning Moses's special function in demanding perfect righteousness. And third, the contrast between the law and the gospel should be understood in terms of relative and not absolute comparison. Grace was indeed present during the Old Testament, but not to the same degree as in the New.[90]

Such responses leave unresolved a number of questions, not least the degree to which the patriarchs received the same covenant blessings as New Testament believers. Did the fathers of Israel not also enjoy freedom, joy, and the Spirit of faith? Calvin addresses this issue with candor, but his answers increasingly seem to depart from his original framework. On the one hand, Calvin claims, the patriarchs did experience the conditions of the Old Testament:

> We shall deny that they were so endowed with the spirit of freedom and assurance as not in some degree to experience the fear and bondage arising from the law.... Hence, they are rightly said, in contrast to us, to have been under the testament of bondage and fear, when we consider that common dispensation by which the Lord at that time dealt with the Israelites.[91]

Yet Calvin affirms, on the other hand, that the patriarchs still shared in God's covenant blessings. And while this position is not inherently incompatible with the statement above, Calvin's particular strategy for harmonizing them involves a surprisingly sharp distinction between the covenants:

89. Ibid.
90. Ibid., 2.11.7.
91. Ibid., 2.11.9. See also 2.11.6.

When through the law the patriarchs felt themselves both oppressed by their enslaved condition, and wearied by anxiety of conscience, they fled for refuge to the gospel. It was therefore a particular fruit of the New Testament *(peculiarem novi Testamenti fructum)* that, apart from the common law of the Old Testament, they were exempted from those evils.[92]

Calvin suggests that the covenant blessings experienced by the patriarchs derived from the New Testament and not the Old. The Old Testament saints were thus a kind of redemptive-historical exception, participating in the new covenant despite their current dispensation.

For a particularly vivid example of this tension in Calvin's thought, we might consider his treatment of Jer. 31:31-34, beginning with the Jeremiah commentary (1563).[93] Calvin begins his exposition, in familiar fashion, by denying that the new covenant is called "new" because it is fundamentally different from the old covenant.[94] Since the first covenant God made with his people was "inviolable *(inviolabile)*," the law was but a "confirmation *(confirmatio)*" of the covenant with Abraham.[95] It is important, then, to be precise about what exactly makes this new covenant new. Calvin writes:

> It being new, no doubt, refers to what they call the form *(formam)*; and the form[96] regards not words only, but first Christ, then the grace of the Holy Spirit, and the whole external way of teaching *(tota docendi ratione externa)*. But the substance *(substantia)* remains the same. By substance I understand the doctrine *(doctrinam)*; for God in the Gospel brings forward nothing but what the Law contains. We hence see that God has so spoken from the beginning, that he has not changed, no not a syllable, with regard to the substance of the doctrine *(doctrinae summam)*. For he has included in the Law the rule of a perfect life, and has also shewn what is the way of salvation, and by types and figures led the people to Christ, so that the remission of sin is there clearly made manifest, and whatever is necessary to be known.[97]

---

92. Ibid., 2.11.9.

93. English translation: *Commentaries on the Prophet Jeremiah*, CTS 9-11. On the date of composition, see Parker, *Calvin's Old Testament Commentaries*, 29.

94. *Comm. Jer.* 31.31.

95. Ibid.

96. I have removed the phrase "or manner," which the CTS translation adds as an editorial explanation.

97. *Comm. Jer.* 31.31.

John Calvin

In short, the *substantia* of the covenant is identified with its unchanging *doctrina,* while the variable *forma* encompasses the expiation of sins and the regeneration of the Holy Spirit.

Having named three differences in form, Calvin proceeds to explicate each. First, Christ accomplished what the law had foreshadowed. The sacrifices "could not of themselves pacify God," but Christ "really fulfilled *(complevit re ipsa)* what God had exhibited under types so that the faithful might have some taste of salvation."[98] Second, the Holy Spirit brings regeneration. "It was, then, in some respects, a new thing *(aliqua novitas),* that God regenerated the faithful by his Spirit, so that it became not only doctrine as to the letter, but also efficacious *(efficax),* which not only strikes the ear, but penetrates into the heart, and really forms us for the service of God."[99] Finally, the outward mode of teaching has been altered, so that "God speaks to us now openly, as it were face to face, and not under a veil."[100]

But the second point in particular poses a challenging question: if the grace of regeneration was a new blessing that accompanied the coming of Christ, did the fathers under the law experience it? In his comments on Jer. 31:33, Calvin answers:

> The Fathers, who were formerly regenerated, obtained this favour through Christ, so that we may say, that it was as it were transferred to them from another source *(illud fuisse quasi translatitium).* The power then to penetrate the heart was not inherent in the Law, but it was a benefit transferred to the Law from the Gospel *(fuit translatitium bonum ab evangelio ad ipsam legem).*[101]

Calvin's language is remarkable: law and gospel are such distinct entities that the benefits of the latter can only be received under the former through redemptive-historical transfer and anachronism. Even more explicit language arises in the Hebrews commentary (1549),[102] where Calvin treats the quotation of Jer. 31:31-34 in Heb. 8:8-13. Here, Calvin's answer concerning the patriarchs is

---

98. Ibid.
99. Ibid.
100. Ibid.
101. Ibid., 31.33.
102. English translation: *Commentaries on the Epistle of Paul the Apostle to the Hebrews,* CTS 22. On the date of composition, see Parker, *Calvin's New Testament Commentaries,* 28.

that the question here is not about persons, but that reference is made to the economical condition of the Church *(oeconomia regendae Ecclesiae)*. Besides, whatever spiritual gifts the fathers obtained, they were accidental as it were to their age *(quasi accidentale fuisse eorum seculo)*; for it was necessary for them to direct their eyes to Christ in order to become possessed of them. Hence it was not without reason that the Apostle, in comparing the Gospel with the Law, took away from the latter what is peculiar to the former. There is yet no reason why God should not have extended the grace of the new covenant to the fathers *(novi foederis gratiam Deus ad patres extenderit)*. This is the true solution of the question.[103]

Again, Calvin so distinguishes between the law and the gospel that he depicts the blessings of the patriarchs as accidental to that era. The patriarchs received New Testament blessings though they lived during Old Testament times.

Drawing on similar observations, Hesselink has rejected a traditional reading of Calvin that presumes there is for the Reformer virtually no difference between the testaments.[104] Indeed, Hesselink argues, parts of Calvin advance an antithesis between law and gospel as stark as Luther's own presentation of their opposition.[105] Hesselink lays particular stress on passages where Calvin speaks of Old Testament believers enjoying only a "suspended grace,"[106] and Calvin's repeated appeal to the law and the gospel in their particularities. Yet for Hesselink, this language is not just superficially discordant with Calvin's emphasis on the unity of the covenant; it raises serious questions about whether Calvin's treatment of the law holds together as an integral whole.[107] Hesselink's own solution is to

---

103. *Comm. Heb.* 8.10.

104. Note the proponents of this view mentioned in Hesselink, *Calvin's Concept of the Law*, 155-56.

105. Hesselink, "Law and Gospel or Gospel and Law?" 25, 29.

106. Hesselink first develops this idea in "Calvin and Heilsgeschichte," but also treats it in "Law and Gospel or Gospel and Law?" 22-23, and *Calvin's Concept of the Law*, 182-84.

107. "The real problem, however, is not that of showing that Calvin takes the accusing, condemning function of the law seriously. Rather, the difficulty is to integrate this concept of the law with his understanding of the law as a whole. (This difficulty is not peculiar to Calvin; contemporary scholars also have a hard time integrating Paul's diverse references to the law, let alone reconciling these references with the portrayal of the law in the Old Testament.) For it could be maintained that Calvin has not thoroughly integrated this aspect of the law into his system as a whole; and that he operates with two concepts of the law,

John Calvin

note Moses's own assumption of two offices (considered above) as both lawgiver and minster of the gospel,[108] and to treat the law's power to condemn as an accidental feature of the law that arises only in response to our sin.[109] These remarks do ameliorate certain difficulties, including the potential problem of God's ordaining an institution that only destroys. Yet Hesselink does not directly address whether the stark differences Calvin draws between law and gospel can plausibly be considered secondary particularities, thus leaving the basic problem he has raised unresolved. I will treat this issue in greater depth later.

For now, it is worth noting that Calvin himself recognized certain complexities in his position. In one important passage in *Institutes,* Calvin attributes certain Scriptural contrasts (figures versus realities, letter versus spirit, bondage versus freedom) to the narrow use of the term "Old Testament" as referring only to the law, and "New Testament" as referring only to the gospel. But, he argues, the Old Testament understood more broadly includes promises as well, including those given before the law. We must therefore distinguish between different meanings of the term "Old Testament," as Augustine, whom Calvin cites in this regard, explains in *Answer to the Two Letters of the Pelagians.* Augustine followed Jeremiah and Paul in defining the Old Testament against the gospel of grace and mercy. Yet he did not preclude the Old Testament saints from spiritual blessings: those children of promise who hoped for eternal reward and believed in the Mediator "belonged to the New Covenant since the world began."[110] So, too, for his own position, Calvin asserts, "All the saints whom Scripture mentions as being peculiarly chosen of God from the beginning of the world have shared with us the same blessing unto eternal salvation."[111]

---

with the more Pauline one playing a subordinate role. This is a very complex problem, for despite his numerous definitions, warnings, and qualifying phrases (the key one being 'in so far as — *quatenus*'), no simple solution is readily apparent" (Hesselink, *Calvin's Concept of the Law,* 194). For another attempt to wrestle with this tension in Calvin's thought, see Benjamin Charles Milner, Jr., *Calvin's Doctrine of the Church,* Studies in the History of Christian Thought (Leiden: Brill, 1970), 87-98. Note also Paul Althaus's remark that "Calvin's covenant teaching kept itself generally in a marked lack of clarity," taken from Lillback, *Binding of God,* 158n96. Lillback concludes that Calvin's thought is less unclear or inconsistent than complex.

108. Hesselink, *Calvin's Concept of the Law,* 196-97.

109. Ibid., 200-201. Opitz adopts a similar solution: "Tötend ist das Gesetz nur akzidentiell, es gehört nicht zu seinem Wesen als regula im Gnadenbund, ein Wesen, das außerhalb des Gnadenbundes gar nicht erfaßt werden kann" (*Calvins theologische Hermeneutik,* 223).

110. *Inst.* 2.11.10.

111. Ibid.

Indeed, "they so lived under the Old Covenant as not to remain there but ever to aspire to the New, and thus embraced a real share in it."[112]

But Calvin's resources for advancing such arguments are not the same as Augustine's, and these differences present a serious challenge for his basic construal of the unitary covenant across the testaments.[113] Augustine could treat the patriarchs as redemptive-historical aberrations precisely because he delineated so sharply between the covenants. Calvin, on the other hand, claims the Old Testament saints participated in the New Testament while also identifying the Old and New Testaments as one and the same covenant. But how could the patriarchs aspire to a new covenant when there is no substantive difference between the testaments in the first place? In the conclusion of this chapter, I will consider this issue more thoroughly. First, though, we must proceed to Calvin's position on Israel and the church.

The Church of the Jews

Calvin categorizes the extension of the covenant from the Jews to the Gentiles as the fifth and final difference between the testaments, but he considers this issue secondary and explicitly waffles on whether the differences should simply number four.[114] This hesitancy arises from his affirmation that Old Testament Israel can be identified with the New Testament church, ethnic differences notwithstanding. Indeed, Calvin goes so far as to call Old Testament Israel "the church of the Jews *(Iudaeorum Ecclesia).*"[115]

Calvin's discussion of this matter is textured and complex, and the difficulties of discerning his position are complicated by the realities that he never wrote a developed treatise on the relationship between Israel

---

112. Ibid.

113. Calvin rightly notes one discrepancy between his and Augustine's understandings of the relation between the testaments, but does not expand on it. "This, then, is the difference between our analysis and his: ours distinguishes between the clarity of the gospel and the obscurer dispensation of the Word that had preceded it, according to that statement of Christ, 'The Law and the Prophets were until John; since then the Kingdom of God is proclaimed' [Luke 16:16, cf. Vg.]; Augustine's division simply separates the weakness of the law from the firmness of the gospel" (*Inst.* 2.11.10).

114. *Inst.* 2.11.1, 2.11.13.

115. Ibid., 2.10.19.

John Calvin

and the church, and that there is no formal section dedicated to the issue in *Institutes*. (Calvin did write a brief essay that engages Judaism called "Response to Questions and Objections of a Certain Jew" *[Ad quaestiones et obiecta Iudaei cuiusdam]*[116] but little can be discerned from these scattered remarks concerning Calvin's larger vision of Old Testament Israel.) For this part, then, I turn to three other loci: his treatment of the covenant with Abraham in the Genesis commentary (1554), his treatment of God's faithfulness to Israel in the Romans commentary (1556 revision), and his treatment of the sacraments in *Institutes*.[117] Each of these texts reveals a strong identification between Old Testament Israel and the church, consistent with Calvin's broader position on the unity of the covenants.

The Covenant with Abraham

Perhaps the most striking feature of the Genesis commentary is the consistency of Calvin's casual references to God's covenant community as the "church." The birth of Seth marked the time when "the face of the Church

---

116. For an English translation of this text, see Mary Sweetland Laver, "Calvin, Jews, and Intra-Christian Polemics" (PhD diss., Temple University, 1987), 229-61, who reproduces the work of Susan Frank. Calvin's essay was not published during his lifetime and cannot easily be dated, but it is typically considered a late text. See discussion in pp. 220-25.

117. English translations: *Commentaries on the Book of Genesis*, CTS 1; *Commentaries on the Epistle of Paul the Apostle to the Romans*, CTS 19. On the dates of composition, see, respectively, Parker, *Calvin's Old Testament Commentaries*, 25-26, and *Calvin's New Testament Commentaries*, 36-37. For recent treatments of Calvin's theology of Jews and Judaism, see Salo W. Baron, "John Calvin and the Jews," in *Harry Austryn Wolfson Jubilee Volume: On the Occasion of His Seventy-Fifth Birthday*, ed. Saul Lieberman, vol. 1 (Jerusalem: American Academy for Jewish Research, 1965), 141-63; Laver, "Calvin, Jews, and Intra-Christian Polemics"; Kraus, "Israel in the Theology of Calvin"; Mary Potter Engel, "Calvin and the Jews: A Textual Puzzle," *Princeton Seminary Bulletin*, Supp. 1 (1990): 106-23; Jack Hughes Robinson, *John Calvin and the Jews*, American University Studies, Series 7: Theology and Religion 123 (New York: Peter Lang, 1992); Dan Shute, *"And All Israel Shall Be Saved*: Peter Martyr and John Calvin on the Jews according to Romans, Chapters 9, 10 and 11," in *Peter Martyr Vermigli and the European Reformations: Semper Reformanda*, ed. Frank A. James III, Studies in the History of Christian Traditions (Leiden: Brill, 2004), 159-76; Achim Detmers, "Calvin, the Jews, and Judaism," in *Jews, Judaism and the Reformation in Sixteenth-Century Germany*, ed. Dean Phillip Bell and Stephen G. Burnett, Studies in Central European Histories 37 (Leiden: Brill, 2006), 197-217; John Hesselink, "Calvin's Understanding of the Relation of the Church and Israel Based Largely on His Interpretation of Romans 9–11," *ExAud* 4 (2006): 59-69.

(ecclesiae facies) began distinctly to appear";[118] the genealogy of Gen. 5 demonstrated God's preservation of a worshiping community, lest "the seed of the Church *(ecclesiae semen)* should fail";[119] and the genealogy of Gen. 10 recounted "the history of the Church *(historiam ecclesiae)* in one continuous narrative," postponing the line of Shem "from which the Church flowed *(unde illa defluxit)*" to the end of the chapter.[120] Though Shem's line was the chief locus where God had preserved the church, his descendants apostatized, such that even Abraham's father and grandfather worshiped idols. Yet God did not forget his people, and the call of Abraham commenced a kind of "renovation of the church *(ecclesiae renovatio),*"[121] such that the family of Abraham was, indeed, "the living representation of the Church *(vivam ecclesiae effigiem).*"[122]

Such blending between the original narrative and later New Testament language characterizes Calvin's subsequent treatment of Abraham. The seed of Abraham, treated in Gen. 12:3, is Christ, for "the covenant of salvation which God made with Abram" could be "neither stable nor firm except in Christ."[123] Abraham builds an altar in Gen. 12:7, and thus "opened for himself a celestial sanctuary, by sacrifices, that he might rightly worship God.... The faith of Abram was directed to the blood of Christ."[124] The strongest link between the New Testament and Abraham's story is, somewhat unsurprisingly, the imputation of righteousness received by faith in Gen. 15:6.[125] Given his Christological/ecclesial reading of Abraham, one might expect Calvin to downplay the significance of Abraham's Jewish particularity, suggesting the promises had to do with Abraham's spiritual, not biological descendants, or with spiritual, not earthly possession. But Calvin's position is far more nuanced and developed, as his comments on "seed" in Gen. 17:7 show:

> Now they are deceived who think that his elect alone are here pointed out; and that all the faithful are indiscriminately comprehended, from whatever people, according to the flesh, they are descended. For, on

---

118. *Comm. Gen.* 4.25.
119. Ibid., 5.1.
120. Ibid., 10.1.
121. Ibid., 11.10. See 12.1.
122. Ibid., 16.5.
123. Ibid., 12.3.
124. Ibid., 12.7.
125. Ibid., 15.6.

John Calvin

> the contrary, the Scripture declares that the race of Abraham, by lineal descent, had been peculiarly accepted by God. And it is the evident doctrine of Paul concerning the natural descendants of Abraham, that they are holy branches which have proceeded from a holy root (Rom. xi. 16). And lest anyone should restrict this assertion to the shadows of the law, or should evade it by allegory, he elsewhere expressly declares, that Christ came to be a minister of the circumcision (Rom. xv. 8). Wherefore, nothing is more certain, than that God made his covenant with those sons of Abraham who were naturally to be born of him.[126]

Calvin rejects a purely spiritual reading of Abraham's seed and dismisses standard tropes in the interpretation of the Old Testament that obscure the genealogical dimension of God's promises.

The key to understanding Old Testament Israel for Calvin is to recognize the difference between "certain distinct degrees of adoption *(certos . . . ac distinctos adoptionis gradus).*"[127] The covenant with Abraham and his physical descendants constituted God's gratuitous adoption of a single people to be separate from the other nations. This covenant was grounded on the Word of God and oriented toward eternal reward — a point of contrast with the promise to Ishmael, who received temporal blessings but not the covenant of eternal life[128] — and its primary blessing was that the Lord would be God to Abraham's children. In that vein, the promise of land can only be considered an "augmentation *(auctarii)*"[129] of the true inheritance. Nevertheless, the covenant with Abraham did not entail that all of Abraham's physical descendants were "legitimate children," and Paul teaches in Rom. 9 that some were of the promise and others of the flesh. There must therefore be a distinction between the outer word of promise and the inward and efficacious seal of the Spirit,[130] and a concomitant distinction between two categories of people amongst the people of God. "Here, then, a twofold class of sons *(duplex filiorum ordo)* presents itself to us, in the Church; for since the whole body of people is gathered together into the fold of God, by one and the same voice, all without exception, are, in this respect, accounted children; the name of the Church is applicable in common to them all: but in the innermost sanctuary of God, none others

---

126. Ibid., 17.6.
127. Ibid., 17.7.
128. Ibid., 16.11.
129. Ibid., 17.7.
130. Ibid.

are reckoned the sons of God, than they in whom the promise is ratified by faith."[131] Thus, the operative distinction for Calvin is not between Old Testament Israel and the New Testament church, but within the church itself, which spans both entities. Just as there are within the New Testament church those who do and do not receive the inward call, so too was there such a distinction within Old Testament Israel.

For Calvin, physical Israel simply was the church during Old Testament times, and the only significant point of distinction between the two communities is the ethnic composition of the people. Christ broke down the wall that divided the Jews and the Gentiles, bringing about the "renovation of the world *(saeculi renovatio)*" whereby the Jews were largely "cast out *(eiecti sunt)*" to make room for the Gentiles.[132] Since most Jews (besides those who received the secret gift of election) did not respond positively to Christ, the church came to adopt a more Gentile character. Nevertheless, this development did not undermine the eternality of the covenant.

> In this way the covenant is called perpetual, as lasting until the renovation of the world; which took place at the advent of Christ. I grant, indeed, that the covenant was without end, and may with propriety be called eternal, as far as the whole Church is concerned; it must, however, always remain as a settled point that the regular succession of ages *(seriem aetatum)* was partly broken *(partim abruptam)*, and partly changed *(partim mutatam)*, by the coming of Christ, because the middle wall being broken down, and the sons by nature being, at length, disinherited, Abraham began to have a race associated with himself, from all the regions of the world.[133]

Calvin's explanation here is a hedge. He first claims the covenant was eternal to the Israelites only in the sense that it would continue until the time of Christ. But he then affirms the eternity of the covenant to the people of God more broadly (believing Gentiles and Jews) according to the more common understanding of the term. As Calvin remarks on Gen. 13:14, "eternity" need not mean eternity: "The change which Christ introduced was not the *abolition (abolitio)* of the old promises, but rather their *confir-*

---

131. Ibid.
132. Ibid.
133. Ibid.

mation (confirmatio). Seeing, therefore, that God has not now one peculiar people in the land of Canaan, but a people diffused throughout all regions of the earth; this does not contradict the assertion, that the eternal possession of the land was rightly promised to the seed of Abraham, until the future renovation."[134]

On the one hand, then, Calvin identifies physical Israel with the church during Old Testament times: the covenant with Abraham was founded on the Word, it was ultimately grounded in Christ, and it set forth eternal and not just temporal blessings. The distinction within Israel between those who were and were not inwardly called is identical to that within the New Testament church. On the other hand, Calvin also asserts that the Israelites have been disinherited such that the Gentiles could be brought into the covenant, and that the covenant with physical Israel was only eternal in the sense that it would last until the advent of Christ. We have here a conundrum: what exactly is the ongoing status of God's covenant with physical Israel? To address this question, we must consider Calvin's treatment of Rom. 9–11.

God's Faithfulness to Israel

Calvin begins his treatment of Rom. 9 with an extended discussion of Paul's quandary concerning the Jews. Given God's promises to Israel, Jewish rejection of Paul's message raises doubts about the veracity of God's words or even Jesus's identity as the messiah, since the messiah was the hope of Israel.[135] The problem is not simply the loss of Israel, though this would be a major concern in and of itself. At stake is the very character of God, who explicitly defined his covenant with the Jews as eternal. Were the Jews not elect after all?[136] On Calvin's reading, Paul cannot accept such a conclusion, and Rom. 9–11 represents the apostle's best effort toward a more acceptable solution.[137] The argument, in short, is that Israel has broken the covenant according to God's own will and prerogative, but God remains faithful to the Israelites.[138] This is a tricky position, but one Calvin can hardly avoid given his commitment, animated by Pauline concerns,

---

134. Ibid., 13.14. Italics in the translation.
135. *Comm. Rom.* 9.1-5.
136. Ibid., 9.3.
137. Ibid., 9.1-5.
138. For summary statements of this position, see ibid., 9.4, 9.6.

to affirm the identity of Christ as the messiah and the ongoing validity of God's promises to physical Israel.[139]

Calvin bases the first plank of his exposition on Paul's argument in Rom. 9 that not all Jews continue to participate in the covenant. As in the Genesis commentary, Calvin distinguishes between two kinds of election: God offered salvation to all the natural descendants of Abraham, but only the children of promise actually received it. Yet this reality does not invalidate God's promises. On Calvin's reading, Paul argues both "that the hidden election of God overrules *(dominari)* the outward calling, and that it is yet by no means inconsistent with it *(et tamen cum ea minime pugnare)*, but, on the contrary, that it tends toward its confirmation *(confirmationem)* and completion *(complementum)*."[140] The choice of Isaac over Ishmael (Rom. 9:7) proves there is a distinction between the children of Abraham. "It hence follows, that some men are by special privilege elected out of the chosen people, in whom the common adoption becomes efficacious and valid."[141]

This distinction within the natural children of Abraham is ultimately rooted in God's own determination, a point particularly manifest in God's choice of Jacob over Esau. Calvin draws three lessons from this story. First, God makes a distinction between the Israelites, predestining some to salvation and others to condemnation. Second, the only basis of this election is God's goodness, without any regard for human works. Third, God is "free and exempt from the necessity of imparting equally the same grace to all."[142] Two implications follow: "that the grace of God is not so confined to the Jewish people that it does not also flow to other nations, and diffuse itself through the whole world, — and then, that it is not even so tied to the Jews that it comes without exception to all the children of Abraham according to the flesh."[143] Commenting on Paul's citation of Hos. 2:23, Calvin explains God's sovereign choice to equalize Gentiles and Jews.

> Since the Jews so provoked God's wrath by their sins, that they deserved to be rejected by him, no hope of salvation remained, except they turned

---

139. The difficulties of interpreting this section of Calvin's commentary have not gone unnoticed. See, for instance, Engel, "Calvin and the Jews," 106.
140. *Comm. Rom.* 9.7.
141. Ibid.
142. Ibid., 9.11.
143. Ibid., 9.24.

John Calvin

to Christ, through whom the covenant of grace was to be restored: and as it was based on him, so it was then renewed, when he interposed. . . . For when the Jews were banished from God's family *(Iudaei e familia Dei exterminati essent),* they were thus reduced to a common class *(redacti erant in vulgarem ordinem),* and put on a level with the Gentiles *(Gentibus pares facti).* The difference being taken away *(post sublatum discrimen),* God's mercy is now indiscriminately extended to all the Gentiles *(Dei misericordia in omnibus Gentibus promiscue locum habet).*[144]

Paul writes that the Jews were rejected because they sought to be justified by works. Calvin acknowledges the presumption of suggesting that the Jews, who assiduously sought to follow the law, should be excluded from righteousness, while the Gentiles, who had no concern for righteousness, received it.[145] He also recognizes that the Jews deserve compassion rather than hatred, since they fell more by ignorance than by malignancy of will: they were, at least, seeking God when persecuting the kingdom of Christ.[146] Nevertheless, we must ultimately affirm God's decision. "They are deservedly rejected *(iuste eos reiici),* who attempt to attain salvation by trusting in their own works; for they, as far as they can, abolish faith, without which no salvation can be expected. Hence, were they to gain their object, such a success would be the annihilation of true righteousness."[147]

The second major plank of this discussion begins at Rom. 11, where Calvin shifts from the rejection of Israel to an apparently contradictory theme: God's ongoing faithfulness to the Jews. As in the Genesis commentary, Calvin explicitly repudiates any attempt to evacuate God's promises to physical Israel of their original meaning. Paul's explicit concern in Rom. 11 is to qualify what he has just said concerning the Jews lest anyone think Christ "had transferred elsewhere *(alio transtulisset)* the promises of God" or that the Jews were "entirely alienated from [God's] kingdom *(alienati sint penitus ab eius regno),* as the Gentiles were before the coming of Christ."[148]

---

144. Ibid., 9.25.
145. Ibid., 9.30.
146. Ibid., 10.2.
147. Ibid., 9.32. A similar view is presented in *Ad quaestiones et obiecta Iudaei cuiusdam,* where Calvin says the covenant was abrogated for many Jews, but not for all. See especially his response to the first question.
148. *Comm. Rom.* 11.1.

Calvin defends God's faithfulness to physical Israel through two strategies. The first concerns God's preservation of a remnant. While Israel as a whole failed to trust in Christ, this does not mean every individual Israelite did. There is a distinction between the collectively disobedient nation and the faithful individuals within her borders.[149] If all the Israelites were cut off, the consistency of God and the validity of his promises might indeed be in question. Yet God rejected Israel such that "no member of the *spiritual body of Christ (spirituali Christi corpore)* was cut off."[150] Commenting on Rom. 11:11, Calvin explains:

> You will be greatly hindered in understanding this argument, except you take notice, that the Apostle speaks sometimes of the whole nation of the Jews, and sometimes of single individuals; for hence arises the diversity, that onewhile he speaks of the Jews as being banished from the kingdom of God, cut off from the tree and precipitated by God's judgment into destruction, and that at another he denies that they had fallen from grace, but that on the contrary they continued in the possession of the covenant, and had a place in the Church of God.[151]

Yet God's faithfulness to Israel extends beyond the preservation of a remnant: for Calvin, the nation at large will actually be restored. Given Israel's widespread rejection of Christ, Paul wonders (according to Calvin's paraphrase) "whether the Jewish nation had so stumbled at Christ, that it was all over with them universally, and that no hope of repentance remained."[152] The apostolic conclusion is unambiguously negative. On Calvin's reading, Paul denies "that the salvation of the Jews was to be despaired of, or that they were so rejected by God, that there was to be no future restoration, or that the covenant of grace, which he had once made with them, was entirely abolished, since there had ever remained in that nation the seed of blessing."[153]

---

149. Ibid., 11.5. See also 3.3.
150. Ibid., 11.2, italics mine. See also 9.27-29.
151. Ibid., 11.11. Calvin emphasizes the distinction between collective Israel and the faithful remnant throughout his remarks on this chapter. See, for instance, his comments on Rom. 11:16, where Paul refers to the Jews as a holy root, in favorable comparison with the Gentiles. Calvin notes that the comparison would not be legitimate if Paul had only individuals in mind, for not all Jewish individuals were holy. Paul must therefore mean God's granting holiness to the whole people descended from Abraham.
152. Ibid., 11.11.
153. Ibid.

John Calvin

"God will again reconcile to himself the first people whom he has divorced."[154] Since Gentile reception of the gospel was intended to make Israel jealous, Israel cannot have fallen into eternal ruin. The restoration of the Jews will rather be a blessing for the Gentiles, and the Gentiles dare not become proud or contemptuous, lest they too be cut off.

In Rom. 11:26, Paul states, rather ambiguously, "All Israel will be saved." Calvin interprets "Israel" to refer to the whole people of God, and not just the Jewish people, but he scrupulously avoids the potential corollary to such a move: a spiritualization of Israel that ducks the question of God's specific faithfulness to the Jews. For Calvin, the restoration of physical Israel is essential to "all Israel" being saved:

> I extend the word *Israel* to all the people of God, according to this meaning, — "When the Gentiles shall come in, the Jews also shall return from their defection to the obedience of faith; and thus shall be completed the salvation of the whole Israel of God, which must be gathered from both; and yet in such a way that the Jews shall obtain the first place, being as it were the first-born in God's family."[155]

The quotation of Isa. 59:20 in Rom. 11:26, "There shall come out of Sion the Deliverer, and shall turn away ungodliness from Jacob" suggests a certain priority of the Jews over the Gentiles.[156] The spiritual people of God encompasses both Jews and Gentiles, but the Jews are nevertheless the firstborn, and Isaiah's words must be fulfilled especially in them. "That Scripture calls all the people of God Israelites, is to be ascribed to the pre-eminence of that nation, whom God had preferred to all other nations."[157]

According to the Romans commentary, then, the Jews have been temporarily rejected from the gospel for the Gentiles to be brought into God's kingdom, and this situation is the result of God's sovereign choice. But God has not finally abandoned the Jewish people, for he has preserved a remnant at the present time and he will restore the nation as a whole at the end of time.[158] "Paul maintains that the purpose of God stands firm and immovable, by which he had once deigned to choose them for himself as a peculiar nation. Since then it cannot possibly be, that the Lord will depart

---

154. Ibid., 11.21.
155. Ibid., 11.26.
156. This translation of Scripture follows the CTS translation of Calvin's commentary.
157. Ibid.
158. For a summary of Calvin's reading of Rom. 9–11, see ibid., 11.28.

from that covenant which he made with Abraham, 'I will be the God of thy seed,' (Gen. xvii. 7) it is evident that he has not wholly turned his kindness from the Jewish nation."[159]

The Old Testament Sacraments

One final point on Calvin's theology of Israel remains: the relative parity of the sacraments across the testaments. In *Institutes* Book 4, Ch. 14, Calvin defines a sacrament as an outward sign that seals our consciences and sustains our faith in the promises of God's favor toward us.[160] Perhaps the most striking feature of Calvin's subsequent exposition of this definition is the network of theological interconnections he draws between the sacraments and other loci: the Word, the Spirit, faith, and ultimately Christ. The sacraments provide a kind of confirmation of God's Word — not, of course, that God's Word needs confirmation, since there is no higher authority, yet they nevertheless represent God's condescension toward our ignorance.[161] The Spirit provides the power of the sacraments, without whom they "can accomplish nothing more in our minds than the splendor of the sun shining upon blind eyes, or a voice sounding in deaf ears."[162] Judas Iscariot demonstrates negatively the indispensability of faith, for he received the sacrament directly from Jesus, yet without benefit.[163] And "Christ is the matter *(materiam)* or (if you prefer) the substance *(substantiam)* of all the sacraments; for in him they have all their firmness *(soliditatem),* and they do not promise anything apart from him."[164] In sum, "the sacraments have the same office as the Word of God: to offer and set forth Christ to us, and in him the treasures of heavenly grace."[165]

It is precisely because these benefits were available during Old Testament times that the Israelites were able to participate salvifically in the ceremonies before the incarnation. Calvin includes a wide range of instances under the broad rubric of sacrament: the tree of life, Noah's rainbow,

---

159. Ibid. CTS locates this passage in *Comm. Rom.* 11.29. The Latin citation can be found at OE 13:250.
160. *Inst.* 4.14.1.
161. Ibid., 4.14.3.
162. Ibid., 4.14.9.
163. Ibid., 4.14.15. Calvin cites Augustine on this point. See Augustine, *Jo. ev. tr.* 26.11.
164. *Inst.* 4.14.16.
165. Ibid., 4.14.17.

Abraham's smoking fire pot, Gideon's fleece, and the changing shadow intended to comfort Hezekiah.[166] But the "ordinary sacraments *(ordinaria sacramenta)*" of the Old Testament are restricted to circumcision, purifications, sacrifices, and other cultic rites, and Calvin insists these practices served the same purpose as baptism and the Lord's Supper do now: "to direct and almost lead men by the hand to Christ, or rather, as images, to represent him and show him forth to be known."[167] The only difference between the sacraments of the Old and New Testament is that "the former foreshadowed Christ promised while he was as yet awaited; the latter attest him as already given and revealed."[168]

Despite their anticipatory role, the Old Testament sacraments did communicate the grace of Christ. "Whatever is shown us today in these sacraments, the Jews of old received in their own — that is, Christ with his spiritual riches. They felt the same power in their sacraments as do we in ours; these were seals of divine good will toward them, looking to eternal salvation."[169] Even if, for instance, the Epistle to the Hebrews seems to denigrate the Old Testament sacrifices, the apostle's true purpose was to show that the efficacy of the Old Testament sacrifices depended on Christ, who was yet to come, and to demonstrate the foolishness of trusting in ceremonies without regard for Christ.[170] To cite Augustine, "the sacraments of the Jews were different in their signs, but equal in the thing signified; different in visible appearance, but equal in spiritual power."[171] This is not to suggest complete parity between the Old and New Testament sacraments: God's fatherly kindness shines brighter and clearer in the New Testament, as do the graces of the Spirit in Christ.[172] Still, the unity of the sacraments is for Calvin fundamental. There is an identity of substance and function between the Old and New Testament sacraments, despite some differences of administration and clarity. The unity of the covenants and the unity of the sacraments are, in short, the same.

As a brief and concluding illustration, we might consider Calvin's discussion of the relation between circumcision and baptism. As Calvin explains, Old Testament circumcision was not an empty symbol, but included

---

166. Ibid., 4.14.18.
167. Ibid., 4.14.20.
168. Ibid.
169. Ibid., 4.14.23.
170. Ibid., 4.14.25.
171. Ibid., 4.14.26. The original reference is from Augustine, *Jo. ev. tr.* 26.12.
172. *Inst.* 4.14.26.

the promise of forgiveness, the hope of eternal life, and the command to walk in uprightness of heart. "We have, therefore, a spiritual promise given to the patriarchs in circumcision such as is given us in baptism, since it represented for them forgiveness of sins and mortification of flesh. Moreover, as we have taught that Christ is the foundation *(fundamentum)* of baptism, in whom both of these reside, so it is also evident that he is the foundation of circumcision."[173] For Calvin, of course, this connection between circumcision and baptism helps legitimate the practice of infant baptism. The more pertinent points for our discussion concern Calvin's presumption of identity between the old and new covenants, and the implications he discerns for Israel.

The former is by now familiar: "The covenant is common *(commune)*, and the reason for confirming it is common. Only the manner of confirmation *(modus confirmandi tantum)* is different — what was circumcision for them was replaced for us by baptism."[174] But this position also bears conspicuously on Calvin's contention with the Anabaptists, whose efforts to dissociate circumcision and baptism, he claims, ultimately denigrate the Jews to the level of carnal beasts. Calvin charges, "A covenant with them would not go beyond the temporal life, and the promises given them would rest in present and physical benefits. If this doctrine should obtain, what would remain save that the Jewish nation was satiated for a time with God's benefits (as men fatten a herd of swine in a sty), only to perish in eternal destruction?"[175] As he proceeds, Calvin insists that heavenly blessing remains for Abraham's physical offspring,[176] drawing upon Rom. 9–11 and rejecting efforts to spiritualize this hope away. "The promise of the covenant is to be fulfilled, not only allegorically *(non allegorice tantum)*, but literally *(ut verba sonant)*, for Abraham's physical offspring *(carnali Abrahae semini)*."[177]

---

173. Ibid., 4.16.3.
174. Ibid., 4.16.6.
175. Ibid., 4.16.10.
176. Ibid., 4.16.12.
177. Ibid., 4.16.15. In the same section, Calvin also affirms a literal interpretation of the promise of the second commandment, that God would bless the offspring of his servants to the thousandth generation. "Shall we take refuge in allegories? That would be too frivolous an evasion! Shall we say that it is abolished? But thus the law would be destroyed, which Christ came rather to establish [Matt. 5:17], in so far as it benefits our life. Let us accept as incontrovertible that God is so good and generous to his own as to be pleased, for their sake, also to count among his people the children whom they have begotten."

John Calvin

Even with such a practical matter as infant baptism, then, the fundamental structures of Calvin's theology emerge. The identity of the testaments grounds the unity of God's people, the security of her hope, and, in this characteristic case, the consistency of her practices.

Scripture and the Knowledge of God

We turn finally to Calvin's doctrine of Scripture. How does Calvin's vision of redemptive history and God's covenant people shape his principles for interpreting the Old Testament? The chief theme in this discussion concerns knowledge of God, which Calvin differentiates between knowledge of God the Creator and knowledge of God the Redeemer. Scripture acts to restore each to us, though in different ways. This part will treat each kind of knowledge in turn before considering the implications of this distinction for Calvin's conception of the literal sense. As will become clear, Calvin's understanding of the literal sense bears the same idiosyncrasies as his understanding of the covenant: there is an identity for Calvin between what might otherwise be called the "literal" and "spiritual," precisely because Christ is the ground of each.[178]

---

178. For studies on Calvin's theology of Scripture and his interpretative practices, in addition to works mentioned above, see Paul L. Lehmann, "The Reformers' Use of the Bible," *ThTo* 3 (1946): 328-44; Alexandre Ganoczy and Stefan Scheld, *Die Hermeneutik Calvins: Geistgeschichtliche Voraussetzungen und Grundzüge* (Wiesbaden: Steiner, 1983); Richard C. Gamble, "*Brevitas et Facilitas:* Toward an Understanding of Calvin's Hermeneutic," *WTJ* 47 (1985): 1-17; idem, "Exposition and Method in Calvin," *WTJ* 49 (1987): 153-65; idem, "Calvin as Theologian and Exegete: Is There Anything New?" *CTJ* 23 (1988): 178-93; idem, "Calvin's Theological Method: Word and Spirit, A Case Study," in Schnucker, *Calviniana,* 63-75; as well as a volume of articles Gamble edited, *Calvin and Calvinism,* vol. 6: *Calvin and Hermeneutics* (New York: Garland, 1992); Elsie Anne McKee, "Exegesis, Theology, and Development in Calvin's *Institutio*: A Methodological Suggestion," in *Probing the Reformed Tradition: Historical Studies in Honor of Edward A. Dowey, Jr.,* ed. Elsie Anne McKee and Brian G. Armstrong (Louisville: Westminster/John Knox, 1989): 154-72; eadem, "Some Reflections on Relating Calvin's Exegesis and Theology," in *Biblical Hermeneutics in Historical Perspective: Studies in Honor of Karlfried Froehlich on His Sixtieth Birthday,* ed. Mark S. Burrows and Paul Rorem (Grand Rapids: Eerdmans, 1991), 215-26; John Lee Thompson, *John Calvin and the Daughters of Sarah: Women in Regular and Exceptional Roles in the Exegesis of Calvin, His Predecessors, and His Contemporaries* (Geneva: Droz, 1992); Susan Schreiner, *Where Shall Wisdom Be Found? Calvin's Exegesis of Job from Medieval and Modern Perspectives* (Chicago: University of Chicago Press, 1994); Peter De Klerk, ed., *Calvin as Exegete: Papers and Responses Presented at the Ninth Colloquium on Calvin and Calvin Studies* (Grand

The Twofold Knowledge of God

The distinction between knowledge of God the Creator and knowledge of God the Redeemer is the structuring principle of *Institutes,* appearing repeatedly throughout Calvin's text and providing the titles for Books 1 and 2, respectively.[179] It thus deserves general consideration before we turn to a more direct assessment of Calvin's doctrine of Scripture. Calvin begins *Institutes* by treating knowledge of God the Creator, but this knowledge is only available for those who also have knowledge of God the Redeemer, and the latter concept exercises more influence over Calvin's theology than the former.

Knowledge of God the Creator concerns what would have been revealed about God if humanity had not fallen, while knowledge of God the Redeemer concerns what has been revealed about God because of our reconciliation in Christ. The latter apprehends God's general goodness, eternity, and power; the latter attests the particulars of God's salvific activity for humanity. This distinction should not be confused with two others. First, the twofold knowledge does not correspond to the difference between the Old and New Testaments. On Calvin's account, Adam, Noah,

---

Rapids: Calvin Studies Society, 1995); David Steinmetz, *Calvin in Context* (Oxford: Oxford University Press, 1995); K. E. Greene-McCreight, *Ad Litteram: How Augustine, Calvin, and Barth Read the "Plain Sense" of Genesis 1-3,* Issues in Systematic Theology 5 (New York: Peter Lang, 1999); eadem, "'We Are Companions of the Patriarchs' or Scripture Absorbs Calvin's World," *Modern Theology* 14 (1998): 213-24; Barbara Pitkin, *What Pure Eyes Could See: Calvin's Doctrine of Faith in Its Exegetical Context* (Oxford: Oxford University Press, 1999); eadem, "John Calvin and the Interpretation of the Bible," in *A History of Biblical Interpretation,* vol. 2: *The Medieval through the Reformation Periods,* ed. Alan J. Hauser and Duane F. Watson (Grand Rapids: Eerdmans, 2009), 341-71; R. Ward Holder, *John Calvin and the Grounding of Interpretation: Calvin's First Commentaries,* Studies in the History of Christian Traditions 127 (Leiden: Brill, 2006); Donald K. McKim, ed., *Calvin and the Bible* (Cambridge: Cambridge University Press, 2006).

179. "The knowledge of God the Creator *(De cognitione Dei creatoris),*" and "The knowledge of God the Redeemer in Christ, first disclosed to the fathers under the law, and then to us in the gospel *(De cognitione Dei redemptoris in Christo, quae Patribus sub Lege primum, deinde et nobis in Evangelio patefacta est)*." The seminal text on the knowledge of God in Calvin is Dowey, *The Knowledge of God in Calvin's Theology,* to which I will make frequent recourse throughout this discussion. This edition includes a reprinting of his earlier article, "The Structure of Calvin's Theological Thought as Influenced by the Two-Fold Knowledge of God," originally published in *Calvinus Ecclesiae Genevensis Custos,* ed. Wilhelm H. Neuser (New York: Peter Lang, 1984), 135-48. For references in *Institutes* to the twofold knowledge of God, see Dowey, *The Knowledge of God in Calvin's Theology,* 43-45.

John Calvin

and Abraham recognized God "not only as Creator but also as Redeemer" in a manner distinct from unbelievers.[180] Old Testament saints, and not just New Testament believers, enjoyed knowledge of God as both Creator and Redeemer. Second, the twofold knowledge of God does not derive from the distinction between the Father and the Son. Calvin chooses somewhat curiously to treat the doctrine of the Trinity in Book 1 (Ch. 13), though the doctrine of the Trinity was only revealed with the coming of Christ, which Calvin treats in Book 2.[181] According to the rubric above, this decision makes natural sense: knowledge of the Trinity would have been possible without the fall, and it is appropriate to treat the topic in some variation from the chronological order of revelation in redemptive history. The treatment in Book 1 focuses primarily on the divinity and relations of the Trinitarian persons, explicitly postponing a discussion of Christ's work as Mediator because this work concerns God's redemptive response to human sin.[182]

The clearest treatment of the distinction between God the Creator and God the Redeemer appears in Book 2, Ch. 6, a turning point in the structure of *Institutes* that figures critically in how Calvin understands the relation between the testaments. Book 2, Chs. 1–5 consists of an extended exposition on the miserable condition of humanity after the fall, with various discussions on providence, original sin, and the corruption of the mind and will. But this section prepares the way for the discussion that will occupy the rest of Book 2, the redemption of humanity in Christ. "The whole human race perished in the person of Adam. Consequently that original excellence and nobility which we recounted would be of no profit to us but would rather redound to our greater shame, until God, who does not recognize as his handiwork men defiled and corrupted by sin, appeared as Redeemer in the person of his only-begotten Son."[183] In our postlapsarian condition, only faith in Christ can restore humanity to knowledge of God.

Logically, this position entails either that there was no knowledge of God during Old Testament times, since Christ had not yet been revealed, or that God was somehow known in Christ even before the incarnation. Somewhat predictably, Calvin opts for the latter position: "Accordingly,

---

180. *Inst.* 1.6.1.
181. See Dowey, *Knowledge of God in Calvin's Theology*, 124-31, 145-46.
182. See paragraphs 9, 11, 23, and 24 of Book 1, Ch. 13.
183. *Inst.* 2.6.1.

apart from the Mediator, God never showed favor toward that ancient people, nor ever gave hope of grace to them. I pass over the sacrifices of the law, which plainly and openly taught believers to seek salvation nowhere else than in the atonement that Christ alone carries out. I am only saying that the blessed and happy state of the church always had its foundation in the person of Christ."[184] On the one hand, God's promise to Abraham would not be fully realized until Christ appeared; on the other hand, even the original adoption of Abraham's descendants was grounded in Christ's mediation. While Calvin acknowledges that the Old Testament authors did not speak of Christ in the most explicit terms, he nevertheless insists that the prophets display widespread hope for a Mediator. As Hannah, David, Isaiah, Jeremiah, Ezekiel, and others reveal, "Since God cannot without the Mediator be propitious toward the human race, under the law Christ was always set before the holy fathers as the end to which they should direct their faith."[185]

For Calvin, then, the chronological fulcrum of the knowledge of God is not the incarnation but the fall.[186] Both forms of this twofold knowledge are possible only through Christ, and both are available during the Old Testament as well as the New. The rest of Book 2 proceeds with discussions on the Law, the relation between the testaments, and especially the work of Christ as Mediator. This last topic bears on the external basis of redemption, leading naturally to Books 3–4, which investigate the application of Christ's redemptive work, first with regard to the internal renewal of the Holy Spirit (Book 3) and then with regard to the external means God uses to promote the Spirit's work (Book 4). In the next two sections, I will first consider Calvin's discussion in Book 1 on Scripture and knowledge of God the Creator and then explore a companion discussion in Book 3, Ch. 2 on Scripture and knowledge of God the Redeemer.

Scripture and the Creator

Knowledge of God the Creator involves not only assent that God exists, but also a posture of religious devotion that looks to God as the fountain of all good things and recognizes the benefits of knowing him: *religio* and

---

184. Ibid., 2.6.2.
185. Ibid.
186. I am grateful for C. Kavin Rowe for helping me to articulate this point.

pietas figure essentially.[187] Quite apart from Scripture, the order of nature reveals God's goodness, providence, and sustenance of the world,[188] and Calvin insists that all people retain this knowledge despite the corruption of humanity after the fall. Internally, "there is within the human mind, and indeed by natural instinct, an awareness of divinity *(divinitatis sensum)*."[189] Externally, God's wisdom can also be seen in the glories of the created order, "a sort of mirror *(speculi)* in which we can contemplate God,"[190] and especially in the marvels that make up humans themselves.[191] Sinful humans suppress and reject this knowledge of God in ignorant, impious, and arrogant expressions of idolatry, superstition, and hypocrisy, with the result that "no real piety remains in the world."[192] Creation is a dazzling theater of God's glory,[193] Calvin writes, but our failure of vision prevents us from perceiving this display.

Scripture is God's privileged means of restoring our sight. "Just as old or bleary-eyed men and those with weak vision, if you thrust before them a most beautiful volume, even if they recognize it to be some sort of writing, yet can scarcely construe two words, but with the aid of spectacles will begin to read distinctly; so Scripture, gathering up the otherwise confused knowledge of God in our minds, having dispersed our dullness, clearly shows us the true God."[194] As this image suggests, the knowledge of God the Creator derived through Scripture is substantially the same as that derived through creation. Both Scripture and creation demonstrate that God is characterized by eternity, self-existence, kindness, goodness, mercy, justice, judgment, truth, power, and might. "Indeed, the knowledge of God set forth for us in Scripture is destined for the same goal as the knowledge whose imprint shines in his creatures, in that it invites us first to fear God, then to trust him."[195] This does not imply the absence of unique knowledge of God the Creator derived from Scripture alone. As

---

187. *Inst.* 1.2.1. On the importance of the metaphor of God as a fountain of good, see B. A. Gerrish, *Grace and Gratitude: The Eucharistic Theology of John Calvin* (Minneapolis: Fortress, 1993), especially pp. 21-49. Gerrish argues that piety, understood as thankfulness to God, is the central concept in Calvin's understanding of true religion.
188. *Inst.* 1.2.1.
189. Ibid., 1.3.1.
190. Ibid., 1.5.1.
191. Ibid., 1.5.2-4.
192. Ibid., 1.4.1.
193. Ibid., 1.5.8, 1.6.2.
194. Ibid., 1.6.1.
195. Ibid., 1.10.2.

mentioned above, Scripture reveals content about the Trinity as well as creation and providence that could not have been known otherwise. Still, the accent of Calvin's discussion is on restoration: Scripture renews our vision to perceive what we could have seen were it not for the fall.[196]

Critical for Calvin's doctrine of Scripture is the relation between Word and Spirit, a theme that occupies much of Book 1, Chs. 7–9.[197] For our purposes, the following points deserve notice. First, Calvin indexes Word and Spirit to the external and internal dimensions of Scripture's authority, respectively.[198] Externally, Scripture is self-authenticating, bearing its own intrinsic authority. Internally, our confidence in Scripture derives from the secret testimony of the Spirit, which generates subjective confirmation of God's voice in the Word.[199] This distinction will figure crucially in Calvin's discussion of Scripture and knowledge of God the Redeemer. Second, Calvin asserts the mutual compatibility of Word and Spirit especially against those who suggest the written character of Scripture somehow constrains the dynamism of the Spirit.[200] The Spirit is the author of Scripture, and his ongoing confirmation of the Word brings completion to that original work.[201] There can thus be no contradiction between Scripture and Spirit,[202] and Paul's remarks about the death-dealing letter (2 Cor. 3:6) should not be taken as a general statement about the Word. Indeed, the letter brings death only when the Spirit, who writes the law upon our

---

196. For more on this point, in dialogue with the debate between Barth and Brunner over natural theology, see Dowey, *Knowledge of God in Calvin's Theology*, 131-46; also Pitkin, *What Pure Eyes Could See*, 144-46.

197. For further discussion of this issue, see Gamble, "Calvin's Theological Method."

198. *Inst.* 1.7.4-5. See also 2.5.5: "God works in his elect in two ways: within, through his Spirit; without, through his Word." For a fuller discussion of the external and internal dimensions of the authority of Scripture, see Dowey, *Knowledge of God in Calvin's Theology*, 89-124. Dowey stresses the priority in Calvin's thought on the internal confirmation of the authority of Scripture, though he also argues that Calvin's position on the external authority of Scripture depends in part on a literal dictation theory of inspiration.

199. This dynamic corresponds to what Brian G. Armstrong calls the "hypothetical" character of Calvin's thought. See his *"Duplex cognitio Dei,* Or? The Problem and Relation of Structure, Form, and Purpose in Calvin's Theology," in McKee and Armstrong, *Probing the Reformed Tradition*, 135-53, based on his earlier "The Nature and Structure of Calvin's Thought according to the *Institutes*: Another Look," in *John Calvin's Institutes: His Opus Magnum* (Potchefstroom, South Africa: Potchefstroom University for Christian Higher Education, 1986), 55-81.

200. *Inst.* 1.9.1.
201. Ibid., 1.9.3.
202. Ibid., 1.9.2.

John Calvin

hearts, is absent.[203] When Calvin treats Scripture and knowledge of God the Redeemer, he will transpose this dynamic into a particularly Christological key. Third, the relation between Word and Spirit holds during Old Testament times as well as New, though this point is more implied than explicit in *Institutes*. Only those who know God as Redeemer can also know him as Creator, but the patriarchs "arrived at both from the Word,"[204] well before incarnation and Pentecost.

Scripture and the Redeemer

By the end of *Institutes* Book 2, Calvin has dedicated much attention to the mediatorial work of Christ as the objective basis for our redemption. The topic of Book 3, then, is the subjective application of Christ's work. "As long as Christ remains outside of us *(extra nos)*, and we are separated from him, all that he has suffered and done for the salvation of the human race remains useless and of no value to us. Therefore, to share with us what he has received from the Father, he had to become ours *(nostrum fieret)* and to dwell with us *(in nobis habitare)*."[205] For Calvin, faith is the means by which the Spirit unites us with Christ, while Scripture is God's designated instrument for generating faith. The opening chapters of Book 3 on the Holy Spirit (Ch. 1) and faith (Ch. 2) are therefore critical for understanding Calvin's discussion of Scripture.

Calvin defines faith as "a firm and certain knowledge of God's benevolence toward us, founded upon the truth of the freely given promise in Christ, both revealed to our minds and sealed upon our hearts through the Holy Spirit."[206] For Calvin, this faith encompasses knowledge, but cannot be reduced to mere intellectual assent. The affirmation of faith "is more of the heart *(cordis)* than of the brain *(cerebri)*, and more of the disposition *(affectus)* than of understanding *(intelligentiae)*."[207] Indeed, faith transcends

---

203. Ibid., 1.9.3.
204. Ibid., 1.6.1.
205. Ibid., 3.1.1.
206. Ibid., 3.2.7.
207. Ibid., 3.2.8. Dowey calls this kind of knowledge "supra-rational." It does not bypass rational processes, and it does include cognitive content. Nevertheless, this knowledge goes beyond comprehension to reach a kind of supernatural certainty concerning God's favor. Faith is therefore just one (albeit essential) element of a broader mystical union with Christ. For further discussion, see his *Knowledge of God in Calvin's Theology*, 181-85, 197-211.

the kind of knowledge we receive through normal sense perception; even when we attain the knowledge of faith, we may not comprehend the assurance we feel.[208] The emphasis in Calvin's understanding of the knowledge of God is thus on the personal and existential rather than on the purely intellectual.[209]

As sinners, we are prone to doubt, but Scripture helps secure our faith. For Calvin, faith and the Word are as inseparable as the sun and its rays,[210] or the fruit of a tree and its living root.[211] "Surely, as often as God commends his Word to us, he indirectly rebukes us for our unbelief, for he has no other intention to uproot perverse doubts from our hearts."[212] While Calvin affirms the general trustworthiness of Scripture, his definition of faith is curiously oriented not toward Scripture at large, but narrowly to the promises. This is a point Calvin feels particularly compelled to defend. "We make the freely given promise of God the foundation of faith because upon it faith properly rests. Faith is certain that God is true in all things whether he command or forbid, whether he promise or threaten; and it also obediently receives his commandments, observes his prohibitions, heeds his threats. Nevertheless, faith properly begins with the promise, rests in it, and ends in it."[213] Calvin lists two reasons for this position against potential critics. First, faith must be firm, and such certainty can only come from God's promises of mercy. Second, faith is that which distinguishes those who are reconciled with God from those who are not. This faith cannot simply consist in the belief that God makes commands or threatens punishment for sin; it is the particular character of saving faith to trust in God's promises of mercy in Christ.

On Calvin's account, all the promises in Scripture, both before and after the incarnation, are ultimately promises of God's love in Christ. "'However many are the promises of God, in him they find their yea and

---

208. *Inst.* 3.2.14. See 3.2.16-28 for a treatment on the relation between doubt and the certainty of faith. In short, Calvin does acknowledge that doubt will accompany faith, but he insists that saving faith eventually conquers doubt. His chief example for this kind of saving faith is David in the Psalms.

209. For arguments against overly intellectualist depictions of Calvin's understanding of faith, see Richard A. Muller, "*Fides* and *Cognitio* in Relation to the Problem of the Intellect and Will in the Theology of John Calvin," *CTJ* 25 (1990): 207-24; and Pitkin, *What Pure Eyes Could See*, 9-40.

210. *Inst.* 3.2.6.
211. Ibid., 3.2.31.
212. Ibid., 3.2.15.
213. Ibid., 3.2.29. See also 3.2.7.

John Calvin

amen' [II Cor. 1:20 p.]."[214] Since every promise in Scripture is a testimony of God's love, and "no one is loved by God apart from Christ,"[215] it follows that all the promises in Scripture are inherently Christological. Calvin recognizes the difficulty of this point, given both Old and New Testament examples that indicate God's favorable disposition toward those who did not know Christ: Naaman the Syrian, Cornelius, and the Ethiopian eunuch. All received some kind of approval despite their ignorance of the Mediator. Yet Calvin argues that "their faith was in some part implicit *(implicitam)*" and that they were surely "instructed in principles such as might give them some taste, however small, of Christ."[216] Naaman must have received some instruction about the Mediator from Elisha, Cornelius had embraced the Jewish religion before Peter found him, and the Ethiopian eunuch recognized the importance of Jerusalem before he met Philip. "Although the knowledge of Christ was obscure among them, it is inconceivable to suppose that there was none at all; because they practiced the sacrifices of the law, which by their very end — that is, Christ — should be distinguished from the false sacrifices of the Gentiles."[217]

Given humanity's fallen condition, the promises of Scripture are not sufficient in and of themselves to engender faith. Calvin therefore stresses the role of the Holy Spirit in internalizing the promises for the believer. This work occurs at two levels. First, the Spirit must penetrate the blindness of the mind to perceive the promises of God. The disciples on the

---

214. Ibid., 3.2.32.
215. Ibid.
216. Ibid.
217. Ibid. A similar discussion arises in Calvin's discussion of implicit faith (3.2.2-5). Calvin rejects the "scholastics" who (as he describes them) hold that those who do not explicitly believe in God's goodness may receive salvation by submitting to the judgments of the church. Yet Calvin also acknowledges the legitimacy of a certain kind of implicit faith, since no one comprehends everything about God. On this point, Calvin cites a number of biblical figures who demonstrated a measure of faith before some experience or encounter with Christ generated a clearer and firmer understanding of what to believe. On these matters, see Dowey, *Knowledge of God in Calvin's Theology*, 167-72; and Pitkin, *What Pure Eyes Could See*, 134-36. The common thread in all Calvin's examples is that Christ is the object of faith. Calvin's concern to define Christ as the object of faith drives both his rejection of the scholastic notion of implicit faith and his willingness to distinguish the promises of Scripture from its other locutions. As Dowey writes, "For Calvin the Scripture is the formal authority of special revelation, but Christ alone is the material of saving faith and the proper object of faith's knowledge" (155). See Dowey, *Knowledge of God in Calvin's Theology*, 58-63 for a discussion on the tension in Calvin's thought between Calvin's emphasis on the authority of all Scripture and the Christocentric orientation of his definition of faith.

road to Emmaus received instruction from Christ himself concerning the mysteries of the Kingdom, but they did not understand what they were taught until Christ opened their minds to comprehend the Scriptures. "Although the apostles were so taught by his divine mouth, the Spirit of truth must nevertheless be sent to pour into their minds the same doctrine that they had received with their ears."[218] Second, the heart must be strengthened with the firmness faith requires. "For the Word of God is not received by faith if it flits about in the top of the brain, but when it takes root in the depth of the heart that it may be an invincible defense to withstand and drive off all the stratagems of temptation."[219] This second step is actually more demanding than the first, since "the heart's distrust is greater than the mind's blindness."[220] The Spirit therefore acts as a seal on our hearts, impressing upon us the certainty of God's promises and our inheritance.

Calvin's treatment of Scripture in Book 3 thus mirrors his treatment of Scripture in Book 1. In both sections, Calvin locates Scripture within the context of redemptive history as God's chosen means to counter the effects of the fall. Both sections also teach that the primary purpose of Scripture is to promote knowledge of God. Finally, both sections trade on a very strong position concerning the unity of the testaments. For Calvin, both the Old and New Testaments restore humanity to knowledge of God the Creator and knowledge of God the Redeemer. The promises of the old covenant, and not just the new, testify to Christ and provide sufficient grounds for salvific faith.

Christ and the Literal Sense

If, as I have argued, Calvin insists that both the Old and New Testaments reveal God the Redeemer and that all the Old Testament promises were Christological and understood as such, a perplexing question arises. Did Calvin in fact support allegory? This would be rather surprising given Calvin's clear and consistent statements against the practice throughout his writings. Calvin writes in *Institutes,* for instance, "Allegories ought not to go beyond the limits set by the rule of Scripture *(praeeuntem habent Scrip-*

---

218. *Inst.* 3.2.34.
219. Ibid., 3.2.36.
220. Ibid.

John Calvin

turae regulam), let alone suffice as the foundation for any doctrines."[221] So too, in his exposition of Paul's allegory of Hagar and Sarah in the Galatians commentary, Calvin remarks:

> Scripture, [the allegorists] say, is fertile, and thus produces a variety of meanings. I acknowledge that Scripture is a most rich and inexhaustible fountain of all wisdom; but I deny that its fertility consists in the various meanings which any man, at his pleasure, may assign. Let us know, then, that the true meaning of Scripture is the natural *(germanus)* and obvious *(simplex)* meaning; and let us embrace and abide by it resolutely. Let us not only neglect as doubtful, but boldly set aside as deadly corruptions, those pretended expositions, which lead us away from the natural meaning *(literali sensu)*.[222]

This curiosity of Calvin's thought has not gone unnoticed by his commentators. In his seminal article, "Calvin's Exegetical Principles," Hans-Joachim Kraus lists eight basic characteristics of Calvin's biblical interpretation, almost all of which stress Calvin's emphasis on straightforward exposition according to the intent of the biblical author.[223] Yet the final principle of Calvin's exegesis concerns the manner in which all Scripture is oriented toward Christ, a point that seems somewhat at odds with the first seven principles.[224] David Puckett's solution to this apparent tension in Calvin's thought is to appeal to the Reformer's dual appreciation for the human and divine sides of Scripture.[225] Calvin's concern for the former pushes him toward a modern, critical approach to Scripture that sometimes looks "Jewish," while his respect for the latter pushes him in a

---

221. Ibid., 2.5.19.
222. *Comm. Gal.* 4:22.
223. The eight principles he lists are: 1) clarity and brevity; 2) seeking the intention of the author; 3) investigating the historical, geographical, and institutional circumstances which determined the author's situation; 4) explaining the "real" (original, true, simple, or grammatical) meaning of a passage; 5) investigating the context of a passage; 6) establishing the extent to which exegesis could go beyond literal biblical wording; 7) dealing properly with metaphorical expressions; and 8) discerning "the scope of Christ" as the aim of all Scripture. For more especially on the first principle, see Gamble, *"Brevitas et Facilitas"*; "Exposition and Method in Calvin"; and "Calvin as Theologian and Exegete: Is There Anything New?"
224. Edmondson, "Christ and History," 16; Muller, "Hermeneutic of Promise and Fulfillment," 76-77.
225. Puckett, *John Calvin's Exegesis of the Old Testament*.

more "Christian" direction that reflects the sometimes troubling manner in which the New Testament appropriates the Old. Calvin seeks a kind of *via media* between historical exegesis that fails to recognize Christ in the Old Testament and fanciful allegory that perceives him behind every nook and cranny of the text. The problem with Puckett's synthesis is the presumption that the historical is for Calvin opposed to the Christological, and that his exegetical practices can be located on a continuum between the two extremes. It is not clear that Calvin would even acknowledge this dichotomy, let alone present his interpretive practices as some kind of middle ground between literal and allegorical reading. Puckett's study provides much textual evidence for a quandary in Calvin's thought, but his proposed solution ultimately reveals the challenges of reading Calvin through a modern hermeneutical lens. Two other studies suggest a more exegetically satisfying way of understanding Calvin's interpretative practices that correlates closely with Calvin's theology of the covenants as outlined above.

The first contribution comes from Richard Muller, who discovers an illuminating pattern in Calvin's interpretation of the Old Testament prophecies of the kingdom.[226] Calvin treats these prophecies with regard to both Old Testament Israel and Christ's kingdom, and the latter itself encompasses a number of distinct events: the first coming of Christ, the present context, and the eschaton. Two rhetorical concepts help Calvin interpret prophecies in such a way. The first is *complexus*, which refers to "a connection in discourse as important to the meaning of a text as the grammatical *sensus*."[227] The *complexus* of Christ's kingdom includes the whole course of the kingdom of Christ from its beginning to end. The second is synecdoche, which refers to "inclusive or extended implication and usually the signification of a larger whole by the naming of a part."[228] Synecdoche can explain, for instance, how a prophecy about the Levites may also refer to the church as a whole. On Muller's account, these two concepts enable Calvin to employ a hermeneutic of multiple fulfillments that encompasses Christ and the church within the literal sense, without appeal to allegory. Such an explanation can account both for Calvin's concern for history and for his complaints against excessively Christological interpretations of the Old Testament that obscure original meaning. Calvin affirms that the Old

---

226. Muller, "Hermeneutic of Promise and Fulfillment."
227. Ibid., 73.
228. Ibid., 75.

John Calvin

Testament should be understood with reference to Christ, but he insists that such reading be grounded in the literal sense — which sense is, in Calvin's use, surprisingly expandable. As Muller concludes, "Calvin's explicit use of rhetorical categories like synecdoche or *complexus* may in this context be seen as a shifting of the mode of analysis out of an allegorical or literal-spiritual mode (which postulated more than one *sensus* of a given text) to a rhetorical mode in which one *sensus* could nevertheless point toward multiple referents."[229]

Stephen Edmondson's work moves one step beyond Muller's study by stressing the redemptive-historical underpinnings of Calvin's hermeneutic. For Edmondson, Calvin's conflation of the literal and Christological interpretations of Scripture is rooted in his theology of the covenant.[230] Calvin holds that there is one covenant across the testaments and that this covenant is enacted by and fulfilled in Christ. Since Scripture is first and foremost a narration of this covenant, biblical interpretation must attend to both history and Christ, between which there is no contradiction but rather interpenetration. Calvin does not seek to read Christ into the Bible; he rather presumes Christ was written into the covenant itself. This explains why, on the one hand, Calvin criticizes Jewish interpreters who fail to discern the Old Testament's witness to Christ, while also rejecting, on the other hand, fairly established ways of discerning Christ in the Old Testament. For Calvin, neglecting the Christological referent of a prophetic statement is quite literally to miss its natural meaning — the meaning the prophet actually intended. Yet he also, for example, ignores the possibility in Genesis 22 that Isaac or the ram prefigures Christ, focusing instead on whether God could fulfill the promise of a mediator through Isaac if Isaac were dead. This approach to the passage is indeed Christological, but it sidesteps figures and allegory for more covenantal concerns. Since the Christological interpretation for Calvin just is the literal, there is no need for multiple senses.

For our purposes, the payoff of Muller's and Edmondson's studies is clear. The relation between the literal and Christological senses is for

229. Ibid., 81. This comment corresponds to Steinmetz's observation that Calvin tended to lump into the "plain" or "natural" sense of the text what medieval theologians would have labeled allegory. Steinmetz suggests, "Perhaps it would therefore be more accurate to say that Calvin stood for a principled reduction of 'spiritual' readings of the text rather than a total and unconditional rejection of them" (David C. Steinmetz, "Calvin as an Interpreter of the Bible," in McKim, *Calvin and the Bible*, 282-91, here 285).

230. In addition to Edmondson, "Christ and History," see also his *Calvin's Christology*, 40-88.

Calvin a unity of identity. Positing two senses of Scripture would be a category mistake, for one cannot move from letter to Spirit when they are, in fact, the same. Calvin's position on Old Testament interpretation thus correlates essentially to his theology of covenant and his understanding of the relation between Israel and the church. There is one covenant and one people, and so also only one sense of Scripture. The divergence between Augustine and Calvin on the shape of redemption and Scriptural interpretation is thus as fundamental as the difference between one and two.

Discussion

In what follows, I consider the key differences that separate Augustine's and Calvin's construals of Scripture and redemptive history while also highlighting difficulties each figure's position raises. The purpose of this part is not primarily comparative, but diagnostic and analytical, setting the stage for the approach to these issues seen in the Epistle to the Hebrews. Before proceeding to the difference between our two figures, I should first acknowledge significant areas of common ground. At the deepest level, Augustine and Calvin both affirm some basic unity between the testaments rooted in the constancy of God and his "moral law" (even if Augustine does not use that particular term) as well as the preparatory character of the Old Testament, which does not contradict but prefigures the revelation of Christ in the New Testament. These are not trivial matters: the identity of the Creator in the Old Testament with the God of Jesus Christ was a central issue in Irenaeus's attacks against the Gnostics and Tertullian's against Marcion. Augustine is not wrong to trace lines of similarity between these earlier heretics, the Manicheans, and the anonymous figure whose writings he opposes in *Answer to an Enemy of the Law and the Prophets*.[231] Both Augustine and Calvin defend the rectitude of God in the Old Testament, the goodness of creation, and the fleshly embodiment of the Son in Christ, and neither considers the abrogation of Old Testament practices to imply any change in the character of God or his moral demands. If one were comparing Augustine and Calvin on the one side, and the Gnostics or the Marcionites on the other, this discussion would look very different.

For our purposes, though, the focus is on the structural difference between Augustine and Calvin that runs like a fault line through their

---

231. *C. adv. leg.* 2.12.40.

John Calvin

respective treatments of redemption and Scripture. What questions and consequences arise from the distinction between a unity of reference and a unity of identity? I consider each of the major loci in turn.

The Relation between the Covenants

The first question concerns the relation between the testaments themselves. Is there one covenant or are there two? Did the Old Testament veil or reveal the hope of the New Testament? Did the Old Testament mediate grace or was it primarily characterized by fear, bondage, and death? As we have seen, Augustine perceives a clear distinction between two covenants, locating their unity decisively in the new. While Catholics do not simply jettison the Old Testament, *contra Faustum,* they retain its commands and promises spiritually and not in practice because the authority of these signs ultimately resides in the realities they prefigured. Calvin defines the unity between the testaments according to the substance of the covenant. Believers before and after Christ shared a common hope, a common law, common promises of reward, and a common knowledge of the same mediator. If Augustine seeks to legitimate the Old Testament according to its figuration of the New, Calvin goes much further and argues that the Old and New Testaments are essentially the same. As a somewhat simplistic analogy, the unity of the testaments is for Augustine like that between the word "ox" and the actual animal; for Calvin, it is like that between a young ox and the same ox when it grows older.

The difference between these positions bears critically on the question of revelation during Old Testament times. Augustine depicts the Old Testament primarily as a time of darkness and opacity, when signs that prefigured the New Testament also obscured what was to come. For Calvin, the testaments are unified because they reveal the same realities; Christ was indeed displayed to the fathers, even if in preliminary, shadowy fashion. We might compare Augustine's understanding of Old Testament revelation to the dynamics of a mystery novel, wherein the author plants clues of some narrative that will make sense of all that has come before, while intentionally keeping the end a surprise. The conclusion's effect trades on prior obscurity, and the final moment of illumination prompts new readings of the text from this fresh perspective.[232] For Calvin, the

---

232. For reflections on such a model, see David C. Steinmetz, "Uncovering a Second Narrative: Detective Fiction and the Construction of the Historical Method," in *The Art*

transition from the Old Testament to the New is more like the repeated presentation of a story, first through radio, then on television, and finally by live performance.[233] Such shifts do not unveil what was formerly hidden, but rather promulgate the same content through new and enhanced media. It is this divergence between Augustine and Calvin that animates their stark opposition concerning the Old Testament promises. Augustine clearly considers the Old Testament temporal in orientation; the difference between earthly and heavenly reward is for him one of the primary dividing lines between the covenants. Yet this is exactly the position Calvin assails in the heretic Servetus before he defends the hope of immortality in the Old Testament and the concomitant parity between Old and New Testament believers. A critical question for our next chapter is whether the Old Testament promised immortality directly or in figures, and how widely this hope was known.

Most fundamental is the basic availability of grace under the old covenant. On Augustine's account, the Old Testament veiled the grace and righteousness of God, bringing the Israelites under bondage to the law, which was able to generate obedience through fear of punishment only, not love for righteousness. Since the Spirit was given to pour out the love of God in our hearts (Rom. 5:5), the general absence of the Spirit before Christ vitiated the possibility of genuine faithfulness. Calvin's theology of covenant cannot permit such a position, and he thus defines the law as a renewal of God's eternal promises to Abraham, and Moses as more fundamentally a mediator of grace than exactor of justice. Jeremiah and Paul force Calvin to acknowledge a narrow sense in which the law did demand obedience and threaten punishment for any defection from God's will. But Calvin still affirms a broader and more basic conception of the law as the mode of administration for God's grace before the incarnation. For both Augustine and Calvin, there is a distinction between the fear of the Old Testament and the love of the New. The issue is whether this contrast is fundamental or supplemental to the covenants.

---

of Reading Scripture, ed. Ellen F. Davis and Richard B. Hays (Grand Rapids: Eerdmans, 2003), 54-65.

233. Randall C. Zachman draws attention to a similar metaphor in Calvin's commentary on Heb. 10:1 whereby the old covenant presents Christ to the Israelites as in a charcoal outline that gradually gets filled in to become a living portrait; see his *Reconsidering John Calvin,* Current Issues in Theology (Cambridge: Cambridge University Press, 2012), 67.

John Calvin

Israel and the Church

Was Israel a sign of the church or simply the people of God before the incarnation? What salvific benefits did the Old Testament saints experience, and what was their relation to Israel at large? What status remains for God's promises to the Jewish people? These questions bring to relief broader decisions about the covenants as well as anomalies in both Augustine's and Calvin's theologies of Jews and Judaism. For Augustine, Israel was a privileged sign which could not simplistically be identified with the earthly city, but still belonged to that side of humanity's divide. Since the old covenant obscured God's grace, the Jews were generally blocked from salvation, despite some significant exceptions. For Calvin, Old Testament Israel was "the church of the Jews," sharing with the New Testament church the same sacraments, the same promises, the same law, the same doctrine, and the same covenant, whose foundation is Christ. Even the distinction between the faithful and the unfaithful in Israel is no different from that within the church. The only substantive difference between Old Testament Israel and the New Testament church — if this should even be considered "substantive" — is that the former was Jewish and the latter includes Gentiles.

Within their respective frames of thought, Augustine and Calvin both struggle with the salvific status of the Old Testament saints. If Abraham was, as Paul teaches, the father of all who believe, it is theologically impossible for either Augustine or Calvin to accept that he was excluded from the gracious covenant revealed in Christ. Augustine's position is that certain Old Testament personages experienced the new covenant by way of redemptive-historical aberration: Moses and others mediated the old covenant as they belonged to the new. But this is a troubling proposal, for it suggests that select individuals bypassed the fear and bondage of the old covenant while deliberately keeping their kinsfolk, the Israelites, in slavery. Calvin's first move is different — the patriarchs and prophets did participate in Christ, but with less clarity of revelation than New Testament believers — but his ultimate conclusion is the same as Augustine's: the Old Testament saints constituted exceptions to their dispensation. Given his construal of the covenants, Calvin's position is perplexing. On his account, the law was an instantiation and renewal of the covenant with Abraham, and not a rival system. Those who belonged to Christ before the incarnation received the benefits of his covenant while experiencing the particularities of the law only in a secondary sense. All, that is, shared the hope of immortality, came to God by grace and not merit, and knew and had Christ as mediator, while also suffering some fear and bondage. It is not clear how such a framework could accommodate a "transfer" of New Testament blessings to the Old Testament saints.

Consider, by way of example, a married couple separated by distance for an extended period of time. They cannot communicate as frequently or directly as otherwise, nor can they share as fully in the same experiences — except, perhaps, a common sense of loneliness. But they are still bound in covenant and able to interact with each other as such, notwithstanding some measure of isolation and dissatisfaction. It would be most odd to call the shared affection they experience through a phone conversation an "aberration" or a "transfer" from their actual relationship. Neither spouse experiences only the love of marriage or only the frustration of distance (understood in their particularities); each experiences both, though marriage more essentially describes their relationship than distance. In his most characteristic statements on the unity of the covenant, this is the image Calvin presents of the Old Testament saints: they participated fundamentally in God's covenant of grace, while also living under shadows. Yet when Calvin confronts passages that present a particularly stark contrast between the testaments — Jer. 31, Gal. 4, 2 Cor. 3 — he resorts to language rather discordant with the basic structures of his thought. Augustine can appeal to redemptive-historical aberration because he affirms the existence of two covenants. But how is it possible to belong to the new covenant and not the old if the new covenant is essentially identical to the old?

Augustine and Calvin also raise a question concerning the character of God's promises to Abraham. In what sense is the covenant "eternal"? Does the covenant pertain to the church as distinct from national Israel? How much weight should be placed on references to land? Neither Augustine nor Calvin completely spiritualizes the Old Testament promises, a point that bears particular weight in their joint affirmation that national Israel will somehow be restored in the end times. While both interpret Paul's "all Israel" as a reference to the church, ethnic Israel does not completely drop from view. Yet both Augustine and Calvin advance what can fairly be called supersessionism, albeit with significant differences. Augustine presents a relatively standard form: the Jews were an earthly people who killed their own messiah, prompting God to cast them off and destroy physical Jerusalem. Israel will be restored only after acknowledging this crime and turning to Jesus. For Calvin, Christ was the foundation of the covenant from the beginning, such that Israel was united with him even

John Calvin

before the incarnation. Since Christ has always mediated participation in the covenant, nothing changes in that regard with the New Testament. By defining Israel as the church during Old Testament times, Calvin sets forth a rather curious form of preemptive supersessionism.

Again, it must be asked whether Calvin's position can finally hold together. From the Reformer's perspective, Israel never had an identity independent of the church. Israel was coterminous with the visible church during Old Testament times by virtue of her participation in Christ through the Mosaic law. In the New Testament, however, the ceremonies have lost their value, such that those who do not participate in Christ according to the new realities have no share in the covenant. But since ethnic demarcation is accidental and not essential to participation in the covenant for Calvin, it is not clear what grounds he can provide for affirming God's ongoing commitment to national Israel, now characterized primarily by rejection of Christ. To be fair, Calvin's chief concern is biblical: his commitment to the literal sense drives his position that the Old Testament promises concern the fleshly descendants of Abraham, not just the visible church, however she may be constituted at different points in the economy of salvation (i.e., by Jews in the Old Testament, by Gentiles primarily in the New). Calvin also makes a valiant effort to decipher Paul's perplexing remarks in Rom. 11 about the restoration of the Jews. Nevertheless, ethnic Israel, as a chosen people distinct from the church in New Testament times, seems for Calvin to materialize in midair. Whence did this people arise if they simply were the church during Old Testament times?

However Calvin or Augustine might address this broad set of issues, Israel is for both a vexed theological question. Both consider non-Christian Jews deficient because of their lack of faith in Christ, but neither reduces Israel to the status of "pagan." That Calvin affirms with Augustine the future restoration of ethnic Israel reveals that each has more than two categories for the world. There are Christians and pagans, but there is also Israel, a mystery.[234] The relation between Israel and church, then, develops and complicates the basic contrast between Augustine and Calvin. In general, the two covenants correspond for Augustine to two peoples. As the Old Testament was a sign for the New, so also was Israel for the church. For Calvin, there is one covenant and one people, despite differences of form and administration. Neither figure, however, completely instrumentalizes

---

234. I am particularly grateful to Paul Griffiths for helping me to think through this matter.

Israel for the sake of the church, precisely to respect the literal sense of God's Old Testament promises to Israel. Israel is not just some non-Christian nation, but remains God's chosen people.

The Senses of Scripture

The difference between Augustine's and Calvin's views on Scripture should not be exaggerated, and it is worth noting for a moment the convictions these figures share concerning the purpose of Scripture. Both locate Scripture against the broader contours of salvation history as a remedy for the fall supplementary to Christ in the process of redemption. Augustine explicitly suggests that those who manifest faith, hope, and love do not need Scripture, since the purpose of Scripture is to prompt enjoyment of God. Calvin is a bit more reticent on this point, but he, too, agrees that Scripture is ultimately designed to direct us to Christ, a judgment that underwrites his (somewhat hesitant) move to define faith according to the promises, as opposed to Scripture more generally. Both figures treat Scripture primarily as it encourages participation in Christ; neither would suggest that the purpose of knowing and loving God is to understand the Bible.

Still, significant differences arise concerning whether the Old Testament fulfilled this purpose before the incarnation, how it speaks toward future events, and whether the text demands spiritual reading. The first issue has largely been addressed above. Since, for Augustine, the incarnation marks the moment when the Old Testament signs would be recognized as such, i.e., as things to be used for the sake of enjoying God in Christ, they could not have united us with Christ before the incarnation (except through special insight reserved for the patriarchs and prophets). For Calvin, the Old Testament promises were not only founded on Christ, but they also revealed him, thus enabling knowledge of God the Redeemer before the incarnation.

The other issues are a bit trickier. Both Augustine and Calvin acknowledge that the Old Testament speaks of the future. Calvin holds no less than Augustine that Old Testament locutions may be taken with reference to Israel, the time of Christ, the contemporary context, or the eschaton. Still, each figure defines these meanings differently, and their structural divergence animates markedly distinct approaches to the biblical text. Augustine indexes figural interpretation to multiple levels of reading. Literal expressions have only one level of signification, from sign to referent, while metaphorical expressions involve a sign that signifies a thing, which in turn signifies some other thing. For Calvin, the literal sense itself contains a plurality of interpretations concerning Christ and the church: a prophecy about Israel could literally refer to Israel, or to the church of the New Testament, or to the church now, or to the church at the end of time. Appeal to the spiritual sense is unnecessary since the Old Testament has already revealed Christ in fairly straightforward fashion. Calvin can thus affirm with Augustine the presence of multiple referents in Scripture without adopting a twofold understanding of the literal and spiritual senses.

For neither figure does the Christological reading obviate the "original" sense. (We cannot use the term "literal" here, since for Calvin the literal encompasses the Christological.) For Augustine, the primary referent of a sign is itself a *res,* even if it also acts as *signum* to another *res;* historical reality must be affirmed since it directs us toward spiritual meanings. So, too, both figures understand the importance of interpretive controls, even if Calvin's chief concern is adherence to the original sense and Augustine's is the promotion of charity. Nevertheless, each thinker's position on the spiritual sense funds an obvious difference of sensibility. Calvin strives to present the clear and plain meaning of the text, and he consistently (though not completely) rejects allegory as fanciful indulgence and speculation. Augustine embraces a wide range of textual play within the boundaries of love, precisely because the process of discovering hidden treasures produces humility, delight, and the enjoyment of God in Christ.

In the fifth chapter, I will consider concrete examples of Augustine's and Calvin's interpretative practices alongside the appropriation of the Old Testament in Hebrews. For now, the first two chapters have established the interconnection between redemptive history and the interpretation of Scripture. Despite their similarities on a number of theological matters, Augustine and Calvin present basically different visions of redemption that animate highly divergent reading practices. There is, for Calvin, one covenant and one people, and so one sense of Scripture. For Augustine, there are two. In the next two chapters, we will consider a different vision of redemptive history and a concomitant mode of Scriptural interpretation unlike what we have seen before. We may now consider the Epistle to the Hebrews.

CHAPTER 3

The Epistle to the Hebrews: God's New Covenant with Israel

Introduction

This chapter and the next function as a hinge in this study. To this point, I have sought to establish a typological distinction between Augustine and Calvin, arguing that their differences concerning the figural reading of the Old Testament are rooted ultimately in different construals of the relation between the testaments and derivatively in the relation between Israel and the church. Yet this descriptive comparison has left open a number of theological questions. Are the old and new covenants fundamentally distinct, or is the new covenant a renewal and continuation of the old? What salvific benefits were available during Old Testament times? To what extent did the Old Testament Israelites participate in the new covenant?

This chapter addresses these issues by turning to the Epistle to the Hebrews, using the concepts and vocabulary Augustine and Calvin provide to reflect constructively upon the questions raised. I advance two primary points. First, Hebrews depicts the establishment of Christ as high priest as a fundamentally new moment in redemptive history. The discontinuity between the testaments should therefore be located in Christ's mediatorial work. Second, Hebrews presents the new covenant as the means by which God brings to fruition the hope of the Old Testament. The continuity of the testaments thus resides in God's ongoing faithfulness to Israel and the common hope of the people of God across the covenants.

The argument of this chapter will proceed in four sections, the first three of which are primarily exegetical in nature. In the first section, I focus on the depiction of the installation of Christ as high priest in Hebrews.

The Epistle to the Hebrews: God's New Covenant with Israel

The second and third sections consider the broader implications of this moment for the establishment of a new covenant and the identity of God's people across the testaments. The fourth section brings Augustine and Calvin back into the conversation to draw out more clearly the epistle's vision of redemptive history and the covenant community.

In this chapter and the next, I draw heavily upon contemporary New Testament scholarship. This methodological decision may be taken as an implicit argument for the fruitfulness of cross-disciplinary inquiry. The rigorous historical work of biblical scholars provides rich material for theological reflection, while the history of biblical interpretation facilitates the incorporation of those insights into a larger theological framework. Nevertheless, my choice to begin in this work with Augustine and Calvin suggests that the dialogue between biblical studies and theological inquiry need not proceed from the former to the latter. My hope in these next two chapters is to demonstrate that beginning with a synthetic theological framework can actually enhance insight into the biblical text. As discussed in the introduction, this methodological approach will not conform to the guild standards of New Testament scholarship. I grant myself the freedom to use later theological categories — not least the very distinction between the "Old Testament" and the "New Testament" — to present Hebrews's unique perspective on the questions this study has sought to address. Still, I hope these chapters reflect my great indebtedness to and appreciation for the work of biblical scholars, even as I direct my remarks toward constructive theological proposal.

I have sought to isolate my reflections on Hebrews from assumptions concerning the provenance of the epistle. The standard literature on Hebrews adequately addresses this question for my purposes, and I do not pretend to advance the discussion.[1] In general, very little can be established

---

1. Harold W. Attridge, *Hebrews,* Hermeneia (Philadelphia: Fortress, 1989); F. F. Bruce, *The Epistle to the Hebrews,* rev. ed., NICNT (Grand Rapids: Eerdmans, 1990); William L. Lane, *Hebrews 1-8* and *Hebrews 9-13,* WBC 47a-b (Dallas: Word, 1991); Paul Ellingworth, *The Epistle to the Hebrews: A Commentary on the Greek Text,* NIGTC (Grand Rapids: Eerdmans, 1993); David A. deSilva, *Perseverance in Gratitude: A Socio-Rhetorical Commentary on the Epistle "to the Hebrews"* (Grand Rapids: Eerdmans, 2000); Craig R. Koester, *Hebrews: A New Translation with Introduction and Commentary,* AB 36 (New York: Doubleday, 2001); Luke Timothy Johnson, *Hebrews: A Commentary,* NTL (Louisville: Westminster John Knox, 2006). See also Barnabas Lindars, *The Theology of the Letter to the Hebrews,* New Testament Theology (Cambridge: Cambridge University Press, 1991); and three recent collections of essays: Gabriella Gelardini, ed., *Hebrews: Contemporary Methods — New Insights* (Leiden: Brill, 2005); Richard Bauckham et al., eds., *A Cloud of Witnesses: The Theology of Hebrews*

concerning the author, date, or recipients of this letter, except that it is not Pauline. Our author appears, like Melchizedek, without father or mother or genealogy, though he leaves behind much material rich for Christological reflection. Greater certainty on whether the letter was written before or after the destruction of the temple in 70 CE would significantly illuminate the epistle's remarks on the Levitical priesthood, but I make no assumptions on this issue. The only important position I adopt concerning provenance is that this letter was written to what may anachronistically be called "Jewish Christians," and not primarily to a Gentile audience. But this is a point I address in greater detail later in this chapter, not one I presuppose. Finally, in my remarks on Hebrews, I move freely between different terms for the object of study: I sometimes speak of "the Epistle to the Hebrews," but at other points refer to "Hebrews," "the epistle," "the author of Hebrews," and so forth. I use the masculine singular pronoun when referring to the anonymous author.[2]

The Establishment of Christ as High Priest

The central theme of Hebrews is the establishment of Christ as great high priest, an event the author identifies with the precise moment when the Father says to the Son, in the words of Ps. 110:4: "Thou art a priest forever, after the order of Melchizedek."[3] Heb. 7–10, the most developed argument of the letter, may be understood as an extended reflection upon the implications of this declaration for the Levitical priesthood and the inauguration of a new covenant. Yet the significance of this moment for Hebrews's understanding of redemptive history is most clearly seen in the narrative sequence the author deploys throughout the epistle to frame his account.

Hebrews highlights at least three primary differences between the priesthood of Christ and that of the Levites.[4] First, the Levitical priesthood was characterized by death, but the priesthood of Christ was characterized by life and immortality. The Levitical priests were prevented from staying

---

in Its Ancient Contexts, LNTS 387 (London: T&T Clark, 2008), and idem, *The Epistle to the Hebrews and Christian Theology* (Grand Rapids: Eerdmans, 2009).

2. See masculine participle in 11:32: διηγούμενον.

3. Heb. 5:6; 7:17, 21; cf. 5:10; 6:20; 7:11.

4. For an exposition of these themes, see Albert Vanhoye, *Old Testament Priests and the New Priest According to the New Testament,* trans. J. Bernard Orchard (Petersham, MA: St. Bede's, 1986).

The Epistle to the Hebrews: God's New Covenant with Israel

in office because they died, but Christ lives to intercede for us forever (7:8, 23-25, 28). Second, the Levitical priesthood pertains to this earth while the priesthood of Christ is heavenly (7:26; 8:1-2). Heb. 9 sets forth a description of the earthly tabernacle (9:1-10), only to proclaim Christ priest of a "greater and more perfect tent" (9:11), the heavenly sanctuary (9:24). Third and most important, the many sacrifices of the Levitical priesthood lacked the efficacy of Christ's once-for-all sacrifice. The gifts and sacrifices of the former could not "perfect the conscience of the worshiper" (9:9), and dealt only with "regulations for the body imposed until the time of reformation" (9:10), that is, those concerning external matters of purity.[5] By contrast, the blood of Christ will "purify your conscience from dead works to serve the living God" (9:14).

This difference in salvific power is particularly evident in the contrast between the repetition of the Levitical sacrifices and the single sacrifice of Christ, efficacious for all time (7:27; 9:12, 25-28). "For since the law has but a shadow of the good things to come instead of the true form of these realities, it can never, by the same sacrifices which are continually offered year after year, make perfect those who draw near" (10:1; cf. 10:11). Indeed, if these animal sacrifices could have cleansed people of sin, then they should have ceased, for then there would be no more consciousness of sin (10:2). These sacrifices instead functioned as a reminder of sin (10:3), in contrast to the sacrifice of Christ, who through a single offering "has perfected for all time those who are sanctified" (10:14).

While a number of these dynamics could be treated in greater depth, the key questions for our purposes are when and how this transition occurred. In his important recent work, *Atonement and the Logic of Resurrection in the Epistle to the Hebrews*,[6] David Moffitt addresses both issues by drawing out the narrative framework that undergirds the broad argument of the epistle. Three passages are of particular pertinence. The first is 2:10, where the author writes, "For it was fitting that he, for whom and by whom all things exist, in bringing many sons to glory, should make the pioneer of their salvation perfect through suffering." The relevant points are, in short: first, Jesus was made perfect; second, this perfection occurred through suffering; and third, Jesus brings about our salvation. The rest of this pericope (2:11-18) develops this sequence further: Jesus

---

5. Attridge, *Hebrews*, 243.
6. David M. Moffitt, *Atonement and the Logic of Resurrection in the Epistle to the Hebrews* (Leiden: Brill, 2011).

took on flesh and blood in order to die, so that he could destroy death's hold upon us. It is because Jesus became human that he can now make expiation for our sins.

The second pertinent passage is 5:5-10, which elucidates 2:10-18. In 5:5-6, the author cites Ps. 2:7 and Ps. 110:4 with regard to Christ's appointment as high priest. Then, in Heb. 5:7-10, the author explains how this process took place.

> In the days of his flesh, Jesus offered up prayers and supplications, with loud cries and tears, to him who was able to save him from death, and he was heard for his godly fear. Although he was a Son, he learned obedience through what he suffered; and being made perfect he became the source of eternal salvation to all who obey him, being designated by God a high priest after the order of Melchizedek.

What 5:7-10 shows more clearly than 2:10 is the chronology of events: it was through Jesus's death that he was perfected; and it was through his perfection that he became high priest. The language in 5:7 concerning the days of Jesus's flesh and his prayer "to him who was able to save him from death" recalls 2:14-15, which also links the assumption of flesh with subsequent death. Likewise, both units connect Jesus's suffering with his being made perfect (2:10; 5:8-9), which produces for both passages the same result: Jesus has become high priest to bring us salvation (2:10, 17-18; 5:9-10).

The final passage, Heb. 12:2, repeats the same themes by encouraging readers to trust in Jesus, "the pioneer and perfecter of our faith, who for the joy that was set before him endured the cross, despising the shame, and is seated at the right hand of the throne of God." As with 2:10, 12:2 explicitly connects the depiction of Jesus as pioneer with the idea of perfection. Like both 2:14 and 5:7, 12:2 also draws attention to Jesus's obedience in death. Finally, like 2:17 and 5:9-10, 12:2 stresses the positive result of Christ's faithfulness, albeit in slightly different terms. The earlier passages focus on Christ's establishment as high priest, while the latter describes Christ's exaltation to the right hand of God. These two ideas, though, are closely linked throughout Hebrews: it is after Christ has been established as high priest and offers himself as a sacrifice that he sits at God's right hand.[7] Heb.

---

7. The connection between Christ's establishment as high priest and his being seated at the right hand of God can be seen in 1:3: "When he had made purification for sins, he sat down at the right hand of the Majesty on high"; 8:1: "We have such a high priest, one who

12:2 thus refers to the priestly ministry of Christ, made possible only after he partook of humanity, suffered and died, and was made perfect.

In three important passages, then, Hebrews invokes the notion of perfection according to a common sequence of events whereby Christ is established as high priest. Still, these passages alone do not elucidate what causal relation exists, if any, between Christ's perfection and his ability to serve as high priest. The next step, then, is Moffitt's provocative but textually supported proposal that perfection should be understood in terms of Christ's resurrection and physical ascent into heaven. It was precisely because Christ took on flesh and received a resurrection body that he was qualified to become high priest.[8] Four critical moves display the outlines of this reading as well as its implications for the narrative above.

First, the opening chapters of Hebrews celebrate the exaltation of Christ by comparing him with the angels.[9] Christ is "Son," his reign is eternal, he sits at the right hand of God, and his enemies are a footstool for his feet (1:6, 8, 12-13). The angels do not participate in such privileges, but rather worship the Son. These angels are, moreover, spiritual — they are "winds," "flames of fire," or "ministering servants" (1:7, 14).

Second, the reference in 1:6 to the moment when God "brings the first-born into the world" and commands, "Let all God's angels worship him," does not refer, as has often been suggested, to the incarnation or the *parousia,* but to Christ's entrance into the heavenly realm. The chief support for this reading is 2:5-9, which depicts Christ as having been made "for a little while lower than the angels" (2:7) only to be crowned with glory and honor, exalted above all things. The "world" Christ enters to the praise of angels in 1:6 corresponds to the "world to come" which has now been subjected to him (2:5; both οἰκουμένη). Since the incarnation

---

is seated at the right hand of the throne of the Majesty in heaven"; and 10:12: "When Christ had offered for all time a single sacrifice for sins, he sat down at the right hand of God . . ." The allusion to God's right hand is derived from Ps. 110:1, cited in full at Heb. 1:13. Ps. 110 also provides Hebrews with the declaration of a new priest in the order of Melchizedek. That "right hand" is explicitly used in Heb. 1:3; 8:1; and 10:12 in connection with Christ's priestly ministry tightens the connections we drew above between Heb. 2:10-18; 5:5-10; and 12:2.

8. In addition to Moffitt, *Atonement and the Logic of Resurrection,* see idem, "'If Another Priest Arises': Jesus' Resurrection and the High Priestly Christology of Hebrews," in Bauckham et al., *A Cloud of Witnesses,* 68-79. For an alternative treatment of perfection, see David Peterson, *Hebrews and Perfection: An Examination of the Concept of Perfection in the 'Epistle to the Hebrews'* (Cambridge: Cambridge University Press, 1982).

9. On this and the next point, see Moffitt, *Atonement and the Logic of Resurrection,* 45-144.

demotes Christ beneath the angels, it would be rather odd for them to be told at this moment to worship him. Nor can the *parousia* be in view, for Christ has already been exalted above all things. As Moffitt rightly argues, then, it must have been after the Son was made lower than the angels in the incarnation and then entered into the heavenlies to receive glory and honor that God commanded the angels to worship him.

Third, it was precisely the fleshly character of the incarnation that enabled the Son to be exalted above the angels.[10] Ps. 8:4-6, cited in Heb. 2:6-8, hints that it was God's intention at creation to elevate humans above angels, but Hebrews observes that this reality has not yet come to fruition. The author resolves this tension by interpreting Ps. 8 as a reference to the subjection of all things to Christ as the representative and forerunner of humanity. By taking on flesh and receiving glory above the angels, Christ paved the way for humanity at large also to be exalted. Heb. 2:10-18 confirms this interpretation by stressing Christ's solidarity with the rest of humanity and depicting him as the pioneer of our salvation. So too, the Son's exaltation over the "spiritual" angels in Heb. 1 appears even more clearly to be based on his status as the one who took on flesh, i.e., became a human.

Fourth, the hero list of 11:1–12:2 stresses the preservation of life from death and the inheritance of incorruptible things, with Christ as the paradigmatic instance of this final hope. Abel still speaks, despite his death (11:4); Enoch was taken up without dying (11:5); Noah preserved his household from death and so became an heir (11:7); Abraham and Sarah received children despite the deadness of their bodies, in hope of a city with foundations (11:10-12); Moses endured ill treatment for the sake of future reward (11:26). Abraham knew with Isaac that God was able to bring life from death (11:19), and other heroes did receive back the dead (11:35). These instances testify to a kind of resuscitation, but the epistle also speaks of a final resurrection and an eternal inheritance: the restoration of Isaac was only a symbol (παραβολή; 11:19), and the saints of old hoped to "rise again to a better life" (11:35), in "a better country, that is, a heavenly one" (11:16). Until the time of Christ, these heroes lived in faith rather than fulfillment, so that "apart from us they should not be made perfect" (11:40). But this has all changed with Jesus, "the pioneer and perfecter of our faith" (12:2), who has persevered in trial to receive the promised inheritance

---

10. On this and the next point, see Moffitt, *Atonement and the Logic of Resurrection*, 145-214.

now available for us. Given the emphasis throughout Heb. 11 on the hope of resurrected life in an incorruptible inheritance, 12:1-2 must mean that Christ did in fact receive these rewards.[11]

We may now return to Christ's perfection in 5:5-10, where the author says Christ offered up prayers and supplications to the one who could save him from death — and "was heard" (5:7). Jesus's faith mirrors Abraham's in 11:17-19, as both trusted in God's ability to bring life from death. As Moffitt suggests, it thus makes sense to understand Jesus's being heard as a reference to his resurrection from the dead. It also follows that the perfection of Christ in 5:9 is a reference to his resurrection.[12] After he suffered and died, Christ was perfected, in part at least, by receiving a glorified body, which allowed him to enter the heavenlies and serve as high priest. The logic of this passage would thereby underscore the assertion of 7:16 that Christ "has become a priest, not according to a legal requirement concerning bodily descent but by the power of an indestructible life."

To summarize, Hebrews utilizes a cluster of consistent images and ideas to narrate the establishment of Christ as high priest. As embodied creatures, humans were intended to be exalted over the angels, who are but ministering spirits. This reality has not yet taken place, except for the Son. He became a human to partake in our nature, and was obedient and suffered, even to death. Through this death, he conquered the devil and released us from fear of death. He also received perfection by means of a glorified body and entered the heavenlies, where he presented before God the single offering of himself and thus provided expiation for our sins, becoming for us an eternal source of salvation such that we too can be made perfect. He then sat down at the right hand of God, where he reigns above the angels and ever lives to intercede for us.

The key point for our purposes is that the salvific benefits of Christ's priestly ministry were not available chronologically prior to the sequence of events that began with his incarnation and concluded with his bodily ascent into heaven. Christ's perfection and ascension were the preconditions of his becoming high priest and source of salvation, but he had to die before he could be perfected, and to take on flesh before he could die. Hebrews praises the Son as the preexisting creator of the world, but it does not suggest his preexistence as high priest. The eternal Son could not act as

---

11. Moffitt, "'If Another Priest Arises,'" 73.
12. Ibid., 74-76.

high priest — that is, he could not take away sins, accomplish forgiveness, purify our consciences, remove our consciousness of sin, or bring us new life — until after his incarnation, death, and exaltation into heaven.

The Establishment of the New Covenant

For the author of Hebrews, the establishment of Christ as high priest necessarily results in the establishment of a new covenant. The epistle emphasizes this point, asserting without apology that the second covenant is better than the first and even that the new covenant implies the abrogation of the old. "Christ has obtained a ministry which is as much more excellent than the old as the covenant he mediates is better, since it is enacted on better promises" (8:6; cf. 7:22; 8:7-13; 9:15-22; 12:24; 13:20). It is necessary, though, to ask what defines this new covenant and how precisely Hebrews considers this covenant to be different from and superior to the old.

The chief Old Testament passage that frames the epistle's vision of a new covenant is Jer. 31:31-34, as cited in Heb. 8:8-12:

> For he finds fault with them when he says: "The days will come, says the Lord, when I will establish a new covenant with the house of Israel and with the house of Judah; not like the covenant that I made with their fathers on the day when I took them by the hand to lead them out of the land of Egypt; for they did not continue in my covenant, and so I paid no heed to them, says the Lord. This is the covenant that I will make with the house of Israel after those days, says the Lord: I will put my laws into their minds, and write them on their hearts, and I will be their God, and they shall be my people. And they shall not teach every one his fellow or every one his brother, saying, 'Know the Lord,' for all shall know me, from the least of them to the greatest. For I will be merciful toward their iniquities, and I will remember their sins no more."

This passage is not cited anywhere else in the New Testament,[13] and this is the most extensive Old Testament quotation in the New.[14] A number of points on how Hebrews here appropriates Jeremiah call for attention.

---

13. R. T. France, "The Writer of Hebrews as a Biblical Expositor," *TynBul* 47 (1996): 264.
14. George H. Guthrie, "Hebrews' Use of the Old Testament: Recent Trends in Research," *CurBR* 1 (2003): 282.

The Epistle to the Hebrews: God's New Covenant with Israel

First, the first covenant was unable to restrain sin. God finds fault with his people (8:8), because those who received the first covenant, established during the exodus, "did not continue in my covenant" (8:9).[15] Second, and by way of contrast, this new covenant will be characterized by the internalization of God's law: "I will put my laws into their minds, and write them on their hearts" (8:10; cf. 10:16). Third, this new covenant will bring about the forgiveness of sins. "For I will be merciful toward their iniquities, and I will remember their sins no more" (8:12). The author further underscores this theme in 10:17-18, where he quotes the same verse and concludes, "Where there is forgiveness of these, there is no longer any offering for sin" (10:18). Fourth, Jer. 31 implicitly predicts the end of the first covenant. The author of Hebrews follows that quotation with the explanation, "In speaking of a new covenant he treats the first as obsolete. And what is becoming obsolete and growing old is ready to vanish away" (8:13).

This last point receives confirmation elsewhere in the epistle, especially 7:11-19, a chiastic unit that presents the most direct affirmation in Hebrews of Christ's qualification to be high priest despite his non-Levitical lineage. For our purposes, the beginning and concluding verses are of particular significance. Both 7:11 and 7:19 deny the possibility of the law bringing perfection, while 7:12 and 7:18 announce a concomitant change of law. We read in Heb. 7:12: "When there is a change in the priesthood, there is necessarily a change in the law as well," and in Heb. 7:18: "A former commandment is set aside because of its weakness and uselessness." For the author of Hebrews, priesthood, law, and covenant form a tight institutional network, and the change effected by Christ involves the replacement of an entire system of earthly, temporal, inefficacious worship by a new system of heavenly, eternal, salvific worship. Christ "abolishes the first in order to establish the second" (10:9).

In her monograph on this issue, Susanne Lehne argues that the author of Hebrews goes beyond any New Testament author, including Paul, in his articulation of a conscious break with the institutions of Israel.[16]

---

15. There is a text-critical issue in 8:8 concerning whether God found fault with the people or with the first covenant. As Hays argues, though, the overall point of the text encompasses both meanings: "The inadequacy of the covenant may be thought to consist precisely in its inability to create an obedient people"; see Richard Hays, "'Here We Have No Lasting City': New Covenantalism in Hebrews," in Bauckham et al., *The Epistle to the Hebrews and Christian Theology*, 151-73, here 160.

16. Susanne Lehne, *The New Covenant in Hebrews,* JSNTSup 44 (Sheffield: Sheffield Academic, 1990).

Hebrews defines the law exclusively in terms of the Jewish cult, and rather paradoxically retains the language and form of the old covenant — blood, sacrifice, high priest, and tabernacle — while rejecting the continuation of its actual practices. Such a treatment of the Levitical system is utterly unique in the Jewish context. In her survey of Second Temple Jewish literature, Lehne finds virtually no material that reflects Jeremiah's prophecy of a new covenant; indeed, she notes, there seems to be a "studious avoidance" of this language.[17] The one notable exception is the Qumran community, which considered the Jerusalem temple system corrupt and so avoided participating in its rites. Nevertheless, the perspective of this sectarian group differs significantly from that of Hebrews: while the Qumran community expresses great devotion to the Law and longs for a purified, material temple system with a legitimate priesthood, Hebrews envisions a radical break from the old cultic system, which the author deems inherently defective.

The abrogation of the Levitical priesthood is a logical corollary of the establishment of Christ as high priest. The former system was inefficacious (7:18-19), unable to take away sin (10:11), characterized by repetitive animal sacrifices (10:1-4), and administered by priests who were themselves sinful (7:27) and constantly needed to be replaced upon their death through a system of succession (7:23). Christ, on the other hand, brings about the forgiveness of sins as a sinless, eternal high priest (7:24-28) through the once-for-all sacrifice of himself (9:25-28). We have noted the oddity of the epistle's retention of Levitical imagery to describe the high priestly ministry of Christ, when Hebrews also asserts the qualitative superiority of Christ's ministry over that of the Levitical priests.[18] Yet the logic of the argument does not begin with the priority of the Levitical priesthood system, which Christ then surpasses, but rather from the opposite direction. The earthly tabernacle that Moses constructed was a copy and shadow of the heavenly sanctuary, and Moses was instructed to build his tabernacle according to an already existing image presented to him (8:5; cf. 9:23-24). In that sense, the heavenly sanctuary has ontological priority over the earthly, even if, from a human perspective, the earthly is epistemologically prior to the heavenly. It is not that Jesus's priestly ministry resembles the Levitical, but the other way around. Since the Levitical priesthood was designed as

---

17. Lehne, *The New Covenant in Hebrews*, 35.
18. See also Deborah W. Rooke, "Jesus as Royal Priest: Reflections on the Interpretation of the Melchizedek Tradition in Heb 7," *Bib* 81 (2000): 92-93.

an image of Jesus, it follows that when he is established as high priest, the Levitical priesthood ceases to serve its purpose.

George Caird's still-valuable article, "The Exegetical Method of the Epistle to the Hebrews,"[19] elucidates this point. Caird argues that the argument of Hebrews is structured around four key Old Testament passages (Ps. 8, Ps. 95, Ps. 110, Jer. 31), and that each receives attention for its confession of the inadequacy of the old covenant. (I will consider these psalms in greater depth in the next chapter.) Jeremiah predicts the establishment of a new covenant because he perceives the problems with the current one; Ps. 110 declares an eternal priest in the order of Melchizedek during a time when the Levitical priests still control the temple cult; Ps. 95 speaks of God's rest when the Israelites already reside in Canaan; and Ps. 8 sets forth a glorious picture of man when we do not see everything in subjection to him. In these arguments, Caird says, "the epistle seeks to establish its main thesis, that the Old Testament is not only an incomplete book but an avowedly incomplete book, which taught and teaches men to live by faith in the good things that were to come."[20] In that regard, the exegetical concern of the author of Hebrews is not "to prove the superiority of the New Covenant to the Old, nor to establish the inadequacy of the old order. His interest is in the confessed inadequacy of the old order."[21] The old covenant was thus a kind of picture that signified, but did not enact a real effect on the world. As Caird writes:

> The priesthood had all the outward trappings of true priesthood, but not the essential quality of enabling men to draw near to God. The sacrifices had the appearance of true sacrifice, but not the power to purify the conscience from dead works. What then is the permanent significance of these outworn institutions? . . . A picture of an unknown fruit resembles the real thing in all except reality: it will not satisfy your hunger, but it may help you to recognize the real fruit if you should come across it. Similarly, the Old Testament priesthood and sacrifices were only shadow pictures of reality, but they prepared men to appreciate the reality when it appeared in Jesus Christ. God spoke to the fathers in the cultus in order that they might become familiar with a picture language

---

19. George B. Caird, "The Exegetical Method of the Epistle to the Hebrews," *CJT* 5 (1959): 44-51.
20. Ibid., 49.
21. Ibid., 47.

without which they could neither apprehend nor convey the full scope of his later word of salvation.[22]

The implication for our purposes is clear: the establishment of Christ as high priest marks the fulcrum in redemptive history that distinguishes the new covenant from the old. The author of Hebrews presents the Levitical priesthood system as an inefficacious sign which was never meant to provide the forgiveness of sins and has now been rendered obsolete by the establishment of Christ as high priest. Given the argument of the previous section that the moment of Christ's installation must occur after his incarnation, death, and exaltation into heaven, the same must be affirmed for the enactment of the new covenant.

Hebrews 11 and the Old Testament Saints

The pivotal locus concerning the identity of God's people across the covenants is Heb. 11, the epistle's celebrated roll call of the Old Testament heroes of faith. While this list may seem to suggest the availability of New Testament benefits before the time of Christ, closer examination of this chapter reveals a very different argument. Heb. 11 does establish a basic narrative continuity between Old Testament Israel and those now called to fix their eyes on Jesus, but it does so by underscoring the incompleteness of the Old Testament dispensation and the deferral of reward before the incarnation.

The fullest study of Heb. 11 remains Pamela Eisenbaum's *The Jewish Heroes of Christian Antiquity,* whose key contribution for our purposes is to highlight the epistle's distinctive and emphatic denial that the Old Testament heroes of faith experienced the blessings now made available in these last days.[23] Three points deserve particular note. First, Heb. 11 lacks any reference to Israel's possession of the land, in striking comparison with recapitulations of Jewish history in the Hebrew Bible. Ps. 105:42-44, for instance, reads: "For he remembered his holy promise, and Abraham his servant. So he brought his people out with joy, his chosen ones with

---

22. Ibid., 50.
23. Pamela Michelle Eisenbaum, *The Jewish Heroes of Christian Antiquity: Hebrews 11 in Literary Context,* SBLDS 156 (Atlanta: Scholars, 1997). For a rhetorical analysis of this chapter, see Michael R. Cosby, *The Rhetorical Composition and Function of Hebrews 11: In Light of Example Lists in Antiquity* (Macon, GA: Mercer University Press, 1988).

singing. He gave them the *lands* of the nations, and they took possession of the wealth of the peoples . . ." Ps. 135:10-12 also deserves note: "He struck down many nations and killed many kings — Sihon, king of the Amorites, and Og, king of Bashan, and all the kingdoms of Canaan — and gave their *land* as a heritage, a heritage to his people Israel."[24] In these and other passages, the inheritance of the land signifies the confirmation of God's covenant with Abraham. Hebrews, by contrast, lays no emphasis on the possession of the land and teaches instead that the heroes of faith looked to a better, heavenly country (4:8; 11:16).

Second, and related, Heb. 11 detaches the faithfulness of the chapter's heroes from their imminent reception of a reward, in significant contrast to Jewish Hellenistic hero lists. 1 Macc. 2:51-60 provides an especially clear example of the association between faithfulness, especially against adversity, and some kind of concrete and public prize: Joseph resists Potiphar's wife, then becomes lord of Egypt; Phinehas roots out sin, then receives the covenant of the priesthood; Elijah defies a sinful king, then ascends to heaven.[25] The lesson in Hebrews is rather different: the heroes of faith "did not receive what was promised" (11:39). This verse, Eisenbaum comments,

> is so out of the ordinary that it is impossible to imagine that it could have been said by a Jew. . . . By saying that the heroes did not receive what was promised them, the author implies that the heroes, relative to his perspective, were somehow disadvantaged. They were not honored and rewarded in their own lifetime. The lack of honor accorded the heroes of Hebrews diverges substantially from the consistent interest of Jewish texts in naming the honors and rewards which the heroes received.[26]

Third, the thread connecting the faith of the heroes of Heb. 11 is not their individual greatness, but their ability to anticipate the future and foresee something better. Abel and Enoch trust in a God who rewards those who find divine approval in this life; Noah builds the ark because he knows what destruction will come; Abraham sojourns patiently, because he awaits a heavenly homeland; Moses rejects the wealth of Egypt for a future reward; and Rahab's actions reflect an awareness of the victory God

---

24. Both passages cited in ibid., 31-32. Italics hers. Eisenbaum also highlights Neh. 9:36; Ezek. 20:42; Ps. 78:55; and Ps. 136:18-22.
25. Ibid., 41-43.
26. Ibid., 82-83.

will grant the Israelites. By contrast, no attention is given to Moses's miracles before Pharaoh or even his leadership in the exodus, deeds that might be expected in a Hellenistic Jewish hero list. Faith in Heb. 11 is connected with eschatology, a point that gains additional support if 11:1 is read in light of 2:5-9. Just as the recipients of the epistle "do not yet see everything in subjection" to Christ (2:8), so also is faith "the assurance of things hoped for, the conviction of things not seen" (11:1).[27]

For the author of Hebrews, Eisenbaum judges, the heroism of the figures

> is not attributable to their achievements in their own time, but to their ability to anticipate a better time (that is the essence of their faith). The heroes of Hebrews function as seers who portend the future, but whose own heroic image is mitigated by their being part of the old world order. Like the levitical system of worship, the tabernacle, the temple, the priests, or other biblical institutions, the author uses the heroes as historical examples for teaching, but at the same time devalues them because they are what made the old covenant old.[28]

We might articulate Eisenbaum's argument slightly differently: Heb. 11 depicts the time before Christ as an age of ongoing expectation and unfulfilled promises, indicating that the full benefits of Christ's work were not available before his establishment as high priest. Not even the greatest of the Old Testament heroes — Noah, Abraham, Moses, and so forth — received new covenant blessings, though they hoped eagerly for them in faith.

Eisenbaum's study of Heb. 11 led her to the curious conclusion that the epistle's depiction of the heroes of faith was an attempt to denationalize biblical history, making room for Gentile Christians to claim this history as their own and thus paving the way for the formation of Christianity as a separate religion from Judaism. But this thesis trades on the assumption that the distinction between Judaism and Christianity was clear and established at a relatively early date, a position recent scholarship has increasingly challenged.[29] Having since developed a greater appreciation for

---

27. On this point, Eisenbaum appeals with qualification to Robert Brawley, "Discoursive Structure and the Unseen in Hebrews 2:8 and 11:1: A Neglected Aspect of the Context," *CBQ* 55 (1993): 81-98.

28. Eisenbaum, *The Jewish Heroes of Christian Antiquity*, 183-84.

29. For bibliography, see notes in the introduction of this work (p. 4 n. 4).

the complexity of early Jewish-Christian relations, Eisenbaum has more recently written:

> Whereas I once would have lumped Hebrews together with Barnabas because of its supersessionist theology, I now see Hebrews' "supersessionism" as possibly a desperate attempt to construct anew a religious heritage that seems to have all but disappeared. It is in some ways neither Judaism nor Christianity and in other ways it represents both — a unique form of Judeo-Christianity that perhaps existed briefly before Rome was the common enemy of Jews and believers in Jesus and before the rhetoric of Christian and Jewish leaders could construct firm boundaries between Judaism and Christianity.[30]

This salutary correction, more historically and exegetically sustainable than Eisenbaum's earlier position, has facilitated new scholarly awareness of the epistle's Jewish contours. In "'Here We Have No Lasting City': New Covenantalism in Hebrews,"[31] for instance, Richard Hays wonders how the epistle might read without the assumption that "Christianity" already existed as a defined, predominantly Gentile movement distinct from "Judaism."[32] After all, Hebrews mentions nothing about the relation between Jews and Gentiles, or the Gentile mission. There is virtually no discussion of circumcision or food laws (except 9:10 and 13:9), nor much polemic against Jewish leaders (except 13:10). And criticism of the Mosaic Law in Hebrews focuses almost exclusively on the Levitical cult.

Hays surveys the epistle's appropriation of Israel's Scriptures and concludes that Hebrews presents the new covenant as one that does not abrogate, but carries forward the narrative of this chosen people. On the appropriation of Jer. 31 in Heb. 8, for instance, Hays discerns no reference to Gentile Christianity or the rejection of the Jews, but rather an eschatological vision of Israel's glorification quite in line with the original force of the prophecy. Neither this passage nor any other suggests that the Old Testament promotes legalism, self-righteousness, or some other defective conception of morality or God. Hebrews embraces and confirms Israel's Scriptures and stories, even if they are incomplete without the final

---

30. Pamela Eisenbaum, "Locating Hebrews within the Literary Landscape of Christian Origins," in Gelardini, *Hebrews: Contemporary Methods — New Insights*, 236-37.

31. See above, p. 123 n. 15.

32. The depiction of Hebrews that follows differs slightly, but not substantively, from that provided by Hays in "'Here We Have No Lasting City,'" 154.

revelation of Christ. Given these considerations, Hays writes, "it may be unhelpful to describe Hebrews' teaching as a form of 'Christianity' over against 'Judaism'; rather, it is better described as a form of Jewish sectarian 'New Covenantalism.'"[33]

Two insightful articles by Matthew Thiessen advance Hays's basic insight.[34] Thiessen takes as his starting point the logic of Heb. 3:7–4:11, which begins thus:

> Therefore, as the Holy Spirit says, "Today, when you hear his voice, do not harden your hearts as in the rebellion, on the day of testing in the wilderness, where your fathers put me to the test and saw my works for forty years. Therefore I was provoked with that generation, and said, 'They always go astray in their hearts; they have not known my ways.' As I swore in my wrath, 'They shall never enter my rest'" (3:7-11).

The brunt of this passage is an extended citation of Ps. 95:7-11, which recalls the rebellion at Meribah and Massah[35] when that generation of Israelites was barred from entering the promised land (Num. 14). Hebrews warns its addressees not to repeat this pattern, urging them to be faithful so that they may enter God's rest.

> Take care, brethren, lest there be in any of you an evil, unbelieving heart, leading you to fall away from the living God. But exhort one another every day, as long as it is called "today," that none of you may be hardened by the deceitfulness of sin. For we share in Christ, if only we hold our first confidence firm to the end, while it is said, "Today, when you hear his voice, do not harden your hearts as in the rebellion" (3:12-15).

Perhaps the most striking feature of this passage is the author's presumption that the Israelites never entered God's rest. Yes, Josh. 21:44 claims that "the Lord gave [the Israelites] rest on every side just as he swore to their fathers." Yes, Solomon rejoiced in 1 Kgs. 8:56 that the Lord "has given rest to his people Israel, according to all that he promised." But Hebrews insists that this rest remains unclaimed: "For if Joshua had given them rest,

---

33. Ibid., 155.
34. Matthew Thiessen, "Hebrews and the End of the Exodus," *NovT* 49 (2007): 353-69; and idem, "Hebrews 12.5-13, the Wilderness Period, and Israel's Discipline," *NTS* 55 (2009): 366-79.
35. Narrated in Exod. 17, and also cited in Deut. 6:16; 9:22; 33:8.

God would not speak later of another day" (4:8). As Hebrews envisions them, the addressees are still in the wilderness wanderings, not yet having entered the promised land.

This context reinforces Eisenbaum's reading of Heb. 11 concerning Old Testament deferral of reward, without adopting her (earlier) suggestion that this chapter seeks to denationalize Israel.[36] Israel remains the people of God, even if she has not yet entered God's rest. Thus, Abraham sojourns as an alien in the land of God's promise, yet he does not receive this land as his inheritance. Joseph's request that his bones be taken to Canaan reveals his hope in the promised land — for his people, if not for himself. Moses receives attention primarily in terms of his identification with Israel and subsequent marginalization in Egypt. Joshua is not mentioned at all — he could not be, for he did not lead the people into the promised land. Just when the Israelites would otherwise be entering Canaan, the list trails off (11:32-38) and the chapter concludes, "All these, though well attested by their faith, did not receive what was promised" (11:39). Then, in 12:1-3, the author introduces Jesus, the pioneer and perfecter of our faith (cf. 2:10). As Thiessen notes, the word "pioneer" is a translation for ἀρχηγός, a term commonly used in the Old Testament with regard to the leaders of Israel in the wilderness (Num. 13:2-3; 16:1-3; 25:1-5). According to Hebrews, Joshua, the first ἀρχηγός, failed to lead God's people into the rest; Jesus, the second ἀρχηγός, will finish the task.

The rest of Heb. 12 bears out this perspective. In 12:5-13, the author urges his readers not to resent the suffering they are currently enduring, but to view it as a form of fatherly discipline. This language is best understood against a longstanding Jewish tradition that considered the wilderness wanderings a period of educational discipline whereby God's people would be prepared to enter the land of promise.[37] Then, in Heb. 12:18-29, the rhetorical climax of the letter, the author situates the addressees in the

---

36. Thiessen, "Hebrews and the End of the Exodus," 360-67. Thiessen depends on Eisenbaum's findings in *The Jewish Heroes of Christian Antiquity*, but significantly departs from her earlier position that Heb. 11 serves to downplay national Israel. According to Thiessen, Hebrews does not separate the heroes of faith from national Israel but rather highlights Israel's history of marginalization, which it considers a sign of belonging to God's people.

37. Thiessen, "Hebrews 12.5-13, the Wilderness Period, and Israel's Discipline," 369-73. As Thiessen notes, this παιδεία could even be likened to an athletic contest, a point that bears resonance with the exhortation in Hebrews to "run with perseverance the race that is set before us" (12:1). See ibid., 374-75.

wilderness, in between Mt. Sinai and Mt. Zion, ready to enter the promised land that Joshua never delivered.

> For you have not come to what may be touched, a blazing fire, and darkness, and gloom, and a tempest, and the sound of a trumpet, and a voice whose words made the hearers entreat that no further messages be spoken to them. . . . But you have come to Mount Zion and to the city of the living God, the heavenly Jerusalem, and to innumerable angels in festal gathering, and to the assembly of the first-born who are enrolled in heaven, and to a judge who is God of all, and to the spirits of just men made perfect, and to Jesus, the mediator of a new covenant, and to the sprinkled blood that speaks more graciously than the blood of Abel (12:18-24).

Thiessen concludes:

> The letter to the Hebrews thus envisions its audience at the very spot that the book of Deuteronomy envisions the people of Israel — at the doorstep of God's promised land of rest. By means of this rewriting and reconfiguration of Israel's history, the author of the letter to the Hebrews demonstrates to his readers that their experience is in continuity with the entire history of Israel, and should be deemed as evidence for the fact that they are God's children, to whom the long-awaited rest is still open.[38]

For our purposes, then, Hebrews contributes two insights concerning the identity of God's people. First, there is a sharp contrast between the Old Testament heroes of faith and those who presently trust in Christ precisely because the redemptive benefits of his salvific work were not available prior to his establishment as high priest. Second, though, this point of discontinuity does not suggest a radical fissure in God's people between Old Testament Israel and the Gentile church of the New Testament. For the author of this Jewish epistle, Christ's establishment as high priest may be taken as a renewal and not an abrogation of God's covenant with the Israelites, founded now as at the beginning on a common hope for an eternal inheritance. We may now return to the conversation with Augustine and Calvin.

---

38. Thiessen, "Hebrews and the End of the Exodus," 369.

The Epistle to the Hebrews: God's New Covenant with Israel

Hebrews in Dialogue

Thus far in this chapter, I have sought to interrogate Hebrews for its answers to the questions of the previous two chapters. This inquiry has involved reading backward to locate Hebrews against the history before and behind the text. How does the Second Temple Jewish context enhance our understanding of the epistle's construal of the covenants and its depiction of God's people across the testaments? This last section reads forward from the text, drawing upon later reflection in the Christian tradition as a source of illumination for the contours of the particular theological vision of Hebrews. For this dialogue with Augustine and Calvin, I begin with the contrast between the covenants, proceed to the identity and character of God's people, and conclude with some remarks on the eschatology of Hebrews.

The Contrast between the Covenants

In comparing Hebrews with Augustine and Calvin, it is important to note, first, what Hebrews does *not* say concerning the old covenant or its people — precisely because the interpretive paradigms we have witnessed especially in Augustine (though also in Calvin) have exercised so much influence over the Western theological tradition. The pivotal decision is to read passages like Jer. 31 in light of Paul. As we saw in *The Spirit and the Letter,* Augustine correlates the teaching of Jer. 31 with the conflation in 2 Cor. 3:6 of the letter with death and the Spirit with life, and the suggestion in Gal. 3 that the law was given to produce transgressors, whether (as Augustine interprets Paul) by inflaming the concupiscence of those who willfully disobey God's will or by producing obedience based solely in fear. Since Paul stresses the role of the "moral law" (to use the term somewhat anachronistically) in bringing about death, the old covenant treated in Jer. 31 must be set against the new according to the slavery and fear of the former, and the freedom and love of the latter. This love for God and neighbor now made possible by the New Testament is precisely what Jeremiah meant concerning our ability to fulfill God's commands as the law is written on our hearts and minds.

In Hebrews, by contrast, Jer. 31 arises in a restricted discussion concerning the Levitical priesthood. The preceding passage (8:1-6) focuses on the superiority of Jesus's tabernacle and high priestly ministry over the old covenant, whose tabernacle was but a shadow and copy of the true one in heaven. The subsequent passage (9:1-10) continues with a description of the earthly sanctuary, again, to stress the superiority of Christ's new high priestly ministry. In this context, the purpose of 8:7-13 is to explain the implications of Jesus's "better" covenant (8:6) for the Levitical priesthood, namely, that this new covenant marks the end of the former. But Hebrews provides no suggestion, as in Augustine's Pauline logic, that the Israelites were in bondage to the old covenant or that the law was given to increase sin. Indeed, the focus of the epistle's argument for the necessity of Christ's priestly ministry is not the "moral" but the "ceremonial" law. As Heb. 10:1-4 reads,

> For since the law has but a shadow of the good things to come instead of the true form of these realities, it can never, by the same sacrifices which are continually offered year after year, make perfect those who draw near. Otherwise, would they not have ceased to be offered? If the worshipers had once been cleansed, they would no longer have any consciousness of sin. But in these sacrifices there is a reminder of sin year after year. For it is impossible that the blood of bulls and goats should take away sins.

For Hebrews, that is, the pivotal Old Testament indicator that the old covenant would come to an end is the inadequacy of the Levitical sacrifices, not our inability to obey God's commands.[39]

Yet the new covenant is indeed different and new, and the affirmation of this point in the epistle distinguishes Hebrews from Calvin as well. In the *Institutes,* Calvin identifies the presence of signs or figures before the

---

39. Note Caird's perceptive remarks: "There is nothing here of the Pauline contrast between the transitory régime which brought condemnation and death and the permanent régime of justification and life, between Mount Sinai in Arabia whose children are slaves and Mount Zion whose children are free. For in Paul's experience the law was not merely incomplete; it had claimed completeness, claimed to be a way of salvation and to give that life which in fact it had no power to give, and just because it had exceeded its God-given function it had become a demonic agency which enslaved its adherents. But in Hebrews part of the validity of the old order is its constant disclaimer of finality. Throughout the Old Testament period men were constantly being warned not to think more highly of their present religious status than they ought to think, and if they were men of faith, they confessed themselves to be strangers and sojourners to whom the old covenant offered no abiding city" ("The Exegetical Method of Hebrews," 46). For a more recent comparison between Paul and Hebrews, see James C. Miller, "Paul and Hebrews: A Comparison of Narrative Worlds," in Gelardini, *Hebrews: Contemporary Methods — New Insights,* 245-64.

The Epistle to the Hebrews: God's New Covenant with Israel

time of Christ as the second of five differences between the testaments. "In the absence of the reality, [the Old Testament] showed but an image and shadow in place of the substance; the New Testament reveals the very substance of the truth as present."[40] But Calvin must reckon on this matter with Hebrews, not just for the epistle's extended treatment of the Mosaic observances but also for its declaration that the old priesthood has been abolished in favor of a new covenant. If these declarations refer to "the substance of the promises *(promissionum substantiam),*" Calvin acknowledges, "there would be great disagreement between the Testaments."[41]

Calvin's solution, in short, is to distinguish between different meanings of the term "covenant" *(foedus* or *testamentum)* such that the abolition of the old covenant in Hebrews refers only to the ceremonies and not to the substance of the promises. These ceremonies are called "covenant" *(foederis nomen habent)* because they constituted the means by which the true and eternal covenant was mediated before the coming of Christ. But their abrogation as secondary and temporary matters of administration (Calvin uses in this context the words *accidentia, accessiones, annexa, accessoria*) does not threaten the integrity of Christ's inviolable covenant, which remains fundamentally unchanged. "The Old Testament of the Lord was that covenant wrapped up in the shadowy and ineffectual observance of ceremonies and delivered to the Jews; it was temporary because it remained, as it were, in suspense until it might rest upon a firm and substantial confirmation. It became new and eternal only after it was consecrated and established by the blood of Christ."[42]

On my reading of Hebrews, something more fundamental is at stake than merely the replacement of figures for a clearer depiction of Christ's mediatorial work. The establishment of Christ as high priest constitutes the basis for our salvation, and this occurrence arises at a very particular moment in the chronology of redemptive history. Jesus Christ could not serve as mediator between God and humanity during Old Testament times because he had not yet been made incarnate to learn obedience,

---

40. *Inst.* 2.11.4: "... illud, absente veritate, imaginem tantum et pro corpore umbram ostentabat; hoc praesentem veritatem et corpus solidum exhibet."

41. Ibid.

42. Ibid. "Quod si malis, ita accipe: vetus fuisse Domini Testamentum, quod umbratili et inefficaci ceremoniarum observatione involutum tradebatur; ideoque temporarium fuisse, quia veluti in suspenso erat, donec firma et substantiali confirmatione subniteretur. Tum vero demum novum aeternumque factum fuisse, postquam Christi sanguine consecratum stabilitumque fuit."

suffer death, and receive perfection. And it was only after Christ presented himself as a single offering in the heavenly realms that he could provide expiation for our sins, participation in his perfection, and the benefits of his ongoing intercession for humanity. On this model, the ceremonies were not just accessories of an eternally functioning covenant; they were the covenant itself, administered uselessly through the blood of animals until a new covenant would be established. The logic of Hebrews precludes the possibility of receiving the benefits of Christ's high priestly work before the incarnation.

The Identity of God's People

In Hebrews, the depiction of the people of God across the testaments challenges Augustine's and Calvin's positions on two fronts. First, in contrast to Augustine, Hebrews provides no grounds for the suggestion that Old Testament Israel has been replaced by a primarily Gentile church, and still less for the depiction of Old Testament Israel as a fleshly people. As we have seen, Augustine repeatedly claims that Israel was a carnal nation that sought only temporal goods, and that this difference in hope constitutes one of the primary differences between the covenants. The Old Testament promised earthly rewards while the New Testament promises eternal life. Indeed, for Augustine, the reason the Old Testament veiled and did not reveal the promise of heavenly rewards is that the Israelites were incapable of receiving it. The natural implication of this position is that those Old Testament figures who understood the true purpose of the temporal promises pertained more to the New Testament than to the Old.

The author of Hebrews categorically rejects the possibility of distinguishing between the testaments according to different hopes. The overriding message of Heb. 11 is that the Old Testament heroes did not receive earthly reward, substantially identified with the physical land of Canaan, yet they continued to walk in faith because they hoped in an as yet unseen but eternal inheritance — the same we also seek. For Hebrews, such personages were not exceptional, redemptive-historical aberrations in Israel's history. It was precisely Moses's identification with God's people that compelled him to reject his Egyptian upbringing (11:24-25), and "time would fail" (11:32) to relate all the exploits of the judges, kings, prophets, and others who through faith performed miracles, conquered foreign armies, and suffered scourging, imprisonment, and torture — even to the point of death. Together, these figures make up "a cloud of witnesses" (12:1) for our encouragement, the most exemplary of God's people before the coming of Christ. The discontinuity in this narrative, then, is neither the identity of God's people nor the object of hope, but the availability of what was promised. The hope of an eternal inheritance had been deferred, but has now been made open to us through Christ, who has displayed the reward of obedience through his entrance into the heavenlies. This marks a radical change in redemptive history, but not by means of Augustine's replacement theology.

The second comparison, with Calvin, is a bit more complex. On the one hand, Calvin converges with Hebrews when he emphasizes the common hope of God's people as a point of unity between the testaments. As we have seen, Calvin dedicates almost his entire chapter in the *Institutes* on the similarity between the testaments to the hope of immortality in the Old Testament.[43] Israel's reception of God's Word presupposed the blessing of eternal life, God's covenant with the Israelites was transparently understood to be eternal, and the suffering of the patriarchs would make no sense if they sought only earthly reward. Calvin acknowledges internal variations concerning the clarity of this promise in the Old Testament — the prophets did present eternal blessing under the lineaments of temporal benefits — but he insists the earthly promises were meant to direct the Israelites to a heavenly heritage. In all of this, Calvin's position confirms the reading of Hebrews advanced above.[44] On my account, the epistle's renarration of Israel's history in 3:7–4:11 infuses the word "rest" with new meaning such that this hope is no longer understood in terms of Canaan but as an eternal blessing made possible by Christ's physical ascent into the heavenly realm. While such a reading of Israel's history may have come as a surprise to the recipients of his epistle, the author of Hebrews insists, not unlike Calvin, that this hope of an eternal reward characterized Israel's heroes from the very beginning.[45]

---

43. *Inst.* 2.10.
44. Indeed, Calvin explicitly cites Heb. 11 in this regard. See *Inst.* 2.10.13.
45. Jon Levenson presents a similar kind of argument as that found in Hebrews (and Calvin) concerning Jewish hope for the resurrection of the dead. While he acknowledges that explicit evidence for this hope does not appear until late in the development of the Jewish canon (Dan. 12:1-3), he argues that the idea had nevertheless developed over the course of centuries before the Second Temple period as a natural outgrowth of several biblical themes, especially God's faithfulness to his promises of life for Israel. See Jon D. Levenson,

On the other hand, this initial point of similarity between Calvin and Hebrews belies a more fundamental difference concerning the availability of salvific benefits during the period of the Old Testament. Does this common hope across the testaments imply the reception of Christ's mediatorial work or its deferral? Calvin, we recall, sets forth two somewhat contradictory ways of understanding the Old Testament saints. At certain points, Calvin identifies Old Testament Israel with the church and explains the blessings of the Old Testament by appeal to relative comparison. The salvific benefits of the New Testament are so much greater than those of the Old that Scripture sometimes speaks as if the Israelites did not experience them during Old Testament times (though they actually did). Yet Calvin also reverts to the same line of argument as Augustine: the patriarchs experienced New Testament blessings by way of transfer, as exceptions, before that dispensation when these blessings would be more widely and appropriately dispersed.

The explanation in Hebrews is quite simple. Just as the Old Testament believers did not receive the promised land, so also did they not receive perfection. Since both blessings were only made possible with the coming of Christ, there is no question of redemptive-historical aberrations or differences of degree or gradation. The establishment of Christ as high priest inaugurates a decisively new age in redemptive history that fundamentally alters the availability of salvific blessings for those who participate in the covenant. This is not to suggest that the Old Testament saints were basically devoid of God's grace, nor that they were excluded from the eventual reception of eternal reward. Such a conclusion would rather undermine the author of the epistle's commendation of their faith and his encouragement to imitate their patience. Still, the accent of the treatment of the Old Testament saints in Hebrews clearly rests on waiting and deferral: "All these, though well attested by their faith, did not receive what was promised, since God had foreseen something better for us, that apart from us they should not be made perfect" (11:39-40). In this regard, Hebrews differs from both Augustine's and Calvin's efforts to assert equivalence between the spiritual experiences of the patriarchs and those of New Testament believers. Such parity would fit uneasily in the epistle's narration of Christ's establishment as high priest.

Resurrection and the Restoration of Israel: The Ultimate Victory of the God of Life (New Haven: Yale University Press, 2006); and Kevin J. Madigan and Jon D. Levenson, *Resurrection: The Power of God for Christians and Jews* (New Haven: Yale University Press, 2008).

The Epistle to the Hebrews: God's New Covenant with Israel

The Last Days

The previous points of comparison direct us toward a final one about the author of the epistle's depiction of his and his addressees' location in redemptive history. The author stresses a contrast of times in his opening words: "In many and various ways God spoke of old to our fathers by the prophets; but in these last days he has spoken to us by a Son, whom he appointed the heir of all things, through whom also he created the world" (1:1-2). This appeal to a new eschatological moment persists throughout the letter, with, for example, the exposition of "today" in 3:7–4:11, the reference to an approaching "day" in 10:25, and the depiction in 12:18-24 of a heavenly Jerusalem populated by angels in festal gathering.

On this matter, Calvin provides a particularly instructive point of comparison, not least because he treats these passages directly in his commentary on Hebrews. Calvin's treatment of Heb. 1:1-2, for instance, acknowledges a contrast between the Son of God and the prophets, but the primary significance of this passage is the unity of the covenant. "In this diversity he still sets before us but one God, that no one might think that the Law militates against the Gospel, or that the author of one is not the author of the other."[46] So too, concerning the "last days," Calvin concludes simply that "there is no longer any reason to expect any new revelation, for it was not a word in part that Christ brought, but the final conclusion."[47] The last days are for Calvin chronologically posterior to earlier times, but not especially climactic.

A similar flattening effect occurs in Calvin's treatment of the "today" language in 3:7–4:11. In his comments on 3:13, Calvin says the author "reminds us that the word *to-day,* mentioned in the Psalm, ought not to be confined to the age of David, but that it comprehends every time in which God may address us. . . . As, then, we know not whether God will extend his calling to to-morrow, let us not delay. To-day he calls us; let us immediately respond to him."[48] Likewise, the exhortation in 3:15 to heed God's call "while it is said, 'To-day if ye will hear his voice'" should be taken, on Calvin's account, "as though [the author] had said, 'Since God never makes an end of speaking, it is not enough for us readily to receive his doctrine, except we exhibit the same teachableness and obedience to-morrow and

---

46. *Comm. Heb.* 1.1.
47. Ibid.
48. Ibid., 3.13. Cf. ibid., 4.16.

every following day.'"⁴⁹ For Calvin, "today" simply refers to any time we may respond to God's salvation, functioning figuratively to warn us against delaying until "tomorrow."

Calvin is not oblivious to the eschatological dynamics in Hebrews. In his treatment of 10:25, for instance, Calvin notes that the exhortation to continue meeting together, as "ye see the day approaching," refers to the second coming of Christ: "Since Christ, after having completed all things necessary for our salvation, has ascended into heaven, it is but reasonable that we who are continually looking for his second manifestation should regard every day as though it were the last."⁵⁰ Nevertheless, Calvin's treatment of the current dispensation goes little beyond acknowledging the basic chronology of redemptive history. Even for the passages where Hebrews most accentuates the contrast between these and the earlier days, Calvin hastens to qualify the opposition between law and gospel. Despite the opposition in 12:18-24 between an earthly and spiritual mountain, for instance, Calvin rejects the implication that the law concerned only earthly matters. The law, he insists, was directed toward spiritual matters, and Christians today continue to practice external religious rites. We should therefore understand the author of Hebrews to be speaking "comparatively *(secundum maius et minus);* and no one can doubt but that the Gospel, contrasted with the Law, excels in what is spiritual, but the Law in earthly symbols."⁵¹

Contemporary New Testament scholarship presents a different perspective on these matters. As C. K. Barrett argued in an influential article, Hebrews is strongly characterized by the paradoxical eschatology typical of early Christian proclamation.⁵² Much of the epistle's focus concerns judgment day, when Christ will appear a second time (9:28), heaven and earth will be shaken and removed (12:27), and willful sinners will face destruction (10:39) and fire (10:27, 12:29) at the hands of the living God (10:31). Yet the author also affirms that Christ's first coming has decisively

---

49. Ibid., 3.15.
50. Ibid., 10.25.
51. Ibid., 12.18.
52. C. K. Barrett, "The Eschatology of the Epistle to the Hebrews," in *The Background of the New Testament and Its Eschatology,* ed. W. D. Davies and D. Daube (Cambridge: Cambridge University Press, 1956), 369-93. For other treatments of eschatology in Hebrews, see Harold W. Attridge, "'Let Us Strive to Enter That Rest': The Logic of Hebrews 4:1-11," *HTR* 73 (1980): 279-88; David A. deSilva, "Entering God's Rest: Eschatology and the Socio-Rhetorical Strategy of Hebrews," *TJ* 21 (2000): 25-43.

inaugurated the final days, a point whose paradigmatic significance may be discerned, as I suggested above, in the author's appeal to "these last days" in the opening verses of his epistle (1:1-2). Christ has already defeated his enemies (2:8ff., 10:12ff.) and the blessings of the new age have already been made available (6:4-6) such that all are called now to respond positively to the offer of salvation (2:1-4) as they approach the heavenly Jerusalem (12:22-24).

On Barrett's reading, the eschatology of Hebrews trades on both temporal and spatial contrasts. While the epistle's references to the heavenly temple, for instance, indicate the existence of an eternally existing tabernacle that functions as an archetype of the earthly tabernacle, the author also depicts Christ's entrance into the heavenly realm as a one-time eschatological event that will be followed by yet another eschatological event, the return of Christ (9:23-28). This mode of thought stands in sharp contrast with the Platonic tendencies in Philo and the Epistle of Barnabas. For Philo, God's charge to Moses to make the tabernacle after the pattern shown him on the mountain (Exod. 25:40) is a call to keep the soul sleepless and wakeful to the incorporeal forms while in the physical body. In Barnabas, the temple is the dwelling place of the human heart. For Hebrews, by contrast, the emphasis is on eschatological event — what occurs in time and space with objective and corporate consequences — and not just timeless reality or subjective religious experience. "Jesus is primarily ... an actor in the eschatological drama of redemption rather than a mediator standing between the real and phenomenal worlds; rather a priest who makes atonement for the sin of mankind than a Gnostic mediator who procures their passage from the material world to the spiritual."[53]

Such dynamics receive little attention in Calvin's muted eschatology, which tends rather to stress the consistency of God's interaction with humans. At every point in redemptive history, humanity is confronted by the same God and called to the same faithfulness. God spoke throughout the Old Testament, even if more clearly in Christ; humanity has always been called to heed God's Word, though with more urgency in these last days. The result for Calvin is a rather static depiction of Christ as the timeless basis for the eternal covenant, the salvific benefits of which are broadly available before and after Christ's earthly life. On this model, the incarnation does not initiate a new covenant so much as enhance the old. Or, as David Steinmetz has stated, Calvin "saw the transition from the old to the new as

---

53. Barrett, "The Eschatology of the Epistle to the Hebrews," 389.

a gentle slope more than as a sharp disjuncture."[54] Again, this rendering of history marks a significant point of difference from Hebrews's theological vision of the contrast between the covenants and the new availability of God's inheritance through the establishment of his Son as high priest.

Conclusion

The vision of redemptive history in Hebrews differs substantially from that of our primary interlocutors. If, for Augustine, the relation between the testaments involves two covenants and two peoples, Calvin acknowledges only one covenant and one people. Hebrews presents another proposal: two covenants, but one people. Here is a unity not of reference or identity, but of transformation. This account affirms with Calvin the continuity of hope across the testaments, but it does not defend the availability of Christ's mediatorial work before the incarnation. It asserts with Augustine the abrogation of the old covenant, but it does not suggest Israel has receded before the church. In Hebrews, the unity of the testaments derives from God's ongoing faithfulness to Israel while the benefits of the new covenant are made available only after and because of Christ's elevation as high priest. If, as I have argued, different construals of redemptive history result in different interpretive practices, Hebrews should read the Old Testament differently from Augustine and Calvin, too. The particular contours of this dynamic in the epistle will be considered in the next chapter.

---

54. David Steinmetz, "John Calvin as an Interpreter of the Bible," in *Calvin and the Bible,* ed. Donald K. McKim (Cambridge: Cambridge University Press, 2006), 286.

CHAPTER 4

The Epistle to the Hebrews: Approaching the Psalms

Introduction

Hebrews famously describes the word of God as "living and active" (4:12), and this expression proves an apt characterization for the author's actual interpretive practices. A broad scholarly consensus has developed around the epistle's propensity for presenting Old Testament locutions, and especially the psalms, as instances of God's direct speech.[1] Eisenbaum counts

---

1. Studies of the use of the Old Testament in Hebrews include: Ronald E. Clements, "The Use of the Old Testament in Hebrews," *SwJT* 28 (1955): 36-45; Robert Rendall, "The Method of the Writer to the Hebrews in Using Old Testament Quotations," *EvQ* 27 (1955): 214-20; Simon Kistemaker, *The Psalm Citations in the Epistle to the Hebrews* (Amsterdam: Soest, 1961); Markus Barth, "The Old Testament in Hebrews: An Essay in Biblical Hermeneutics," in *Current Issues in New Testament Interpretation: Essays in Honor of Otto A. Piper*, ed. William Klassen and Graydon F. Snyder (New York: Harper, 1962), 53-78; Kenneth J. Thomas, "The Old Testament Citations in Hebrews," *NTS* 11 (1965): 303-25; George Howard, "Hebrews and the Old Testament Quotations," *NovT* 10 (1968): 208-15; H. J. B. Combrink, "Some Thoughts on the Old Testament Citations in the Epistle to the Hebrews," *Neot* 5 (1971): 22-36; Graham Hughes, *Hebrews and Hermeneutics: The Epistle to the Hebrews as a New Testament Example of Biblical Interpretation* (Cambridge: Cambridge University Press, 1979); J. C. McCullough, "The Old Testament Quotations in Hebrews," *NTS* 26 (1980): 363-79; Karen H. Jobes, "The Function of Paronomasia in Hebrews 10:5-7," *TJ* 13 (1992): 181-91; Thomas Ladd Blackstone, "The Hermeneutics of Recontextualization in the Epistle to the Hebrews" (PhD diss., Emory University, 1995); Dale F. Leschert, *Hermeneutical Foundations of Hebrews: A Study in the Validity of the Epistle's Interpretation of Some Core Citations from the Psalms*, National Association of Baptist Professors of Religion Dissertation Series 10 (Lewiston, NY: Edwin Mellen, 1995); Pamela Michelle Eisenbaum, *The Jewish Heroes of Christian Antiquity: Hebrews 11 in Literary Context*, SBLDS 156 (Atlanta: Scholars, 1997); George H. Guthrie, "Old Testament in Hebrews," in *Dictionary of the Later New Testament and Its Devel-*

thirty-one scriptural citations: twelve from the Pentateuch, seven from the Prophets, and twelve from the Writings, with all but one of the latter coming from Psalms (the exception is Prov. 3:11-12 in Heb. 12:5-6).[2] The author never uses the name of a biblical book, nor even the word "Scripture," and one searches in vain for the Pauline formulation, "It is written," or the Matthean, "As it was spoken by the prophet." The emphasis is rather on orality and unmediated communication.[3] Almost all the citations involve quotations of direct speech,[4] the vast majority are introduced by

---

opments, ed. Ralph P. Martin and Peter H. Davids (Downers Grove, IL: InterVarsity, 1997), 841-50, "Hebrews' Use of the Old Testament: Recent Trends in Research," *CurBR* 1 (2003): 271-94; idem, "Hebrews," in *Commentary on the New Testament Use of the Old Testament*, ed. G. K. Beale and D. A. Carson (Grand Rapids: Baker Academic, 2007), 919-95; A. T. Hanson, "Hebrews," in *It Is Written: Scripture Citing Scripture: Essays in Honour of Barnabas Lindars, SSF*, ed. D. A. Carson and H. G. M. Williamson (Cambridge: Cambridge University Press, 1998), 292-302; Stephen Motyer, "The Psalm Quotations of Hebrews 1: A Hermeneutic-Free Zone?" *TynBul* 50 (1999): 3-22; Harold W. Attridge, "The Psalms in Hebrews," in *The Psalms in the New Testament*, ed. Steve Moyise and Maarten J. J. Menken (London: T&T Clark, 2004), 197-212; Luke Timothy Johnson, "The Scriptural World of Hebrews," *Int* 57 (2004): 237-50; A. J. M. Wedderburn, "Sawing Off the Branches: Theologizing Dangerously *Ad Hebraeos*," *JTS* 56 (2005): 393-414; Susan E. Docherty, *The Use of the Old Testament in Hebrews: A Case Study in Early Jewish Interpretation*, WUNT 2. Reihe 260 (Tübingen: Mohr Siebeck, 2009); Ken Schenck, "God Has Spoken: Hebrews' Theology of the Scriptures," and Daniel J. Treier, "Speech Acts, Hearing Hearts, and Other Senses: The Doctrine of Scripture Practiced in Hebrews," in *The Epistle to the Hebrews and Christian Theology*, ed. Richard Bauckham et al. (Grand Rapids: Eerdmans, 2009), 321-36 and 337-50, respectively. See especially Docherty, *The Use of the Old Testament in Hebrews*, 9-82 for an overview of scholarship on this issue. A recent collection of essays on the history of the interpretation of Hebrews is Jon C. Laansma and Daniel J. Treier, eds., *Christology, Hermeneutics, and Hebrews: Profiles from the History of Interpretation* (London: T&T Clark, 2012).

2. Eisenbaum, *The Jewish Heroes of Christian Antiquity*, 92. A citation is defined (e.g., against an allusion) according to a formal introductory formula and the integrity of the citation. For other ways of counting the citations, see Blackstone, "The Hermeneutics of Recontextualization in the Epistle to the Hebrews," 16-23. See also Guthrie, "Old Testament in Hebrews," 846-49 for a comprehensive chart of Old Testament references in Hebrews that distinguishes between quotation, allusion, summary, and reference to a name/topic.

3. For a rhetorical analysis that stresses oral dynamics in Hebrews, see Michael R. Cosby, *The Rhetorical Composition and Function of Hebrews 11: In Light of Example Lists in Antiquity* (Macon, GA: Mercer University Press, 1988). See also his "The Rhetorical Composition of Hebrews 11," *JBL* 107 (1988): 257-73, as well as Jobes, "The Function of Paronomasia in Hebrews 10:5-7."

4. The two exceptions are Gen. 2:2, cited in Heb. 4:4 with reference to the meaning of "rest"; and Gen. 5:24, cited in Heb. 11:5 with regard to Enoch's avoiding death. See Eisenbaum, *The Jewish Heroes of Christian Antiquity*, 92 n. 14.

The Epistle to the Hebrews: Approaching the Psalms

verbs of speaking (typically in the present tense), and the original human speaker is hardly ever named.[5] For Hebrews, Old Testament quotations are not primarily expressions of the original prophet or psalmist but the very words of God,[6] communicated directly to the covenant community in the present moment: "In many and various ways God spoke (λαλήσας) of old to our fathers by the prophets; but in these last days he has spoken (ἐλάλησεν) to us by a Son" (1:1-2).

This chapter explores how Hebrews treats three critical Old Testament passages in dialogue with Augustine and Calvin. As mentioned in the previous chapter, Caird has suggested that the argument of the epistle is structured according to Ps. 8, Ps. 95, Ps. 110, and Jer. 31, in order.[7] Since I have already considered Jer. 31 at some length, I focus here on the psalms. Ps. 95 presents the epistle's fundamental redemptive-historical structures, Ps. 110 depicts Christ's establishment as high priest, and Ps. 8 narrates this moment according to the humiliation and exaltation of a "son of man." I treat the psalms in this sequence rather than their order of appearance in Hebrews. For our historical interlocutors, I draw primarily from Augustine's *Expositions of the Psalms* and Calvin's commentary on Psalms, though I also provide supplementary remarks from Calvin's commentary on Hebrews. This comparison would, of course, have been enhanced by an Augustine commentary on Hebrews, but such does not exist. Still, this chapter will reveal the hermeneutical difference redemptive history makes: Hebrews relies for its appropriation of the Psalms on neither allegorical speculation (contra Augustine) nor some static literal sense (contra Calvin), but on a dynamic identification between Old Testament locutions and God's address to his covenant people. The author thus attends to the literal sense while transforming it according to theological and redemptive-historical controls.

---

5. Ibid., 94-96. The two significant exceptions are 4:7 (David) and 9:19-20 (Moses), both of which stress the speaker's particular context for the sake of the larger argument. The other exception is 12:21, where Moses simply says that he was afraid.

6. Though in two distinct passages, the speaker is Christ: Heb. 2:12-13, citing Ps. 22:22 and Isa. 8:17, 18; and Heb. 10:5-7, citing Ps. 40:6-8. Note also the references to the Holy Spirit in Heb. 3:7 and 10:15. On the psalms as responsive expressions of Jesus and his followers, see Attridge, "The Psalms in Hebrews," 208-12.

7. For slight variations on this proposal, see Richard N. Longenecker, "Hebrews and the Old Testament," in *Biblical Exegesis in the Apostolic Period,* 2nd ed. (Grand Rapids: Eerdmans, 1999), 140-65; R. T. France, "The Writer of Hebrews as a Biblical Expositor," *TynBul* 47 (1996): 245-76.

TODAY WHEN YOU HEAR HIS VOICE

Psalm 95

Psalm 95 provides the basis for the exhortation to faithfulness in Heb. 3:7–4:11. The author presents the Israelites in the wilderness wanderings as an example of unfaithfulness, urging his readers not to imitate them but to enter God's rest through obedient perseverance. The entire psalm reads as follows:

> 1O come, let us sing to the Lord; let us make a joyful noise to the rock of our salvation! 2Let us come into his presence with thanksgiving; let us make a joyful noise to him with songs of praise! 3For the Lord is a great God, and a great King above all gods. 4In his hand are the depths of the earth; the heights of the mountains are his also. 5The sea is his, for he made it; for his hands formed the dry land.
>
> 6O come, let us worship and bow down, let us kneel before the Lord, our Maker! 7For he is our God, and we are the people of his pasture, and the sheep of his hand.
>
> O that today you would hearken to his voice! 8Harden not your hearts, as at Meribah, as on the day at Massah in the wilderness, 9when your fathers tested me, and put me to the proof, though they had seen my work. 10For forty years I loathed that generation and said, "They are a people who err in heart, and they do not regard my ways." 11Therefore I swore in my anger that they should not enter my rest.

In what follows, I consider first Augustine's, then Calvin's exposition of this psalm, before returning in greater depth to Hebrews. In my comments on Augustine and Calvin, I focus primarily on passages cited by our epistle. Since Augustine, Calvin, and Hebrews are working with different Latin and Greek versions of the text, and these texts do not always correspond with the English translation provided above, I will frequently supply the verses they are commenting upon in the course of my exposition. For the sake of simplicity and clarity, I retain the chapter/verse numbering system of contemporary English translations throughout the chapter. The citations in the footnotes will thus vary from the references found in the body of the text.

The Epistle to the Hebrews: Approaching the Psalms

Augustine

Augustine treats Ps. 95 as a song for the New Testament church, understood primarily but not exclusively to be Gentile.[8] This orientation is especially clear in his comments on two passages. The first is a text found in Augustine's Old Latin version but not in the Hebrew, "The Lord will not reject his people,"[9] which Augustine reads in light of Paul's discussion of Israel in Rom. 11. The Jews have been rejected as the Gentiles have been grafted in, but God has preserved a remnant among the Jews through those who have believed in Christ. This psalm is thus fulfilled in the church, which consists of both Jews and Gentiles, and not in God's faithfulness to Israel per se. A second example concerns Ps. 95:7: "We are the people of his pasture, the sheep of his hands,"[10] which triggers Augustine's memory of a passage from Song of Songs: "Your teeth are like newly-shorn flocks, coming up from their washing. All of them bear twins; there is never a barren one among them (Sg 4:2; 6:5)."[11] This passage is an allegory of the church, which is like God's teeth as the means by which he speaks; she is newly shorn because she has shed the burdens of the world; she comes up from her washing in baptism; she bears twins in the twofold love commandment. By treating "sheep" figurally, using Song of Songs 4:2 as an intertext, Augustine transfers the referent of the term from Israel to the New Testament community.[12]

These considerations set the stage for Augustine's treatment of the critical passage in Hebrews, "If you hear his voice today . . . ,"[13] which he takes

---

8. Augustine's expositions on the psalms are notoriously difficult to date. He probably began preaching on the Psalms around 392 and completed the entire collection around 421-22. See Michael Cameron, *"Enarrationes in Psalmos,"* in *Augustine through the Ages: An Encyclopedia,* ed. Allan D. Fitzgerald (Grand Rapids: Eerdmans, 1999), 290-91, and the general introduction by Michael Fiedrowicz in *Expositions of the Psalms 1–32,* trans. Maria Boulding, WSA 3.15 (Hyde Park, NY: New City, 2000), 15-16.

9. *En. Ps.* 94.7. See *Expositions of the Psalms 73–98,* trans. Maria Boulding, WSA 3.18 (Hyde Park, NY: New City, 2002), 415 n. 10.

10. *En. Ps.* 94.11.

11. Ibid.

12. This allegorical move also arises at a paradigmatic moment in *doc. Chr.* (2.6.7-8), where Augustine considers the purpose of obscurities and concludes that it is more pleasing and elegant to learn truths through figures than through straightforward teaching. Augustine's exposition of Ps. 95:7 thus adheres to his own instruction in his handbook on biblical interpretation. Augustine's interpretation in *doc. Chr.* is substantially the same as here, though he suggests differently that the teeth signify the way the church tears people away from errors, and softens such people, as in mastication, to enter the church.

13. *En. Ps.* 94.12.

to address not just the Israelites of the Old Testament but all God's people through Christ. "Long ago you heard his voice through Moses, and you hardened your hearts. He spoke again through his herald, and you hardened your hearts. Now at last, when he speaks with his own lips, let your hearts become tender. He sent heralds ahead of him, time and time again, but now he graciously comes himself. He who used to speak through the mouths of the prophets speaks here with his own."[14] The phrase, "For forty years I stayed very close to this generation,"[15] refers in the first place to the signs and acts of power by which God demonstrated his presence with the Israelites. Yet the years should not be understood only in terms of that literal duration but also as "the whole course of the ages, as though time reached its fullness at the number forty."[16] Forty days represents the time of Jesus's testing as well as the duration of his stay with the disciples after his resurrection: the first forty represents temptation, while the second forty signifies consolation. By the term "forty," the church understands that she must endure temptations in this world, but her consoler remains with her.

Concerning God's oath, "They shall never enter my rest,"[17] Augustine warns that it is already a great matter for God to speak, even more for God to swear. God swears by himself because there is none greater by which to swear.[18] Augustine then suggests the oath applies not just to the Israelites of old, but to anyone who now rejects God: "As you must be utterly sure about gaining rest, happiness, eternity, and immortality, if you have kept his commandments, so you must be equally sure of perdition, the heat of eternal fire, and damnation with the devil, if you have despised his commandments."[19] Since the promise of rest cannot go unfulfilled, it must remain for the church to enjoy what the Israelites of old could not. "They have been disqualified," Augustine exhorts, "but we shall enter it. Some of the branches were broken off because they had lost their likeness to God and were unfaithful, but let us be grafted in through faith and humility. Let us enter into his rest."[20]

---

14. Ibid.
15. Ibid., 94.14.
16. Ibid.
17. Ibid., 94.15.
18. Note the illusion here to Heb. 6:13, though Augustine changes the referent of the oath in Hebrews from the promise to Abraham that God would bless and multiply him, to the threat that the Israelites would not enter God's rest.
19. *En. Ps.* 94.15.
20. Ibid.

The Epistle to the Hebrews: Approaching the Psalms

Augustine's treatment of this psalm thus reflects the same lines of thought we have sketched in prior chapters. While he does acknowledge some import for Old Testament Israel, he treats the passage primarily with regard to the church addressed "today" in Christ.

Calvin

Though Calvin, like Augustine, treats Ps. 95 with reference to the church, he does not resort to allegory to do so.[21] Since Israel simply was the church during Old Testament times, God's manner of addressing Israel in Ps. 95 is substantially the same as his manner of addressing the church today. Calvin's comments on Ps. 95:6, for instance, clearly concern the Israelites, calling them the "children of Abraham," acknowledging their "pre-eminence among the nations," and reading the command to kneel before "the face of the Lord" as an injunction for the Israelites to "prostrate themselves before the Ark of Covenant, for the reference is to the mode of worship under the Law *(de legali cultu).*"[22] Yet Calvin's remarks on the next verse address the "church," with no explanatory transition from Israel to the New Testament community: "While it is true that all men were created to praise God, there are reasons why the Church is specially said to have been formed for that end."[23] God's protection of "the children of Abraham" means that he is "the Shepherd of the Church *(ecclesiae suae pastorem)*"[24] because there is for Calvin no distinction between these two communities. Both are set apart from the world, and both receive God's special favor.

Calvin's comments on "today," "forty years," and "rest" also reflect an orientation toward Old Testament Israel and the literal sense. The psalm warns the Israelites to persevere and obey the law; "today" stresses their ongoing access to God's voice, a certain sign of their election.[25] "Forty years" means the forty years God contended with the Israelites in the wilderness,[26]

---

21. Calvin's Psalms commentary was written from 1553-57 and published in 1557. T. H. L. Parker, *Calvin's Old Testament Commentaries* (Louisville: Westminster/John Knox, 1986), 15, 31.
22. Comm. Ps. 95.6.
23. Ibid., 95.7.
24. Ibid.
25. Ibid.
26. Ibid., 95.10.

and "rest" simply means land.[27] Abraham and his posterity had been wanderers in Canaan, and Egypt represented a time of exile; when the Israelites were poised to return to the land, God "very properly *(merito)*" called it his rest. While Calvin does acknowledge the psalm's pertinence for other contexts, he always roots the generalizing move in the history of Israel. Thus, the Israelites were warned against imitating their predecessors because they often boasted in their fathers;[28] but hardness of heart afflicts all people when they show contempt for the Word of God. The incident at Meribah was especially foolish given God's proofs of power before the Egyptians; yet this lesson is "equally applicable to ourselves *(aeque ad nos pertinet)*,"[29] for we receive all manner of blessings from God yet still demand proof of his goodness.

Calvin considers the appropriation of Ps. 95 in Heb. 3–4 in his commentaries on both Psalms and Hebrews. For our purposes, his remarks are conceptually consistent with each other and emphasize the following themes. First, the appeal in Hebrews to "today" stresses the continuity of God's revelation to his people. As we saw in the previous chapter with the Hebrews commentary, Calvin thinks this word "ought not to be confined to the age of David, but that it comprehends every time in which God may address us."[30] Similar remarks arise in the commentary on the Psalms: "today" should not be confined to the time of the law, for it applies also to the gospel, when God has begun to speak more openly.[31]

Second, "rest" applies first to physical Canaan and only derivatively to some better hope. In the Psalms commentary, Calvin says Hebrews cannot be "considered as undertaking professedly to treat this passage *(neque enim ex professo tractandum locum suscipit)*," but only as focusing *(insistit)* on the words "today" and "rest."[32] According to Calvin, by observing the implied promise of the text, the author of Hebrews deduces that

> there must have been some better rest promised to the people of God than the land of Canaan. For, when the Jews had entered the land, God held out to his people the prospect of another rest, which is defined by the Apostle to consist in that renouncing of ourselves, whereby we

27. Ibid., 95.11.
28. Ibid., 95.9.
29. Ibid.
30. *Comm. Heb.* 3.13.
31. *Comm. Ps.* 95.11.
32. Ibid.

rest from our own works while God worketh in us. From this, he takes occasion to compare the old Sabbath, or rest, under the Law, which was figurative, with the newness of spiritual life.[33]

The Hebrews commentary describes a similar logic. On the one hand, "the land of Canaan was to be, according to the promise, [the Israelites'] perpetual inheritance; and it was in reference to this promise that God called it *his* rest: for nowhere can we have a settled dwelling, except where we are fixed by his hand."[34] On the other hand, the Old Testament Israelites had always known to seek a rest beyond this physical land:

> [The author of Hebrews] meant not to deny but that David understood by rest the land of Canaan, into which Joshua conducted the people; but he denies this to be the final rest to which the faithful aspire, and which we have also in common with the faithful of that age; for it is certain that they looked higher than to that land; nay, the land of Canaan was not otherwise so much valued except for this reason, because it was an image *(imago)* and a symbol *(symbolum)* of the spiritual inheritance.[35]

By alluding to Sabbath, Hebrews seeks "to reclaim the Jews from its external observances; for in no other way could its abrogation be understood, except by the knowledge of its spiritual design.... He shews us in passing what is the true design of the Sabbath lest the Jews should be foolishly attached to the outward rite."[36]

Third and related, Calvin distinguishes Hebrews's creative appropriation of Ps. 95 from a literal understanding of the text. Hebrews does not expound, but "reasons from the *rest,* to an extent which we are not to suppose that the words of the Psalmist themselves warrant *(de requie subtilius disputat quam ferant prophetae verba)*."[37] From Heb. 4:3, the author

> begins to embellish *(exornare)* the passage which he had quoted from David. He has hitherto taken it, as they say, according to the letter *(secundum literam)*, that is, in its literal sense *(in genuino sensu);* but he now amplifies and decorates it *(expoliendo amplificat);* and thus he rather

33. Ibid.
34. *Comm. Heb.* 3.11.
35. Ibid., 4.8.
36. Ibid., 4.10.
37. *Comm. Ps.* 95.11.

alludes *(alludit)* to than explains *(interpretetur)* the words of David. This sort of decoration (ἐπεξεργασία) Paul employed in Rom. x. 6, in referring to these words of Moses, "Say not, who shall ascend into heaven!" &c. Nor is it indeed anything unsuitable, in accommodating *(accommodetur)* Scripture to a subject in hand, to illustrate by figurative terms *(similitudinum . . . coloribus illustrare)* what is more simply delivered. However, the sum of the whole *(summa omnium)* is this, that what God threatens in the Psalm as to the loss of his rest, applies also to us, inasmuch as he invites us also to this day to a rest.[38]

In sum, and as expected, Calvin applies Ps. 95 first to Old Testament Israel and only derivatively to the New Testament church; the epistle's hermeneutical innovation should be taken as an illustration and not an explanation of the text. There is, however, no impropriety in this mode of embellishment, and the author of Hebrews stresses the continuity of hope between the Old Testament Israelites and current readers. If Augustine reads Ps. 95 primarily for how it bears upon the contemporary church, without denying some purchase in the history of Israel, Calvin begins with the original meaning for Israel, and then expands this sense for all God's people.

The Epistle to the Hebrews

Calvin is right to consider the appropriation of Ps. 95 in Hebrews an innovation, but recent New Testament scholarship suggests different categories for characterizing this hermeneutical novelty than the Reformer could have recognized. Susan Docherty's recent application of "form analysis" to Hebrews illuminates the epistle's interpretive moves.[39] Form analysis

---

38. *Comm. Heb.* 4.3-10.

39. Docherty, *The Use of the Old Testament in Hebrews*. For other treatments of the use of Ps. 95 in Hebrews, see Harold W. Attridge, "'Let Us Strive to Enter That Rest': The Logic of Hebrews 4:1-11," *HTR* 73 (1980): 279-88; A. T. Lincoln, "Sabbath, Rest, and Eschatology in the New Testament," in *From Sabbath to Lord's Day: A Biblical, Historical, and Theological Investigation,* ed. D. A. Carson (Grand Rapids: Zondervan, 1982), 197-220; Peter Enns, "The Interpretation of Psalm 95 in Hebrews 3.1-4.13," in *Early Christian Interpretation of the Scriptures of Israel,* ed. Craig A. Evans and James A. Sanders, JSNTSup 148 (Sheffield: Sheffield Academic, 1997), 352-63; Jon Laansma, *'I Will Give You Rest': The Rest Motif in the New Testament with Special Reference to Mt 11 and Heb 3-4* (Tübingen: Mohr Siebeck, 1997); David A. deSilva, "Entering God's Rest: Eschatology and the Socio-Rhetorical Strategy of Hebrews," *TJ* 21 (2000): 25-43; Randall C. Gleason, "The Old Testament Background of

(to be distinguished from form criticism) is a mode of studying midrash that begins with the identification of small literary units and then explores the interrelation between these units in more complex forms of literature. Much rabbinic literature consists of the arrangement of individual biblical citations into new literary units such that the same words are used for different purposes than in their original context. Since the "co-text," or "the purely linguistic environment of a text," counts more than the "context," or the text's "non-linguistic setting,"[40] the statement (*Aussage*) remains the same while the meaning (*Bedeutung*) changes. "The editors of the rabbinic works were in fact not interested in what their citations were meant to say in their original contexts, but in what they can say now, presumably regarding this new meaning as being inherent in the original words."[41] As Docherty suggests, this practice reflects a view of Scripture less concerned with the events recorded in the text than with the interplay of individual linguistic signs. "Whilst the number of graphic signs is finite, determined by the limits of the written text of scripture, the meaning of the signs is infinite, as they remain open to constant interpretation and are understood as polysemic by divine intent."[42]

This discussion provides a useful vocabulary for understanding the use of the Old Testament in Hebrews, though the epistle exhibits greater theological controls than form analysis might suggest. Heb. 3:7–4:11 reflects close fidelity to the author's Greek source text, and virtually all the differences between the epistle's quotation and the majority of Septuagint witnesses could reflect an alternate Greek tradition.[43] Yet this textual

---

Rest," *BSac* 157 (2000): 281-303; Matthew Thiessen, "Hebrews and the End of the Exodus," *NovT* 49 (2007): 353-69. Note also two earlier pieces: Ernst Käsemann, *The Wandering People of God*, trans. Roy A. Harrisville and Irving L. Sandberg (orig. 1939; Minneapolis: Augsburg, 1984); Gerhard von Rad, "There Remains Still a Rest for the People of God: An Investigation of a Biblical Conception," in *The Problem of the Hexateuch and Other Essays*, trans. E. W. Trueman Dicken (New York: McGraw-Hill, 1966), 94-102.

40. Docherty, *The Use of the Old Testament in Hebrews*, 107.

41. Ibid., 103. In this and the next quotation, Docherty is describing Arnold Goldberg's position, which she approves with qualification.

42. Ibid., 105.

43. Ibid., 137-39. The most significant point where the author seems deliberately to have altered his source is 3:10, where the addition of διό ("therefore") revises the referent of "forty years" such that the expression refers to the time when the Israelites tested God, as opposed to the time of their punishment. For various explanations of this change, see Enns, "The Interpretation of Psalm 95 in Hebrews 3.1–4.13"; Harold W. Attridge, *Hebrews*, Hermeneia (Philadelphia: Fortress, 1989), 115.

integrity brings to relief the creativity of the epistle's appropriation of the Old Testament, which is overwhelmingly characterized by first-person direct speech. As Docherty argues, the act of removing a text from its original context and placing it in a new co-text works particularly well for direct speech passages, "because their original contextual links are often weak or ambiguous, and because it is very easy to provide new co-text for them simply by means of specifying more precisely a speaker and/or addressee."[44] Where Hebrews appropriates Ps. 95, the psalm no longer addresses the original hearers, but the recipients of the epistle. The speaker of the scriptural text remains God, but the "you" are those whom the author of Hebrews addresses now.

The use of "today" and "rest" in Hebrews exploits this dynamic. In the new co-text, "today" is associated both with "every day" (3:13), which stresses the ongoing relevance of God's message, and with the general sense of eschatological expectation throughout the letter. The "today" of Ps. 95/Heb. 3–4 may also be linked to the citation of Ps. 2:7 in Heb. 1:5a: "Thou art my Son, *today* I have begotten thee" (italics mine). If this passage refers to Christ's exaltation to the right hand of God, as Docherty thinks, then the "today" of Ps. 95 further underscores the present reality of God's activity through Christ, and so also the urgency of responding positively to God.[45] For "rest," Docherty highlights a rabbinic technique that the form-analytical school calls "opposition resources," whereby one biblical word is heavily stressed so as to exclude the opposite.[46] On this model, the statement, "They shall never enter my rest," means not just that the Israelites of the wilderness will *not* enter it, but also that other people *will*. Since God's oath was binding on that earlier generation alone, and not on anyone else, Hebrews can transpose the psalm into a promise: the addressees dare not harden their hearts — precisely because the rest remains open for them.

Hebrews wonders how there can remain a promise for rest when the people have already entered the land of Canaan (4:8). In particular, Ps. 95 speaks of "*my* rest," which, Docherty suggests, prompts the author of Hebrews to search for another text that refers to God's resting.[47] Gen. 2:2 functions well in this regard, especially because it describes this rest in terms of

---

44. Docherty, *The Use of the Old Testament in Hebrews*, 147.
45. Ibid., 151.
46. Ibid., 191.
47. For a helpful exposition of the traditions concerning "rest" that shape the treatment of it in Hebrews, see A. T. Lincoln, "Sabbath, Rest, and Eschatology in the New Testament," 205-14.

The Epistle to the Hebrews: Approaching the Psalms

the works of creation, a theme Ps. 95 also stresses in its reference to God's works (Ps. 95:9/Heb. 3:9) and God's status as "Maker" (Ps. 95:5). Although the use of *gezera shawa* with Ps. 95 and Gen. 2 focuses primarily on the term "rest," the unstated thematic and linguistic points of contact between these passages strengthen the intertextual resonances, while also suggesting the epistle's attention to the larger context of the texts used. The interpretation of "rest" in Hebrews also demonstrates the author's interest in chronology: the term must refer to a Sabbath rest and not Canaan because the psalm continued to speak of rest long after the people had entered the physical land. As Docherty notes, such arguments are not unusual in the New Testament: Paul argues in Rom. 4 that Abraham was reckoned righteous before he was circumcised, and in Gal. 3 that the law, which came 430 years after God's promise to Abraham, could not overturn the earlier covenant. They are, however, unique in early Jewish interpretation, which stresses the independence of scripture from the particularities of time. "In general, early post-biblical Jewish exegesis does not make use of the same kind of temporal argument in interpreting scripture as occurs here, perhaps because the eschatological outlook of the New Testament writers encouraged them to see God's revelation in a more linear way than other contemporary Jewish exegetes, as leading to its fulfillment in Christ."[48]

Hebrews thus exploits while also affirming the literal sense. "Rest" is no linguistic cue for speculative association (contra Augustine), nor does it encompass several meanings across the one covenant of grace (contra Calvin). The meaning is strictly defined according to the theological context of the epistle, with its repeated references to an eternal inheritance and the heavenly sanctuary where Christ has now been exalted as high priest. Indeed, this context is the only way to make sense of the Old Testament locutions, whose internal difficulties already suggested some other meaning. How could David speak so long after the wilderness generation of another day, "today," to enter God's rest (4:7-8)? There must be a different rest than the physical land of Canaan. And since God speaks through David of "my rest," this must be tied to God's resting after the works of creation, which in turn functions as a model for our eschatological hope, when we will rest from our labors as God did from his.[49] The burden of

---

48. Docherty, *The Use of the Old Testament in Hebrews*, 192.
49. See Attridge, "'Let Us Strive to Enter That Rest'" for a helpful discussion of the relation between antitype (eschatological rest), type (Canaan), and even more original type (God's rest).

Heb. 11 to identify this eternal inheritance with Israel's longstanding hope may thus be taken as an argument that the new interpretation of Ps. 95 is not so new after all. The original sense is largely retained, though theologically transformed.

Psalm 110

In Ps. 110, we consider the promise of a new priesthood in the order of Melchizedek. This psalm is the most cited Old Testament passage in the New Testament, and Attridge judges it "undoubtedly" the most important text quoted in the epistle.[50] The first verse presents the exaltation of the Son, while the fourth animates the author's discussion of Christ's establishment as high priest. The English translation of the psalm reads thus:

> A Psalm of David.
> ₁The LORD says to my lord: "Sit at my right hand, till I make your enemies your footstool." ₂The LORD sends forth from Zion your mighty scepter. Rule in the midst of your foes! ₃Your people will offer themselves freely on the day you lead your host upon the holy mountains. From the womb of the morning like dew your youth will come to you. ₄The LORD has sworn and will not change his mind, "You are a priest for ever after the order of Melchizedek." ₅The Lord is at your right hand; he will shatter kings on the day of his wrath. ₆He will execute judgment among the nations, filling them with corpses; he will shatter chiefs over the wide earth. ₇He will drink from the brook by the way; therefore he will lift up his head.

Augustine

Augustine considers Ps. 110 an obvious prophecy of Christ, and his exposition of the text stresses Christ's unique qualification to act as mediator through his humanity and divinity. Augustine begins his comments with an extended introduction on redemptive history and the dynamics of promise and fulfillment across the testaments.[51] Jesus is the ultimate pledge of

---

50. Attridge, "The Psalms in Hebrews," 197.
51. *En. Ps.* 109.1-3.

The Epistle to the Hebrews: Approaching the Psalms

God's favor toward us as well as the "Way" by which we may return to God. Augustine then considers the text at hand: "Our psalm deals with these promises. It speaks prophetically of our Lord and Savior Jesus Christ with such certainty and clarity that we cannot doubt that it is he who is proclaimed here."[52] In particular support of this point is the conflict over Ps. 110 recorded in the gospels: the Jews knew that the Christ would be the son of David, but they had no response when Jesus asked them how the Christ could also be David's Lord. For "David in spirit calls him Lord, saying, The Lord said to my Lord, Sit at my right hand, until I put your enemies under your feet."[53]

The distinction between "David's son" and "David's Lord" acts as a cipher for Augustine for the humanity and divinity of Christ. The Jews were not wrong to confess that the Christ would be the son of David. Matthew's first words confirm that Jesus did descend from David, as do several other passages in Scripture.[54] The problem was that the Jews did not go far enough: they confessed the Christ as David's son, but not as David's Lord — as man, but not as God. Augustine distinguishes between "transient acts *(aliud . . . transitorium)* performed by the Lord" and "the stable reality *(aliud stabile)* of the Lord."[55] The Lord was transitory in his incarnation, birth, maturation, miracles, suffering, death, resurrection, and ascension, doing these things in the course of time before he disappeared. But Jesus is also the Word, who in the beginning was with God and was God, through whom all things were made. He was thus David's son in the incarnation, but David's Lord from eternity. Augustine preaches:

> In the beginning you were the Word, and as the Word you were with God, and you, the Word, were God. All things were made through you, and in this we know you to be David's Lord. But because of our weakness, because we lay prostrate, hopeless flesh, you, the Word, were made flesh in order to dwell among us; and in this we know you to be David's son. Being in the form of God you certainly deemed it no robbery to be God's equal: lo, you are David's Lord. But you emptied yourself and took on the form of a slave: lo, you are David's son. When you put to us the question, *Whose son is he?* you were not denying this but seeking to

---

52. Ibid., 109.3.
53. Ibid., citing Matt. 22:43-45.
54. Ibid., 109.4-5. Augustine also cites Rom. 1:3; 2 Tim. 2:8; and Matt. 20:30.
55. Ibid., 109.5.

draw from us a confession of how it came about. *David calls him Lord, you say. How can he be David's son?* I am not repudiating that title, says Christ, but tell me how it came to be mine.[56]

Ps. 110:1 says Christ has now sat down at the right hand of the Father. Augustine asks how David's son could also become David's Lord. In human affairs, it is possible for a man's son to be exalted as king while the father remains an ordinary citizen. It is also possible in the church for a man's son to become the father's father, i.e., if the son becomes a bishop. Since Jesus was in the flesh when he ascended to heaven, we may conclude that he retained this flesh when he sat at the right hand of the Father. Even now, then, Jesus remains both David's son and David's Lord, both man and God.[57] The reference in Ps. 110:4 to Melchizedek advances a similar point. "By his birth from the Father, as God with God, co-eternal with his Begetter, he is not a priest. He is a priest only because of the flesh he assumed, the body he received from us to offer as a sacrificial victim for us."[58] Christ was not priest from eternity, but could only become one by taking on flesh and thus establishing a priesthood that would never end.

The psalmist's reference to the irrevocability of God's oath indicates a contrast between the order of Aaron and that of Melchizedek. Unlike humans who may regret some prior decision, Augustine explains, God can neither repent nor change. When Scripture speaks of God's repenting, it refers only to God's changing something in a way humans do not expect, and this always involves God's foreknowledge and wisdom. The abolition of the former priesthood must be understood accordingly, and not taken to imply repentance or variation in God. In the new priesthood, Christ intercedes for us at God's very side, "like the priest entering the innermost place, the holy of holies, the secret recess of heaven, and cleansing us easily from sins because he has no sin himself."[59] The implications for the old priesthood are by now familiar:

> But what kind of priesthood is envisaged? Will it require those victims and sacrifices offered by the patriarchs, altars running with blood, and

56. Ibid., 109.6.
57. Ibid., 109.7.
58. Ibid., 109.17.
59. Ibid., 109.18.

the sacred tent, and all the other emblems of the first covenant, the old one? By no means. All those things have been swept away *(illa sublata sunt)* with the destruction of the temple *(euerso iam templo)*, the abolition of the old priesthood *(remoto illo sacerdotio)*, and the disappearance of the victims and sacrifices that belonged to them *(pereunte uictima eorum et sacrificio)*. Not even the Jews have these now. They see that their priesthood according to the order of Aaron has ceased to exist *(perisse)*, and they fail to recognize the priesthood according to the order of Melchizedek.[60]

For Augustine, then, it is the humanity and divinity of Christ that brings the Aaronic priesthood to an end, for Jesus's retention of flesh and his exaltation as God uniquely qualifies him as the mediator of a priesthood that will never end.

Calvin

Calvin begins his treatment of Ps. 110 by setting forth four chief points in the text: first, that God conferred upon Christ supreme dominion and power to subjugate his enemies; second, that God would extend widely the boundaries of Christ's kingdom; third, that Christ is established as both priest and king; and fourth, that the new order according to which Christ is priest would be eternal and bring to an end the Levitical priesthood, which was only temporary. Calvin then defends the identity of Christ as the referent of the psalm. Even without Jesus's explicit testimony in the gospels that this psalm refers to himself, it would still be obvious that this is the proper interpretation. The language of the psalm could not be asserted of David or any of his successors, for none enjoyed such wide dominion while also being established as priest forever in the order of Melchizedek. Plus, no mortal person could assume such an honor, by definition, since it would be terminated immediately upon death. It must be Christ whom the psalmist has in view.

Commenting on the first verse, Calvin acknowledges that God's establishment of a kingly figure could to some extent be applied to David, or any king for that matter, since all rule and authority comes ultimately by God's decree. But the scope of this psalm extends beyond David, who

60. Ibid., 109.17.

must have spoken this psalm as part of the church, "a member of the body under the same head."[61] David foresaw the future reign of Christ when Jesus would be made manifest as supreme head of the church. "There is something in Christ more excellent than his humanity, on account of which he is called the Lord of David his father."[62] The reference to Jesus's sitting at the right hand of the Father confirms this point, indicating that "one king is chosen in a peculiar manner, and elevated to the rank of power and dignity next to God, of which dignity the twilight only appeared in David, while in Christ it shone forth in meridian splendour."[63] Christ has been exalted above all powers, including the angels and principalities; David never enjoyed such honor, nor has any earthly king.

The reference to Melchizedek prompts a discussion of Christ's identity as both king and priest. Israelite kings were not allowed to adopt for themselves priestly duties. Uzziah was struck with leprosy for trying to offer incense to God (2 Chr. 26:21). But Melchizedek was divinely appointed as both priest and king, and this peculiar combination is what made him distinct, since Salem was a small, obscure town, and Melchizedek would not otherwise have merited much attention.[64] That God sealed Christ's appointment by oath underscores the importance of this event and confirms Christ's elevation above all priests. It follows for Calvin that the Levitical priesthood must be abrogated. "Because, while that remained entire, God would not have sworn that there should be a new order of priesthood unless some change had been contemplated. What is more, when he promises a new priest, it is certain that he would be the one who would be superior to all others, and would abolish the then existing order."[65]

Calvin's commentary on Hebrews elaborates these points. Again, Calvin stresses the particularity of one person acting as both priest and king, making repeated reference to Uzziah.[66] Yet he also distinguishes between Melchizedek's "private capacity" and those features according to which he acts as an image of Christ. Melchizedek did have biological parents, for instance, but Scripture obscures this genealogy for the purpose of making

---

61. *Comm. Ps.* 110.1.
62. Ibid.
63. Ibid.
64. Ibid., 110.4.
65. Ibid.
66. *Comm. Heb.* 1.13, 5.6.

him prefigure Christ's eternity.[67] Melchizedek was not an angel, or Christ, or the Holy Spirit; he was only a human who happened to be both king and priest. Calvin lists five specific points of similarity between Melchizedek and Christ.[68] First, Melchizedek was called "the king of righteousness"; Christ brings righteousness, in both allowing us to be reckoned righteous before God and renewing us by the Spirit to live godly lives. Second, Melchizedek was associated with peace; Christ brings that inward peace which calms our consciences of anxiety or inquietude. Third, Melchizedek had no genealogy; Christ is eternal. Fourth, Melchizedek received tithes from Abraham and, derivatively, from the Levites; Christ bears greater dignity than all the house of Levi. And finally, Melchizedek blessed Abraham; Christ also excels the patriarch with whom God established the covenant of eternal life. The offering of the bread and wine does not constitute a point of similarity, against the "extremely ridiculous" Papists who "yet prattle about the sacrifice of bread and wine."[69]

The references in Hebrews to Melchizedek's eternity must be treated according to these considerations. Scripture does not mention Melchizedek's death, but this was only to provide an image of Christ's eternal priesthood. Melchizedek did actually die.[70] Still, the eternity of Melchizedek's priesthood presents a contrast with the Levitical priesthood and the Mosaic law, both of which came to an end with Christ. Commenting on Heb. 7:11, Calvin explains, "No covenant between God and man is in force and ratified, except it rests on a priesthood."[71] Since God has replaced the Levitical priesthood, it follows that the Mosaic law must also be abolished. "As the authority of the Law and the priesthood is the same, Christ became not only a priest, but also a Lawgiver; so that the right of Aaron, as well as of Moses, was transferred to him."[72] This development must, of course, be understood according to the distinction between the law in its peculiarity and the law as it contains the rule of life and the covenant of grace. Christ abolishes only the former, not the latter. Within this context, though, Christ's establishment as priest does mean the Levitical and Mosaic structures have lost all force.

67. Ibid., 7.3.
68. Ibid., 7.1-10.
69. Ibid., 7.10.
70. Ibid., 7.8.
71. Ibid., 7.11.
72. Ibid., 7.12.

The Epistle to the Hebrews

The engagement with Ps. 110 in Hebrews is pervasive and unique.[73] Citations or allusions to Ps. 110:1 appear throughout the epistle at significant junctures in the text: the exordium (1:3-4), the concluding verse of the subsequent scriptural catena (1:13), two important summary passages (8:1 and 10:12-13), and the climactic exhortation of 12:2.[74] The epistle's application of this verse to Jesus is not itself unusual: the New Testament witnesses indicate the psalm was understood messianically from a very early juncture,[75] and the gospels attribute this tradition to Jesus himself.[76] What makes the contribution in Hebrews distinct is the affirmation of a new priesthood through Ps. 110:4, first cited in 5:6, alluded to in 5:10 and 6:20, and discussed at length in Heb. 7, with two citations at 7:17 and 7:21.[77] Since the addressee of Ps. 110:1 is easily identified with Jesus, it makes natural sense that Ps. 110:4 also be understood in this regard. If Jesus is the exalted Lord, he must be priest forever, too, after the order of Melchizedek.

The treatment of Melchizedek in Hebrews has attracted a fair amount of scholarly discussion and debate, especially concerning the relation between Hebrews and other Jewish traditions.[78] For our purposes, the fol-

---

73. The following paragraph depends on Attridge, "The Psalms in Hebrews," 197-98.

74. There are no differences between the epistle's explicit citations of Ps. 110:1 and the major Septuagint witnesses, though slight variations arise when the author alludes to the passage instead of citing it. See Docherty, *The Use of the Old Testament in Hebrews*, 168-71.

75. Acts 2:34-35; Rom. 8:34; 1 Cor. 15:25; Eph. 1:20; Col. 3:1.

76. Matt. 22:41-46; Mark 12:35-37; Luke 20:41-44. For a survey of early Christian interpretation of Ps. 110, see David M. Hay, *Glory at the Right Hand: Psalm 110 in Early Christianity*, SBLMS 18 (Atlanta: Society of Biblical Literature, 1973).

77. The citations of Ps. 110:4 depart only slightly from the main Septuagint witnesses. Craig R. Koester, *Hebrews: A New Translation with Introduction and Commentary*, AB 36 (New York: Doubleday, 2001), 287.

78. For a recent treatment of this matter, see Gareth Lee Cockerill, "Melchizedek without Speculation: Hebrews 7:1-25 and Genesis 14:17-24," in *A Cloud of Witnesses: The Theology of Hebrews in Its Ancient Contexts*, ed. Richard Bauckham et al. (London: T&T Clark, 2008), 128-44. This study draws upon his earlier work, "The Melchizedek Christology in Heb. 7:1-28" (PhD diss., Union Theological Seminary in Virginia, 1976). See also Joseph A. Fitzmyer, "'Now this Melchizedek . . .' (Heb 7, 1)," *CBQ* 25 (1963): 305-21; as well as idem, "Further Light on Melchizedek from Qumran Cave 11," *JBL* 86 (1967): 25-41; and idem, "Melchizedek in the MT, LXX, and the NT," *Bib* 81 (2000): 63-69; M. Delcor, "Melchizedek from Genesis to the Qumran Texts and the Epistle to the Hebrews," *JSJ* 2 (1971): 115-35; David M. Hay, *Glory at the Right Hand*, 134-53; Fred L. Horton, *The Melchizedek Tradition: A Critical Examination of the Sources to the Fifth Century A.D. and in the Epistle to the Hebrews* (Cambridge:

The Epistle to the Hebrews: Approaching the Psalms

lowing (relatively non-controversial) points bear mentioning. First, the interest in Melchizedek displayed by the author of Hebrews does not arise in a vacuum. Though Melchizedek appears at only two points in the Old Testament (Gen. 14:18-20 and Ps. 110:4), he attracts a wide range of attention in Second Temple Jewish literature: Jubilees, 1 Maccabees, the Assumption of Moses, various Targumim, Josephus, and Philo, as well as the oft-discussed Melchizedek Scroll from Qumran (11QMelch). Second, the epistle's appropriation of Melchizedek is quite distinct from the kind of allegorical speculation found in Philo.[79] While Philo does present Melchizedek as a historical human figure, his chief concern is to depict Melchizedek as the eternal Logos. Melchizedek's identity as "king of righteousness" and "king of peace," for instance, means that reason is a good pilot for the proper conduct of life, able to bring order to unruly passions.[80] Reason brings forth "food" full of cheerfulness and joy, and "wine" to intoxicate the soul with sober virtue. The treatment of Melchizedek in Hebrews is, by contrast, thoroughly Christological and historical in orientation. Third, whether or not 11QMelch influenced Hebrews, there are significant differences between the two in their depictions of Melchizedek.[81] The Qumran community seems to have identified Melchizedek with the archangel Michael as a kind of heavenly redeemer-warrior figure, who with the assistance of other angels will bring judgment upon the wicked and salvation for God's elect. Hebrews treats Melchizedek as a prefiguration of Christ,

---

Cambridge University Press, 1976); Richard Longenecker, "The Melchizedek Argument of Hebrews: A Study in the Development and Circumstantial Expression of New Testament Thought," in *Unity and Diversity in New Testament Theology: Essays in Honor of George E. Ladd,* ed. Robert A. Geulich (Grand Rapids: Eerdmans, 1978), 161-85; Mikael C. Parsons, "Son and High Priest: A Study in the Christology of Hebrews," *EvQ* 60 (1988): 195-215; Anders Aschim, "Melchizedek and Jesus: 11QMelchizedek and the Epistle to the Hebrews," in *The Jewish Roots of Christological Monotheism: Papers from the St. Andrews Conference on the Historical Origins of the Worship of Jesus,* ed. Carey C. Newman, James R. Davila, and Gladys S. Lewis, Supplements to the Journal for the Study of Judaism 63 (Leiden: Brill, 1999), 129-47; Deborah W. Rooke, "Jesus as Royal Priest: Reflections on the Interpretation of the Melchizedek Tradition in Heb 7," *Bib* 81 (2000): 81-94; Eric F. Mason, *'You Are a Priest Forever': Second Temple Jewish Messianism and the Priestly Christology of the Epistle to the Hebrews,* STDJ 74 (Leiden: Brill, 2008).

79. The standard refutation of Philo's influence on Hebrews is Ronald Williamson, *Philo and the Epistle to the Hebrews* (Leiden: Brill, 1970). See especially pp. 434-49 for his discussion on Melchizedek.

80. *Legum Allegoriae* 3.79-82.

81. Cockerill, "Melchizedek without Speculation," 136-41.

not the actual agent of eschatological deliverance,[82] and repeatedly stresses Christ's superiority over the angels. The Qumran scroll also reveals little interest in Gen. 14:18-20 and Ps. 110:4, the chief foci of the epistle's attention.[83]

These observations illuminate the kind of scriptural reasoning exhibited in Heb. 7, the entirety of which may be understood as a reflection upon Ps. 110:4. Hebrews treats the affirmation of Christ's priesthood as a performative act, spoken at that temporal juncture when he was in fact installed as high priest in the heavenlies.[84] As in the scriptural catena of Heb. 1, Ps. 110 presents a dialogue between God and the Son, and the moment of Ps. 110 corresponds more or less with that described in Heb. 1:6, when God "brings the first-born into the world." Heb. 7:20-21 stresses the solemnity of this declaration: "Those who formerly became priests took their office without an oath, but this one was addressed with an oath, 'The Lord has sworn and will not change his mind, "Thou art a priest for ever."'" On the reading of Hebrews advanced in the previous chapter, this moment could only occur after the incarnation, death, and bodily ascent of the Son into heaven. Ps. 110 thus bears within itself the marks of incompletion, speaking in advance of some future event when God would establish a new priest, in the order of Melchizedek and not of Levi.

Ps. 110 naturally leads Hebrews to Gen. 14:18-20, the only other Old Testament reference to Melchizedek. Hebrews indicates that Melchizedek, by virtue of his name and location in Salem, is a king of righteousness and peace.[85] Hebrews then stresses two revelatory events in the narrative of Gen. 14: Abraham paid Melchizedek a tithe, and Melchizedek blessed Abraham. The tithe is a significant point for the author, for the law prescribes that the descendants of Levi receive a tithe from the Israelites. In this case, there is a sense in which Levi is tithing to Melchizedek, which indicates the superiority of Melchizedek's priesthood over the Levitical. So too does Melchizedek's blessing of Abraham, since "it is beyond dispute that the inferior is blessed by the superior" (7:7). Finally, Melchizedek "is without father or mother or genealogy, and has neither beginning of

---

82. On this point, see Longenecker, "The Melchizedek Argument of Hebrews," 176-79.
83. See Fitzmyer's early judgment on these issues in "Further Light on Melchizedek," 31. For an alternate view, see Aschim, "Melchizedek and Jesus."
84. Attridge, "The Psalms in Hebrews," 209.
85. See Rooke, "Jesus as Royal Priest," 84-85 for an argument that "righteousness" and "peace" were deliberately flagged to stress the messianic character of Jesus's royal priesthood.

days nor end of life, but resembling the Son of God he continues a priest for ever" (7:3). As scholars have noted, this is an argument from silence, following the rabbinic principle, *quod non in thora non in mundo* ("what is not in the Torah is not in the world"),[86] and it is difficult to discern whether the author means to affirm Melchizedek's actual eternity, or to present his lack of recorded genealogy as a prefigurement of Christ.[87] In either case, the author's interest in this issue clearly derives from the reference in Ps. 110:4 to an eternal priesthood.

In the remainder of Heb. 7, the author shifts to Jesus's new Melchizedekian priesthood. For our purposes, there are two points of particular importance. First, the author deduces from Ps. 110:4 the abrogation of the Levitical system. Since Melchizedek was a priest, Levitical descent cannot be a requirement for priesthood, and Jesus can also be a priest despite his descent from Judah. This new priesthood must be superior to the old, not just in light of Gen. 14 (Abraham paid Melchizedek a tithe; Melchizedek blessed Abraham), but also because Melchizedek's priesthood has been declared to be eternal, grounded not in lineage, but in "the power of an indestructible life" (7:16). Unlike those priests who die and must be replaced, Christ "is able for all time to save those who draw near to God through him, since he always lives to make intercession for them" (7:25). Since Christ's priesthood surpasses the Levitical, there must have been some deficiency in the old system which would eventually spell its end: "Now if perfection had been attainable through the Levitical priesthood (for under it the people received the law), what further need would there have been for another priest to arise after the order of Melchizedek, rather than one named after the order of Aaron?" (7:11).

Second, Hebrews demonstrates (again) keen interest in chronology. In the concluding remarks of Heb. 7, the author says, "Indeed, the law appoints men in their weakness as high priests, but the word of the oath, which came later than the law, appoints a Son who has been made perfect for ever" (7:28). The oath here corresponds to the words of Ps. 110:4, which declared Christ to be high priest after his bodily ascent into heaven. That this event took place temporally after the establishment of the Levitical

---

86. See, for instance, Longenecker, "The Melchizedek Argument of Hebrews," 276, or James Kurianal, *Jesus Our High Priest: Ps 110, 4 as the Substructure of Heb 5, 1-7, 28* (Frankfurt am Main: Peter Lang, 2000), 92.

87. See discussion in Cockerill, "The Melchizedek Christology in Heb. 7:1-28," 39-41. Attridge's judgment seems fair: "The author [of Hebrews] studiously avoids any direct claims about the mysterious figure of Psalm 110 and Genesis 14" ("The Psalms in Hebrews," 198-99).

priesthood prompts the author to reevaluate the earlier priesthood. What could it mean that God declared the Son to be priest according to a different order than the earlier one established in the law? The answer must be that the older priesthood was somehow inadequate, intended to give way to this new priesthood. Only by reading Gen. 14 in light of this conclusion can the author discern textual hints that Melchizedek was superior to Abraham and, derivatively, to the descendants of Levi. The silence on Melchizedek's genealogy and the problem that the Levitical priests die further reinforce the point in Ps. 110:4 that Christ's new priesthood is better because it is eternal.

In sum, Hebrews treats Ps. 110 as a literal reference to Christ, in some respects analogously to Augustine and Calvin. None of the figures we have considered takes seriously the possibility that this passage refers to an earthly king, and Augustine needs no allegory for his interpretation: the psalm refers directly to Jesus, not to some earthly king who signifies Jesus. But the epistle's most dramatic maneuver derives from a particular approach to the literal sense that identifies Old Testament locutions with particular moments in redemptive history. The Lord addressed in Ps. 110:1 is declared only three verses later to be priest in the order of Melchizedek. This pronouncement is a very recent event that seals the fate of the Levitical priesthood. Yet the epistle's conclusion does not undermine but again affirms the ongoing relevance of the biblical text, even as later declarations assume greater hermeneutical weight than earlier ones. For the identification of Ps. 110:4 with the very oath that established Christ's priesthood testifies to the epistle's conviction that God continues to speak in the words of the earlier prophets.

Psalm 8

Our final passage is Ps. 8, which Heb. 2:5-9 treats as an image of the humiliation and exaltation of Jesus. The English translation of Ps. 8 reads as follows:

> To the choirmaster: according to The Gittith. A Psalm of David.
> 1O LORD, our Lord, how majestic is thy name in all the earth! Thou whose glory above the heavens is chanted 2by the mouth of babes and infants, thou hast founded a bulwark because of thy foes, to still the enemy and the avenger. 3When I look at thy heavens, the work of thy

fingers, the moon and the stars which thou hast established; 4what is man that thou art mindful of him, and the son of man that thou dost care for him? 5Yet thou hast made him little less than God, and dost crown him with glory and honor. 6Thou hast given him dominion over the works of thy hands; thou hast put all things under his feet, 7all sheep and oxen, and also the beasts of the field, 8the birds of the air, and the fish of the sea, whatever passes along the paths of the sea. 9O LORD, our Lord, how majestic is thy name in all the earth!

Augustine

Augustine's exposition of Psalm 8 focuses on the division in humanity between the righteous and unrighteous, and the extension of this division into the church. Ps. 8:4 presents this division in the distinction between its two halves: "What is a mere man that you remember him, or a son of man that you visit him?"[88] Had the psalmist written "and" *(et)* instead of "or" *(aut),* "son of man" could have been identified with "man." But the two words are clearly meant to be distinguished, and it appears that every son of man is a man, but not the other way around. "Man" must refer to those who bear the image of the earthly man, while "sons of men" are those who bear the image of the heavenly man. "Man" and "son of man" are thus synonyms for "old man" and "new man," respectively: since a man becomes a new man through spiritual regeneration, it is appropriate to call this new man a "son of man." "Men" are far from God while "sons of men" are close, so God is said to "visit" the latter, but only to "remember" the former, as from a distance.

These anthropological considerations set up a Christological shift, on the grounds that Jesus is the paradigmatic son of man.

> The "son of man" is visited in the first instance *(primo)* in the person of the Lord-man himself, born of the virgin Mary. On account of his fleshly weakness, which the wisdom of God condescended to bear, and on account of the humility of his suffering, scripture rightly says of him, *You have made him a little lower than the angels.* But mention is made too of his glorification, in that he rose and ascended into heaven: *with glory*

---

88. *En. Ps.* 8.10. Boulding inexplicably leaves off the "or," so I have added it to the translation above. Italics mine. See Boulding, *Expositions of the Psalms 1–32,* 134.

and honor you have crowned him; and you have set him above the works of your hands, says the psalm.

As the Son was set a little below the angels during the incarnation, so also will he be exalted above them in his glorification, since angels, too, are the works of God's hands.

Augustine struggles with the next line in the psalm: "All sheep and cattle, and even beasts of the field, birds of the air, and fishes of the sea, who roam the pathways of the deep."[89] The psalmist seems to have set the angels aside to focus on animals, but animals are far lower in the order of being, so they must be treated figurally. Perhaps the sheep and the cattle are holy souls, both human and angelic, who yield fruit and make the earth fruitful by producing the fruit of innocence and drawing earthly humans to new life. But the other animals seem to represent something else, since "beasts of the field" are mentioned separately from sheep or oxen (though the latter also reside in fields), and "even" *(insuper)* before the second list of animals suggests a distinction between the beasts, birds, and fish, and those animals already named. Augustine reminds the reader of the preface to the psalm: "To the end for the presses, a psalm of David himself." These presses, Augustine had commented, can produce both grape skins and wine, just as a threshing floor contains both chaff and grain. They thus present an image of the church, which includes for the time being both good and evil people, until the judgment of God when they will finally be separated.

If the sheep and oxen represent holy people (and angels), then, the beasts, birds, and fish represent evil people who can nevertheless be found in the church. The beasts can be understood as those who indulge fleshly pleasures, since such a life involves no precipitous mountain climb, but only a field — like the broad road that leads to death, or the open place where Abel was killed. The birds are the proud, those who boast in their eloquence, wafted high by the wind. The fish are the unduly inquisitive who seek profundities in temporal things which disappear as quickly as the evanescent waves of the sea. These animals thus correspond to three

---

89. *En. Ps.* 8.12. "Oues et boues universas, insuper et pecora campi; uolucres caeli, et pisces maris, qui perambulant semitas maris." For consistency, I have modified the translation slightly here and throughout my description of Augustine's exposition. Boulding translates *pecora campi* in one place as "wild beasts," and at other points as "beasts of the field." She also translates *insuper* as both "even" and "what is more." Sometimes she includes the articles, sometimes not. These changes obscure the force of Augustine's remarks.

paradigmatic vices: the indulgence of the flesh, pride, and inquisitiveness, as described in 1 John 2:16.[90] They also match the temptations of Christ: to make the stones bread (lust of the flesh), to receive the kingdoms of the world (empty boasting), and to test the angels by throwing himself off the pinnacle of the temple (inquisitiveness).

As a whole, then, this psalm concerns the *corpus permixtum*. The distinction between "men" and "sons of men" is that between earthly people and heavenly people; Christ is the ultimate "son of man," who rules over the church; and the church consists of both good and evil individuals. Augustine acknowledges the possibility of interpreting individual words differently in other contexts, but judges for himself that he has provided the best reading for this particular psalm.[91]

Calvin

Calvin's treatment of Ps. 8 demonstrates considerably less allegorical imagination: this psalm is simply a tribute to God's power and splendor in the created order, and principally in humanity. The juxtaposition of Ps. 8:3, *"When I see thy heavens, the works of thy fingers; the moon and the stars which thou hast arranged,"* with the following verse, *"What is man, that thou art mindful of him? and the son of man, that thou visitest him?"* highlights God's condescension to our lowly species. Humanity is "miserable" and "vile," "but dust and clay," and those not astonished that God would take note of us are "more than ungrateful and stupid."[92] Unlike Augustine, Calvin sees no contrast between "man" and "son of man," or "remembering" and "visiting." God's being "mindful" of us signifies his fatherly love in defending, cherishing, and governing us. "Visiteth" means much the same, reflecting a tendency in the Psalms to communicate one thought in different words. Both terms remind us to marvel in God's continuous care for humanity.

---

90. On the importance of this verse for Augustine's delineation of sin, see *conf.* 10.30.41-10.39.64. James J. O'Donnell argues that 1 John 2:16 plays a structuring role in the earlier books of *conf.* as well; see his remarks in *Augustine: Confessions,* 3 vols. (Oxford: Clarendon, 1992), 1.xxxv-xxxvi.

91. *En. Ps.* 8.13.

92. *Comm. Ps.* 8.4-5. The *Calvini Opera* numbers the title of the Psalm as the first verse, creating a discrepancy with CTS. I follow the Latin numbering system, but the English references may be found by looking one section before what I list, e.g., *Comm. Ps.* 8.4-5 = CTS 8.3-4.

On the phrase, *"For thou hast made him little lower than God; and hast crowned him with glory and honour,"*[93] Calvin focuses his comments on humanity as image-bearers of God, created for immortality and blessedness, and exalted even to resemble celestial glory. Calvin notes a variant reading in the Septuagint, and especially in Hebrews, where one finds the word "angels" instead of "God," but favors the latter as more natural and better supported by Jewish interpreters. Concerning this textual discrepancy in Hebrews, Calvin says,

> We know what freedoms *(quam libere)* the apostles took in quoting texts of Scripture; not, indeed, to wrest them to a meaning different from the true one *(non quidem ut torquerent in alienum sensum)*, but because they reckoned it sufficient to show, by a reference to Scripture, that what they taught was sanctioned *(sancitum)* by the word of God, although they did not quote precise words. Accordingly, they never had any hesitation in changing the words, provided the substance of the text *(summa rei)* remained unchanged.[94]

A trickier problem concerns the propriety of applying this passage to the humiliation *(exinanitio)* of Christ, as Hebrews does, when the psalm speaks instead of humanity's excellence *(praestantia)*.[95] Calvin sets forth two issues of difficulty: first, the general legitimacy of applying to Christ what is said about humanity; and second, the epistle's particular use of this passage with regard to the death and resurrection of Christ. On the former issue, Calvin first acknowledges the basic propriety of referring predications made of the body's members (individuals in the church) also to the head (Christ),[96] but then suggests a more textured explanation. David's remarks about humanity must refer to the prelapsarian condition, since we certainly do not experience the liberty David describes. Christ, the image of God in the fullest sense, restores this image within us. "But as the heavenly Father hath bestowed upon his Son an immeasurable fulness of all blessings, that all of us may draw from this fountain, it follows that whatever God bestows upon us by him belongs of right to him in the highest degree; yea, he himself is the living image of God, according to

---

93. *Comm. Ps.* 8.6.
94. Ibid.
95. Ibid.
96. Ibid.

which we must be renewed, upon which depends our participation of the invaluable blessings which are here spoken of."[97]

The second issue reveals that Hebrews is treating the psalm by way of illustration rather than explanation.

> What the apostle therefore says in that passage concerning the abasement of Christ for a short time, is not intended by him as an explanation *(non est exegeticum)* of this text; but for the purpose of enriching and illustrating the subject on which he is discoursing, he introduces and accommodates to it what had been spoken in a different sense (κατ' ἐπεξεργασίαν *ad suum institutum deflectit quod alio sensu dictum fuerat*). The same apostle did not hesitate, in Rom. x. 6, in the same manner to enrich and to employ *(per amplificationem ornare)*, in a sense different from their original one, the words of Moses in Deut. xxx. 12: "Who shall go up for us to heaven and bring it to us, that we may hear it and do it?" &c. The apostle, therefore, in quoting this psalm, had not so much an eye to what David meant; but making an allusion to those words, *Thou hast made him a little lower;* and again, *Thou hast crowned him with honour,* he applies this diminution to the death of Christ, and the glory and honour to his resurrection. A similar account may be given of Paul's declaration in Eph. iv. 8, in which he does not so much explain *(non tam interpretatur)* the meaning of the text, (Ps. lxviii. 18,) as he devoutly applies it, by way of accommodation, to the person of Christ *(quam pia deflexione ad Christi personam accommodat)*.[98]

In short, the use of Ps. 8 in Hebrews transgresses the boundaries of the literal sense and cannot be legitimated through the connection between humanity and Christ, or between body and head. Calvin must therefore appeal to a different mode of reading the Old Testament: illustration, not explanation.

Calvin's remaining remarks on the psalm reflect a similar pattern. God has set humanity over all creation, but our rule over creation has not yet been brought to fruition. It remains for Christ, the lawful heir of creation, to take complete possession of this dominion after which point we too will rule the world.[99] The sheep, oxen, beasts, birds, and fish are examples of

---

97. Ibid.
98. Ibid. Calvin presumes here that Paul is the author of Hebrews.
99. Ibid., 8.7.

our rule that also direct our minds toward heavenly reward, though again, this idea must be qualified by the fall. We have degenerated far from our prelapsarian condition, and it is only through God's grace to the church that we may receive some fragments of what Adam enjoyed.[100]

The Hebrews commentary advances similar points. On the general application of the psalm to Christ, Calvin appeals to the same argument as above: humanity has largely lost its dominion over the world, but we may regain our original blessing by turning to Christ. And the most vexing issue concerns βραχύ τι ("a little"), which originally concerned humanity's status below God but now refers to the brief period of Christ's humiliation. As in the Psalms commentary, Calvin explains:

> It was not the Apostle's design to give an exact explanation of the words *(genuinam verborum expositionem)*. For there is nothing improperly done, when verbal allusions are made to embellish a subject at hand *(si allusiones in verbis quaerat ad ornandam praesentem causam)*, as Paul does in quoting Rom. x. 6, from Moses, "Who shall ascend into heaven," &c., he does not join the words "heaven and hell" for the purpose of explanation *(non interpretationem)*, but as ornaments *(sed exornationem)*. The meaning of David is this, — "O Lord, thou hast raised man to such a dignity, that it differs but little from divine or angelic honour; for he is set a ruler over the whole world." This meaning the Apostle did not intend to overthrow, nor to turn to something else; but he only bids us to consider the abasement of Christ, which appeared for a short time, and then the glory with which he is perpetually crowned; and this he does more by alluding to expressions *(alludens magis ad verba)* than by explaining what David understood *(quam exprimens quid intellexerit David)*.[101]

In familiar fashion, then, Calvin demonstrates a willingness to apply the Old Testament to Christ, yet only as an extension of the literal sense. There is in Calvin's interpretation a kind of circular movement: the "man" God remembers is all of humanity; but in a greater sense Christ, the paradigmatic representative of humanity; and in yet another sense the church, which just is humanity as it participates in Christ. Calvin's hesitance with the epistle's appropriation of the psalm concerns not the shift from hu-

---

100. Ibid., 8.8-10.
101. *Comm. Heb.* 2.7.

manity to Christ, but the particular application of David's words to the death and resurrection of Christ. On that point, the author of Hebrews is not explaining the psalm at all.

The Epistle to the Hebrews

The treatment of Ps. 8 in Hebrews differs in obvious ways from the expositions of the text by both Augustine and Calvin, but all three share a significant point of contact: the perception that what is affirmed about humanity can also be affirmed about Christ. In context, the epistle's exposition serves to explain why "it was not to angels that God subjected the world to come" (2:5). The author introduces the psalm with a rather ambiguous introductory formula, "It has been testified somewhere" (2:6a), and then quotes the text in 2:6b-8, following his Greek source text closely. The line, "You have set him over the works of your hands" (Ps. 8:6a), is omitted, perhaps to facilitate the application of this passage to Christ.[102] Then in 2:9, the author explicitly makes this connection: "But we see Jesus, who for a little while was made lower than the angels, crowned with glory and honor because of the suffering of death, so that by the grace of God he might taste death for every one." Scholarly debate over the epistle's appropriation of Ps. 8 concerns where the author begins to treat the psalm Christologically, and whether the phrase "son of man (υἱὸς ἀνθρώπου)" should be taken as a Christological title. According to the anthropological reading, the psalm is cited primarily with regard to humanity, and only applied to Christ in 2:9; according to the Christological reading, the author has Jesus in view during the citation of the psalm, and not just from 2:9.[103]

---

102. Attridge, *Hebrews*, 71.
103. For a recent defense of the anthropological view, see Craig L. Blomberg, "'But We See Jesus': The Relationship between the Son of Man in Hebrews 2.6 and 2.9 and the Implications for English Translations," in Bauckham, *A Cloud of Witnesses*, 88-99. For a recent defense of the Christological view, see George H. Guthrie and Russell D. Quinn, "A Discourse Analysis of the Use of Psalm 8:4-6 in Hebrews 2:5-9," *JETS* 49 (2006): 235-46. For other treatments of Ps. 2:5-9, see Brevard S. Childs, "Psalm 8 in the Context of the Christian Canon," *Int* 23 (1969): 20-31, also found in his *Biblical Theology in Crisis* (Philadelphia: Westminster, 1970), 151-63; Geoffrey W. Grogan, "Christ and His People: An Exegetical and Theological Study of Hebrews 2:5-18," *VE* 6 (1969): 54-71; Robert L. Brawley, "Discoursive Structure and the Unseen in Hebrews 2:8 and 11:1: A Neglected Aspect of the Context," *CBQ* 55 (1983): 81-98; S. P. Brock, "Hebrews 2:9b in Syriac Tradition," *NovT* 27 (1983): 236-44; Thomas G. Smothers, "A Superior Model: Hebrews 1:1–4:13," *RevExp* 82 (1985): 333-43; L. D.

In its original setting, the psalm expresses wonder at the care and privilege God has bestowed upon humanity: lower than the angels,[104] higher than the beasts, crowned with honor and glory. As we have seen in Calvin, the innovation in Hebrews is to turn this passage into a statement about Jesus, one concerned less with the unchanging ontological status of humanity than with the sequence of events of Jesus's incarnation and exaltation. This move depends upon an ambiguity in the Greek citation of Ps. 8:5. Heb. 2:7 reads: "Thou didst make him for a little while (βραχύ τι) lower than the angels." While the phrase βραχύ τι could suggest a small measure of distance or substance — as the psalmist probably intended with these words — Hebrews chooses instead to treat the term temporally: the son of man was not "a little bit lower than the angels," but "for a little while lower than the angels."

This Christological move depends upon the continuity of argument between Heb. 1 and 2. In the previous chapter, I discussed Moffitt's recent assessment that "the world (οἰκουμένη) to come" in 2:5 refers to the same οἰκουμένη mentioned in 1:6, the heavenly realm Christ entered in accordance with his establishment as high priest. Here I note the connection between Ps. 8 and Ps. 110:1. The latter verse is quoted in Heb. 1:13 as the concluding citation of the catena in 1:5-13, which treats the psalm as evidence for the Son's superiority over the angels: "But to what angel has he ever said, 'Sit at my right hand, till I make thy enemies a stool for thy feet'?" (1:13). Ps. 8 is regularly associated in the New Testament with Ps. 110:1 (1 Cor. 15:25-27; Eph. 1:20-22), since Ps. 110:1 speaks of enemies being made a footstool, while Ps. 8:6 promises that "all things will be put under his feet."[105] In Heb. 2, the author draws upon this point of contact as well as Ps. 8's reference to angels to advance the argument of the first chapter: the way the Son was exalted over the angels (Ps. 110) was by first becoming lower than them (Ps. 8). Since the author takes Ps. 110:1 as evidence for the superiority of the Son over the angels, Ps. 8 naturally commends itself in complementary fashion.

Hurst, "The Christology of Hebrews 1 and 2," in *The Glory of Christ in the New Testament: Studies in Christology in Memory of George Bradford Caird*, ed. L. D. Hurst and N. T. Wright (Oxford: Clarendon, 1987), 151-64; Lanier Burns, "Hermeneutical Issues and Principles in Hebrews as Exemplified in the Second Chapter," *JETS* 39 (1996): 587-607; Randall C. Gleason, "Angels and the Eschatology of Heb 1-2," *NTS* 49 (2003): 90-107.

104. The Greek text resolves an ambiguity in the Hebrew, by rendering as "angels" what could also be translated "gods" or "God." Guthrie and Quinn, "A Discourse Analysis of the Use of Psalm 8:4-6 in Hebrews 2:5-9," 236.

105. Ibid., 237-39. William L. Lane, *Hebrews 1-8*, WBC 47a (Dallas: Word, 1991), 46-47.

Hurst argues in line with Caird's earlier suggestion that the use of Ps. 8 controls the material of 1:3-13.[106] Against the tendency to read Heb. 1 with regard to a heavenly being who became a man, Hurst suggests that the emphasis of this chapter lies in the opposite direction: how a man was elevated over the angels. In other words, the author's primary concern is not the divinity, but the humanity of Jesus. Most of the texts cited in this chapter are royal psalms that stress the qualities of an ideal king who acts as a representative of the people. This is especially obvious in the citations of Ps. 2:7 and 2 Sam. 7:14 in Heb. 1:5, and in the citation of Ps. 45:6-7 in Heb. 1:8-9. Yet even the citation of Ps. 102:25-27 in Heb. 1:10-12, which sounds as if it must refer to God ("Thou, Lord, didst found the earth in the beginning, and the heavens are the work of thy hands . . ."), might be understood as a reference to an earthly king who possesses divine, creative wisdom.[107] In light of these observations, Hurst concludes, "The emphasis of chapter one is the same as that of chapter two: it concerns a figure who, *qua* man, is exalted above the angels and leads those whom he represents, as their ideal king, to an appointed destiny."[108] "The author's *main* interest was not in a uniquely privileged, divine being who becomes man; it is in a human figure who attains to an exalted status."[109]

This reading of Heb. 1 legitimates the application of Ps. 8 to Jesus's identity as a representative of humanity. "The reversal of conditions in the future age will result in the supremacy over these angels by redeemed humanity rather than exclusively by a single individual."[110] The verses following the epistle's citation of Ps. 8 confirm this point. Jesus tasted death "for every one" (2:9), "bringing many sons to glory" as "the pioneer" of humanity's salvation (2:10). Because "he who sanctifies and those who are sanctified have all one origin," Jesus is "not ashamed to call them brethren" (2:11). Jesus partook "in flesh and blood" (2:14); he is concerned "not with angels but with the descendants of Abraham" (2:16); and he was "made like his brethren in every respect" (2:17). To use the terms of contemporary scholarly debate, the Christological and anthropological dimensions are mutually implicative at the deepest level. The author of Hebrews treats

---

106. Hurst, "The Christology of Hebrews 1–2."

107. Hurst appeals especially to Wisdom 7–9 for this point. See discussion in ibid., 160-62.

108. Ibid., 157.

109. Ibid., 163.

110. Ibid., 154. For a similar view, see David M. Moffitt, *Atonement and the Logic of Resurrection in the Epistle to the Hebrews* (Brill: Leiden, 2011), 45-144.

Ps. 8 both as an image of the exaltation of Christ and as a promise for the rest of humanity. Those who remain faithful will also rule over angels in the world to come, but one representative has already entered this realm as our pioneer.

The argument of Heb. 2:8b-9 focuses on the final phrase of Ps. 8 quoted in 2:6-8a, "putting everything in subjection under his feet," which the author cannot apply to humanity: "Now in putting everything in subjection to him, he left nothing outside his control. As it is, we do not yet see everything in subjection to him" (2:8b). The person in view must therefore be Jesus, first named in 2:9, "who for a little while was made lower than the angels, crowned with glory and honor because of the suffering of death, so that by the grace of God he might taste death for every one." Lane describes the logic like this: "The author found in the quotation [of Ps. 8] a prophecy that will eventually be fulfilled. He regards Ps 8:7b as a legal decree, the realization of which is yet deferred. The recognition of the present unfilled state of affairs prepares him to see that the promised subjection has reference not to humankind in general (v. 8) but to Jesus (v. 9), whom God has appointed 'heir of everything' (1:2)."[111] There is thus in Heb. 2 a rich and lively interchange between humanity and Jesus: the psalm originally refers to humanity, but the psalmist's vision has not yet been actualized; instead, we see Jesus crowned with glory and honor, embodying this psalm as one exalted individual; yet by virtue of Christ's participation in and representation of humanity, we, too, will receive such glory; then the psalm will reach its fullest consummation. On this matter, Caird's early judgment seems right: Heb. 2 advances the author's purpose from the opening catena of 1:5-14 "to illustrate the theme of the psalm that man has been destined by God to a glory excelling that of the angels and that this destiny has been achieved by Christ, both individually and representatively, as the pioneer of man's salvation who came to lead many sons into their desired glory."[112]

On this reading, Hebrews does attend to the literal sense, but adds a Christological twist that ventures further from the psalmist's original meaning than the other passages we have considered thus far. The move to treat βραχύ τι temporally rather than substantivally alters the contours of the psalm to such an extent that the psalm's locutions refer to the se-

---

111. Lane, *Hebrews 1-8*, 47-48.
112. George B. Caird, "The Exegetical Method of the Epistle to the Hebrews," *CJT* 5 (1959): 49.

quence of events involving the humiliation and exaltation of Christ rather than to humanity's ontological status in the created order. Nevertheless, this radical transformation is theologically congruent with the psalm's own trajectory. If the psalmist's vision of humanity describes not our present reality but our eschatological hope — which it must, given our postlapsarian condition — then the original sense invites the reader to consider how we might attain that end. Hebrews insists such glory awaits us through the man Jesus, whose participation in humanity allowed him to act as our representative and pioneer into the heavenly realms. This appropriation of the psalm remains miles away from Augustine's allegorical treatment of the beasts, birds, and fish, or even the distinction between men and sons of men. But it does resemble Calvin's account of the movement from humanity to Christ to church, even if Hebrews does at points favor "illustration" over "explanation." Most foundationally, the epistle shares with both Augustine and Calvin the conviction that Christ is the ultimate representative of humanity who directs us to our final end.

Conclusion

This chapter began with a typological distinction between Augustine's two levels of meaning and Calvin's Christologically expansive literal sense. In Hebrews, we have witnessed a third approach that identifies earlier instances of divine speech with God's present address to contemporary hearers by focusing and transforming Old Testament locutions according to the new theological situation. "Today" refers to the eschatological finality of these "last days" (Ps. 95). The announcement of Christ's priesthood (Ps. 110) occurs just after his entrance into our "rest" (Ps. 95 again). And Ps. 8 makes fullest sense as a picture of the humiliation and exaltation of Christ, the twofold event that enacted God's new covenant with his people (Jer. 31). This approach does not discredit the literal sense but displays its true meaning. Only within the Christological framework Hebrews develops do these locutions declare God's present word to his people. Yet even within this new context, the literal meaning is largely preserved: there *does* remain a rest; Christ *is* a priest in the order of Melchizedek; humanity *will* be exalted over the angels.

The appropriation of the Old Testament in Hebrews generates a dynamic immediacy that neither Augustine nor Calvin fully displays. Augustine's appeal to multiple senses creates a division between straightforward readings of the text and a wide field for interpretive play whose alternate level of meaning is so discontinuous with the original sense that the text no longer bears straightforwardly on its hearers. A similar phenomenon arises with Calvin, whose reading of the Old Testament derives from a relatively static understanding of redemptive history wherein covenant, church, and Christ function almost as constants to which Scripture can be universally applied. In Hebrews, the literal sense speaks straight to the current situation. The call to enter God's rest comes *now*, not at any given moment in redemptive history, but at the very recitation of God's Word, with increased intensity and richer theological valence in this final, climactic dispensation. So too, Ps. 110 is not some general principle for understanding the Son, but an actual declaration that occurred in time, long after the writing of the psalm, at a specific juncture in history after Jesus's ascension into the heavenlies. Such readings were not available during the Old Testament period; only in these last days has the Word of living address revealed the divine intent.

Taken together, these psalms weave an image of the Old Testament as a time characterized by unfulfilled promises, generating anticipation of something better but as yet mysterious. Some rest remains "long after" the Israelites have entered Canaan; a new priesthood is declared while the Levitical priesthood is still in place; and the proclamation of a new covenant implicitly declares the old one "old." The rest of the epistle shares this perspective: the heroes of faith long for reward, yet never receive what was promised; the repetition of animal sacrifice prefigures some better offering; the priests' mortality and guilt allude to some eternal, sinless mediator; the earthly tabernacle is designed after a heavenly tabernacle that demands a heavenly priest. All this hope and longing finally resolve in Jesus, who establishes a new priesthood, forges into the promised land, and makes possible the glorification of humanity as its first representative in the heavenlies. This transformation means some things must be left behind: there is no more animal sacrifice, the earthly sanctuary is past its time, and Canaan is no longer the promised rest. Yet Christ's fulfillment of the Old Testament does not extinguish but extends God's engagement with his people, and the same applies for God's speech through the prophets: there remains a living Word today. The implications of this claim will be considered theologically in the following two chapters.

CHAPTER 5

Hearing the Living Word: Scripture and the Divine Address

Introduction

This chapter marks a transition from the historical and exegetical to the constructive theological. In the previous two chapters, I argued that the chief interpretive strategy in Hebrews is to present Old Testament locutions as God's direct address to the covenant people in the redemptive-historical present. I now explore the possibility of generalizing this pattern for a doctrine of Scripture, and the way such a model might address a series of longstanding questions: the necessity and limitations of interpretive freedom, the legitimacy of multiple senses of Scripture, the place of historical criticism in the theological reading of Scripture, and the mode of God's self-revelation after the apostolic age. This chapter provides a theological sketch of Scriptural authority according to the notion of divine address. The next considers the implications of such an account for the relation between Scripture and tradition.

I begin by considering the dynamics of fixity and flexibility in divine self-revelation, and then suggest two boundaries for interpretive freedom: the fidelity of God's promises to Israel, and the necessity of reading Scripture in light of Christ. This discussion leads to a treatment of "figural" reading as well as an exploration of the concrete particularity of the divine address. A final section considers the divine address in relation to authorial intent and the historical method, which I argue play an important but qualified role in receiving God's self-revelation in Scripture.

TODAY WHEN YOU HEAR HIS VOICE

Scripture as Divine Address

When one examines how the author of Hebrews appropriates the Old Testament, three salient features of how he construes Scriptural authority according to the divine address emerge. First, the address is direct and immediate, i.e., without mediation. The author of Hebrews does not engage in the two-step process of discerning original meaning (identified with human authorial intent) and then applying the text to the contemporary situation. There is no operative distinction between what the text "meant" and what it "means," to borrow Stendahl's language;[1] there is only what God says now. Second, the address is dynamic. Despite the author's conflation of the original communication ("as the prophet said long ago . . .") and the contemporary reprisal ("so God says now . . ."), we can at least theoretically differentiate how an Old Testament reader might have received various locutions from the meanings they assume in the new context. If "today" adopts fresh valence in these "last days," the significance of the psalmist's words could not have been exhausted in the original moment. New meanings are possible for new contexts, within certain semantic and theological boundaries. Third, the determinative context for discerning divine intent is the contemporary and not the original setting. The viability of the epistle's hermeneutical decisions depends on the legitimacy of its theological claims, e.g., whether these are the last days, whether Christ was established as high priest. If the present situation has indeed effected the theological revolution Hebrews claims, the meaning of the original locutions must concomitantly be transformed.

In recent years, John Webster has advanced a dogmatic account of Scripture very much compatible with the dynamics observed in Hebrews.[2] Webster locates Scripture against the activity of the triune God in the economy of salvation. This activity begins with revelation, which Webster defines as *"the self-presentation of the triune God, the free work of sovereign mercy in which God wills, establishes and perfects saving fellowship with himself in which humankind comes to know, love and fear him above all things."*[3]

---

1. Krister Stendahl, "Biblical Theology, Contemporary," in *The Interpreter's Dictionary of the Bible: An Illustrated Encyclopedia,* ed. George Buttrick, vol. 1 (Nashville: Abingdon, 1962), 418-32.

2. John Webster, *Word and Church: Essays in Christian Dogmatics* (Edinburgh: T&T Clark, 2001); and idem, *Holy Scripture: A Dogmatic Sketch,* Current Issues in Theology (Cambridge: Cambridge University Press, 2003).

3. Webster, *Holy Scripture,* 13. Unless otherwise specified, all italics his.

Webster's definition advances three claims. First, God is both the content and agent of revelation: God presents *himself,* and *God* presents himself. Revelation derives from God's triune activity in creation, whereby the Father originates the divine self-presence actualized by the Son, and perfected and made effective by the Spirit. Second, revelation reflects God's free, sovereign mercy — spontaneous, uncaused, unexpected, and undeserved. Since God makes himself present on his own terms, revelation is not completely accessible for our own classification and use. Third, revelation has the soteriological purpose of establishing fellowship between God and us. Because this fellowship embraces the relational dimension as well as the cognitive, revelation should not be construed primarily as a means of addressing epistemological questions or the sources and norms of Christian discourse. Rather, "the proper doctrinal location for talk of revelation is the Christian doctrine of the Trinity, and, in particular, the outgoing, communicative mercy of the triune God in the economy of salvation. Revelation is the corollary of trinitarian theology and soteriology."[4]

For our purposes, the central point for emphasis is that this revelation continues in the contemporary context. God has not simply presented himself once, e.g., in the inspiration or canonization of Scripture, only to fall silent for the remainder of redemptive history. God continues to work for the salvation of his people, and this soteriological activity preeminently involves God's revelation of himself in Scripture. The question, then, is how to affirm the freedom of God in the divine address while also acknowledging the fixity of Scripture as the privileged means of this communication. What is the relation between ongoing revelation and the written, sealed Word? Webster's provocative suggestion involves the concept of sanctification, a term traditionally associated with soteriology, but one he appropriates for the doctrine of Scripture. Webster defines sanctification as "the act of God the Holy Spirit in hallowing creaturely processes, employing them in the service of the taking form of revelation within the history of the creation."[5] On his account, Scripture is the creaturely context in which God reveals himself, while sanctification names the non-competitive means by which God appropriates the text for himself. This dynamic bypasses the traditional dilemma between historical naturalism and its photographic negative, the denial of creaturely contribution to the Bible, such that texts with an obviously human, "natural" history can effect divine action in the economy of salvation.

4. Ibid., 16-17.
5. Ibid., 17-18.

Webster's proposal can be distinguished from other efforts to articulate the relation in Scripture between the human and divine. One might, for instance, liken Scripture to the hypostatic union: the Bible is both human and divine, just like Jesus. For Webster, this position threatens the uniqueness of the incarnation by characterizing all God's activity in the world as a union between the human and the divine. By divinizing the Bible, the model also obscures the instrumental character of Scripture's relation to God. A second account might appeal to testimony: as prophetic or apostolic witness, the biblical texts refer to God but are not themselves divine. But this (Barthian) view falters because it presents "little intrinsic relation between the texts and the revelation to which they witness. In this way, the annexation of the Bible to revelation can appear almost arbitrary: the text is considered a complete and purely natural entity taken up into the self-communication of God. The result is a curious textual equivalent of adoptionism."[6] Sanctification, by contrast, understands Scripture as divine communication through creaturely elements. Scripture is not therefore "natural"; the biblical texts are privileged fields of the Spirit's revelatory activity within the realm of all human activity. Still, "it is *as* — not *despite* — the creaturely realities that they are that they serve God."[7]

This position commends a qualified distinction between Scripture and revelation. Exegesis does not fully circumscribe God's communicative activity in the world, yet Scripture is not accidental to God's purposes either. Scripture is the uniquely authoritative, divinely chosen means of God's self-revelation, demarcating but also submitting to God's freedom in the economy of salvation. The fixity of the text's verbal form secures stability and consistency in divine authority. It is the selfsame God, without change or alteration, who presents himself as the content of revelation by means of those particular texts set apart for this purpose. Yet God's priority over Scripture in revelation also funds the possibility of his ongoing self-disclosure throughout redemptive history. God can take up canonical texts in new and fresh ways as he continues to guide, challenge, and edify the church in her progressive growth.

Kevin Vanhoozer's *The Drama of Doctrine* develops this perspective by appeal to speech-act theory and a theatrical metaphor.[8] For Vanhoozer,

---

6. Ibid., 24.
7. Ibid., 28.
8. Kevin J. Vanhoozer, *The Drama of Doctrine: A Canonical-Linguistic Approach to Christian Theology* (Louisville: Westminster John Knox, 2005).

God's self-revelation in Scripture consists of a series of verbal, communicative acts that present God's voice to the covenant people and prescribe the proper response. "Behind all the particular things God says and does in Scripture lies one overarching purpose: to communicate the terms, and the reality, of the new covenant. Scripture summons the church to be God's covenant partner; Scripture communicates a share in the triune life."[9] Speech-acts consist of three elements: locutions (what is said), illocutions (what the locutions do), and perlocutions (what the locutions effect). Different locutions perform a variety of illocutions: questions, commands, assertions, complaints, and requests. Illocutions may or may not produce desired perlocutionary effects: a command could be rejected, a request denied, and so forth. Scriptural speech-acts bear a particularly Trinitarian shape, as the Father initiates communication of which the Son is the content and the Spirit the efficacy.[10] Two implications follow. First, the doctrine of inspiration encompasses the entire speech-act, from locutions and illocutions through perlocutionary effects. There is thus an unbreakable relation between Spirit and text: "When the Spirit speaks in Scripture today he is not speaking *another* word but ministering the written words: '[The Spirit] will not speak on his own, but will speak whatever he hears' (John 16:13). The Spirit is active not in producing new illocutions but rather in *ministering* the illocutions that are already in the text, making them efficacious."[11] Second, Scripture is an extension of the Trinitarian missions. If the Son is the embodied expression of triune communicative action, Scripture is the verbalized expression of the same as it continues to recount and enact God's work in the world.

The hermeneutical upshot is a model of Scriptural authority that can encompass continuity without rigidity, stability of identity alongside development and growth. Vanhoozer invokes the practice of improvisation as an example for biblical interpretation. Though improvisation involves spontaneity, it also depends on prior training and discipline. Improvisers do not seek complete originality, for this would rupture the organic connection between the new elaboration and the original script. Readiness for the new derives from deep internalization of the old. The improviser's most important skill is reincorporation, which involves *"remembering and capitulating past elements in the narrative in order to make of the scene a whole*

---

9. Ibid., 67.
10. Ibid., 65.
11. Ibid., 67. Unless otherwise specified, all italics his.

and unified action."¹² On Vanhoozer's application, ecclesial fidelity consists of a similar kind of continuity: "*ipse*-identity," not "*idem*-identity."¹³ The church participates in a drama of redemption, and she is called throughout this journey to discover and exploit Scripture's "meaning potential."¹⁴ Authority resides in canon, not community, but this does not preclude the possibility of drawing from the text meanings that previously lay hidden. Much to our purposes, Vanhoozer perceives this dynamic most clearly in the relation between the testaments:

> The greatest divine improvisation is, of course, the incarnation, when the word of the Lord comes in a way that is different yet at the same time continuous with previous words. Indeed, one might say that the whole New Testament is an improvisation upon the Old. For, *what makes the whole Bible a unified canon is the unified action at its heart, and what gives the unified action closure is the recapitulation of all that has gone before in Christ.* All the significant persons and events in the earlier scenes — creation, exodus, temptation, prophets, priests, kings, sacrifice, sin offerings, miracles, wisdom — are reincorporated into the word-act that is the gospel of Jesus Christ.¹⁵

Recent treatments of the theology of Scripture evident in Hebrews confirm the correspondence between Vanhoozer's proposals and the epistle's actual interpretive practices.¹⁶ According to Ken Schenck, Hebrews operates with a kind of λόγος theology whereby written texts are understood not as identical with God's word but only as particular instantiations of it. It is first and foremost God who speaks — though this address also proceeds through various media, e.g., the law (2:2), the prophets (1:1), and especially the Son (1:2, 2:3). The meaning of God's address arises through the interplay between original meaning and contemporary eschatological context. "It is because of the eschatological context of the salvation

---

12. Ibid., 340.
13. Ibid., 127-28, drawing upon Paul Ricoeur, *Oneself as Another,* trans. Kathleen Blamey (Chicago: University of Chicago Press, 1992), 116.
14. Vanhoozer, *The Drama of Doctrine,* 352, drawing upon the work of Mikhail Bakhtin.
15. Ibid., 340-41.
16. Ken Schenck, "God Has Spoken: Hebrews' Theology of the Scriptures," and Daniel J. Treier, "Speech Acts, Hearing Hearts, and Other Senses: The Doctrine of Scripture Practiced in Hebrews," in *The Epistle to the Hebrews and Christian Theology,* ed. Richard Bauckham et al. (Grand Rapids: Eerdmans, 2009), 321-36 and 337-50, respectively.

story and because the audience is understood to be the most important 'addressee' of the scriptural texts, that the Scriptures come to take on the meanings that they do."[17] Daniel Treier highlights the utility of speech-act theory for elucidating this dynamic. The meaning of speech-acts cannot be determined by semantic considerations alone; various contextual factors, sometimes unstated, can extend and reconfigure textual meaning within the linguistic boundaries of a given locution. In particular, recontextualization generates new performances of the original communicative act according to various functions latent in the text's semantic possibilities. Thus, Hebrews can appropriate David's assertion, "They shall never enter my rest," as both a promise and a warning in the present situation. What once functioned as a declaration of judgment has now become a sign of God's patience with the epistle's audience, though the consequences of disobedience are even more frightful than before. For Treier, this is not to suggest complete "hermeneutical promiscuity,"[18] but to acknowledge the reality that fixed locutions can speak afresh in new contexts. The integrity of the biblical speech-act remains. "However, a dynamic dimension is also present whereby, with movement in redemptive history, texts can enact new divine speech-acts by extension.... The biblical text's theology has spiritual-ethical motion."[19]

The results of the previous chapter suggest two additional points. First, the impetus for such hermeneutical innovation derives from the biblical text itself. Each of the blessings now enacted in Christ received shadowy reference in messages spoken long before. But these images did not make sense in the original context, which is precisely why Hebrews perceives them to signal fresh readings in light of Christ. Scriptural locutions thus invite their own reappropriation; they are not just passive objects of some alien theological frame. Second, the effect of the epistle's interpretive practices is not to multiply but to specify meaning. While new significations cannot simplistically be identified with the original sense, they do not invite interpretive plurality either. In the cases we have considered, it is actually the determination of propositional content embedded in the original locutions that enables them to adopt new force. "Today" means these "last days," "rest" means our eternal inheritance, and the new priest is, in fact, Jesus. Such precision animates the immediacy of the divine address, as

---

17. Schenck, "God Has Spoken," 336.
18. Treier, "Speech Acts, Hearing Hearts, and Other Senses," 341.
19. Ibid., 349-50.

readers encounter very God — and not just some record of how he spoke before. Divine speech thus operates through original locutions, analogous illocutionary intent, and situational particularity.

The Divine Address and Redemptive History

If there is a certain openness in God's self-revelation, questions immediately arise about the limits of that openness. Such limits, of course, must be understood as self-limitations: God's freedom to reveal himself in redemptive history is constrained only by God's fidelity to his own character and promises. These limitations may nevertheless be determinate and discernible, serving as boundaries for how humans may receive the divine address. In this section and the next, I argue that the dynamic between continuity and discontinuity in revelation must be indexed to two central facts of redemptive history: the radical newness of the Christ event, and the fidelity of God's promises to Israel. This section will defend the theological construal of redemptive history in Hebrews. The next will consider the implications of this construal for the interpretation of Scripture.

In his magisterial *Medieval Exegesis,* Henri de Lubac explicitly acknowledges the theological interconnections between the spiritual reading of Scripture, a particular construal of the covenants, and the ongoing relation between Israel and the church.[20] Given the importance of this work, it is worth considering his delineation of these dynamics in some detail. De Lubac's position on the unity of the testaments resembles what we have witnessed in Augustine: the spirit is not separate from the letter, but hidden within it; the letter is good in that it leads to the spirit, but is ultimately an instrument and servant to greater realities. De Lubac acknowledges what we have noted in previous chapters, namely, that this is an odd kind of unity. Yes, the Old Testament announced the incarnation as "an outline, a rough sketch, a 'first draft,' as it were," of the things to come.[21] But this new moment also catalyzed a rupture — an abrupt, decisive transition when Truth replaced shadow, and the kingdom

---

20. Henri de Lubac, *Exégèse médiévale: Les quatre sens de l'écriture,* 4 vols. (Paris: Aubier, 1959-64). English translation: *Medieval Exegesis: The Four Senses of Scripture,* Retrieval and Renewal: Ressourcement in Catholic Thought (Grand Rapids: Eerdmans): vol. 1, trans. Mark Sebanc, 1998; vols. 2-3, trans. E. M. Macierowski, 2000 and 2009, respectively.

21. De Lubac, *Medieval Exegesis,* 1.235.

of God surpassed the law and the prophets. "The first Testament found itself surpassed, obsolete, outdated — 'antiquated' in all the parts of its writings that were not in conformity to the new.... Henceforth this Old Testament no longer exists for the believer except in its relation to the New Testament, which is to say that henceforth it has to be understood in its entirety 'according to the spirit.'"[22]

This assertion is foundational for de Lubac's account of the Scriptural senses. According to de Lubac, the four senses are ultimately two: the literal and the spiritual, with the latter encompassing the allegorical, tropological, and anagogical senses. The first sense, sometimes called *historia,* concerns the record of events that transpired in time and does not appeal to mystical or hidden signification. This sacred history constitutes the foundation of all interpretation. The second sense enacts a kind of conversion of the literal.[23] Since the allegorical meaning is Christ (and/or the church), this spiritual sense is essentially historical and not a matter of atemporal, philosophical speculation. Yet the object of allegorical reference ultimately transcends history, generating what de Lubac calls an "infinite qualitative difference" between the testaments.[24] Thus, allegory is not a new literal sense, but genuinely spiritual. While typology seeks historical correspondences between events,[25] allegory leads to the historical reality of Christ, who is no mere historical personage. "Everything culminates in one great Fact, which, in its unique singularity, has multiple repercussions; which dominates history and which is the bearer of all light as well as of all spiritual fecundity: *the Fact of Christ.*"[26]

The implications for Israel follow naturally. Failure to recognize the qualitative difference between the testaments "would not be to promote 'the Synagogue' to the level of the Church; it would rather be to change the Church once again into a synagogue. By merely affirming the succession and not the difference of the times one would suppress the difference at the heart of the legitimate heritage of the 'Christian people' regarding the 'Jewish people.'"[27] Indeed, de Lubac says, the distinction between the testaments almost inexorably produces conflict between Israel and the church.

22. Ibid., 1.228.
23. Ibid., 2.83-84.
24. Ibid., 2.98.
25. Ibid., 1.259.
26. Ibid., 2.101.
27. Ibid., 2.99.

Under the opposition of the letter and the spirit, or of the shadow and the truth, in its varied and sometimes, for us, paradoxical expressions, there is therefore always the opposition of two peoples, of two ages, of two régimes, of two "economies," which is affirmed. There are two peoples, two ages, two states, two régimes, two economies, which, however, are opposed to each other in a real contradiction properly speaking only once they have come to coexist, *the first not having wished to disappear on the arrival of the one for which its whole task was to prepare, because it had not understood that it was merely the means of getting ready for it.* Henceforth, therefore, the two peoples, the Jewish and the Christian, meet face to face. Each of them sucks at one of the two breasts of Scripture: the one is "the letter" . . . and the other is "allegory"; the two breasts are none other than the Two Testaments, which are both, today, equally the heritage of the Church, and the second contains within it the whole substance of the first.[28]

De Lubac is certainly not the first to reason from the existence of two covenants to the existence of two peoples.[29] We have witnessed much the same perspective in Augustine, whose writings reflect widespread assumptions in the early church. Justin argues on the basis of Isa. 51:4-5 and Jer. 31:31-32 that the Mosaic law was intended only for the Jews, while the new covenant concerns (primarily Gentile) Christians.[30] Tertullian also draws upon these passages to contrast the old covenant for the Jews with the new covenant for the Gentiles.[31] These positions largely reflect apologetic concerns: the need to defend the Old Testament as Scripture (against Marcion or the Manicheans), or the need to explain why Christians do not practice ceremonial observances (against the Jews). But in the heat of such polemics, a serious question is lost: what might a prophecy of the new covenant mean for the Jews themselves, the original recipients of this promise? For much of the Christian tradition, that which was intended to encourage the Jewish people becomes pretext for disregarding or even denying God's continued commitment to Israel. If de Lubac is right to perceive the connection between redemptive history and the spiritual reading of Scripture,

---

28. Ibid., 2.54. Italics mine.
29. Nor is de Lubac simplistically supersessionist. See, for instance, *Catholicism: Christ and the Common Destiny of Man,* trans. Lancelot C. Sheppard and Elizabeth Englund (San Francisco: Ignatius, 1988), 217-45.
30. *Dialogue with Trypho* 11.1-5.
31. *Adversus Marcionem* 4.1.

he has seriously misconstrued the economy of salvation concerning the ongoing status of Israel.

Few scholars have more poignantly considered the consequences of such a position than Daniel Boyarin. *A Radical Jew* presents Paul, somewhat by way of thought experiment, as a first-century, self-identifying Jew who adopts extreme Hellenistic positions in essential tension with Judaism.[32] Foundational for Boyarin's account is Gal. 3:28, where, he claims, Paul most clearly expresses his desire for a universal human essence beyond all difference and particularity: "There is neither Jew nor Greek, there is neither slave nor free, there is neither male nor female, for you are all one in Christ Jesus." Like de Lubac, Boyarin perceives a connection between this judgment and hermeneutics. Paul's universalism corresponds to both a dualistic opposition between body (particularity) and spirit (universalism), and an interpretive dualism between literal and allegorical interpretation. The spiritual reading of Israel's Scripture mobilizes a posture of indifference toward Jewish practices — which, Boyarin insists, results in simply disregarding Jewish difference. Paul cared very little about Jews remaining Jewish, "although Paul, were he here, would probably argue that he was redefining Jewishness in such a way that everyone could be Jewish."[33]

Paul's depiction of the law in Gal. 3–4 brings this issue to relief. Paul does not oppose the law as if it were inherently evil, neither does he condemn law observance as such. But he denies that the law could bring life, and he depicts the law as a pedagogue, given only as a temporary babysitter until the child is prepared for adulthood, at which point the pedagogue is no longer necessary. This image illustrates Paul's low estimation of the law and the Jewish people. Jews and Judaism had value during the childhood of humanity, but that time is now over and the signified has superseded the signifier. Israel therefore has no further role in history. Boyarin acknowledges Paul's grief and concern for the Israelites, and his hope that the Jews will be redeemed by faith in Christ. But "if the only value and promise afforded the Jews . . . is that in the end they will see the error of their ways, one cannot claim that there is a role for Jewish existence in Paul. It has been transcended by that which was its spiritual, allegorical referent always and forever: faith in Jesus Christ and the community of the faithful in which

---

32. Daniel Boyarin, *A Radical Jew: Paul and the Politics of Identity* (Berkeley: University of California Press, 1994).

33. Ibid., 10.

there is no Jew or Greek."[34] Paul is neither anti-Semitic nor anti-Jewish; he loves his brethren and believes they will receive salvation. Yet "this salvation . . . is precisely for the Jews a bitter gospel not a sweet one, because it is conditioned precisely on abandoning that to which we hold so dearly, our separate cultural, religious identity, our own fleshy and historical practice, our existence according to the flesh, our Law, our difference. Paul has simply allegorized our difference quite out of existence."[35]

As Boyarin argues, the very passage where Paul warns most clearly against Gentile boasting over the Jews actually underwrites a particular version of supersessionism. In Rom. 11, Paul urges the Gentiles to recognize that they are like wild olive branches grafted onto a cultivated olive tree where other branches have been cut off. The problem is that "the Jewish root which supports them has been continued solely in the Jewish Christians. The branches which have been lopped off — for all Paul's confidence that they may be rejoined some day — are those Jews who remain faithful to the ancestral faith and practice and who do not accept Jesus as the Messiah. We thus see the peculiar logic of supersession at work here. *Because* Israel has not been superseded, therefore most Jews have been superseded."[36] Boyarin acknowledges a difference between Paul's supersessionism and the view that God has rejected *all* Jews and replaced them entirely with Gentile Christians. Paul does not claim that there was any inherent fault in the Jews or Judaism that prompted their rejection. Yet he still redefines "Israel" such that it is no longer understood as a community of flesh, with concomitant entailments of genealogy and circumcision, but as a community of faith. This is a radical departure from the prophetic literature, which consistently depicts faithful Israelites as a remnant that would secure salvation for the rest of Israel and humanity. For the prophets, this remnant would display faithfulness through works. Paul proposes a new election characterized by faith in Christ, such that those who trust in Jesus at least temporarily replace those who were faithful to the original covenant.[37] Paul has, in short, adopted the prophetic perspective to reverse it.

Boyarin's criticisms deserve to be taken seriously by those who receive Jesus as the fulfillment of the Old Testament. It is a troubling form of imperialism so to lay claim upon another people's Scripture that the original

---

34. Ibid., 151.
35. Ibid., 152.
36. Ibid., 201-2. Unless otherwise specified, all italics his.
37. Ibid., 203.

recipients of its promises are no longer of any concern, but simply cast aside or even condemned. Boyarin raises probing questions about not just the value of Jewish particularity but the faithfulness of God — a problem Paul himself recognized. That said, it is hard to imagine any Christian reading of Scripture that does not somehow affirm the novelty and centrality of Christ in the mediation of God's grace, and de Lubac's survey of medieval exegesis highlights the virtual unanimity of the Christian tradition that the change of testaments effects a radical rupture in redemptive history. The question, then, is to what extent Jewish particularity and God's faithfulness to Israel can be preserved while affirming the newness of the new covenant.

This is precisely the question Hebrews helps address. Free from concerns about Gentile Christianity or the unity of all people, the epistle sets forth a relatively straightforward understanding of the new covenant with reference to the Jewish people: it is theirs. The author does not challenge the ongoing validity of distinctive Jewish practices like circumcision, Sabbath observance, or food laws. And he certainly never suggests that the new covenant gives rise to a new people unrelated to and radically distinct from the Jews. The abrogation of the Levitical priesthood is, in fact, an affirmation of God's continuing faithfulness to Israel. The old covenant centered on a shadowy, temporal arrangement that could not provide forgiveness of sins. This new covenant enables the Jews to be more, not less faithful to the covenant originally established with Abraham, so that they might enter the rest and seize the hope of their fathers from long ago. Only the priesthood has been superseded, not the people or the promises; the new covenant remains with the original people.

This does not mean Hebrews presents no challenge to the Judaism(s) of its day or the modern context. Jesus is the culmination of Jewish history, surpassing the things of old — greater than the prophets, greater than Moses, greater than Joshua, reality to the ceremonies' shadows. Because Hebrews addresses only Jews (and not Gentiles), it actually focuses the relation between Judaism and Christianity more sharply than the Pauline epistles. In his survey of secondary literature on Paul, Boyarin addresses briefly what he calls the "Gaston-Gager Hypothesis," that Paul never intended to replace the law with Christ in the salvation of the Jews, but only to present Christ as a means of salvation for the Gentiles. According to this view, ethnic Jews were not required to accept Christ, and Paul's remarks on the law were directed not toward Jews, but to Judaizers who insisted Gentiles convert to Judaism and keep the Jewish law. Boyarin rejects this position as exegetically unconvincing and deems especially untenable Gager's claim that "gentiles could become part of Israel without observing the law, *and that this would not result in a fundamental redefinition of what being part of Israel meant!*"[38] First, "the notion that one could be part of Israel and not subject to the Law issues in a fundamental redefinition of Israel."[39] Second, such a mixed community would be structurally unworkable, and it was not, in any case, the practice at Antioch. Third, this position contradicts Paul's claims that neither circumcision nor uncircumcision matters in Christ (Gal. 5:6).

On the reading of Hebrews presented here, the Gaston-Gager Hypothesis is even less of an option. Salvation has been made possible through Christ's establishment as high priest, and this salvation is for the Jews. No other community is considered that would allow Christ to be siphoned off for the Gentiles while leaving the law for the Jews. Yet the epistle's insistence on Christ as the only source of salvation also suggests a point of finally irreconcilable difference between Jews who do and do not affirm Jesus as the culmination of Israel's history. This is not an anti-Judaic position, at least in Boyarin's terms: "I treat Paul's discourse as indigenously Jewish, thereby preempting (or at least recasting) the question of the relationship between Paul and anti-Semitism. This is an inner-Jewish discourse and an inner-Jewish controversy."[40] Despite the intensity of modern debates between Orthodox and Reform Jews on the Torah, "no one doubts the Jewishness of either group, nor considers the other 'anti-Semitic'!"[41] Boyarin's analogy lends itself even more readily to Hebrews than Paul. For the unknown author, Jesus is now the necessary conduit for participation in the covenant, the means of entrance to the Jewish inheritance. Yet it is first and foremost the Jews whom God calls to enter his rest, the Jews and not the Gentiles who may now receive the promise. If this depiction of redemptive history is to be called supersessionism, this is a charge the Christian cannot completely escape.[42]

The Divine Address and Figural Reading

The next question, then, is how these redemptive-historical considerations bear on the freedom of God in revelation. I suggest God's ongoing fidelity

---

38. Ibid., 272 n. 9. See discussion on p. 42.
39. Ibid., 272 n. 9.
40. Ibid., 205.
41. Ibid.
42. For a similar sentiment, see John David Dawson, *Christian Figural Reading and the Fashioning of Identity* (Berkeley: University of California Press, 2002), 216-18.

to Israel secures his self-commitment to Scripture's literal sense while the novelty of Christ in salvation history legitimates the identification of God's address with an extension of that sense. This proposal bears significant similarities to traditional accounts of the figural interpretation of Scripture, though it also differs from them in important respects. To construe Scriptural authority according to divine address is not to distinguish between the senses as concurrent, coexisting modes of interpreting Scripture. Yet the basic dynamics of figural reading can still be affirmed as a mode of receiving the divine address in Scripture.

Perhaps the most textured recent defense of figural reading is John David Dawson's *Christian Figural Reading and the Fashioning of Identity*, which draws heavily upon Origen while engaging at length with Boyarin's work.[43] Dawson critiques Boyarin's overemphasis on binary oppositions for obscuring the complexity of Paul's thought on continuity and discontinuity in God's redemptive activity. Concerning Rom. 11, for instance, Boyarin depicts Paul's use of the term "Israel" as a disingenuous substitution of its proper referent (the historical community of Israel) for a generic, universal community defined by faith in Christ. Dawson rejects this reading. Paul's words in this chapter are not some linguistic trick; they articulate his conviction that "God has expanded Israel by including gentiles in a way that preserves the continuity of that community's identity with the Israel made up of Jews who practiced Jewish law without belief in the messiahship of Jesus."[44] Boyarin misses this possibility because he denies it out of hand. While Paul claims that Christianity represents the fulfillment, not the repudiation of his Jewish identity, Boyarin assumes that Jews who become Pauline Christians necessarily abandon membership in the Israel of the flesh. Boyarin thus preemptively forecloses the possibility that Jewish Christianity could, in fact, manifest itself in a visible community.

Dawson turns to Origen for an alternative to Boyarin's radical dualism. Origen's emphasis on spirituality focuses on transformation, not abstraction. When he speaks of a "spiritualized body," for instance, he does not mean that the old body is annihilated to make room for the new, but that the old body is transformed into something better, though still continuous with the old. There is an intrinsic relation between apparent opposites: visible/invisible, corporeal/incorporeal, manifest/hidden, earthly/heavenly.

43. Ibid., 19-64.
44. Ibid., 21.

Origen does not suggest that the soul is radically other than or trapped in the body, but that the body is just what cooled souls become. Indeed, he "revalues the bodily realm" by making "the body the soteriologically necessary site of the soul's recovery of its former status as mind or spirit."[45] Our final end is thus spiritualized embodiment, not disembodied spirithood; we leave behind corruption, not bodies.[46] Given this possibility of the spiritualized body, Dawson suggests that Christianity, too, can accommodate a transformed Judaism, one that claims Christ as the fulfillment of Israel's history without leaving Jewish identity behind.

This understanding of redemptive history animates a vision of Scriptural interpretation whereby figural reading "extends rather than effaces" the literal sense, leading to its "intensification rather than its supersession."[47] On this matter, Dawson draws heavily on the work of Hans Frei, especially *The Eclipse of Biblical Narrative*.[48] Frei stressed the importance of biblical realism, a feature of Western biblical interpretation before the eighteenth century that understood the text as oriented toward both the literal (or historical) and the doctrinal (or edifying).[49] Individual biblical narratives were taken to refer to actual historical occurrences, while figural reading served to unite those narratives into a single cumulative story that brought coherence to the whole canon. By treating earlier biblical stories as types of later stories, interpreters could relate the Old and New Testaments as figure and fulfillment of one consistent narrative. On this rubric, Frei argued, literal and figural interpretation were not in conflict; rather, "figuration or typology was a natural extension of literal interpretation. It was literalism at the level of the whole biblical story and thus of the depiction of the whole of historical reality."[50]

For Dawson, Frei's treatment of figural reading provides a strategy for resisting Boyarin's binary oppositions between flesh and spirit, or literality and nonliterality. Frei saw Calvin as perhaps the interpreter *par excellence* who recognized the "natural coherence" between literal and figural reading and "the need of each for supplementation by the other." Frei could also

---

45. Ibid., 63.
46. Ibid., 78-79.
47. Ibid., 141.
48. Hans W. Frei, *The Eclipse of Biblical Narrative: A Study in Eighteenth and Nineteenth Century Hermeneutics* (New Haven: Yale University Press, 1974). For Dawson's discussion, see *Christian Figural Reading and the Fashioning of Identity*, 141-85.
49. Frei, *The Eclipse of Biblical Narrative*, 1.
50. Ibid., 2.

describe the two senses as bearing a "family resemblance" to each other, belonging together even if they were neither strictly identical nor mutually substitutable.[51] Dawson explains:

> Various entities may be members of the same group in the way that different members of a family resemble one another — not because some single trait or essence is shared by all members but because the members share clusters of overlapping features. Frei argues that such "family resemblance" between literal and figural reading "permits a kind of extension of literal into figural interpretation" through "work[ing] out a common meaning among a number of diverse texts" by emphasizing different but not contradictory aspects of narrative. In other words, to say that literal meaning extends into figural meaning is to reject the idea that what is figural must be nonliteral, or that in the figural, the literal can no longer be present. Instead, when a narrative is read figurally, the reader stresses a certain feature of the text that differs from, but does not contradict, the feature of the narrative that would be stressed in a literal reading.[52]

Figural reading, to be clear, is not nonliteral, but a different kind of literal.

Dawson agrees with Frei that such reading presupposes a theological judgment about the nature and dynamics of redemptive history. Figural interpretation is not an arbitrary imposition of the reader upon the text, but arises from the internal dynamics of the text itself.[53] This practice reads forward, from figure to fulfillment, affirming that Old Testament people, institutions, and events were actually figures during Old Testament times and not just by retroactive literary judgment. As Frei said, "The meaning pattern of reality is inseparable from its forward motion; it is not the product of the wedding of that forward motion with a separate backward perspective on it, i.e. of history and interpretation joined as two logically independent factors.... The only spiritual act is that of comprehension — an act of mimesis, following the way things really are — rather than of creation, if it is to be faithful interpretation."[54] Dawson acknowledges that Jewish readers may consider such reading a distortion of the text. But

---

51. Ibid., 27.
52. Dawson, *Christian Figural Reading and the Fashioning of Identity*, 146-47, citing Frei, *The Eclipse of Biblical Narrative*, 27.
53. Frei, *The Eclipse of Biblical Narrative*, 34-35.
54. Ibid., 36.

he nevertheless affirms that "from the classical Christian point of view, such distortion can only be apparent."[55] Christians assert that "the figural reading of the Old Testament is precisely the reading that extends the meaning of Hebrew Scripture when that meaning is adequately grasped. Rather than some sort of misreading, Christian figural reading is actually the reading that aptly discerns the way the Old Testament is 'leading *as it were by its own thrust* to its climactic fulfillment in the New.'"[56]

For our purposes, Dawson's proposals provide a rich vocabulary for understanding figural reading as well as a contrast for the dynamics of Scriptural authority we have witnessed in Hebrews. I have argued, very much in line with Dawson, that the legitimacy of figural interpretation hinges on whether Jesus did in fact fulfill the Old Testament, and that the New Testament can draw fresh interpretive possibilities from Old Testament locutions without effacing their original meaning. Yet the task of discerning the divine address differs significantly from the traditional figural reading practices that Dawson's hero, Origen, exemplifies. It may be helpful to distinguish between figural *reading* and the supposition of a figural *sense* different from (though related to) the literal. Figural reading involves the practice of interpreting Old Testament locutions in light of Christ, but need not presume a second level of meaning that coexists with the literal. Hebrews consistently points to curiosities, inconsistencies, or lacunae in Old Testament locutions that only make sense in light of Christ, the new covenant, and the new inheritance. There cannot be two senses, literal and figural, that are simultaneously retained. The "figural sense" rather specifies the "literal sense" according to the dynamics of redemptive history. Hebrews does not, for instance, consider the literal sense of Ps. 95 to have urged the Israelites into Canaan, and the figural sense to urge contemporary hearers into the eternal inheritance. The argument is rather that "rest" could *not* refer to Canaan, since the Israelites were already in the land when the message was originally delivered. It can only mean *God's* rest, now made available to us through Christ's establishment as high priest. Hebrews extends and intensifies the literal, transposing the literal sense into Christological key (to borrow a musical metaphor) while also asserting that this "new" meaning was the true meaning all along. This move does not depend on the existence of multiple senses, though it is an instance of figural reading.

---

55. Dawson, *Christian Figural Reading and the Fashioning of Identity*, 163.

56. Ibid., 163-64, citing Hans W. Frei, *Types of Christian Theology*, ed. George Hunsinger and William C. Placher (New Haven: Yale University Press, 1992), 59. Italics Dawson's.

This distinction — figural reading versus figural sense — invites a more dynamic understanding of Scriptural authority than the traditional method. Augustine's account of figural reading in *De doctrina Christiana* provides a paradigmatic point of contrast. For Augustine, there is a distinction between signs and things. Signs signify things, while things, inasmuch as they are things, do not so refer. Metaphorical signs signify things that in turn signify other things. In *Summa Theologiae*, Thomas Aquinas will adopt and systematize this rubric to defend the fourfold method:

> The author of Holy Writ is God, in whose power it is to signify His meaning, not by words only (as man also can do), but also by things themselves *(in cuius potestate est ut non solum voces ad significandum accommodet... sed etiam res ipsas)*. So, whereas in every other science things are signified by words, this science has the property that the things signified by the words have themselves also a signification *(ipsae res significatae per voces, etiam significant aliquid)*. Therefore that first signification whereby words signify things belongs to the first sense, the historical or literal *(sensus historicus vel litteralis)*. That signification whereby things signified by words have themselves also a signification is called the spiritual sense *(sensus spiritualis)*, which is based on the literal, and presupposes it *(super litteralem fundatur, et eum supponit)*.[57]

Thomas considers the objection that these senses might produce confusion through the accretion of meaning, and responds, "The multiplication of these senses does not produce equivocation *(aequivocationem)* or any other kind of multiplicity *(aliam speciem multiplicitatis)*, seeing that these senses are not multiplied because one word signifies several things *(una vox multa significet)*; but because these things signified by the words can be themselves types of other things *(ipsae res significatae per voces, aliarum rerum possunt esse signa)*."[58] His treatment of this matter thus resembles Augustine's:

Signs → things → other things

---

57. ST I.1.10. Latin edition: Sancti Thomae de Aquino, *Summa Theologiae* (Cinisello Balsamo, Italy: San Paolo, 1988). English translation: Thomas Aquinas, *Summa Theologica*, trans. Fathers of the English Dominican Province, 6 vols. (Notre Dame, IN: Christian Classics, 1948).

58. ST I.1.10 ad 1.

The individual word is the central unit of interpretation in this framework.[59] A given word-sign refers to some person, practice, or event in redemptive history that in turn refers to some other person, practice, or event, or multiple persons, practices, or events. Since one thing in redemptive history can signify many other things, individual word-signs can figurally refer to many things as well. Allegory thus produces a multiplication of meaning, not with respect to the original referent of a sign, but according to the many things that referent can signify.

For Hebrews, the locus of interpretation is quite different. The author draws correspondences between various things in redemptive history — Jesus is greater than Moses, he is the second Joshua, he resembles Melchizedek, and so forth — but he demonstrates almost none of the early or medieval Christian's interest in particular word-signs. The meaning of "Melchizedek," for instance, receives passing mention (he is king of righteousness and king of peace), but it plays a minimal role in the rest of the author's argument. "Rest" receives greater attention, but not according to Augustine's account of signs. The author does not teach that the Israelites entered Canaan, the land that signified the eternal inheritance. He rather suggests that "rest" should not be understood with reference to Canaan at all.

Augustine: "rest" → Canaan → eternal inheritance

Hebrews: "rest" → eternal inheritance

This is a radically different approach from Augustine's suggestion in *De doctrina Christiana,* considered in the first chapter, that "land" could refer to Canaan, or the church, or heaven. There is one true meaning, and it is the eternal inheritance to which Jesus has paved the way.

De Lubac, who generally follows Augustine's emphasis on word-signs, displays the significance of these distinctions. De Lubac argues that allegory is properly found in the realities narrated by the text, and not in the text itself — "not in history as recitation, but in history as event."[60] Yet he so closely associates words and deeds that the legitimacy of correspondences between events extends rather freely to correspondences between

---

59. For conceptual problems with Augustine's definition of sign according to individual word unit, see Christopher Kirwan, *Augustine* (London: Routledge, 1989), 35-59.

60. De Lubac, *Medieval Exegesis,* 2.86.

utterances as well. "Scripture is in a way doubly the Word of God, since God speaks to us in it with words about what he has spoken to us in deeds. Biblical allegory is therefore essentially *allegoria facti*. More precisely, it is *allegoria facti et dicti*."[61] Individual word units become occasions for maximizing meaning, and Scripture exists in large measure to encourage contemplation. Scripture is a vast world, "undecipherable in its fullness and in the multiplicity of its meanings," "a deep forest, with innumerable branches, 'an infinite forest of meanings,'" "a table arranged by Wisdom, laden with food, where the unfathomable divinity of the Savior is itself offered as nourishment to all. Treasure of the Holy Spirit, whose riches are as infinite as himself. True labyrinth. Deep heavens, unfathomable abyss. Vast sea, where there is endless voyaging 'with all sails set.' Ocean of mystery. Or raging torrent . . ."[62]

De Lubac amasses a venerable line of proponents for this reading throughout the early and medieval church, and his presentation bears significant appeal. A fuller study might explore the compatibility of Scripture as divine address and the fourfold method, which do not seem to me obviously antithetical. For our epistle, however, it must be acknowledged that a different hermeneutical strategy is at work. Hebrews is not concerned with contemplation but action, and its appropriation of the Old Testament is oriented toward not individual words but broader locutions: declarations, commands, promises, threats, warnings, and exhortations. Such verbal units do not correspond one to one with things as do word-signs; they are complex linguistic structures that perform particular communicative acts. The clarity and efficacy of such expressions depend on a certain fixity, not multiplication, of meaning. For the church must know what God demands in order to submit obediently.

The model of this chapter thus identifies the divine address with the new meaning revealed in Christ and not with the original sense. Scriptural authority primarily derives from what God communicates now and not from how particular locutions were presented or received in earlier contexts. The epistle's appropriation of Scripture does not trade on two coexisting senses, literal and figural; there is only one meaning that counts as authoritative for the church, namely, that which God communicates through Christ. This vision of Scriptural authority may be considered a species of figural interpretation in its extension of the literal sense. The

61. Ibid., 2.88-89.
62. Ibid., 1.75.

meaning now revealed is continuous with earlier appropriations of the same locution. Yet this new signification also enacts such a transformation of the text that the figural sense basically replaces the literal — or rather, the figural reading imposes itself as what the original locution must have meant all along. The literal sense just is the Christological, though its meaning would not have been recognized in earlier times.

Receiving the Divine Address

The imposition of God's address into the present situation suggests a model of revelation oriented toward the concrete particular. The appropriation of the Old Testament by the New is an extraordinarily privileged instance of the divine address, but not entirely discontinuous with God's guidance of his covenant people after the apostolic age. The church exists in the penultimate stage of redemptive history, and thus expects no new revelation of eschatological significance before the final return of Christ. Yet she still listens in obedience and submission for God's voice in the contemporary moment. The following chapter will consider the implications of this perspective for the relation between Scripture and tradition. The purpose here is to develop further the conceptual apparatus for this understanding of Scripture.

In *Church Dogmatics* 1/1, Karl Barth delineates the Word of God according to its threefold form, advancing an account of God's ongoing self-revelation that bears significant affinities with the construal of Scriptural authority presented in this chapter.[63] Barth distinguishes between the Word of God preached, the Word of God written, and the Word of God revealed. The Word of God preached refers first and foremost to the authoritative proclamation of the prophets and the apostles, but derivatively to the contemporary proclamation of the church. That which makes proclamation "real proclamation," or that which enables proclamation to communicate God's address, is the Word of God, which Barth sets forth as the commission, theme, judgment, and event of proclamation. It is, in short, the Word of God that initiates proclamation — and this proclamation concerns the Word, submits to the Word, and enacts the Word's presence.

---

63. Karl Barth, *Die Kirchliche Dogmatik* 1/1 (Munich: Kaiser Verlag, 1932). English translation: *Church Dogmatics* 1/1, trans. G. W. Bromiley, 2nd ed. (London: T&T Clark, 1975). I draw especially here on §4.

Hearing the Living Word

While there is a certain identity between the forms of the Word of God, they also exist in hierarchical relation to each other. In particular, that proclamation recorded in Scripture, the Word of God written, stands over contemporary church proclamation according to the status of canon. Scripture is

> the deposit of what was once proclamation by human lips. In its form as Scripture, however, it does not seek to be a historical monument but rather a Church document, written proclamation. The two entities may thus be set initially under a single genus, Scripture as the commencement and present-day preaching as the continuation of one and the same event, Jeremiah and Paul at the beginning and the modern preacher of the Gospel at the end of one and the same series. . . . In this similarity as phenomena, however, there is also to be found between Holy Scripture and present-day proclamation a dissimilarity in order, namely the supremacy, the absolutely constitutive significance of the former for the latter, the determination of the reality of present-day proclamation by its foundation upon Holy Scripture and its relation to this, the basic singling out of the written word of the prophets and apostles over all the later words of men which have been spoken and are to be spoken to-day in the Church.[64]

Scripture thus exercises determinative authority over future church proclamation as the privileged locus of God's self-revelation. The proclamation of the prophets and apostles is of a piece with contemporary proclamation by present-day preachers, yet the written character of the former establishes a relation of fundamental asymmetry with the latter.

Barth famously differentiates the Bible from the Word of God, or the Word revealed. Scripture cannot be identified with past revelation, but rather witnesses to it, pointing beyond itself to another. Similarly, the authority of Scripture does not rest in the biblical witnesses but in that to which they testify. Such a distinction enables Barth to affirm the human quality of the Bible while nevertheless asserting God's freedom to enliven Scripture in the act of self-revelation.

> The direct identification between revelation and the Bible which is in fact at issue is not one that we can presuppose or anticipate. It takes

---

64. *Church Dogmatics* 1/1, 102.

place as an event when and where the biblical word becomes God's Word, i.e., when and where the biblical word comes into play as a word of witness, when and where John's finger does not point in vain but really indicates, when and where we are enabled by the means of his word to see and hear what he saw and heard. Thus in the event of God's Word revelation and the Bible are indeed one, and literally so.[65]

Since the Bible becomes the Word of God only in the event of revelation, there is a sense in which the Bible is only "derivatively and indirectly" God's Word, and must "continually become" it.[66] This event is not defined primarily by human reception, "as though our reaction to this event or attitude toward it could be constitutive for its reality and content."[67] Barth's concern is rather the freedom of God, namely, God's gracious prerogative to reveal himself as he chooses, according to no other authority than his own. The event of revelation occurs "where and when God, in speaking once and for all, wills according to His eternal counsel that it be true, where and when God by His activating, ratifying and fulfilling of the word of the Bible and preaching lets it be true."[68] Human effort cannot finally control God's freedom in revelation. It is the very character of Scriptural authority to impose itself upon God's people at his pleasure.

Barth's threefold delineation of the Word provides a useful articulation for the relation between divine freedom and canonical mediation proposed here. Canon names the textual expression of God's self-commitment to his Word, but the Word continues to reveal himself through the church's ongoing proclamation of Christ. As Webster argues, such inscription does not restrict God: "inspiration is a mode of the Spirit's freedom, not its inhibition by the letter."[69] Yet God's activity in revelation has a particularly textual character. "The relation of the words of Scripture to the communicative self-presence of God is not merely contingent; what revelation impels is writing."[70] It is therefore possible to locate Scriptural authority in God's present address while affirming the essential relation between fresh events of revelation and their original locutions. The divine address is continuous with yet extends the literal sense; it abides fixity of written form,

---

65. Ibid., 113.
66. Ibid., 117.
67. Ibid.
68. Ibid., 120.
69. Webster, *Holy Scripture*, 33.
70. Ibid., 38.

but imposes the text on new situations with fresh power and meaning. To adopt the language of the creeds and confessions, the Spirit "has spoken through the prophets";[71] but the Word of God preached is the Word of God.[72] Our understanding of divine address can thus affirm Barth's basic conviction that Scripture speaks with God's authority as God makes himself vitally and actively present in the contemporary moment.[73]

For a particularly familiar illustration of these dynamics, we might consider *Confessions* 8.[74] While Augustine's conversion in the garden of Milan bears no direct connection with questions concerning the relation between the testaments, the critical role Scripture plays in his narrative invites reflection upon the nature of God's self-revelation in the biblical text.[75] The incident in the garden is actually the last of four such interlocking stories. Augustine recounts a series of conversion accounts that climaxes in his own, with each individual instance illuminating the contours of his own submission to continence. The first narrative concerns Marius Victorinus, a prominent rhetorician-philosopher who by "reading holy scripture and intensively studying all the Christian writings" first grew interested in Christianity, but still feared his pagan friends and refused to receive baptism.[76] The turning point comes through his continued reading of Scripture: "Later he drank in courage from his avid reading and came to fear that he might be disowned by Christ before his holy angels if he feared to confess him before men and women. In his own eyes he was guilty of a great crime in being ashamed of the holy mysteries instituted

---

71. The third article of the Niceno-Constantinopolitan Creed.

72. Second Helvetic Confession, Ch. 1.

73. The preceding paragraph accepts Webster's remarks as a corrective to Barth's doctrine of inspiration, an area some evangelicals have found problematic. For Webster's proposal that inspiration encompasses the formation of the canonical text in addition to its ongoing reception, see *Holy Scripture*, 26-27, 30-39. One recent evangelical assessment of Barth's doctrine of Scripture is Kevin J. Vanhoozer, "A Person of the Book? Barth on Biblical Authority and Interpretation," in *Karl Barth and Evangelical Theology: Convergences and Divergences,* ed. Sung Wook Chung (Grand Rapids: Baker Academic, 2006), 26-59.

74. Note the prominence of this example also in Nicholas Wolterstorff, *Divine Discourse: Philosophical Reflections on the Claim That God Speaks* (Cambridge: Cambridge University Press, 1995), discussed below.

75. James J. O'Donnell has argued that the entirety of *conf.* 8 is structured as a reading of Paul. See *Augustine:* Confessions, 3 vols. (Oxford: Clarendon, 1992), 3.3. As instances, he cites: *conf.* 8.1.2: Rom. 1:21-22; *conf.* 8.4.9: Rom. 4:17; *conf.* 8.5.11: Rom. 7:16-17; *conf.* 8.5.12: Rom. 7:22-25; *conf.* 8.10.22: Rom. 7:17, 20; *conf.* 8.12.29: Rom. 13:13; *conf.* 8.12.30: Rom. 14:1.

76. *Conf.* 8.2.4.

by your humble Word, while feeling no shame at the sacrilegious rites of proud demons, whose likeness he had been proud to assume himself."[77] Finally emboldened to become a Christian, Victorinus humbles himself and submits to public baptism, much to the joy of the Christian community in Rome.

The next two stories appear in Ponticianus's account of his colleagues' conversions. Two Roman officials are walking in the gardens when they come across a copy of *The Life of Antony*. One of the officials hears in the story of Antony's conversion his own call to renounce secular pursuits. He "directed his eyes back to the page, and as he read a change began to occur in that hidden place within him *(et legebat et mutabatur intus)* where you alone can see; his mind was being stripped of the world, as presently became apparent. The flood tide of his heart leapt on, and at last he broke off his reading with a groan as he discerned the right course and determined to take it."[78] Antony, of course, experienced a dramatic conversion through a gospel reading in church that moved him to renounce his wealth. Now, the account of his conversion has impelled another rich young man, centuries removed from the gospel's original context, to reject worldly ambition — again, through reading.

The Life of Antony reappears in *Confessions* 8 at a critical moment in Augustine's own conversion. Augustine has tried but failed to embrace Lady Continence, and now laments his condition in tears, exhausted by his own helplessness. Suddenly he hears the voice of a child singing, *"Tolle lege, tolle lege,"* words he interprets as "nothing other than a divine command *(divinitus mihi iuberi)* to open the Book and read the first passage I chanced upon."[79] Antony immediately comes to mind, for "he happened to arrive when the gospel was being read, and took the words to be addressed to himself *(tamquam sibi diceretur quod legebatur)* when he heard, *Go and sell all you possess and give the money to the poor: you will have treasure in heaven. Then come, follow me.* So he was promptly converted to you by this plainly divine message."[80] The rest of Augustine's story is well known:

> Stung into action, I returned to the place where Alypius was sitting, for on leaving it I had put down there the book of the apostles' letters.

77. Ibid.
78. Ibid., 8.6.15.
79. Ibid., 8.12.29.
80. Ibid.

I snatched it up, opened it and read in silence the passage on which my eyes first lighted: *Not in dissipation and drunkenness, nor in debauchery and lewdness, nor in arguing and jealousy; but put on the Lord Jesus Christ, and make no provision for the flesh or the gratification of your desires.* I had no wish to read further, nor was there need. No sooner had I reached the end of the verse than the light of certainty flooded my heart and all dark shades of doubt fled away.[81]

In every developed instance of conversion in *Confessions* 8, Scripture plays a critical role. It was Antony's encounter with the gospel reading that prompted his immediate conversion; it was his example, itself a form of biblical interpretation, that prompted Ponticianus's colleagues to follow suit; and it was again Antony's example, mediated through the conversation with Ponticianus, that prompted Augustine to turn to Paul. Meanwhile, Victorinus's conversion through Scripture has already paved the way for Augustine's conversation with Ponticianus. For the great Latin father, divine speech moves the heart, rendering it incapable of resisting God's call. The address is so unavoidably direct that every effort to escape it ultimately fails. Yet the power of this address invariably demands a Scriptural locution. While Augustine recounts two instances of divine speech in his own conversion, the first through the child and the second through Paul, it is only the latter that releases him from the bondage of sin to receive the certainty of God's light. God can indeed speak through some juvenile ditty, but only Scripture effects submission to the divine will.

It is not entirely clear why Augustine considered continence necessary before receiving baptism.[82] His mother, Monica, did not share this conviction, having secured him a wife to marry at the proper time, and Augustine himself demonstrates great forbearance toward Verecundus, who cannot join the Cassiciacum community because he is bound to a wife.[83] Yet Paul's words in Romans become for Augustine an unambiguous command to sexual chastity, one he never doubts, even if he does not consider this requirement applicable for all Christians. God's message to Augustine is not even the same as that to his closest friends. Alypius's transformative experience occurs at virtually the same moment, in the same garden, but it is not nearly so dramatic, and it derives from a different source. Alypius

---

81. Ibid.
82. For discussion, see O'Donnell, *Augustine:* Confessions, 1.xxxvii-xl.
83. *Conf.* 9.3.6.

reads beyond Rom. 13:13 to Rom. 14:1 *("Make room for the person who is weak in faith"),* applying this passage to himself *(quod ille ad se rettulit)*[84] as a call simply to join Augustine in continence — never much of a struggle for Alypius anyway.[85] The same God speaks, yet he speaks differently to different people according to their individual needs.

In none of these accounts does the reception of Scripture diverge dramatically from how a given passage might have been intended or received in the original setting. Yet the way these texts speak varies in each instance. God addresses individuals directly in their particular situations, prompting specific convictions and concrete obedience. The words of Scripture are the very words of God, applied precisely to the concerns at hand. The literal sense is not thereby abandoned, but adopts greater specificity and power as Scripture is taken up in the divine address. One may thus confess Scripture as the privileged locus of God's self-revelation while also affirming God's ongoing address to his people, continuous with but distinct from earlier moments of revelation. God's chosen mode of self-revelation in redemptive history, at least on Augustine's terms, is the enlivening of Scripture for the recipients of God's grace.

Divine Address, Authorial Intent, and the Historical Method

Given the hermeneutical priority of the contemporary moment for my proposal, a methodological question arises concerning the role of historical inquiry in discerning God's voice. As I conceive it, the model of Scriptural authority advanced in this chapter qualifies but does not undermine the value of historical inquiry. The divine address operates in continuity with the original sense, even if the original sense does not fully constitute divine communication. Historical inquiry provides a necessary control against unrestrained applications of the text, ensuring continuity between contemporary efforts to discern God's will and the reception of divine revelation in earlier contexts. This principle does not function as a restriction upon God's freedom in self-revelation, since God has chosen to bind himself to the canonical text. Yet Scripture also expresses the consistency of God's activity in redemptive history, and historical inquiry illuminates the shape of that saving work.

---

84. Ibid., 12.30.
85. Ibid., 6.12.21-22.

As mentioned in the introduction of this book, the relation between historical inquiry and theological interpretation is a vibrant area of study in contemporary scholarship. In what follows, I fill out the details of my model of Scriptural authority to indicate where my sympathies lie in the broader discussion. My proposals are tentative, and the basic contours of Scriptural authority sketched above could, I think, be retained with other accounts of the original sense. But I will especially focus my approach on authorial intent as a constitutive element of the historical method. In particular, I commend Nicholas Wolterstoff's *Divine Discourse* as a sophisticated (though not unproblematic) effort to speak coherently about the divine address in Scripture, whose account of authorial discourse provides a serviceable conceptual base for the proposals of this chapter. If a more persuasive account of the original sense can be found to secure comparable fixity in biblical interpretation, the locus of Scriptural authority will remain unchanged, though perhaps construed in somewhat different terms.

It is worth observing, by way of background, just how much the historical method relies on claims about authorial intent. One of the earliest progenitors of the historical method was Baruch Spinoza, whose *Theological-Political Treatise* advocated the practice of interpreting Scripture like nature.[86] Though this text was published anonymously in 1670, its proposals on Scriptural interpretation are strikingly familiar to those acquainted with the practice of historical criticism today. Spinoza stresses the importance of acquiring biblical languages, investigating words for their range of possible meanings, and analyzing individual books of the Bible according to their distinctive themes and phrases. Yet he considers just as fundamental as these practices the study of provenance:

> It is important to know of the life, character and concerns of each writer, so that we may know which statements are meant as laws and which as moral doctrine; we are more readily able to explain someone's words, the better we know his mind and personality. It is crucial to know on what occasion, at what time and for what people or age the various texts were written so that we may not confuse eternal doctrines with

---

86. Benedict de Spinoza, *Œuvres III, Tractatus Theologico-Politicus, Traité théologico-politique,* ed. Fokke Akkerman (Paris: Presses Universitaires de France, 1999). English translation: *Theological-Political Treatise,* ed. Jonathan Israel, trans. Michael Silverthorne and Jonathan Israel (Cambridge: Cambridge University Press, 2007). I have not been able to secure a copy of the Akkerman edition and include the bibliographic information only for the sake of reference.

those that are merely temporary or useful only to a few people. It is essential, finally, to know all the other things mentioned above, so that, apart from the question of authorship, we may also discover, for each book, whether it may have been contaminated with spurious passages or not; whether mistakes have crept in, and whether the mistakes have been corrected by unskilled or untrustworthy hands. It is vital to know all this, so that we will not be carried away by blind zeal or just accept whatever is put in front of us. We must acknowledge exclusively what is certain and unquestionable.[87]

Given the ongoing vitality in contemporary biblical studies of Spinoza's basic method, we may indeed ask to what degree authorial intent continues to define historical criticism. Harold Attridge's commentary on Hebrews provides a representative example.[88] Naturally enough, the first section of this work is dedicated to questions of authorship. As Attridge judges, little can be determined except that the author was male; well educated in Greek rhetorical and philosophical traditions, and especially in Greek-language Jewish exegetical practices; not a witness to Jesus; probably of Jewish ancestry; perhaps of a radical Gentile-oriented wing of the church to which Paul belonged; and not likely or not obviously Paul, Barnabas, or Apollos. The rest of the commentary investigates what this author intended to communicate at the level of individual words and phrases. Concerning the "son of man" in Heb. 2:5-9, for instance, Attridge writes the following:

> It is likely that the designation "Son of Man" was applied to Jesus as a title in the early church in connection with the belief in his exaltation or parousia. If our author presupposed familiarity with that eschatological title, the image of Jesus "crowned with honor and glory" could have been designed to evoke it. Yet lack of any development of the images most closely associated with the "Son of Man" renders this suggestion problematic. Furthermore, in all the varied references to Jesus in the text, this title appears nowhere. It is quite possible that the author simply did not know the Son of Man tradition.[89]

---

87. Spinoza, *Theological-Political Treatise*, 7.5.
88. Harold W. Attridge, *Hebrews*, Hermeneia (Philadelphia: Fortress, 1989).
89. Ibid., 74.

Similar considerations characterize Attridge's comments on Heb. 10:1, concerning the Platonic background of the shadow/image contrast:

> There is on the surface of this Platonic imagery an element of paradox. For how can an "image" cast a "shadow"? If the terms are understood in the highly metaphorical sense that their technical philosophical usage suggests, this paradox is diminished. Yet it would appear that our author exploits the simple sense of the surface imagery as well as its philosophical connotations. For ultimately the ideal or spiritual paradigm of the old sacrifices is the offering of Christ in his "body" (10:10), and bodies, rather than "images" or ideal forms, are the sorts of things that cast shadows. Our author indulges to the full his penchant for dramatically exploiting the polyvalence of his language. Precisely that playful delight in language makes it clear that he cannot be neatly categorized as a philosopher or apocalyptist.[90]

In both these quotations, exegetical judgments operate in conjunction with conjectures about the author's philosophical training, religious background, and other factors. Attridge's goal is to ascertain exactly what the author intended: whether he did or did not invoke the "son of man" language of the gospel traditions; whether he did or did not draw upon Platonic categories in his language about shadows and images; whether he did or did not allude to technical philosophical categories in exploiting Platonic language. The operating assumptions are, so far as I can tell, that the meaning of a text is relatively fixed, it can be determined with reasonable certainty, and it corresponds essentially with what the author intended. Such assumptions are not at all unique within biblical scholarship; they may indeed be considered guild standards. The question, then, is whether such assumptions can be defended.

This is precisely the issue Wolterstorff addresses in *Divine Discourse*, which provides a rigorous philosophical account of human authorial discourse as a means of communicating divine authorial discourse.[91]

---

90. Ibid., 271.

91. I use the term "discourse" and not "intent" here to reflect Wolterstorff's practice. Wolterstorff understands intent to be a constitutive element of authorial discourse, but distinguishes between the intentional performance of a speech act and the intention to perform that act. Authorial-discourse interpretation concerns itself primarily with the former. See Wolterstorff's discussion in *Divine Discourse,* 197-99 as well as his brief remarks in "Resuscitating the Author," in *Hermeneutics at the Crossroads,* ed. Kevin J. Vanhoozer, James K. A.

Wolterstorff's account of authorial discourse draws upon speech-act theory, focusing upon the distinction, considered above, between locutions and illocutions. In particular, he argues that locutions acquire communicative force by means of normative ascriptions that adhere to both speaker and recipient. What it means for a speech-act to be ascribed to an agent is that the agent adopts a set of *prima facie* obligations toward his or her locution, and that this speech-act entails a set of *prima facie* obligations on the part of the recipient toward the same locution. A promise, for instance, places the promise-maker under obligation to fulfill his or her pledge. So also, an assertion presupposes a binding responsibility to the truth. The recipient of a promise or assertion has, in turn, a moral obligation to trust the communicator, and a right to expect fidelity to the speech-acts communicated.

These obligations are, of course, only *prima facie* and can be undercut. Wolterstorff lists three conditions under which malformed speech acts do not entail *prima facie* normative obligations. First, a speech-act may not correspond properly to the mental states of the speaker, e.g., if the agent asserts a statement without believing it, or issues a promise with no intent of fulfilling it. Second, a speech-act may not correspond properly to the facts of the world, e.g., if a statement is simply mistaken on what it asserts. Finally, a speech-act may not correspond properly to social norms, e.g., if someone makes a pronouncement without any right to do so. Only a judge can pronounce guilt or innocence, and only clergy can pronounce a couple married in a religious wedding ceremony. These qualifications do not undermine Wolterstorff's claim that communication involves normative obligation: it is morally wrong to assert what one does not believe because "at bottom, it is our dignity as persons that requires that we be taken at our word, and take ourselves at our word."[92] But they do reveal conditions when *prima facie* obligations no longer apply. The upshot of Wolterstorff's discussion is that authorial discourse need not involve an inexhaustible search into the morass of the writer or speaker's mind, inaccessible as such knowledge may be due to insincerity, falsehood, or confusion. An affirmation of authorial discourse simply suggests that readers and hearers may ascribe meaning to a given speech-act, that it is possible for agents to communicate, and that their communicative acts are not completely subject to the interpretive community.

Smith, and Bruce Ellis Benson (Bloomington: Indiana University Press, 2006), 48-49. I am grateful to Daniel Treier for bringing this distinction to my attention.

92. Ibid., 94.

To speak is not, as such, to express one's inner self but to take up a normative stance in the public domain. The myth dies hard that to read a text for authorial discourse is to enter the dark world of the author's psyche. It's nothing of the sort. It is to read to discover what assertings, what promisings, what requestings, what commandings, are rightly to be ascribed to the author on the ground of her having set down the words that she did in the situation in which she set them down. Whatever be the dark demons and bright angels of the author's inner self that led her take up this stance in public, it is that stance itself that we hope by reading to discover, not the dark demons and bright angels.[93]

Wolterstorff's account of authorial discourse does not address in significant depth the particularities of biblical interpretation: how, for instance, discourse may be ascribed to an authorial community and not just a single author; how text-critical issues affect our ability to discern authorial discourse; how discourse may be ascribed to texts that reflect the presence of multiple authors operating relatively independently of each other, with later authors possibly redacting the work of earlier ones. These are not easy questions, and it is striking that perhaps the chief twentieth-century progenitor of "canonical criticism" himself confessed that the Christian Bible is the object of an "ongoing *search*," the impossibility of whose final discovery "appears to be constitutive for Christian faith."[94] Even the most rigorous theological and philosophical accounts of authorial intent confront the vagaries and contingencies of historical research. Still, Wolterstorff does make a substantive case that texts actually communicate, that an author's intent can indeed be expressed and understood in substantial continuity with what was meant. The basic conviction that texts represent the author's design seems an almost inescapable intuition and a necessary condition for affirming God's ability to communicate through Scripture. That the Spirit "has spoken through the prophets" need not entail that the biblical texts reflect no human influence or that human response plays no role in the reception of Scriptural discourse. It must, however, mean that the canon somehow exercises God's authority over his people, that Scripture can be trusted to communicate the divine message faithfully, and that the ultimate voice behind the biblical locutions is God's. These are the chief points Wolterstorff helps secure.

---

93. Ibid., 93.
94. Brevard S. Childs, *Biblical Theology of the Old and New Testaments: Theological Reflection on the Christian Bible* (Minneapolis: Fortress, 1992), 67. Italics his.

The question, then, is precisely how the biblical texts relay the divine intent, and here Wolterstorff proves less helpful. Wolterstorff's strategy is to distinguish between two hermeneutics, one concerning human discourse (that mediates divine discourse), and another concerning divine discourse (which is mediated through human discourse). The first is relatively straightforward: well-formed sentences have meanings, and these meanings can be discerned according to practices basic to communication.[95] The second is more theologically fraught because it introduces the notion of two authors (one human and the other divine). Wolterstorff suggests conceiving the relation between human and divine discourse according to an appropriation model whereby one person's speech is adopted *mutatis mutandis* by a second person as his or her own. A human example might be a board meeting where one trustee proposes a motion and another concurs. Canon is the privileged object of appropriated divine discourse, and the canonization process is the (extended) event of divine appropriation whereby God claims the Bible as his own speech. On this model, we may adopt a presumption of coincidence between appropriated and appropriating discourse in the absence of good reason not to do so. The interpretation of divine discourse will thus proceed "with convictions in two hands: in one hand, our convictions as to the stance and content of the appropriated discourse and the meanings of the sentences used; in the other, our convictions concerning the probabilities and improbabilities of what God would have been intending to say by appropriating this particular discourse-by-inscription."[96] Included in the latter are various positions concerning the consistency, nature, and purposes of God.

Wolterstorff seems to consider the resolution of most potential discrepancies between appropriated and appropriating discourse a relatively straightforward task.[97] It is important, for instance, to distinguish between the main point of some passage and the author's way of making that point. Thus, we need not adopt a geocentric cosmology just because a psalmist sees in the stability of the physical world evidence for the majesty and strength of God. So, too, the blessing in Ps. 137 upon those who would dash the Babylonian infants against the rocks may express the literal intent of the human author, but we must take those words to convey God's

---

95. Wolterstorff, *Divine Discourse*, 189-97.
96. Ibid., 204.
97. Ibid., 208-18.

general opposition to whatever resists his will.[98] Most discrepancies fall within a limited number of recognizable patterns; more difficult cases are addressed on a case-by-case basis. Yet this is precisely where Wolterstorff's approach loses appeal. While his specific prescriptions for dealing with biblical phenomena are not especially objectionable, his basic rubric for distinguishing between human and divine discourse is rather schematic. In principle, it seems rather optimistic to suggest that a handful of techniques will resolve almost any potential discrepancy between human and divine discourse. And even the examples Wolterstorff considers relatively uncomplicated resist the somewhat simplistic solutions he offers. (Ps. 137 in particular seems to me far less soluble than his three-quarter-page discussion might suggest.[99]) More fundamentally, Wolterstorff's approach is from this chapter's perspective methodologically backwards. God's speech is not discerned by ascertaining the meaning of human locutions and then determining whether God was likely so to have communicated. God freely addresses his people, here and now, in a manner recipients cannot expect or control. Indeed, God must speak in ways that could not previously have been understood, precisely because of the New Testament. Those who consider the Old Testament in light of Christ discover fresh speech-acts that enliven and explain the text beyond its original reception. The biblical authors spoke of things they did not know; we receive these illocutionary mysteries with Christological insight. The movement is thus not from human discourse to possibly distinct divine meaning. It is rather from God through Scripture to his people according to the contours of redemptive history. Since the divine address operates in the context of God's fidelity to his Word, new illocutionary acts will function in a manner continuous with the original sense. But human authorial discourse is not basically identical to divine discourse as Wolterstorff suggests.

Wolterstorff does consider instances in which one locution bears multiple illocutionary acts.[100] Nathan's story about the rich man stealing the lamb of a poor man functioned at one level as a narrative, but at another level as a rebuke for David's sin with Bathsheba. So, too, a common locution may communicate the different intents of multiple authors. The

---

98. Ibid., 212-13.

99. For one alternate treatment of this passage, see Ada María Isasi-Díaz, "'By the Rivers of Babylon': Exile as a Way of Life," in *Reading from This Place*, vol. 1: *Social Location and Biblical Interpretation in the United States*, ed. Fernando F. Segovia and Mary Ann Tolbert (Minneapolis: Augsburg Fortress, 1995), 149-63.

100. Wolterstorff, *Divine Discourse*, 212-15.

human author of the Song of Songs may have intended to write a simple love song about two humans, but divine appropriation has transformed this song into a depiction of God's love for the church. Yet these examples are not exceptions to an otherwise uniform identity between divine and human discourse (a point Wolterstorff does to some extent recognize in his suggestion that biblical narrative as a whole reflects the presence of multiple authors with different illocutionary intent). Such illocutionary diversity is in fact a constitutive feature of the New Testament's use of the Old Testament and, indeed, an essential condition for the unity of Scripture. The Old Testament is a paradigmatic collection of locutions that bear multiple meanings, and the revelation of God in Christ enacts a transformation in the proper reception of the prefiguring text. On the reading of Hebrews above, Old Testament locutions were designed to prompt questions and confusion. How could the psalmist speak of humans having already been exalted over the angels? Why did David speak of "rest" when the Israelites had already entered Canaan? These locutions were not intended to produce a satisfying perlocutionary effect. The desired response was confusion and curiosity, a sense of incompleteness and longing. Only when God spoke through his Son could the true illocutionary force of these speech-acts be unveiled. Divine appropriation of human discourse was not simply a matter of course — or canonization. It demanded the fullness of times.

The suggestion that human authorial intent does not fully constitute divine communication is not new in the Christian tradition, nor is it the function of prevailing scholarly winds. Augustine presumed the importance of the human author, but broadened the notion of authorial intent beyond one fixed meaning. In his discussion of this matter in *Confessions* 12, Augustine admits his inability to discern with certainty Moses's intent in Gen. 1, but rejects the notion that the text is therefore of no value to him.[101] The quest for authorial intent is an act of love, an effort to honor God's servant, inspired as he was by the Spirit for the promulgation of Scripture. But Moses may have had multiple meanings in mind, and there is no loss in receiving all these meanings according to their varied benefits for the individual reader. For the ultimate task of interpretation is not to discern the author's meaning but to discover truth, and Augustine would also be encouraged if his readers found in *Confessions* whatever truths speak best to them. Thus, Augustine can say, "I am convinced that when [Moses]

---

101. *Conf.* 12.30.41–12.32.43.

wrote those words what he meant and what he thought was all the truth we have been able to discover here, and whatever truth we have not been able to find, or have not found yet, but which is nonetheless there to be found."[102] Yet he can also admit the possibility that Moses had only one meaning in mind.

> If he did, by all means let that one which he intended be taken as paramount. But as for us, Lord, we beg you to point out to us either that sense which he intended or any other true meaning which you choose, so that whether you take occasion of these words to make plain to us the same thing that you showed him, or something different, you still may feed us and no error dupe us. . . . For this is the assurance on which I make my confession: that if I manage to expound the sense intended by the writer who served you, that will be correct and the best course I could take, and that I must endeavor to do; but if I do not succeed in that, I may at least say what your Truth wills to reveal to me through the words of Moses, since it was your Truth who communicated to him also whatever he willed.[103]

Augustine's position on authorial intent displays striking nuance. The goal of interpretation is truth, which we can trust the biblical author to communicate faithfully. But Moses may have had multiple meanings in mind, and God can communicate truths through Moses's words that Moses did not originally intend. So long as the particular interpretation chosen fits God's overall purposes, Augustine will be content.

Thomas Aquinas adopts a different perspective. In his treatment of the possibility of Scriptural words bearing multiple senses, considered above, Thomas remarks: "Since the literal sense is that which the author intends *(quem auctor intendit),* and since the author of Holy Writ is God, Who by one act comprehends all things by His intellect *(omnia simul suo intellectu comprehendit),* it is not unfitting, as Augustine says *(Confess.* xii), if even according to the literal sense, one word in Holy Writ should have several senses *(etiam secundum litteralem sensum in una littera Scripturae plures sint sensus).*"[104] Like Augustine, Thomas affirms the importance of authorial intent while imbuing it with plurality. Yet Thomas lays primary stress on the

---

102. Ibid., 12.31.42.
103. Ibid., 12.32.43.
104. ST I.1.10.

divine authorship of Scripture with hardly any reference to human intent, and he locates multiplicity of meaning in the spiritual senses: the literal sense secures a fixity of meaning, but those things to which the literal sense refers can, in turn, signify other things according to God's governance of sacred history. Augustine, by contrast, understands the literal sense itself to contain multiple meanings, even if he also affirms the existence of spiritual senses that further multiply these meanings. There is for Augustine a correspondence, if not direct identity, between Moses's conscious intent and what God would have us believe.

From the perspective of this chapter, Augustine is closer to the mark. Multiplicity of meaning does not reside first and foremost in the spiritual senses, but in God's free, sovereign address through the words of the biblical text. This is not to draw Barth's distinction between Scripture and the Word of God, nor to suggest that the divine address has only a contingent or arbitrary relation with Scriptural locutions. It is rather to confess that God speaks dynamically through the words of Scripture, here and now, according to the contours of redemptive history, and in a manner consistent with but not fully constituted by the original sense, defined at least provisionally according to the historical method and a qualified affirmation of human authorial intent. Within this model of Scriptural authority, the historical method informs the interpretive process in a variety of ways: it provides valuable information on the background and circumstances of individual writings; it sheds light on original meaning; it provides a reference point for hermeneutical disputes; it helps readers avoid supersessionist moves that evacuate God's promises to Israel of their straightforward meaning. Yet the results of the historical method cannot fully constitute the divine address, precisely because God continues to reveal himself in Scripture in ways that could not previously have been understood. Indeed, one of the chief benefits of the historical method is to raise consternation concerning what Old Testament locutions could have meant to the original recipients. The text will be full of oddities, discrepancies, and confusion that would not have made sense in earlier contexts. Yet these curiosities should be highlighted, not glossed, for they ultimately direct the reader toward Christ. True meaning will not be identified with the results of scientific study, but will arise spiritually from the text in a manner that explicates, extends and animates what had formerly served as an occasion for perplexity. The dynamics of Scriptural authority thus embrace both continuity and discontinuity. The locutions that mediate God's speech remain canonically constant, but the illocutions adopt new force according to the contours of redemptive history. God is faithful to his unchanging Word, but this Word is living, not static.

Two implications follow. First, we may remove some pressure from the historical method to secure God's ongoing message for his people. The historical method plays an important, even essential role in biblical interpretation, but the locus of Scriptural authority does not ultimately reside in the original sense. Thus, while new historical insights to the text may in principle challenge current doctrinal positions, the ecclesial reception of Scripture is not desperately contingent upon the latest results of the critical method, nor hopelessly impossible given the limitations of historical inquiry. Since the divine address will reflect God's fidelity to his Word, we must attend to the original sense to discern how God may now be speaking. But the original sense does not so constitute the divine address that we can receive it only after exhausting the historical method (as if such a task were even possible). Second, even contemporary readers find themselves only at a particular moment in redemptive history. They have not yet reached the final end when they will experience the beatific vision and see God face-to-face. As such, they cannot claim to have understood Scripture fully, even if they have proleptically received the fullness of God in Christ. The question of the next chapter, then, concerns God's ongoing speech throughout redemptive history, after the incarnation and before the final return. We must therefore turn to issues of Scripture and tradition.

CHAPTER 6

Witnessing the Living Word: Scripture and Tradition

Introduction

This chapter moves beyond the relation between the testaments to consider the character of God's address after the apostolic age. On my model of Scriptural authority, the use of the Old Testament in the New is one particular, albeit privileged instance of divine self-revelation. As the Spirit continues to illuminate Scripture, the covenant people gains new understandings of the text that may be expressed in various creeds, conciliar formulations, and doctrinal statements. Tradition is thus a witness to the divine address necessary for the interpretation of Scripture, but not a distinct authority independent from or normative over the biblical text.

I begin this chapter by considering the dynamics of redemptive history after the incarnation, and the implications of these dynamics for the relation between Scripture and tradition. I then trace the development of fourth-century Trinitarian theology as a test case for my model of Scripture and tradition as well as an opportunity to explore the relation between interpretive communities and the literal sense. A final section, which may be considered a kind of appendix, addresses the ecclesial conditions necessary for a proper understanding of Scripture and tradition, focusing especially on issues that continue to divide Protestants and Catholics.

Redemptive History after the Incarnation

If Scriptural authority derives from the activity of the triune God in the economy of salvation, we must consider how God continues to reveal himself in the post-apostolic era. Is God's self-revelatory activity restricted to the formation of the canon or does it extend also to subsequent reception history? What redemptive-historical considerations govern how Scriptural authority is to be construed in our contemporary context? In the previous chapter, I suggested that the figural reading of Scripture must be indexed to two non-negotiable Christian convictions, namely, the fidelity of God's promises to Israel and the radical newness of the Christ event. Here the determinative issue is another constitutive Christian confession: the Holy Spirit's ongoing guidance of the church. The question of Scripture and tradition ultimately hangs on pneumatology, particularly with reference to the relation between the work of the Spirit and the revelation of the Word. In this section, I argue that the Spirit's task is to minister the revealed Word, not by providing new revelation but by enlightening the church for deeper understanding of the apostolic deposit. In the next, I defend Scripture's correlative authority over tradition, whose role is to serve as witness to the living Word.

In *De trinitate,* Augustine sets forth a conceptual framework for distinguishing between the Trinitarian persons according to the divine relations. Against Arian suggestions that the Father and Son must be distinguished according to disparity of substance, Augustine argues that the distinctions within the Godhead derive rather from the eternal relation of each person to the other.[1] The Father begets the Son, but is not begotten; the Son is begotten of the Father, but this relationship cannot be reversed. The point here is not just semantic, but ontologically fundamental: the Father is not the Son precisely because he begets and is not begotten, and the Son is not the Father precisely because he is begotten and does not beget the Father. Nevertheless, such distinctions do not suggest any difference of power, wisdom, or goodness; they simply affirm a certain plurality within the context of a self-consciously Nicene emphasis on divine simplicity and the unity of divine will and action. In general, Augustine devotes less attention in his discussion of these issues to the Spirit, but such categories can be extended to the third person of the Trinity as well. While the Father and the Son are distinguished as begetter and begotten, the Spirit is the bond of love between the Father and the Son. There is thus a special sense in which the Spirit may be called "charity";[2] he receives the name "Holy

---

1. *Trin.* 5.2.3–5.14.15. The most substantive recent treatment of Augustine's trinitarian theology is Lewis Ayres, *Augustine and the Trinity* (Cambridge: Cambridge University Press, 2010).

2. Ibid., 6.5.7.

Spirit" because both the Father and the Son are "holy" and "spirit";[3] and he figures consistently in the analogies of the second half of *De trinitate* as an agent of union and desire — akin to the will, for instance, that prompts some object of recollection to be brought from the storehouses of memory before the intellect.[4]

The intra-Trinitarian relations bear concretely upon the visible manifestations of God in redemptive history. While Augustine attributes the Old Testament theophanies to angelic activity, he identifies the missions of the Son and the Spirit primarily with the incarnation and the giving of the Spirit at Pentecost (or the appearance of the dove at Jesus's baptism), respectively.[5] As the Father sent the Son to become man, so also did the Father and the Son send the Spirit in the flames of fire. The Spirit's most important task is encapsulated in Rom. 5:5: to pour the love of Christ into our hearts.[6] Augustine's suggestion that the missions of the distinct persons of the Godhead reflect their relations presages the eventual adoption of the *filioque* clause in the West. The more pertinent point for our purposes is that the missions are, like the relations, irreversibly ordered: the Son and the Spirit are sent, but the Father is not, just as the Son is begotten of the Father, but not the other way around.[7] This distinction does not imply subordinationism; the economic sendings derive from the relations of the immanent Trinity, in whom each of the persons is coeternal and coequal. Nor is modalism in view: all of God's work in redemptive history reflects the consensus and activity of all three persons. Nevertheless, it is necessary to affirm some kind of qualified differentiation in God's activity in redemptive history according to the distinctions of the intra-Trinitarian relations.

Calvin elaborates on the dynamics between the Son and the Spirit, especially with regard to Scripture. For Calvin, the particular role of the Spirit in salvation is to unite believers with Christ by prompting faith in the promises of Scripture.[8] Christ has accomplished the external, objective grounds for salvation; the Spirit's task is to interiorize this work through subjective application. It was not the Spirit who took on flesh, died on the cross, and rose to new life for the forgiveness of sins. The Spirit serves instead to bring Christ's work to completion, enabling be-

---

3. Ibid., 5.11.12.
4. Ibid., 9.6.9–9.12.18, 10.11.17–10.12.19.
5. Ibid., 2.5.7–2.6.11.
6. See especially *spir. et litt.* for the importance of this passage for Augustine.
7. *Trin.* 4.20.27-29, 4.21.32.
8. See discussion in chapter 2.

lievers to receive the promises of Scripture as their own such that Christ may dwell in their hearts by faith. This is the reason Calvin resists those "fanatics" who attempt to separate Word and Spirit.[9] The Spirit directs Christians toward the Scriptures he himself inspired and continues to illuminate, such that the agreement between Word and Spirit is simply the Spirit's conformity with himself. The Word without the Spirit would be fruitless and inert; yet the Spirit is so intimately bound to the Word that independent agency would be a contradiction in terms. The work of the Spirit, then, is essentially referential, aimed not at the original accomplishment of salvation, but toward its fulfillment. If Calvin frames his treatment of this issue somewhat differently from Augustine, the core theological point remains: the Spirit and the Son adopt different roles in redemptive history according to the distinctions of the intra-Trinitarian relations. The Spirit directs us to Christ because he is the bond of unity between the Father and the Son.

Such considerations form the basis for a properly Trinitarian understanding of the Spirit's superintendence over Scripture, which may in a strong sense be identified with the Word of God. As has often been noted, the term "Word" is ambiguous, referring first to the eternal Son, but derivatively to Scripture as a witness to Christ. Scripture should not be hypostasized as if it were the second person of the Godhead, but may legitimately be called "Word" as the privileged means of God's self-revelation. Given this qualification, the Spirit's activity with reference to the written Word is properly understood as a subset of his more general role in redemptive history: to direct believers toward the eternal Son. The first step in this movement was the Spirit's inspiration of Scripture, which brought glory to the Son through the Old Testament's prophetic anticipation of Christ's redemptive work, and the New Testament's retrospective celebration of the same. Yet the Spirit continues to glorify the Son by illuminating and enlivening Scripture with reference to the eternal Word. Again, the work of the Spirit is referential: his task is not to establish new salvific realities, but to interiorize what has been received. The absence of the Spirit's activity in the church would leave Scripture powerless to communicate the divine address. But if the Spirit has not abandoned the church in the post-apostolic age, reception history must exercise some role in the interpretation of Scripture. The ongoing work of the Spirit thus provides *prima facie* theological grounds for the legitimacy of tradition. Scripture is the

---

9. *Inst.* 1.9.

completed prophetic and apostolic testimony to Christ, while tradition is a record of the Spirit's continued activity in bringing glory to the Son in the church.

This is the basic position adopted by Yves Congar in his *Tradition and Traditions,* which remains arguably the most significant Roman Catholic treatment of Scripture and tradition since the period surrounding Vatican II.[10] For Congar, the relation between Scripture and tradition hinges on the ordered relationships between Christology, pneumatology, and ecclesiology as manifested in redemptive history. God's saving work has not ceased with the closing of the canon; the realities of the apostolic age remain in some sense present with us. This means, on the one hand, that tradition does not entail fundamental change or modification from the original deposit; it rather preserves the identity through time of what was once received. Yet God's ongoing activity in redemption also suggests the possibility of "continual renewal and fertility *within* this given structure, which is guaranteed by a living and unchanging principle of identity."[11] Tradition is not a matter of stasis or stagnation, "the simple permanence of a structure," but the application of Christ's work by the Spirit for the church.[12] Christ established the apostolate, the sacraments, and the church; the Holy Spirit infuses within this structure "its vitality, the inner movement of its life, and interiorizes in men the gifts which Christ has acquired for them."[13] It is therefore theologically possible to locate Christ at the origin of "a finally established and supratemporal deposit" while also affirming the Spirit's role in actualizing and personalizing this deposit for the church throughout her history.[14]

The Johannine promises of the Spirit are of great importance in this regard: "The Counselor, the Holy Spirit, whom the Father will send in my name, he will teach you all things, and bring to your remembrance all that I have said to you" (John 14:26). "I have yet many things to say to you, but you cannot bear them now. When the Spirit of truth comes, he will guide you into all the truth; for he will not speak on his own authority, but

---

10. Yves M.-J. Congar, *La Tradition et les traditions,* 2 vols. (Paris: Librairie Artheme Fayard, 1960 and 1963). English translation: *Tradition and Traditions: The Biblical, Historical, and Theological Evidence for Catholic Teaching on Tradition,* trans. Michael Naseby (original vol. 1) and Thomas Rainborough (original vol. 2) (San Diego: Basilica, 1966).

11. *Tradition and Traditions,* 265. Unless otherwise specified, all italics his.

12. Ibid., 264.

13. Ibid., 265.

14. Ibid.

whatever he hears he will speak, and he will declare to you the things that are to come. He will glorify me, for he will take what is mine and declare it to you" (John 16:12-14).[15] For Congar, these assurances of the Spirit's role in testifying alongside the apostles to the incarnate Son secure confidence that future generations will faithfully guard the deposit they have received.[16] Yet they also pose a challenge to Protestants who seek to identify the Spirit's work exclusively with the original inspiration of Scripture and not with subsequent reception of the biblical text. As Congar insists, there are two stages of God's self-revelatory action in redemptive history: "the definitive formation of an objective deposit," and "the Gospel's flowering in a personal human subject, throughout an endlessly varied history."[17] The first has been completed in the canonization of Scripture, which acts as the external point of reference for the Word of God throughout the church's history. The second entails a new act whereby God grants efficacious understanding of the Word to his people, as, for instance, with the disciples on the road to Emmaus or the Ethiopian eunuch to whom Philip was sent.[18] Protestants, Congar suggests, implicitly acknowledge this distinction in their appeal to the inner testimony of the Spirit. Yet their aversion to any sort of development or creative progress from the original deposit has kept them from fully appreciating this dynamic. Again, a proper understanding of the Trinitarian missions mitigates such concerns. Because the mission of the Spirit is to complete and fulfill the mission of the Son, there is no question of an autonomous tradition. The Spirit's work augments but does not replace or challenge the work of the Son; tradition unfolds the meaning of Scripture but not as a rival authority.

Fifty years after its publication, Congar's work continues to merit serious consideration, and contemporary scholarship reflects burgeoning Protestant interest to embrace the notion of tradition more than previous generations have. The overarching aim of Vanhoozer's *The Drama of Doctrine* is to invite creative new appropriations of Scripture that retain fidelity to the biblical witness. According to his theatrical metaphor, redemptive history demands ongoing ecclesial "performances" both to develop and to preserve consistency with earlier "movements."[19] Failure to retain the

---

15. Both passages in ibid., 16.
16. Ibid., 18-19.
17. Ibid., 401.
18. Ibid., 400-401.
19. Kevin J. Vanhoozer, *The Drama of Doctrine: A Canonical-Linguistic Approach to Christian Theology* (Louisville: Westminster John Knox, 2005).

right balance risks two extremes: the effort, on the one hand, to address the problems of the contemporary context by simply re-creating the past (complete knowledge of which is, in any case, epistemologically inaccessible), and a propensity, on the other hand, to correlate the canonical script without qualification to contemporary concerns, inviting revisionism ultimately incommensurate to the original performance. Against these alternatives, Vanhoozer argues, Christians seek neither "slavish repetition" nor "sovereign originality," but "bound fidelity" or "creative freedom."[20] As mentioned in the previous chapter, Vanhoozer invokes the practice of improvisation as an image for this mode of Scriptural engagement.[21] Christians are called to a kind of improvisation that draws upon prior trajectories in the text to address the challenges of the contemporary context faithfully; some creative tension between past and present is necessary. Yet the requirement for Christian improvisation is not radical autonomy or independent authorship, but the development of virtues that will cultivate the *habitus* of Christ and a readiness to perform new renditions of the gospel.

Vanhoozer's proposal does not ultimately depend on the appeal of his dramatic model, but, as with Congar, on a series of Trinitarian and ecclesiological convictions concerning the relation between Scripture and tradition. On the analogy of the canonical drama, the Son is the primary agent who "performs" the Father's script. The "transcript" of Christ's life, death, and resurrection then becomes a script for God's continued activity in the church through the activity of the Spirit, who empowers the church for subsequent performances of the Son's prior and paradigmatic performance of the Father's will.[22] For Vanhoozer, "canon" is ultimately a Christological, not ecclesiological term. It was Christ who provided the authoritative interpretation of the Old Testament, Christ who commissioned the apostolate to speak on his behalf, and Christ who established the canon as a privileged instrument for his ongoing lordship over the church. The Spirit's role, by contrast, is ministerial: he is not just any spirit, but the Spirit of Christ (Rom. 8:9), and his commission is not to bear witness to himself, but to the Son. Such a position does not imply subordinationism, for the

---

20. Ibid., 253.

21. For another suggestion along these lines, see Richard B. Hays, *The Moral Vision of the New Testament: A Contemporary Introduction to New Testament Ethics* (San Francisco: HarperSanFrancisco, 1996), 6. See also Samuel Wells, *Improvisation: The Drama of Christian Ethics* (Grand Rapids: Brazos, 2004).

22. Vanhoozer, *The Drama of Doctrine*, 189.

concern here is not the divinity but the particular role of the Spirit. Yet it does underscore the importance of properly ordering the particular roles of the economic Trinity. Thus construed, the relation between the Son and the Spirit obviates the possibility of post-canonical revelation that does not ultimately derive from or submit to the canonical witness to Christ. "In the final analysis, the supreme theological warrant for *sola scriptura* can only be *solus Christus*. To practice *sola scriptura* with the Reformers is to recognize that Jesus Christ is the ultimate content, author, and interpreter of Scripture.... However, just as *sola scriptura* does not imply 'without tradition,' so *solus Christus* does not entail 'without the Spirit.'"[23]

The ecumenical importance of this discussion should not be minimized. In Congar and Vanhoozer, we discern a growing consensus that the relation between Scripture and tradition must be grounded in a proper understanding of the immanent relations and economic missions of the triune Godhead. This perspective secures the Roman Catholic position, as Congar expounds it, that the Spirit's task is not to produce new words of Scripture, and that tradition is witness to and not rival of the original apostolic deposit. Yet it also enables a Protestant evangelical theologian to affirm the Spirit's ongoing ministry of the Word such that fidelity to Scripture need no longer be defined as a kind of rote repetition. The traditional stereotypes of Protestants wholly allergic to doctrinal development since the apostolic age, or of Roman Catholics recklessly devoted to tradition over and against Scripture, can no longer be sustained without qualification. The door has been opened on both sides for a measured affirmation of tradition as a privileged witness to Scripture, and the development of doctrine as a fruit of the Spirit's commissioned testimony to the Son.

Scripture and Tradition

The Trinitarian framework for Scripture and tradition sketched above provides theological warrant for understanding the Spirit's illumination of Scripture as the primary mode of God's direct address in the post-apostolic age. From this perspective, tradition may be understood as a record of God's ongoing speech to the church, a testimony to the Spirit's ministerial work whose consistency derives from God's faithfulness to himself. Since the Spirit cannot direct the church away from the one to whom he bears

---

23. Ibid., 197.

witness, his presentation of the divine address will necessarily result in deeper reverence for the Word. Yet the referential character of the Spirit's witness does not render his testimony superfluous to the interpretive task, and this naturally raises questions concerning the relative weight of Scripture and tradition. In the previous section, I stressed significant areas of convergence on this matter of longstanding controversy between Protestants and Roman Catholics. This section concretizes that discussion while also flagging remaining barriers to ecumenical consensus. For his ongoing influence and importance, I continue the dialogue with Congar, noting both the insights and challenges of his position from a Protestant perspective.

We begin with areas of common ground. Recent Protestant scholarship has been characterized by newfound appreciation for the importance of tradition. Increasingly, *sola scriptura* is understood not to preclude engagement with reception history, but in a sense to demand it, against the presumption that contemporary readers may operate as autonomous individuals with little to learn from the past. Again, Vanhoozer provides a useful example of this approach. His particular defense of tradition appeals to Bakhtin's concept of meaning potential, according to which texts contain trajectories that can only be realized later in their reception history.[24] The meanings that arise derive from the text itself, and not the authority of the interpreting community, but they can nevertheless be considered new by virtue of the fresh insight they provide into the text. The paradigmatic demonstration of this dynamic is, as we have considered, the relation between the testaments. But such a model can also be extended to redemptive history after the incarnation: *"Christian doctrine is the realization of canonical potential."*[25] Christians may thus distinguish between *sola scriptura*, a constitutive Protestant position, and *"'solo' scriptura"* or *"nulla traditio,"* which Vanhoozer considers a distortion of the Reformers' original intent.[26] According to his interpretation, *sola scriptura* did not entail the rejection of all authorities outside Scripture; it was a modernist distortion to place virtually exclusive emphasis on the individual in biblical interpretation. A proper understanding of the Reformation slogan embraces a more measured valuation of other theological norms: *sola scriptura* is the ecclesial practice whereby Scripture exercises supreme rule over Christian thought

---

24. Ibid., 352.
25. Ibid.
26. Ibid., 154, 233.

and life, but this is compatible with the assistance of historical testimonies to its power and meaning. "Church tradition enjoys the authority not of the judge but of the *witness*. Better: tradition enjoys the authority that attaches to the testimony of *many* witnesses."[27]

Such Protestant gestures mirror complementary shifts, or at least clarifications, in Roman Catholic thought on this issue since the Second Vatican Council. Congar, too, depicts doctrinal development as a realization of biblical themes and trajectories, and not as an accretion to the Scriptural witness. On his narration, the fathers and councils were forced to produce new conceptual forms and language in response to contemporary challenges and concerns, but they perceived themselves only to be drawing out the implications of what was once received. They saw the church as a flowering of the original event of the apostles and Pentecost — a propagation from a single seed, or a vine spreading its branches across the world from a single stock — and considered the entirety of Christianity a transmission, a spiritual reality that arose from but remained the same as the one apostolic source derived from Christ.[28] The early church thus preserved the primacy of the original foundation, while also affirming the continuity of later developments. Tradition developed as a kind of commentary on Scripture — a vital, but derivative witness. "Scripture, as the prophetic and apostolic witness to God's plan *explains itself* in tradition; in this respect, there is *more* in the ecclesial explanation (and, on occasion, in a 'definition' of the extraordinary magisterium) than in the text of Scripture, understood at the purely philological and historical level. But the magisterium and the Church must always come back to the normative fountainhead which is the transmitted deposit: there is *more* in this source of their life than they can fully take in or express."[29]

This perspective, Congar acknowledges, poses a challenge to traditional understandings of the Council of Trent, which declared that the gospel was passed down in both Scripture and unwritten traditions, and affirmed the reception and veneration of each "with a like feeling of piety and reverence."[30] Congar admits that certain controversialists during the time of the Reformation spoke of tradition as an authority independent

---

27. Ibid., 234.
28. Congar, *Tradition and Traditions*, 24-25.
29. Ibid., 267.
30. "Pari pietatis affectu ac reverentia suscipit et veneratur." This important phrase appears in the first decree of Session 4 of the Council of Trent. For Latin text and English translation, see Norman P. Tanner, ed., *Decrees of the Ecumenical Councils*, vol. 2 (Washington, DC: Georgetown University Press, 1990), 663.

of Scripture. While Trent remained circumspect on this matter, some of its signatories did not, defending the existence of truths in the deposit of faith that were not also revealed by Scripture.[31] For Congar, however, their position represented a polemical overreaction that superseded the teachings of the early and medieval church. Irenaeus, Tertullian, and others presumed an identity of content between Scripture and tradition, while also acknowledging the existence of unwritten apostolic traditions concerning relatively secondary matters of liturgy, discipline, or custom. None of these figures asserted a fundamental dualism in sources of knowledge, nor did Trent determine a new position on this matter.[32] For Congar, the proper Catholic understanding was, and still is, to affirm the material sufficiency of Scripture and its formal insufficiency. "Scripture contains, at least in the form of suggestion or principle, the entire treasury of truths necessary to believe in order to be saved."[33] Yet "Scripture by itself cannot adequately present its true meaning; it is only understood correctly in the Church and in its tradition."[34]

At first blush, Congar's remarks on these matters seem substantially compatible with the Protestant developments considered above. But closer inspection reveals a stronger, if somewhat inconsistent, position than his measured statements might suggest, and this point should be pressed for ecumenical honesty. For Congar's position is not simply that Scripture is "the highest authority in matters of faith" while tradition is "indispensable to the interpretation of the Word of God," according to the language of Pope John Paul II's 1995 encyclical, *Ut unum sint*.[35] The French Dominican also affirms the assertion of Trent's authors, as he understands it, that "that which the Church regards as normative and which would seem not to appear in Scripture, deserves the same respect as what has explicit scriptural warrant if it bears upon matters of faith or discipline: for the apostolic heritage has come to us through unwritten traditions as well as by Scripture."[36] Congar is quick to qualify this point with the observation that "it was widely, if not commonly, admitted that all the truths necessary to salvation are at least outlined in Scripture,"[37] but his defense

---

31. Congar, *Tradition and Traditions*, 376.
32. Ibid., 410-12.
33. Ibid., 116.
34. Ibid., 117.
35. *Ut unum sint* 79 (1995).
36. Congar, *Tradition and Traditions*, 412.
37. Ibid.

of doctrinal positions with only a loose connection to Scripture reveals a significant difference of perspective from the Protestant viewpoint. The following quotation is illustrative:

> The Church gradually acquired an awareness, sometimes one that went beyond the explicit letter of the text, of the content of the Christian mystery by which it lives. It unfolded, into a synthesis, certain elements which had been more or less left aside by the textual witnesses. . . . Catholics cannot adequately justify their position by appeal to explicit texts, but, holding these positions as elements of the Christian reality which they have received through tradition, they can rediscover and point out their points of insertion, their connections and support in Scripture. Hence the Church justifies its belief by scriptural texts without ever being restrictively limited to what they state expressly. . . . The text regulates the Church, but the Church in turn casts light on the text: the text is never anything but a witness to the facts and realities by which the Church lives.[38]

Congar alludes several times in this regard to contemporary developments concerning the virgin Mary, which he seems to consider the best test case for whether the church has ever set forth dogmatic definitions *"sine Scripturis."*[39] Yet his defense of such positions is rather forced and awkward. Again, I present Congar's remarks at length:

> If we seek a critical justification of a particular article of faith by an express witness (for example, the bodily assumption of the Mother of God) we may, perhaps, not find this in Scripture, but only distant references, general outlines, which demand a long and subtle process of reasoning in the light of the analogy of faith before we can arrive at the article in question. Despite this, however, the process of Tradition and of theological development animated by the whole Church's Christian sense under the twofold and harmonious direction of the Church and the assisted pastoral ministry, is never without some connexion with the scriptural witness, nor without some reference to the inspired Text.[40]

---

38. Ibid., 408-9.
39. Ibid., 413 n. 2.
40. Ibid., 413.

Protestants are unlikely to accept such explanations, not least when they concern the only matters upon which the magisterium has ever invoked papal infallibility, and this raises unavoidable challenges for ecumenical progress between Protestants and Roman Catholics. For the Protestant, the question is not just whether a doctrinal proposal may be hung upon some tenuous Scriptural hook. This is to flip the irreversibly ordered relations between Word and Spirit, or revelation and reception. The issue is rather the twofold conviction that Scripture is the uniquely privileged and authoritative locus of divine revelation, and that tradition is the means by which the Spirit illuminates the biblical text. The experience of the church cannot trump the divine address through Scripture, nor may doctrinal positions with only obscure Scriptural warrant be granted the weight of dogma on the grounds of unwritten traditions. The authority of experience derives from the authority of Scripture, and the experience of the church carries weight only to the degree that it proves illuminative of Scripture. Congar's judgment is thus too cavalier that "doubtless the debate will only be concluded when the Spirit has aided our separated brethren to understand that which the Church believes he has in fact enabled her to understand."[41] Scripture is not a rubber stamp for experience, and Protestants cannot compromise the unique authority of the biblical text over church practice, regardless of the latter's duration and extent. To concede this position would be to abandon the basis for "protest" and the possibility of ecclesial reform.

At various points, Congar appears sympathetic to such concerns. In the conclusion of a significant chapter on Scripture, tradition, and the church, immediately following a lengthy treatment of *sola scriptura,* Congar writes, "Scripture and Tradition are not on the same level. Scripture has an absolute sovereignty; it is of divine origin, even in its literary form; it governs Tradition and the Church, whereas it is not governed by Tradition or by the Church."[42] One also notes in this regard Congar's salutary warning not to ascribe independent authority to the magisterium over the apostolic deposit: "In speaking of the magisterium as *fons fidei* one might forget that the magisterium itself presupposes a source on which it draws and without which it would be absolutely NOTHING. The magisterium is a *channel* by which revelation is presented to the faithful with the value of a rule of faith. It is not itself a source, save in the apostles, and then in virtue of a charism which has not been transmitted to the inheritors of

---

41. Ibid., 403.
42. Ibid., 422.

their ministry. The help guaranteed to the Church is not the inspiration given to its apostolic foundation."[43] Nevertheless, Congar still approves the basic principle that "the Church, filled and assisted by the Holy Spirit, cannot be wrong on a matter of faith,"[44] as well as particular nineteenth- and twentieth-century developments concerning magisterial authority that paved the way for the dogmatic declarations on papal infallibility, the immaculate conception, and the bodily assumption of Mary.[45] The question arises whether Congar can hold with consistency his own affirmations of the supremacy of Scripture over tradition and the magisterium's "secondary and dependent" role in relation to the actual sources of revelation.[46]

In the final section of this chapter, I will set forth various ecclesial preconditions necessary for the vision of Scripture and tradition presented here to obtain. Here, it might simply be noted that the issues that continue to separate Protestants and Roman Catholics ultimately concern the locus of Scriptural interpretation. While the Trinitarian foundations for a proper valuation of Scripture and tradition have received growing ecumenical assent, the ecclesiological discussion remains a theological morass; there remains much for Protestants and Roman Catholics to learn from one other. Protestants insist on the primacy of Scripture because they believe the church can err. Experience may be embraced as a theological authority, but only as a *norma normata* under Scripture's preeminent rule. This does not imply the elevation of the autonomous individual as the primary locus of Scriptural interpretation, in isolation from the community of faith. As I will argue, the challenge remains for Protestants to articulate a substantive position on the role of the church in the reception of God's Word. Still, Protestants may encourage their Roman Catholic brothers and sisters to take more seriously Scripture's sober presumption that the people of God may fall into serious sin, and the implications of this teaching for ecclesial authority. At this point, then, we may celebrate ecumenical progress in a broadly shared affirmation of the authority of Scripture over tradition, and the legitimacy and necessity of tradition for the interpretation of the biblical text. The degree to which tradition must be generated by and submissive to Scripture remains a matter of dispute. The position adopted here is that the authority of tradition derives from Scripture alone.

43. Ibid., 205. Capital "RIEN" in the original French. Congar, *La Tradition et les traditions*, 1.257.
44. Congar, *Tradition and Traditions*, 203.
45. Ibid., 196-203.
46. Ibid., 205.

Scripture and Nicea

The vision of Scripture and tradition presented above may be illustrated by closer consideration of the Trinitarian developments of the fourth century. The value of this particular example arises from several factors: the doctrinal centrality of the theological locus; the broad, longstanding ecumenical consensus Nicene grammar continues to generate, even among ecclesial communities not typically associated with adherence to tradition; and the evident challenge Scripture posed for those fourth-century thinkers who sought a satisfactory formulation for the unity of the divine persons. Fair-minded historical inquiry reveals that the doctrine of the Trinity did not emerge uncontested from the biblical text, but that its framers at least perceived themselves to be drawing their conclusions from Scripture. My argument advances a more theological proposal: Nicea presents a paradigmatic instance of the divine address in the fourth century, and the authority of the Council derives from the Spirit's binding testimony to the Son. The development of Trinitarian doctrine was therefore not the product of eisegetical speculation or ecclesial fiat, but the fruitful discovery of God's Word as mediated through the biblical text.

Two recent proposals concerning the relation between Scripture and Nicea may be found in the work of David Yeago and C. Kavin Rowe.[47] For Yeago, the Nicene declaration that the Son is *homoousios* with the Father was not imposed upon the biblical texts nor simplistically deduced from them, but rather described a pattern of judgment present in the texts. Philippians asserts that Jesus has been granted "the name which is above every name" (2:9), to which "every knee should bend, in heaven and on earth and under the earth, and every tongue confess that Jesus Christ is Lord, to the glory of God the Father" (2:10-11). Paul's language clearly alludes to Isaiah 45:21-24 and the name YHWH, demonstrating the practice even among the earliest Christians of attributing to Jesus the closest possible relation to the God of Israel. Nicea expressed the same judgment in different conceptual terms, with the understanding that this intimate bond between the Father and the Son must be eternal. The task of biblical exegesis, Yeago infers, is not the historical examination of various biblical

---

47. David S. Yeago, "The New Testament and the Nicene Dogma: A Contribution to the Recovery of Theological Exegesis," in *The Theological Interpretation of Scripture: Classic and Contemporary Readings,* ed. Stephen E. Fowl, Blackwell Readings in Modern Theology (Oxford: Blackwell, 1997; original essay, since revised, published in 1993), 87-100. C. Kavin Rowe, "Biblical Pressure and Trinitarian Hermeneutics," *ProEccl* 11 (2002): 295-312.

terms in their original context, but inquiry into the "content and unity of the biblical *teaching*" in an effort to discern "unifying common judgments which may be rendered in very diverse ways, attempting to redescribe or re-render those judgments so as to do justice to the significance of their various articulations across the range of the canon."[48]

Rowe adopts a slightly different approach, drawing upon Brevard Childs's work on the bipartite character of the canon as generative of the Nicene formulations. It was precisely because both testaments were held as normative that the early church was forced to synthesize the Old Testament insistence that God is one with the New Testament's indications that God exists as Father, Son, and Spirit. The biblical text pressures readers to make judgments about the nature of the triune God, moving the interpretive task from questions of original sense to those of ontological reality: just who is this one God of Israel whom the New Testament identifies with Jesus Christ? On Rowe's account, this pressure may be understood as a form of divine self-revelation. "It is in fact the divine will mediated through God's own Word that compels us to speak in trinitarian terms about God. We may even say that it is the presence of God himself in his Word that wills and moves us to speak in this way about God."[49] Further, Rowe asserts, the ontological identification of the God of Israel with Jesus Christ legitimates a kind of qualified backward reading from dogma to text whereby Old Testament terms like "YHWH" and "Elohim" can be understood in terms of the Trinity.

The basic lesson of both proposals is that Scripture may be coordinated with later theological developments such that the latter is understood not as a foreign intrusion upon the text but as a faithful synthesis of biblical trajectories. Scripture drives the formation of doctrine, not the other way around, even if the process takes time and debate. Indeed, this dynamic can be observed in the actual development of Trinitarian thought from the apologists through the fourth-century writers.[50] In general, pre-Nicene

---

48. Yeago, "The New Testament and the Nicene Dogma," 96. Italics his.

49. Rowe, "Biblical Pressure and Trinitarian Hermeneutics," 309.

50. For introductions to this period, see J. N. D. Kelly, *Early Christian Doctrines*, 5th ed. (New York: Continuum, 1977); R. P. C. Hanson, *The Search for the Christian Doctrine of God: The Arian Controversy, 318-381* (New York: T&T Clark, 1988); John Behr, *Formation of Christian Theology*, 2 vols. (Crestwood, NY: St. Vladimir's Seminary Press, 2001 and 2004); Lewis Ayres, *Nicaea and Its Legacy: An Approach to Fourth-Century Trinitarian Theology* (Oxford: Oxford University Press, 2004); Khaled Anatolios, *Retrieving Nicaea: The Development and Meaning of Trinitarian Doctrine* (Grand Rapids: Baker Academic, 2011).

treatments of the relation between the Father and the Son were characterized by diversity and ambiguity. Justin and his contemporaries tended to favor the term "Logos" over "Son," conceiving a two-phase mode of being whereby the Word originally existed as the Father's mind or reason before creation, and then received some kind of external begetting for the creation of the world.[51] Tertullian adopted similar lines of thought by locating the begetting of the Son just prior to the moment of creation,[52] and construing the Son as distinctly visible from the Father.[53] Origen's Trinitarian theology, of course, would produce a quagmire of confusion for the fourth-century controversies, asserting on the one hand that the Son was eternally begotten of the Father,[54] while suggesting on the other that the Word was not "*the* God," but only "God" (in some lesser, non-articular sense).[55]

The debates of the following century testify not just to an increasingly precise terminology concerning the unity and diversity of God, but also to Scripture's presumptive normativity as the ultimate arbiter of orthodoxy.[56] In *Orations against the Arians*, Athanasius likens the "Arians" to the devil for veiling false teaching in Scriptural language.[57] He then dedicates almost

---

51. See Justin Martyr, *Dialogue with Trypho* 61-62, *Second Apology* 6. English translations: *Dialogue with Trypho*, trans. Thomas B. Falls, rev. Thomas P. Halton, ed. Michael Slusser (Washington, DC: Catholic University of America Press, 2003); *The First and Second Apologies*, trans. Leslie William Barnard, Ancient Christian Writers 56 (New York: Paulist, 1997). For discussion, see Alasdair Heron, "'Logos, Image, Son': Some Models and Paradigms in Early Christology," in *Creation, Christ, and Culture: Studies in Honour of T. F. Torrance*, ed. Richard W. A. McKinney (Edinburgh: T&T Clark, 1976), 43-62.

52. *Against Praxeas* 5-7. See also *Against Hermogenes* 3. English translations: *Tertullian's Treatise against Praxeas*, trans. Ernest Evans (London: SPCK, 1948); *Against Hermogenes*, ANF 3.

53. *Against Praxeas* 14-16.

54. *First Principles* 1.2.2-4. English translation: *Origen on First Principles*, trans. G. W. Butterworth (Gloucester, MA: Peter Smith, 1973).

55. *Commentary on the Gospel according to John* 2.12-18. English translation: *Origen: Commentary on the Gospel according to John, Books 1-10*, trans. Ronald E. Heine, Fathers of the Church 80 (Washington, DC: Catholic University of America Press, 1989). The issues surrounding Origen's Trinitarian theology and his influence on the fourth-century debates are notoriously complex. For further discussion, see Rowan Williams, *Arius: Heresy and Tradition*, rev. ed. (Grand Rapids: Eerdmans, 2001), 131-57; Behr, *Formation of Christian Theology*, 1:163-206; Ayres, *Nicaea and Its Legacy*, 20-30.

56. For general remarks in this regard, see Ayres, *Nicaea and Its Legacy*, 31-40.

57. *Orations against the Arians* 1.8. English translation: $NPNF^2$ 2.4. For a more recent translation of selected writings from Athanasius, including the *Orations*, see Khaled Anato-

all of his treatise to refuting Arian readings of contested passages, with the majority of the second oration devoted to Proverbs 8:22 alone. A similar impulse animates his defense in *De decretis* of the use of non-Scriptural terms in the Council of Nicea: "Let it be known to anyone who wishes to learn, that even if the words are not as such in the Scriptures, yet, as has been said before, they contain the sense *(dianoian)* of the Scriptures and they express this sense and communicate it to those who have ears that are whole and hearken unto piety."[58] Later in the fourth century, Basil's *On the Holy Spirit* engages in detailed discussions of Scripture's use of various conjunctions and prepositions, with extended sections dedicated to Scriptural testimonies of the divinity of the Spirit (even if Basil avoids using the term *homoousios* of the third person of the Trinity).[59] In one curious chapter, Basil does defend the value of unwritten traditions passed down from the apostles, but the purpose of this discussion seems largely to defend the legitimacy of liturgical practices that reflect Scriptural teaching but do not match exactly the language of Scripture — an important argument in his support of a traditional doxology whose precise formulation does not appear in the biblical text.[60] Certainly, the brunt of Basil's treatise focuses on Scripture as the primary support for his theological claims.[61]

As Scripture furnishes the warrant for various doctrinal conclusions, these positions come, in turn, to establish rules for reading Scripture. One of the most pressing concerns in the fourth-century debates is the proper interpretation of passages indicating some kind of limitation, subordination, or progress in Christ. Athanasius's strategy, which would exercise considerable influence over subsequent writers in both the Greek-speaking

---

lios, *Athanasius* (New York: Routledge, 2004). For discussions of Athanasius's interpretation of Scripture, see James D. Ernest, *The Bible in Athanasius of Alexandria,* The Bible in Ancient Christianity (Leiden: Brill, 2004); Anatolios, *Retrieving Nicaea,* 99-156; Peter J. Leithart, *Athanasius,* Foundations of Theological Exegesis and Christian Spirituality (Grand Rapids: Baker Academic, 2011), 27-55.

58. *De decretis* 21. English Translation: Anatolios, *Athanasius.*

59. E.g., *On the Holy Spirit* 19.48–23.54. English translation: *On the Holy Spirit,* trans. Stephen Hildebrand, Popular Patristics Series 42 (Yonkers, NY: St. Vladimir's Seminary Press, 2011).

60. Ibid., 27.65-68. For discussion, see Darren Sarisky, *Scriptural Interpretation: A Theological Account,* Challenges in Contemporary Theology (Oxford: Wiley-Blackwell, 2013), 111-28.

61. See, for instance, Basil's remark concerning the coordinated doxology at *On the Holy Spirit* 7.16: "But we are not content simply because this is the tradition of the Fathers. What is important is that the Fathers followed the meaning of Scripture" (as quoted in Sarisky, *Scriptural Interpretation,* 119 n. 33).

East and the Latin-speaking West, is to appeal to a narrative of divine descent whereby the eternal Word took on fleshly lowliness.[62] If Scripture teaches that Christ suffered, hungered, thirsted, and was even created, these testimonies must be attributed to the humanity of Christ in the incarnation, and not to the preexistent Word — an interpretive strategy that presupposes both humanity and divinity in Christ, albeit in only incipiently Chalcedonian terms.[63] Later authors utilize similar rules with striking consistency. In his *Theological Orations*, Gregory of Nazianzus affirms the practice of referring Scripture's lofty and lowly language of Christ to the divinity and humanity, respectively,[64] while also advancing another rule to differentiate between the Son's equality with the Father, and the Son's relational distinction from the Father. "The 'greater' refers to the origination, while the 'equal' refers to the nature."[65] Augustine adopts the same "canonical rules" in *De trinitate,* relying heavily on Paul's distinction in Phil. 2:6-7 between Christ in the form of God and Christ in the form of a servant.[66] Some statements in Scripture concerning the Father and the Son "indicate their unity and equality of substance"; others "mark the Son as the lesser because of the form of a servant, that is, because of the created and changeable human substance he took"; and finally, others "mark him as neither less nor as equal, but only intimate that he is from the Father."[67] While some locutions are ambiguous and could theoretically fit the second or third categories, irresolvable passages may be taken either way, so long as the basic Trinitarian grammar is preserved.[68]

62. For further discussion, see Behr, *Formation of Christian Theology,* 2:208-15; Anatolios, *Athanasius,* 66-74.

63. Anatolios judges, "We have here not only the introduction of the crucial strategy of 'partitive exegesis' into the fourth-century doctrinal debates, but also a prototype of the Chalcedonian christological framework, inscribed in the framework of scriptural narrative. Grounding the later ontological vocabulary of two natures and one person, we have here the exegetical categories of two dimensions of the scriptural christological narrative and a single agent of whom this narrative is predicated." *Retrieving Nicaea,* 124.

64. *Orations* 29.18, 30.9, 30.15-16. English translation: *The Theological Orations,* trans. Charles Gordon Browne and James Edward Swallow, in *Christology of the Later Fathers,* ed. Edward Rochie Hardy, in collaboration with Cyril C. Richardson, Library of Christian Classics (Louisville, KY: Westminster John Knox, 1954). See Behr, *Formation of Christian Theology,* 1:347-52 for further discussion.

65. *Orations* 30.7. See also 29.15. For a similar move in Athanasius, see *Orations against the Arians* 1.58.6, cited in Behr, *Formation of Christian Theology,* 1:348 n. 40.

66. *Trin.* 1.7.14, 1.11.22–1.12.24, 2.1.2–2.2.4.

67. Ibid., 2.1.3.

68. Ibid., 2.1.2, 2.2.4.

These examples illustrate both the fluidity of doctrinal development and the persistence of Scriptural authority. From the apologists through Augustine, the biblical text plays a determinative role for the language and concepts adopted to describe the relations between the divine persons. The authors employ a variety of philosophical and linguistic tools to explain these concepts, but Scripture remains the immovable reference point, or, to borrow Lewis Ayres's phrase, "the fundamental resource for the Christian imagination."[69] As stated above, this is not to suggest that Nicene terminology materialized from Scripture in a ready-made box. The ambiguities of second- and third-century theology and the heated debates of the fourth century make clear that the teaching of Scripture on the unity of the divine persons required elucidation. Yet the textual evidence also demonstrates that the chief combatants at least assumed there was some teaching to be sought. The biblical text as a whole had to support one position or another, and potential difficulties could and must be resolved. In time, with halting progress, there would arise growing consensus on the proper construal of the divine relations, such that rules derived from Scripture could provide a filter and guide for how the text should be read. But the prerequisite of these developments was a basic presumption of canonical authority and unity.

The historical particularities of this process indicate the complexities of such gains. Ayres has documented the vagaries and shifting political dynamics of the fourth-century debates, arguing in line with his mentor, Rowan Williams, that Athanasius's construction of the "Arians" was a fiction. There was no established Arian party, and Arius's supporters would not have considered themselves disciples of his thought.[70] Williams suggests the condemnation of Arius arose in part from changing relations in ecclesial and civil power structures, such that charismatic, speculative teachers could increasingly fall afoul of now state-sanctioned episcopal authorities. Early Christianity's arch-heretic was, at least to some extent, the victim of unfortunate timing.[71] Moreover, Williams argues, Arius was at core a theological conservative who sought to preserve the freedom and self-subsistence of God within the context of disparate Alexandrian

---

69. Ayres, *Nicaea and Its Legacy*, 39.

70. Ayres, *Nicaea and Its Legacy*, 13-14. See Williams, *Arius*, 82-83.

71. Williams, *Arius*, 87: "If we call these two approaches the 'Catholic' and the 'Academic' (in the classical sense) respectively, it seems that Arius, like his great Alexandrian predecessors, is essentially an 'Academic'; and, like those predecessors, he might have survived tolerably well in a different ecclesiastical and political climate."

traditions he had received, even if his particular synthesis meant reducing the Word to a distinct *hypostasis* fundamentally outside the life of God.[72] His concern was not first and foremost to denigrate the Son.

Williams's purpose is not to defend Arius's theological conclusions per se, but he does suggest that a proper evaluation of the fourth-century controversy, purged of Athanasius's distorting polemic, may yield fresh perspective on the historical development of Trinitarian thought as well as the very nature of doctrine. The Arian controversy was not simply a matter of the church's defense against radical innovation. Athanasius, too, was aware that *homoousios* represented a new event and that "the lost innocence of Pre-Nicene trinitarian language" could not be restored.[73] The defining question was which particular innovations best represented fidelity to the past. "Athanasius' task is to show how the break in continuity generally felt to be involved in the creedal *homoousios* is a necessary moment in the deeper understanding and securing of tradition; more yet, it is to persuade Christians that strict adherence to archaic and 'neutral' terms alone is in fact a potential betrayal of the historic faith."[74] Athanasius's model becomes a pattern for the church: subsequent ecclesial history would demonstrate that "some kind of doctrinal hermeneutics had come to stay; continuity was something that had to be re-imagined and recreated at each point of crisis."[75]

> There is a sense in which Nicaea and its aftermath represent a recognition by the Church at large that *theology* is not only legitimate but necessary. The loyal and uncritical repetition of formulae is seen to be inadequate as a means of securing continuity at anything more than a formal level; Scripture and tradition require to be read in a way that brings out their strangeness, their non-obvious and non-contemporary qualities, in order that they may be read both freshly and truthfully from one generation to another. They need to be made more *difficult* before we can accurately grasp their simplicities. Otherwise, we read with eyes not our own and think them through with minds not our own; the 'deposit of faith' does not really come into contact with *ourselves*. And this 'making difficult,' this confession that what the gospel says in Scripture

---

72. Ibid., 175-78.
73. Ibid., 235.
74. Ibid.
75. Ibid., 237.

and tradition does not instantly and effortlessly make sense, is perhaps one of the most fundamental tasks for theology.[76]

Williams's reflections reveal why questions of Scripture and tradition are so fraught with consternation and debate. At stake are the very core of social and religious identity, and the mechanisms by which this identity will be negotiated between competing desires for contemporary relevance and fidelity to received teaching.[77] In such discussions, wisdom resists the temptation to promote a partisan vision of Christianity that denigrates the legitimate concerns of other traditions. That said, the theologian has little choice but to make judgments about the relative valuation of various theological norms, and this demands some position on the dynamics of Scriptural authority vis-à-vis tradition. The Protestant suggestion of this chapter is that a proper understanding of the Trinitarian missions and the contours of redemptive history will assign supremacy to Scripture as the primary locus of divine revelation, while also acknowledging the secondary and derivative authority of tradition as a guide for the interpretation of Scripture. The interpretation of Nicea in this section supports such a proposal. The fourth-century formulations do not represent an imposition on the text but a distillation of Trinitarian trajectories in Scripture that demanded further explication in the midst of theological controversy. The result was a richer and more satisfying understanding of the biblical authors' original meaning.

There is a sense, then, in which the early church did not fully comprehend the import of John 1:1 until the fourth century, even if pre-Nicene authors did, of course, grasp somewhat inchoately the exalted status of

---

76. Ibid., 236. Italics his.

77. It is worth noting in this regard that the kinds of controversies that divide Protestants and Roman Catholics are not unique to Christianity. Muslim theology is characterized by similar disputes concerning the relative weight and contemporary application of the Qur'an and sunna — is the Prophet's length of beard or the order in which he cut his fingernails normative? — as is American legal scholarship in the area of constitutional interpretation, which also wrestles with questions of authorial intent, original meaning, and the practice of precedent. On Islam, see Daniel W. Brown, *Rethinking Tradition in Modern Islamic Thought,* Cambridge Middle East Studies (Cambridge: Cambridge University Press, 1996); and Daniel A. Madigan, *The Qur'ân's Self-Image: Writing and Authority in Islam's Scripture* (Princeton: Princeton University Press, 2001). On constitutional interpretation, see Sanford Levinson, *Constitutional Faith* (Princeton: Princeton University Press, 1988); and Antonin Scalia, *A Matter of Interpretation: Federal Courts and the Law,* The University Center for Human Values Series (Princeton: Princeton University Press, 1997).

the Logos. The Trinitarian debates were the means by which the Spirit revealed the broader implications of such locutions, with the result that the Nicene interpretation came to acquire binding status. In this new context, as much for the contemporary church as for the fourth-century writers, "In the beginning was the Word, and the Word was with God, and the Word was God," means quite literally that the Son is eternally begotten of and *homoousios* with the Father, God from God, Light from Light, true God from true God — even if the original biblical authors would not have recognized such formulations. In Congar's terms, the development of Nicene categories demonstrates the role of tradition in making more precise the fuzzy lines of Scripture, of filling out what was once a rough image, outline or sketch.[78] Or, to invoke Barth, Nicea presents an instance of the revelation of the Word of God through Scripture that brings glory to that self-same Word, precisely by demonstrating his equality with the Father.[79]

Still, the authority of tradition cannot trump the authority of Scripture, and this implies the perpetual possibility that Scripture will judge traditional formulations and find them wanting. Athanasius, the Cappadocian fathers, Augustine, and others did not advance Nicene dogma as a matter of pure decree; they considered the results of the Council the natural consequence of Scriptural consistency, and they were willing to revise their positions if their arguments were found contrary to the biblical text. For our purposes, their example represents a model for seeking the divine address as well as an instance of the Spirit's imposition of the Word upon the church. In practice, any theologian who considers himself or herself reasonably orthodox will hardly be inclined to challenge creedal declarations with extraordinary historical and ecumenical consensus. Yet the freedom of God in the divine address entails that even such venerable conciliar formulations as those of Nicea must, in principle, be open to correction. The consistency of divine self-revelation with Scripture arises from God's fidelity to his own Word; the relative contingency of tradition arises from the authority of God to rule and challenge his people, as well as the reality that the church can err and sin. In this respect, Nicea constitutes the paradigmatic instance of tradition as a record of God's direct address to his people as well as an argument for the supremacy of Scripture

---

78. Congar, *Tradition and Traditions*, 21-22.

79. Barth is not far from such a description when he narrates the early Reformation as the "great historical example" of the "discovery of the Canon." *Church Dogmatics* 1/1, trans. G. W. Bromiley, 2nd ed. (orig. 1932; London: T&T Clark, 1975), 108-9.

over tradition. As Vanhoozer suggests, the authority of tradition is ministerial and not magisterial because the role of tradition, like the role of the Spirit, is to direct the people of God to the Word of God.[80] Again, the relative valuation of Scripture and tradition derives from Trinitarian and redemptive-historical considerations.

The Literal Sense Revisited

This depiction of Nicea raises questions about the literal sense. To what extent can the literal sense be identified with ecclesial consensus? Does the identification of Scriptural authority with the Spirit's ongoing revelatory activity undermine the primacy of the literal sense in biblical interpretation? Protestants have historically appealed to the literal sense to secure the authority of Scripture over and against the doctrinal accretions of later church teaching, and Congar implicitly acknowledges the legitimacy of this concern in his insistence that the Roman Catholic position on Scripture and tradition is not to equate history and revelation.[81] Yet recent scholarship has sought to reject or to seriously redefine the literal sense, and the suggestion that tradition may prescribe normative interpretations of Scripture seems to relocate doctrinal authority from the canonical text to postbiblical ecclesial developments. I have argued that the appropriation of the Old Testament in the New necessitates a reconfiguration of the literal sense. The question of this section is whether the development of doctrine legitimates the same dynamic.

Perhaps the dominant trend among scholars who defend the legitimacy of the literal sense as a theological category is to connect the concept to community reception and a concomitant plurality of meaning. The initial impulse for this trajectory was Hans Frei's seminal article, "The 'Literal Reading' of Biblical Narrative in the Christian Tradition: Does It Stretch or Will It Break?"[82] Frei identified the literal sense as "the closest

---

80. Vanhoozer, *The Drama of Doctrine*, 207-10.
81. Congar, *Tradition and Traditions*, 490-91.
82. Hans W. Frei, "The 'Literal Reading' of Biblical Narrative in the Christian Tradition: Does It Stretch or Will It Break?" in *Theology and Narrative: Selected Essays*, ed. George Hunsinger and William C. Placher (Oxford: Oxford University Press, 1993), 117-52. Essay originally published in 1986. For history and analysis of Frei and the postliberal school, see Paul J. DeHart, *The Trial of the Witnesses: The Rise and Decline of Postliberal Theology*, Challenges in Contemporary Theology (Malden, MA: Blackwell, 2006), especially pp. 111-28.

one can come to a consensus reading of the Bible as the sacred text in the Christian church," emphasizing the historic roots of this position in early Christian strategies for appropriating Jewish Scripture as the Old Testament.[83] On the one hand, some kind of allegorical interpretation was necessary to establish the unity of the Old and New Testaments. On the other hand, this allegorical move ultimately assigned primacy to the literal sense of the New Testament, particularly for the gospels, but also for other New Testament writings that describe Jesus. In this way, the literal sense "became" the plain sense, namely, that which bears normative primacy for a given community. "There is no a priori reason why the 'plain' reading could not have been 'spiritual' in contrast to 'literal,' and certainly the temptation was strong. The identification of the plain with the literal sense was not a logically necessary development, but it did begin with the early Christian community and was perhaps unique to Christianity. The creed, 'rule of faith,' or 'rule of truth' which governed the Gospels' use in the church asserted the primacy of their literal sense."[84]

While Frei's article engaged at some length with contemporary hermeneutical theory, he ultimately rejected such efforts for a "less ambitious," "low-level theoretical effort"[85] that located textual meaning in the immediate cultural and linguistic contexts where the texts exercised authority. "Established or 'plain' readings are warranted by their agreement with a religious community's rules for reading its sacred text. It is at best questionable that they are warranted, except quite provisionally, under any other circumstances."[86] Frei acknowledged Christianity's historic adoption of virtually universal rules for interpretation, but his primary concern was to advocate latitude within varying contexts for community definition of the plain sense. Minimally, any Christian reading of Scripture must affirm both the literal ascription to Jesus of the gospels and other New Testament writings that describe him; and the unity of the testaments and the congruence of this unity with the principle of literal ascription. Otherwise, flexibility was Frei's norm: "Any readings not in principle in contradiction with these two rules are permissible, and two of the obvious candidates would be the various sorts of historical-critical and literary readings."[87]

83. Frei, "The 'Literal Reading' of Biblical Narrative," 118.
84. Ibid., 122.
85. Ibid., 139, 146.
86. Ibid., 144. Lindbeck's influence becomes especially clear toward the end of Frei's article.
87. Ibid., 144-45.

Subsequent years have witnessed a number of scholarly efforts to develop Frei's vision from a "postliberal" perspective. In one widely cited article, Kathryn Tanner defines the "plain sense" as a "function of communal use," "the obvious or direct sense of the text according to a *usus loquendi* established by the community in question,"[88] contrasting this view with the position that the plain sense is a property of the text and might thus be identified with "'what the text simply says,' the 'text's own immanent sense,' the 'text's sense when the expositor is a purely passive or transparent recorder of objective meaning,' or the 'text's sense without the imposition of extratextual categories.'"[89] Following Frei, she also appeals to narrative as a means of preserving flexibility and plurality in the plain sense across varying geographical and historical contexts. In a fuller study of this issue, Kathryn Greene-McCreight surveys Augustine, Calvin, and Barth's interpretations of Genesis 1-3 to advance similar judgments, concluding that the plain sense ultimately arose for each figure from a negotiation between the "verbal sense" of the text and "Ruled reading."[90] On the one hand, the plain sense must be disciplined by the semantic and grammatical constraints of the text's fixed arrangement of lexical units. On the other hand, some measure of hermeneutical flexibility is permitted within the broad constraints of the Rule of Faith, whose limited scope encourages a kind of expansion of meaning. Within these guidelines, the plain sense should not be identified with the verbal sense per se, but with a measured ecclesial practice that seeks to avoid either the potential for arbitrary communal judgment or the reduction of textual matter to some sort of pristine, objective meaning independent of reception history.

One final proposal comes from Eugene Rogers, who locates himself within Frei and Tanner's trajectory but stresses more explicitly the importance of virtue in the interpretive process.[91] For Rogers, the literal sense generates an "ordered diversity" of readings, a phenomenon that derives directly from the divine authorship of Scripture. Rogers leans heavily for

---

88. Kathryn E. Tanner, "Theology and the Plain Sense," in *Scriptural Authority and Narrative Interpretation,* ed. Garrett Green (Philadelphia: Augsburg Fortress, 1987; repr. Eugene, OR: Wipf and Stock, 2000), 59-78. Quotations from p. 63.

89. Ibid., 62. The quotation marks indicate representative positions with no named representatives provided.

90. K. E. Greene-McCreight, *Ad Litteram: How Augustine, Calvin, and Barth Read the "Plain Sense" of Genesis 1-3,* Issues in Systematic Theology 5 (New York: Peter Lang, 1999).

91. Eugene F. Rogers, "How the Virtues of an Interpreter Presuppose and Perfect Hermeneutics: The Case of Thomas Aquinas," *JR* 76 (1996): 64-81.

this point on Thomas Aquinas's remarks on the literal sense in the *Summa Theologiae,* where the Dominican identifies the literal sense with what God intended and then concludes that this sense may encompass multiple meanings of one passage of Scripture.[92] Further defense of interpretive plurality comes from Thomas's *De potentia,* in another passage Rogers quotes at length:

> Thus it is also to be avoided ... that anyone confine [*cogere*] scripture so to one sense, that other senses be entirely excluded, that in themselves contain truth and are able to be adapted to scripture, preserving the way the words run [*salva litterae circumstantia*]; for this pertains to the dignity of divine scripture, that it may contain many senses under one letter, in order that one may marvel that they are able to find in divine scripture the truth that they conceived by their minds — and by this also defend more easily against the infidels, since if anything which someone wants to understand out of sacred scripture appears to be false, recourse is possible to another of its [literal!] senses. ... Whence all truth [*omnis veritas*] which, preserving the way the words run, can be adapted [*potest adaptari*] to divine scripture, is its sense [or, 'is a sense of it'].[93]

Thomas's point is not that the literal sense encompasses all manner of exegetical fancy, but that interpretation remains, within certain constraints, underdetermined. The question is how to fill this hermeneutical gap, and Rogers's provocative proposal is to defer evaluative decisions to the "in-

---

92. ST I.1.10. This passage was considered briefly in the previous chapter.
93. Taken in full from Rogers, "How the Virtues of an Interpreter," 74, including explanatory remarks and a minor parenthetical discrepancy from the Latin, which actually reads *salva circumstantia litterae.* The Latin quotation is as follows: "Aliud est, ne aliquis ita Scripturam ad unum sensum cogere velit, quod [alii] sensus qui in se veritatem continent, et possunt, salva circumstantia litterae, Scripturae aptari, penitus excludantur; hoc enim ad dignitatem divinae Scripturae pertinet, ut sub una littera multos sensus contineat, ut sic et diversis intellectibus hominum conveniat, ut unusquisque miretur se in divina Scriptura posse invenire veritatem quam mente conceperit; et per hoc etiam contra infideles facilius defendatur, dum si aliquid, quod quisque ex sacra Scriptura velit intelligere, falsum apparuerit, ad alium eius sensum possit haberi recursus. ... Unde omnis veritas quae, salva litterae circumstantia, potest divinae Scripturae aptari, est eius sensus." I have taken this text from the *Corpus Thomisticum,* but have replaced *alios* with *alii* for the bracketed word. The former is almost surely a text-critical error, which will hopefully be corrected in the forthcoming edition of the Leonine Commission. http://www.corpusthomisticum.org/qdp4.html.

terests and purposes" of moral virtue.[94] Since interpretation is a human act, it is subject on Thomistic grounds to two modes of evaluation: one according to external art, or intellectual virtue, and another according to internal or moral virtue.[95] Priority clearly rests in Thomas with the latter. For Rogers, the implication is that interpretive skill plays some role in the hermeneutical task, but the weightier considerations concern wisdom and prudence. "If readers instruct themselves along Thomas's lines then they will attend not only to an interpretation's truth but also to its goodness, not only to its art and skill but also to its use and fruit. . . . It falls to method, by purpose and function, to promote diversity; to evaluate the products and choose among them, on the other hand, falls to ethical reflection."[96]

This chapter shares the postliberal concern to uphold the normativity of the literal sense while acknowledging the theological complexities of identifying its boundaries and function within the Christian community. I have also followed these scholars in a general affirmation of the communal dimension of interpretation, a measure of flexibility in the literal sense, and the relation between virtue and proper reading. Yet the dominant thrust of these authors' work is to blur the lines of demarcation for what counts as authoritative across different Christian contexts, and this impulse raises a number of concerns for construing Scriptural authority according to the divine address. I should therefore note three points that distinguish my position from the postliberal trajectory and thus draw the particular proposals of this chapter into sharper relief. The first concerns the importance of historical inquiry in the determination of the literal or plain sense. In the line of scholarship above, the descriptor, "the way the words run" (or some variation thereof), has come to function as a kind of catchphrase definition for the literal sense. So far as I can discern, the phrase originated with Bruce Marshall as a loose translation of Thomas's reference in *De potentia* to the *litterae circumstantia,* a genitive Latin construction which does not, in and of itself, provide a particularly high degree of specificity on the proper controls for interpretation.[97] The scholars in question largely follow suit. While Rogers, Tanner, and others acknowledge the legitimacy

---

94. Rogers, "How the Virtues of an Interpreter," 64. Rogers takes this phrase from Jeffrey Stout, "What Is the Meaning of a Text?," *New Literary History* 13 (1982): 1-12.

95. Rogers, "How the Virtues of an Interpreter," 76.

96. Ibid., 77.

97. Bruce D. Marshall, "Absorbing the World: Christianity and the Universe of Truths," in *Theology and Dialogue: Essays in Conversation with George Lindbeck,* ed. Bruce D. Marshall (Notre Dame, IN: University of Notre Dame Press, 1990), 101 n. 38.

of some checks on the literal sense, they tend functionally to assign little role to historical inquiry as a constitutive element of Scriptural interpretation. Such a lacuna reveals the complexities of drawing upon premodern authors to address contemporary concerns. It is certainly helpful to recognize that earlier thinkers acknowledged a degree of openness and flexibility in the literal sense. My previous chapter largely did the same. But in the contemporary context, the prescriptions of a thirteenth-century author on the boundaries of interpretation — even from so venerable an authority as Thomas — cannot be adopted without also accounting for genuine developments in biblical exegesis since the rise of the historical method.[98] The principle that Scriptural interpretation should accord with "the way the words run" can no longer function as some *pro forma* concession that not just any interpretation goes (if this is what Thomas meant anyway). On the contrary, the *litterae circumstantia* depends significantly on the semantic range of possible meanings in the original setting. Without some kind of contextual analysis, little determination can be achieved for which readings a lexical unit may or may not support. This is not to suggest that the meaning of a text is restricted to what the original author intended for the original audience. As I argue here, words contain meaning potential that may be actualized through new events for later communities. Still, the value and legitimacy of the historical method in establishing boundaries for interpretation cannot be rejected out of hand. In its proper use, the historical method functions as a means of securing fidelity to the literal sense.

A second question concerns the degree of interpretive diversity that may be countenanced, and whether such minimalist rules for interpretation as Frei's cohere with a Trinitarian account of Scripture and tradition. If tradition can be understood as a form of the Spirit's testimony to the Son, the development of doctrine may result in the specification, and not just expansion, of meaning. At Nicea, for example, the fourth-century debates produced a creed that established stricter guidelines for reading Scripture than before, disambiguating key biblical loci that had previously been ap-

---

98. For a more developed argument along these lines, see Joseph Cardinal Ratzinger, "Biblical Interpretation in Crisis: On the Question of the Foundations and Approaches of Exegesis Today," in *Biblical Interpretation in Crisis: The Ratzinger Conference on Bible and Church*, ed. Richard John Neuhaus, Encounter (Grand Rapids: Eerdmans, 1989), 1-23, cited in the introduction to this work. A more popular presentation of this position can be found in the foreword to Joseph Ratzinger/Pope Benedict XVI, *Jesus of Nazareth: From the Baptism in the Jordan to the Transfiguration*, trans. Adrian J. Walker (New York: Doubleday, 2007), also cited in the introduction to this work.

propriated for a much wider range of positions on the relation between the Father and the Son. The councils did leave various areas of obscurity open (the relation between the person and natures of Christ, for instance), but they also endorsed more than Frei's two informal rules of interpretation. If the only principles were the unity of the testaments and the literal ascription of the gospels to Christ, the church would not have progressed much beyond the second-century controversies. A more defensible account is that something akin to Frei's rules necessitated a decision on how to describe the relation between the Father and the Son, which, in turn, gave rise to further rules of Scriptural interpretation derived from that more basic set. From this perspective, narrative may indeed provide a helpful device for negotiating the tension between fidelity and creativity in diverse contexts, but the Spirit's rule over the church may also produce increasingly specific boundary markers for participation in a received tradition.

Rogers's emphasis on virtue proves valuable on this point, though not necessarily in the terms he sets forth. For Rogers, the literal sense lends itself to such a wide range of possible readings that virtue must become the arbiter between interpretive options: "When hermeneutics leaves interpretation underdetermined . . . interests and purposes take over."[99] The argument of this chapter suggests the opposite: virtue enables the literal sense to be received with more force and particularity. The contemporary academic context often operates on the presumption that scholars enjoy pride of place as arbiters of textual meaning. Scientific learning is taken to secure Scriptural insight, as if such knowledge were simply a matter of historical and linguistic training, and the suggestions of nonspecialists could be dismissed for lack of erudition. But this perspective cannot account for Jesus's repeated criticism of the Pharisees' interpretations of the law and his attribution of their failings to moral deficiencies. Those who cannot comprehend Jesus's words are not the exegetically untutored, but the hardened of heart, hearing but not understanding, seeing but not perceiving. If the proper end of biblical interpretation is obedience, the best readers will not be scholars but saints — those most sensitive and responsive to the voice of God in the text. Indeed, this is the difference between Scripture *qua* Scripture and the biblical text as historical artifact: the Word of God written is not an object of study but the privileged mode of God's address to humanity, which can rightly be received only from a posture of humility and submission.

99. Rogers, "How the Virtues of an Interpreter," 75.

Such a perspective enables fresh appreciation for the role of moral appeal in earlier theological discourse. As de Lubac observes, the *disciplina* of ethical and spiritual formation was understood throughout the early and medieval church as prerequisite for the spiritual reading of Scripture. For Hugh of St. Victor, for instance, "Scripture is given to us with a view to 'education in morals.'" It follows that "in the cultivation of knowledge extreme care should be taken not to neglect discipline, and that discipline is no less in keeping with Scripture than knowledge."[100] Gregory of Nazianzus begins his *Theological Orations* with these striking remarks:

> Not to everyone, my friends, does it belong to philosophize about God; not to everyone — the subject is not so cheap and low — and, I will add, not before every audience, nor at all times, nor on all points; but on certain occasions, and before certain persons, and within certain limits. Not to all men, because it is permitted only to those who have been examined, and are past masters in meditation, and who have been previously purified in soul and body, or at the very least are being purified. For the impure to touch the pure is, we may safely say, not safe, just as it is unsafe to fix weak eyes upon the sun's rays.[101]

The suggestion of this warning is not to reject the legitimacy of historical scholarship, far less to recover the practice of *ad hominem* attack in contemporary theological discourse. It is rather to locate the role of scholarship as but one element of the interpretive process, the end of which must involve the fruit of the Spirit, since, after all, it is the Spirit who guides the church into a deeper understanding of the text. Gregory displays a concern for both moral formation and theological orthodoxy, but he prioritizes the former decisively before the latter. For the theologian, hermeneutical ambiguities do not give way to the "interests and purposes" of the reader. Those with the wrong interests and purposes cannot even broach the text for its true meaning.

This consideration directs us to a final question and our original concern, namely, the authority of Scripture over the interpretive community.

---

100. Henri de Lubac, *Exégèse médiévale: Les quatre sens de l'écriture*, 4 vols. (Paris: Aubier, 1959-64). English translation: *Medieval Exegesis: The Four Senses of Scripture*, Retrieval and Renewal: Ressourcement in Catholic Thought (Grand Rapids: Eerdmans): vol. 1, trans. Mark Sebanc, 1998; vols. 2-3, trans. E. M. Macierowski, 2000 and 2009, respectively. Here 1:17.

101. *Theological Orations*, 27.3.

That Scripture enjoys final authority over ecclesial communities seems to me a constitutive Protestant position, and the scholars above would, I believe, generally agree. For Tanner, the formal identification of the plain sense with communal use does not prejudge the material or normative questions of how the plain sense is or ought to be construed. Few communities simply define the plain sense as the object of general agreement.[102] Indeed, "part of the functional import of privileging the plain sense is the denial of a semantic equivalence between text and interpretation: interpretive accounts, in other words, cannot capture without remainder what the text conveys, and therefore none of them can take its place.... [The plain sense] functions critically even with respect to consensus readings of a text; it works to evacuate the pretensions of communal discourse generally."[103] Yet this qualification is often obscured in Frei and his followers' depiction of the plain sense as a means of encompassing the cultural variability of Scriptural interpretation, and this move threatens the essential function of the literal sense. While the plain sense may be defined sociologically as that which bears normative primacy for the ecclesial community, the authority of Scripture cannot be reduced theologically to communal consensus. The legitimacy of the community's readings derives from their coincidence with the divine address, here identified with the Spirit's illumination of the biblical text. The literal sense does not become normative because the community recognizes it as such. Acknowledging the primacy of the literal sense is a non-negotiable condition for any community that considers itself Christian.

In Marshall's terms, this means Scripture enjoys "justificatory primacy" in the Christian community.[104] Christians ought not presume they have correctly identified the plain sense in the face of powerful counterevidence from other sources; it may well be that the accepted understanding of a given text demands revision in light of challenging new considerations. Still, if no interpretation of Scripture can accommodate the alternate position according to "the way the words go," Christians have no choice but to accept Scriptural teaching and to revise in one way or another their evaluation of these external truth claims. "To say that the plain sense is primary in the order of justification is to say that one does not take Scripture to be false, although what we identify as its plain sense may at any

---

102. Tanner, "Theology and the Plain Sense," 65.
103. Ibid., 72.
104. Marshall, "Absorbing the World," 73.

given point be false." Yet "it is possible to retain the primacy of the plain sense in the order of justification, while still allowing that external arguments may lead to a change in the way the plain sense is construed."[105] To adopt such a perspective is not to restrict the literal sense to reconstructed historical meaning, nor to suggest that Scripture admits no variability in interpretation. It is rather to ground the literal sense first and foremost in God's address to humanity, and to locate hermeneutical novelty and creativity in the discovery of that which was already latent in the text. The affirmation of this chapter that tradition can mediate the divine address does not, then, conflate the distinction between Scriptural authority and community judgment. While my model acknowledges the importance of virtue and communal wisdom for the interpretation of Scripture, I understand the utility of such factors according to their ability to display and not to determine the literal sense. The question, then, hitherto postponed, is how this community that stands under Scripture should be characterized, particularly from a Protestant perspective. We must therefore consider issues of ecclesiology.

Whither the Church?

Thus far, this chapter has operated on the assumption that the term "church" signifies some reasonably identifiable reality to which the theological proposals presented might be understood to refer. Closer inspection reveals more confusion on this matter than one might prefer. For the Protestant who does not define ecclesial bounds according to strict visible markers (e.g., communion with the Bishop of Rome), claims about the character and obligations of the church may seem ambiguous and theoretical, without application for any actual community. Indeed, contemporary scholarship is characterized by strong appeal to the visible church coupled with a curious lack of definition concerning just where this church may be found. This is one of Richard Hays's chief criticisms of Stanley Hauerwas in an otherwise appreciative appraisal of his thought. According to Hays's assessment, Hauerwas's theology should direct him to Roman Catholicism, yet he "chooses instead to live, anomalously, as a Protestant with no clear theological rationale for his ecclesial practice and no empirical community to exemplify his vision of ecclesial politics. There is no tradition of high-

---

105. Ibid., 94.

church Mennonites; the idealized tradition to which Hauerwas appeals is an idiosyncratic fiction."[106] Hauerwas is himself aware of this irony. To those who ask him where he derives his authority to preach, he replies, "I wish I had a good answer to that troubling question."[107] For other scholars, such imprecision seems less a challenge to overcome than a tool to embrace. In *Engaging Scripture,* Stephen Fowl responds at length to critics of an earlier book, cowritten with L. Gregory Jones, concerning its frequent reference to some undefined "Christian community." Fowl admits to terminological ambiguity, but defends its value for encompassing virtually any manifestation of the church local or universal, whether in recognized ecclesial contexts or *ad hoc* interdenominational gatherings. Vagueness is Fowl's preferred option: "Whether or not any particular grouping counts as a Christian community can only be worked out in conversation and debate."[108]

Such formal designations mask the complexities of Scriptural interpretation. For Francis Watson, this is a significant blind spot in Brevard Childs's appeal to canon as a means of securing the authority of Scripture over the interpretive community. As Watson argues, the abstract invocation of canon does not bring to tidy conclusion the messiness of hermeneutical morass; it simply demarcates new boundaries for further contention. Watson delineates a number of questions the theological notion of canon leaves unanswered: the normative privilege of certain strands of the biblical witness over others; the relation between canon and other authorities; the canonicity of Greek-language Jewish texts; and the relation between the testaments. Even for texts commonly acknowledged as canonical, the history of interpretation reveals widely divergent strategies that result in radically different theological conclusions: Genesis alone has been understood variously to legitimate polygamy, supersessionism, and young-earth theories, among other positions. On Watson's account, the reason Childs fails to acknowledge these unresolved problems is that he is "operating with a concept of an *ideal* community of faith to which real communities only occasionally and imperfectly correspond."[109] Scripture exists

---

106. Hays, *The Moral Vision of the New Testament,* 265.

107. Stanley Hauerwas, *Unleashing the Scripture: Freeing the Bible from Captivity to America* (Nashville: Abingdon, 1993), 10, cited in Hays, *The Moral Vision of the New Testament,* 265.

108. Stephen E. Fowl, *Engaging Scripture: A Model for Theological Interpretation,* Challenges in Contemporary Theology (Malden, MA: Blackwell, 1998), 2 n. 1.

109. Francis Watson, *Text, Church, and World: Biblical Interpretation in Theological Perspective* (London: T&T Clark, 1994), 44. Italics his.

for Childs in a relative vacuum, undisturbed by the vagaries of history, such that a legitimate argument for the necessity of the canon becomes an untenable assertion of canonical sufficiency. "Childs' important hermeneutical proposal locates the texts in their proper ecclesial context, but misconstrues that context as a self-contained autonomous space isolated from the world. In fact, the world permeates that space, and the 'truthful witness' offered by the canonical text cannot simply be read off its surface but must be given and discovered in the midst and in the depths of the conflict-ridden situations in which it is inevitably entangled."[110]

Watson provides a salutary check for theological proposals, like the one presented here, that look to advance broad analytic judgments somewhat abstracted from historical particulars. The synthetic move is a necessary step for advancing normative claims; yet the persistent challenge for theologians to identify the objects of theoretical reflection indicates the importance of concrete definition even for the speculative task. In particular, the proposals of this chapter depend on certain ecclesial conditions hitherto left undefined; some explication concerning the vision of the church presupposed seems unavoidable. In what follows, I consider a series of questions that demand at least preliminary judgments for my understanding of canonical authority to gain purchase on actual interpretive communities. The suggestions put forward function primarily as invitations for exploration rather than definitive determinations; conclusions at this juncture would be premature. Nevertheless, the complexity of the issues addressed should demonstrate the need for serious Protestant reflection on the nature of the church as well as the value of ongoing ecumenical dialogue. I focus my comments in particular on issues that divide Protestants and Catholics, both because Protestant ecclesiology has historically been characterized by opposition to Catholic understandings of the church, sometimes to the point of distortion, and because of a burgeoning interest in contemporary theological discussion in matters Roman.[111] While the posture adopted here will draw upon Reformation themes and convictions, the discussion will, I hope, demonstrate the degree of respect presumed toward those who do not share this heritage.[112]

---

110. Ibid., 44-45.

111. For two recent examples of this scholarly trend, see Gerald W. Schlabach, *Unlearning Protestantism: Sustaining Christian Community in an Unstable Age* (Grand Rapids: Brazos, 2010); Christian Smith, *How to Go from Being a Good Evangelical to a Committed Catholic in Ninety-Five Difficult Steps* (Eugene, OR: Cascade, 2011).

112. The importance of ecumenical dialogue is an implicit and explicit element of

The first area for further exploration concerns the relation between the individual Christian and the corporate body of Christ. In the concluding chapter of *Tradition and Traditions,* Congar highlights exclusive Protestant emphasis on the individual as arguably the primary point of divergence between Roman Catholic and Reformation traditions. On his reckoning, the very character of God's relation with humanity hangs on this question. "The Reformers wished this to depend on God *alone* and to be established *directly* (vertically) between God and sinful man, as a pure salvation by grace through faith."[113] The result was the "elimination of the reality 'Church' as a constitutive element of the covenant relationship. . . . It seems that what is required is a Scripture which is *self-*communicating, and a tradition which owes none of its value to a Church given life by the Holy Spirit, but depends solely on Scripture, and so on."[114] For Congar, this lacuna ultimately derives from a functional disregard for the public dimension of revelation and the promises of the Spirit's ongoing assistance to the church. It also relates to the rejection of the magisterium, which Congar considers constitutive of the covenant relation between God and humanity. On the one hand, Congar acknowledges the existence of the *sensus fidelium* whereby the church as a whole, laity and clergy alike, participates in a kind of common consciousness about matters of faith. The faithful are agents irreducible to the magisterium and capable of contributing their own testimony to the collective wisdom of the church. On the other hand, this common consciousness does not imply equal levels of roles and responsibilities concerning teaching authority. All are called to preserve and transmit the apostolic deposit, but the magisterium determines its meaning. "The definition of Tradition, either by the promulgation of its meaning, or by the fixing of it in 'dogmas' properly so called, that is, as a rule for belief having the force of law, has always been the task of the bishops and was traditionally exercised in a solemn way in the councils.

Geoffrey Wainwright's suggestion that liturgy is the "hermeneutical continuum" of Scripture. The continuity of tradition derives not just from God's faithfulness to his Word but also from the ongoing worship of his people across time. Wainwright, *Doxology: The Praise of God in Worship, Doctrine, and Life* (Oxford: Oxford University Press, 1980), 149-81; and idem, "Reading Scripture Together," in *Embracing Purpose: Essays on God, the World and the Church* (Peterborough, UK: Epworth, 2007), 85-104, originally published as "Towards an Ecumenical Hermeneutic: How Can All Christians Read the Scriptures Together?," *Greg* 76 (1995): 639-62.

113. Congar, *Tradition and Traditions,* 463.
114. Ibid.

In the councils, the whole of the Church's communion is expressed in that of the bishops, its unanimity is theirs and its consciousness also. They are the 'judges of the faith' and they define it."[115]

Recent ecumenical discussion has revived interest in the magisterium, not least because of John Paul II's 1995 encyclical, *Ut unum sint,* which noted with refreshing candor that the papal office, which was intended to function as a "visible sign and guarantor of unity," instead "constitutes a difficulty for most other Christians, whose memory is marked by certain painful recollections."[116] John Paul requested forgiveness for his own and his predecessors' complicity in this result, while also inviting dialogue on "a way to exercise the primacy which, while in no way renouncing what is essential to its mission, is nonetheless open to a new situation."[117] Many Protestants have responded positively to these overtures, recognizing the necessity and legitimacy of a teaching office with binding authority while also acknowledging the pragmatic unavoidability of the bishop of Rome exercising a certain prominence within the universal Christian community. As one representative example, "In One Body through the Cross," the Princeton Proposal for Christian Unity sponsored by the Center for Catholic and Evangelical Theology and published in 2003, both affirmed the Pope as "the only historically plausible candidate to exercise an effective worldwide ministry of unity" and encouraged him to exercise this office in a manner amenable toward those beyond the Roman Catholic communion.[118] Specifically, the document urged, the Pope should avoid pre-Vatican II forms of theology; demonstrate a spirit of sacrificial service toward non-Roman Catholics; and receive regular counsel from non-Roman

---

115. Ibid., 322.

116. *Ut unum sint* 88. English text taken from http://www.vatican.va/holy_father/john_paul_ii/encyclicals/documents/hf_jp-ii_enc_25051995_ut-unum-sint_en.html.

117. Ibid., 95.

118. Carl E. Braaten and Robert W. Jenson, eds., *In One Body through the Cross: The Princeton Proposal for Christian Unity* (Grand Rapids: Eerdmans, 2003), quotation taken from p. 65. See also Carl E. Braaten and Robert W. Jenson, eds., *Church Unity and the Papal Office: An Ecumenical Dialogue on John Paul II's Encyclical* Ut unum sint *(That All May Be One)* (Grand Rapids: Eerdmans, 2001), and an important series of dialogues that preceded *Ut unum sint:* Paul C. Empie and T. Austin Murphy, eds., *Papal Primacy and the Universal Church,* Lutherans and Catholics in Dialogue 5 (Minneapolis: Augsburg, 1974); and Paul C. Empie, T. Austin Murphy, and Joseph A. Burgess, eds., *Teaching Authority and Infallibility in the Church,* Lutherans and Catholics in Dialogue 6 (Minneapolis: Augsburg, 1978, 1980).

Catholic consultants.[119] Such recommendations presupposed significant progress on these matters through a series of bilateral dialogues involving the Roman Catholic Church, as well as the work of the Faith and Order Commission of the World Council of Churches especially in the decades immediately following Vatican II.[120]

These developments reflect the new ecumenical landscape that has emerged in the last half-century. Contemporary Protestant thought is not characterized by the kind of reductionist individualism that once concerned Congar, and recent Protestant theology reveals an encouraging recognition of the church as a constitutive element of the covenant relation between God and humanity. The interpretation of *sola scriptura* presented here does not understand the Reformation slogan as free license for individuals to interpret Scripture in isolation from church tradition. Indeed, I have argued largely on Congar's grounds that Protestants can affirm the authority of later doctrinal formulations as a manifestation of the Spirit's ongoing work to interiorize and deepen the work of the Son, so long as this authority is understood as secondary to and derivative of Scripture. This perspective bears affinities with Barth's oft-cited appeal to the Fifth Commandment: contemporary interpreters are no more at liberty to disregard their theological predecessors than their own parents.[121] Nevertheless, the model of Scriptural authority presented here does not permit the community simply to absorb the individual. The freedom of God in the divine address precludes the restriction of the locus of revelation to institutional ecclesial structures, for God may choose to exercise this freedom through unexpected means — even the enlightened reception of Scripture by the individual Christian over and against established teaching authorities. This was one of Luther's genuine insights, polemical hyperbole and excesses notwithstanding, and it remains a basic Protestant impulse, even if one that requires nuance and care. The possibility that the individual Christian may challenge the church is a natural implication of God's rule over his people. It also undergirds the Protestant affirmation of the priesthood of all believers, a point whose Scriptural warrant Congar himself acknowledges: "But you have been anointed by the Holy One, and you all know . . . but

---

119. *In One Body through the Cross*, 66.
120. Ibid., 16.
121. Karl Barth, *Credo: A Presentation of the Chief Problems of Dogmatics with Reference to the Apostles' Creed*, trans. J. Strathearn McNab (London: Hodder & Stoughton, 1936), 181; and idem, *Church Dogmatics* 1/2, trans. G. T. Thomson and Harold Knight (London: T&T Clark, 1956), 585.

the anointing which you received from him abides in you, and you have no need that any one should teach you; as his anointing teaches you about everything . . ." (1 John 2:20, 27).[122] The theological correlate of canonical authority is the church's submission to and humility before Scripture. It follows that any teaching authority can possess only provisional oversight of the biblical text.

Still, crass individualism is not the only alternative to complete conformity with the magisterium. Protestants must recognize better than they often have that union with Christ presupposes union with the body of Christ and that Christian identity and ecclesial communion are mutually implicative. Orthodox theologian John Zizioulas strikes the right balance on this issue in his vigorous argument against the Western intellectual pattern of dividing being and communion. Substance is not some basic principle of reality to which personhood is only adjunct. God's subsistence as Trinity demonstrates instead that relationship is constitutive of being. Love is *"the supreme ontological predicate,"*[123] a point that bears heavily on theological anthropology. Baptism signifies new birth into the Trinitarian life and a restoration of personhood in the ultimate sense. Given the dynamics of the intra-Trinitarian relations, this means the Christian can no longer exist as an isolated individual but only in ontological relation with the communion of saints. While retaining a "unique" and "unrepeatable" identity, she also becomes catholic in the deepest sense, receiving adoption into an ecclesial family that transcends even biological relations.[124] For the vision of canonical authority proposed in this chapter to obtain, something like Zizioulas's vision must be affirmed whereby both the individual and the community retain their proper place. On the one hand, the Spirit continues to guide the church through the illumination of Scripture, and tradition is a record of God's ongoing speech to the corporate body of Christ. On the other hand, this tradition must in principle remain open to challenge and correction through new insight into the text, which may arise through the individual Christian. Any failure to acknowledge both dynamics will naturally result in a distorted understanding of God's active governance of the church in the postapostolic era.

---

122. Congar, *Tradition and Traditions,* 326. I quote directly from his text.
123. John D. Zizioulas, *Being and Communion: Studies in Personhood and the Church* (Crestwood, NY: St. Vladimir's Seminary Press, 2002), 46. Italics his.
124. Ibid.

A second area of exploration arises from the first, namely, whether the church may err, or sin more broadly. This latter topic was the subject of some debate within mid-twentieth-century Roman Catholic theology,[125] and has received fresh consideration in recent discussion triggered by John Paul II's designation of a Day of Pardon in the Jubilee Year 2000. In a remarkable homily delivered at St. Peter's Basilica, the Pope asked for the forgiveness of sins throughout the church's history, including the contributions of her members to ecclesial division, violence for the sake of truth, and hostile attitudes toward those of other religions. This act was almost entirely unprecedented, and the document of the International Theological Commission issued in preparation for the request had to reach back to Pope Adrian VI in 1522 for any similar instance before Vatican II.[126] Nevertheless, the request and the rationale provided for it stopped noticeably short of acknowledging the church's own complicity in sin, drawing upon a careful but controversial distinction preserved in Vatican II between the holiness of the church and the sins of the church's members.[127] As successor to Peter, John Paul II asked only that the church "implore forgiveness for the past and present sins of her sons and daughters,"[128] and not the sins of the church herself. This language prompted frustration from several quarters, including many Roman Catholics disappointed by the lack of explicit acknowledgement that these "sons and daughters" also encompassed the hierarchy — popes, cardinals, and bishops authorized to speak in the name of the church.[129] The Day of Pardon seemed to imply that the church

---

125. Still worth reading in this regard are the remarks at Vatican II by Stephen Laszlo, then Bishop of Eisenstadt, Austria: "Sin in the Holy Church of God," in *Council Speeches of Vatican II*, ed. Hans Küng, Yves Congar, Daniel O'Hanlon (Glen Rock, NJ: Paulist, 1964), 44-48. Brief remarks on twentieth-century Catholic discussion of ecclesial sin can be found throughout Avery Dulles, "A Half Century of Ecclesiology," *TS* 50 (1989): 419-42. For a fuller study, see Bernard E. Yetzer, "Holiness and Sin in the Church: An Examination of *Lumen gentium* and *Unitatis redintegratio* of the Second Vatican Council" (STD diss., Catholic University of America, 1988).

126. International Theological Commission, *Memory and Reconciliation: The Church and the Faults of the Past* (December 1999), 1.1. http://www.vatican.va/roman_curia/congregations/cfaith/cti_documents/rc_con_cfaith_doc_20000307_memory-reconc-itc_en.html.

127. *Lumen gentium* 8; *Unitatis redintegratio* 3.

128. For the full text of this homily, see http://www.vatican.va/holy_father/john_paul_ii/homilies/documents/hf_jp-ii_hom_20000312_pardon_en.html. John Paul II quotes here *Incarnationis Mysterium* 11.

129. See, for instance, Francis A. Sullivan, "The Papal Apology," *America*, April 8, 2000, http://www.americamagazine.org/content/article.cfm?article_id=657. For a fuller account

had promulgated official policies and practices contrary to the gospel. To assert at the same time that the church did not sin was confusing at best and disingenuous at worst. How could the church ask for forgiveness for the Inquisition; the divisions with the East as well as with Protestants; and hostility toward the Jews and indifference toward their plight in Nazi Germany — all matters discussed in the preparation for the Day of Pardon — and yet have sinned only in her members?

In his treatment of ecclesial repentance, Mennonite theologian Jeremy Bergen challenges the official Roman Catholic position while also highlighting resources within Catholic discourse for a more textured account of the church's complicity in sin. In particular, Bergen flags the hidden presupposition in such public declarations as the Day of Pardon that the church actually existed at the point when sin occurred.[130] The communion of saints indicates an identity of agency across time such that the past sins for which the church asks forgiveness just are the sins of that same church. Yet the church did not disappear when she sinned, and the Spirit did not entirely abandon her even in her worst betrayals. Indeed, the presence of the Spirit in the church is seen precisely in her repentance, and the holiness of the church can concomitantly be identified with the action of the Spirit in conforming her to the body of Christ. On this model, the continuity of the church does not ultimately rest in the human response, as if holiness were a matter of the church's possession or property, but upon the triumph of God's grace over his erring and recalcitrant people.[131] Repentance is the means by which the Spirit preserves the church's continuity with her sinful past while also liberating her for the future, and it signals both the persistence of the church across time and her direct complicity in sin. Correction and conversion do not destroy the church; they enable her progress toward her eschatological end.

This understanding of the ecclesial condition draws considerable support from the practice of reading the Old Testament narration of Israel figurally with reference to the New Testament church, a strategy that most prominently entered contemporary scholarly discussion through George Lindbeck.[132] Lindbeck stressed the primacy of narrative for iden-

---

of reactions to the "apology," see Jeremy M. Bergen, *Ecclesial Repentance: The Churches Confront Their Sinful Pasts* (London: T&T Clark, 2011), 136-50.

130. Bergen, *Ecclesial Repentance*, 224-26.

131. To paraphrase Rowan Williams in *A Ray of Darkness: Sermons and Reflections* (Cambridge, MA: Cowley, 1995), 114-15. Cited in Bergen, *Ecclesial Repentance*, 234.

132. George Lindbeck, "The Story-Shaped Church: Critical Exegesis and Theological Interpretation," in Green, *Scriptural Authority and Narrative Interpretation*, 161-78.

tity determination to demonstrate the continuity between Israel and the church and to elucidate its implications for contemporary ecclesiology. Israel's history was for the earliest Christians their only history and Israel's Scripture their only ecclesiological text. They understood the inclusion of the Gentiles into the covenant not as a replacement but as an expansion of the existing community, and they considered the entirety of Israel's history to be their own, not just the favorable parts. Indeed, the relation between Israel and church is not that of shadow and reality, or of promise and fulfillment. Both Israel and church are types of the kingdom of God in Christ, and the church continues but does not complete Israel's story. Given this narrative identity, Lindbeck warned, the church must with sobriety confess that Israel's pattern of infidelity could also become her own. Perhaps the clearest New Testament support for this position arises in Paul's admonitions in 1 Cor. 10:5-11 not to rebel as the Israelites in the desert, whose failings were written as warnings for us, or in Rom. 11:21 that God might cut off the unfaithful church just as he has the unfaithful synagogue. Yet a similar dynamic animates the severe warnings of Galatians, Hebrews, and the letters of Revelation to various churches that they not depart from the gospel to the point where they could not be redeemed.[133] "There is nothing in the logic of this hermeneutic to deny that the bride of Christ, like the betrothed of Yahweh (Ezekiel 16 and 23), can be a whore worse than the heathen. The typological transfer is not actually made, but then, the responsible narrative exegete will note, situations as extreme as the one Ezekiel confronted did not develop until later in church history."[134]

From the perspective adopted here, Hebrews may lend even weightier support for such a position than the Pauline correspondences provide. Previous chapters have stressed the epistle's assumption of continuity between its addressees and the community of Israel before the time of Christ. Here it is worth underscoring the gravity of this presupposition in the warning passages for which Hebrews is preeminent in the New Testament canon. While the author presents Christ's establishment as high priest as the inaugural moment of a radically new covenant, he does not presume this altered situation renders the danger of infidelity impossible. Quite the opposite, the new covenant heightens the urgency of obedience and the consequences of sin. Hebrews repeatedly sets forth Old Testament Israel

---

133. Ibid., 176 n. 5.
134. Ibid., 166.

as a negative example for the contemporary addressees, with the warning that the latter could well meet the same fate as their predecessors. "Who were they that heard and yet were rebellious? Was it not all those who left Egypt under the leadership of Moses? And with whom was he provoked forty years? Was it not with those who sinned, whose bodies fell in the wilderness? And to whom did he swear that they should never enter his rest, but to those who were disobedient? So we see that they were unable to enter because of unbelief. Therefore, while the promise of entering his rest remains, let us fear lest any of you be judged to have failed to reach it" (3:16–4:1).[135]

For our purposes, the question is whether such warnings against moral faithlessness may also be appropriated with reference to doctrinal error. Such a move seems *prima facie* possible: truth and holiness are essentially related, and the very history of the church bears ample witness to perilous moments for her theological integrity. Even when defending papal infallibility, Avery Dulles rejected the position held by Gasser and others that divine providence entailed persistent preservation from error, noting in this regard the extended periods of time when the identity of the legitimate pope was uncertain, and the acknowledgement by theologians from the medieval period through the present that the pope may fall into heresy or schism.[136] Roman Catholic affirmation of papal infallibility derives in part from the presumption that God has provided the church the effective means by which she will remain in truth until the end of times.[137] Protestant resistance to such notions is not a denial of God's faithfulness to his people or the presence of his Spirit in the church. The concern is rather to take seriously that such gifts do not secure persistent rectitude in matters of doctrine or morality, and to recognize that the Spirit's preservation of the church occurs through correction, repentance, and

---

135. See also 2:1-4; 10:26-31; 12:18-29. The warning passages in Hebrews are well-trodden in the secondary literature. See any of the standard commentaries on the epistle listed in the bibliography for further references.

136. Avery Dulles, "Moderate Infallibilism: An Ecumenical Approach," in *A Church to Believe In* (New York: Crossroad, 1982), 141-42, originally published in Empie, Murphy, and Burgess, *Teaching Authority and Infallibility in the Church,* 81-100. See also idem, "Toward a Renewed Papacy," in his *The Resilient Church: The Necessity and Limits of Adaptation* (Garden City, NY: Doubleday, 1977), 126. This essay is a revision of "Papal Authority in Roman Catholicism," in *A Pope for All Christians: An Inquiry into the Role of Peter in the Modern Church,* ed. Peter J. McCord (New York: Paulist, 1976), 48-70.

137. Dulles, "Moderate Infallibilism," 135.

renewal. To affirm the growth of God's people in truth and holiness is not to presume that such development has unfolded in a straight line. From this perspective, the Protestant question for Roman Catholic theology is whether an appropriate concern for the indefectibility of the church has obscured the confession that she could fall into serious doctrinal error. To what extent is fallibility fatal to the church, and could correction from falsehood be one mechanism of the Spirit's preservation of the church in truth?

The third and related area of exploration is the visible unity of the church, a matter many Protestants have not taken as seriously as they ought. The Scriptural foundation for ecumenism is Jesus's prayer in John 17:21 "that they may all be one," the passage from which John Paul II derived the title of his encyclical, *Ut unum sint,* and one he understood to be at the center of the church's identity. The importance of this passage may be seen in the connection Jesus draws between the unity of the church and that of the triune God ("even as thou, Father, art in me, and I in thee"), and the stress he lays on the visibility of the church for the efficacy of her mission ("that the world may believe that thou hast sent me"). As John Paul II wrote, "This unity, which the Lord has bestowed on his Church and in which he wishes to embrace all people, is not something added on, but stands at the very heart of Christ's mission. Nor is it some secondary attribute of the community of his disciples. Rather, it belongs to the very essence of this community. God wills the Church, because he wills unity, and unity is an expression of the whole depth of his *agape*."[138] For our purposes, the challenge of this passage is whether it is possible to bear credible witness to apostolic truth without visible church unity. The Princeton Proposal understood this difficulty well, noting the way church division especially in North America has undermined evangelical proclamation such that generative, binding truths are taken merely as consumer options available for comparison with those of alternate Christian communities. "In these circumstances, even the most sincere efforts to establish and enforce norms of faithfulness to the apostolic message lose credibility. The very fact of division insinuates doubt as to whether such norms are really based on discernment of the one gospel or arise rather from institutional or cultural self-maintenance."[139]

Yet the effect of division is not pragmatic alone. In recent years,

---

138. *Ut unum sint* 9.
139. Braaten and Jenson, *In One Body through the Cross,* 42.

Ephraim Radner has advanced the troubling suggestion, not without Scriptural warrant, that the Spirit has actually responded to ecclesial division by abandoning the church as in the Babylonian exile.[140] Radner's provocatively titled text, *The End of the Church*, not only defends the theoretical possibility that the church could err in extraordinarily serious ways, but asserts that the church has already fallen into such a situation, and that she cannot even understand Scripture properly now because she will not repent. Radner's text focuses on the divisions of Western Christianity and the concomitant and empirically observable impasse between Roman Catholics and Protestants on the locus of the Spirit's illumination of Scripture. By identifying the Spirit's work primarily with either the individual or the corporate body of Christ, Protestants and Catholics have functionally had to deny the presence of the Spirit in the other.[141] This fragmentation has led to a failure to discern God's address not unlike the degeneration of the priestly and prophetic offices in Israel after the division of the kingdoms into competing and deceptive claims for the truth. Disunity, Radner carefully clarifies, was not in and of itself the cause of God's judgment upon Israel; the division of Israel was itself an act of judgment for various forms of apostasy since the Exodus. Still, the rending of Israel was inextricably intertwined with the ongoing movement of sin and judgment that characterized the course of her history until the final paroxysm of godlessness that resulted in the Assyrian and Babylonian exiles. There are no theological grounds for denying the same possibility for the contemporary church. The division of Israel precipitated the acceleration into sin wherein the people became increasingly unable to heed God's warnings, respond with repentance, or even discern where God was speaking. As Israel resisted the Spirit, so also did God harden her heart, and her prophets became as drunkards or blind, staggering in a stupor until they fell into a deep sleep. On this sobering analogy, Radner warns, Western Christianity may thus hear herself addressed: "And the vision of all this has become to you like the words of a book that is sealed. When men give it to one who can read, saying, 'Read this,' he says, 'I cannot, for it is sealed.' And when they give

---

140. Ephraim Radner, *The End of the Church: A Pneumatology of Christian Division in the West* (Grand Rapids: Eerdmans, 1998), 26-39, drawing heavily on Lindbeck's proposals concerning the practice of treating Old Testament Israel as a figure for the church. I have not been able to incorporate his most recent work into this text: *A Brutal Unity: The Spiritual Politics of the Christian Church* (Waco: Baylor University Press, 2012).

141. Ibid., 21-22.

the book to one who cannot read, saying, 'Read this,' he says, 'I cannot read'" (Isa. 29:11-12).[142]

Radner notes the prominence of this figure among the Reformation controversialists. Because the New Testament does not explicitly address the question of a firmly divided church, Protestants and Catholics alike had to turn to the Old Testament for paradigms to explain the contemporary situation.[143] In his *Reply to Sadoleto,* Calvin compared the Reformers to the faithful remnant of Israel called to challenge the prophets and priests who ruled Israel. The Roman Pontiff and his followers naturally invited comparison with Zedekiah and Jehoiakim, whose reign could hardly be likened to the flourishing of Israel under David and Solomon, and whose end was ultimately to preside over the destruction of the nation.[144] Catholic writers also made use of this image, though more with reference to a chosen people assaulted by her own children. On Radner's account, both appropriations of Israel's history failed to appreciate the broader scope of the Scriptural narrative. While the prophets do acknowledge the presence of a remnant, these faithful Israelites are not set apart from the rest of the nation as the uniquely elect. They suffer together with the unrighteous Israelites, and their hope for restoration concerns the whole of the nation of Israel — "not the unveiling, let alone the vindication, of the 'true church' from amid its travails, but rather the gracious action of recreating a united people out of the dust of their past obliteration (cf. Ezek. 11:14-21)."[145] By and large, Protestants have not treated such suggestions with the seriousness they deserve. Some fifty years ago, Congar noted positively a trend in Protestant theology to rediscover the church as a necessary context for reading Scripture. Yet, he complained, this church was understood largely as a "spiritual *locus,*" and the community in question lacked clear definition.[146] "What is this 'Church'? Is it simply the sum-total of individuals each of whom is separately and independently made a Christian, or is it a unique reality in which and through which individuals become Christians?"[147] These questions remain as pertinent as they did during Congar's

---

142. Cited in ibid., 38, though I quote a slightly different selection of verses.

143. Ibid., 34-35.

144. J. K. S. Reid, ed., *Calvin: Theological Treatises,* Library of Christian Classics 22 (Louisville: Westminster John Knox, 1956), 231 and 249. Cited in Radner, *The End of the Church,* 30, though I use a different translation.

145. Radner, *The End of the Church,* 36.

146. Congar, *Tradition and Traditions,* 475.

147. Ibid., 478.

time. Where, in the fragmented ecclesial context, is teaching authority to be found? What limitations and frustrations impede the interpretation of Scripture when the text is read only in the context of a relatively isolated ecclesial community? What judgment might the church currently be experiencing, even if unaware, in disobedience to her Lord's insistence and prayer for visible church unity? In the end, the question of Scripture and tradition depends essentially on broader questions of ecclesiology. It remains therefore unlikely that the project of reclaiming the canonical witness to Christ for the church can succeed without further ecumenical progress.

Conclusion

This study began with the basic observation that Christian Scripture consists of two parts but that the relation between these two parts has not received consensus definition in Christian tradition. I have subsequently considered the implications of this ambiguity for the relation between Israel and church, the figural reading of the Old Testament, and the dynamics of Scriptural authority. Augustine, Calvin, and the author of Hebrews present three different understandings of the relation between the testaments and the interpretation of Scripture. While each is generally self-consistent, the key manifestation of the difference between Hebrews and the other two figures is the question of Israel. Neither Augustine nor Calvin adopts an unqualified supersessionism that understands the church entirely to have replaced Israel, rendering the covenant with the Jews totally null and void. Both respect the literal sense too much to allegorize God's promises to Israel completely away, and thus retain some place for ethnic Israel's restoration at the end of times. Yet Israel also presents a stumbling block for both figures, each of whom struggles to provide a satisfactory account of the salvific status of Israel and the Old Testament saints, the continuity of God's people across the testaments, or the grounds for God's plan to restore the Jewish people.

Hebrews provides a singular contribution to the canonical witness by insisting that the new covenant begins with and cannot bypass Israel. The author of Hebrews is not, of course, alone on this matter, but his unvarying orientation toward the Jews and his total inattention to the Gentile mission nevertheless distinguish his theological vision. If Paul stresses the nations' inclusion in Israel's hope, Hebrews responds that the covenant remains with the Jewish people despite this new development. The interpretive consequences have been considered by contrast: Augustine's twofold understanding of Israel and church funds a twofold understanding of the literal and spiritual senses (what I have called a unity of reference), while Calvin's conflation of Israel and church accords with his emphasis on the unitary and unchanging *sensus litteralis* (a unity of identity). Hebrews presents an instance of redemptive-historical and hermeneutical transformation that identifies the literal sense with God's direct address in the contemporary moment. The author's interpretation of Scripture is continuous with the way Israel would have received the original locutions, but Scripture also adopts fresh meaning that could not formerly have been perceived. Jesus makes an interpretive difference.

The proposal I have drawn from the epistle's example is that Scriptural authority is not constrained to original historical meaning, but resides in God's direct self-communication in the redemptive-historical present. This suggestion does not undermine the determinative character of the apostolic witness. The Spirit's ongoing testimony to the Son deepens and does not divert the church's understanding of Scripture, and the unbreakable relation between Word and Spirit inflects all interpretation with Christological valence. Similarly, my proposal relativizes but does not repudiate the importance of historical criticism and authorial intent. I have acknowledged the importance of historical inquiry as an interpretive control and stressed the continuity between the Spirit's inspiration and ongoing illumination of the text as a function of God's consistency to himself. Yet it bears noting that none of the figures treated in this work restricts the interpretive task to the discernment of the original sense, narrowly defined according to human authorial intent. If Augustine's penchant for allegory disqualifies his authority on this matter, Calvin, a champion of the literal sense, will not serve the role either. And our canonical author who composed Hebrews is, according to historical-critical consensus, certainly not a historical critic. The hermeneutic of Scripture and tradition is not the hermeneutic of the Enlightenment.

These conclusions raise at least four issues that deserve further consideration. First, even if the author of the epistle's vision of redemptive history is defined by God's covenant faithfulness to ethnic Israel, his voice is just one within the variegated canonical witness. The church today is, in fact, primarily composed of Gentiles, and this condition has been characteristic since shortly after her inception. Can Hebrews facilitate theological reflection upon the current constitution of the church, or must we turn to Paul? A full treatment of this matter is obviously out of the question here,

Conclusion

but I would simply gesture toward Paul's own concern for God's commitment to Israel. The apostle rejects the possibility that Israel's unfaithfulness could nullify God's faithfulness (Rom. 3:3-4); he retains his concern for her hallowed history and continued possession of sonship, the covenants, and the promises (Rom. 9:4-5); and he reminds the grafted branches that they were once a wild olive shoot and have unnaturally been adopted into the cultivated tree (Rom. 11:24). "The gifts and the call of God are irrevocable" (Rom. 11:29). Read canonically, in the context of a largely Gentile church, Hebrews may be taken as a reminder of Paul's still-pertinent admonition: "Do not boast over the branches. If you do boast, remember it is not you that support the root, but the root that supports you" (Rom. 11:18). Indeed, Paul's warning to the Gentiles sounds at certain points very much like the voice of Hebrews: "Note then the kindness and the severity of God: severity toward those who have fallen, but God's kindness to you, provided you continue in his kindness; otherwise you too will be cut off" (Rom. 11:22).

The second issue concerns another limitation in this study, namely, my almost exclusive attention to the Psalms. This decision received some warrant from the orientation of Hebrews, but the Psalms are not the only locus in the author's view. Eisenbaum has noted a significant difference between the epistle's quotations of the Old Testament and its narrative retellings of Old Testament texts. Unlike contemporary rabbinic interpreters, Hebrews does not seek to resolve perceived contradictions in the scriptural text; it purposefully sets texts against each other such that quotations of direct speech testify against various parts of the biblical narrative.[1] Scripture as God's present word thus challenges historical events and institutions like temple and priesthood. Eisenbaum somewhat overstates the contrast between quotations and retellings,[2] but her general point seems to me substantially right: Hebrews assigns different hermeneutical weight to different parts of Scripture. A fuller study might thus consider several more things, including the propriety (or impropriety) of applying the model of divine address to different parts of Scripture, how different Old Testament

---

1. Pamela Michelle Eisenbaum, *The Jewish Heroes of Christian Antiquity: Hebrews 11 in Literary Context,* SBLDS 156 (Atlanta: Scholars, 1997), 131-33.

2. Eisenbaum's central example of how the retellings in Hebrews denigrate parts of the biblical narrative is Heb. 11. As I have discussed in the third chapter, and as Eisenbaum has herself conceded, Heb. 11 does not undermine the national distinctiveness of Israel. More broadly, I have argued that the Old Testament locutions in Hebrews invite their own reappropriation. Thus, the challenge that quotations of direct speech pose to historical events and institutions receives warrant from the events and institutions themselves.

genres might generate different modes of appropriation, and the fruitfulness of alternate models of Scriptural interpretation. Here especially the fourfold method comes to mind. On the other hand, the Psalms bear a venerable history as the worship book of God's people, and their wide applicability invites fresh appropriations in new contexts. Without reducing Scripture to a crude canon within a canon, is it possible to acknowledge a certain privilege for particular parts of the biblical witness?

The third issue concerns the value of interpreting the Bible in dialogue with theology. Chapters three and four constituted an experiment in the fruitfulness of employing later figures in the history of interpretation as theological interlocutors for the canonical witness. At one level, this is formally no different from appealing to various forms of, e.g., literary theory to elucidate the dynamics of an ancient text. One rubric will in principle work as well as another; there is no intrinsic or internal connection between the theoretical framework and the text explored. From a theological perspective, however, one may ask whether the communion of saints legitimates and even necessitates the practice of reading Scripture in light of later tradition. According to reigning guild practices, New Testament scholars do not seek the meaning of biblical texts according to later ecclesial interpretation. A word study might investigate the meaning of a given term in other writings by the same author, in the New Testament, in Second Temple Jewish literature, or in the wider Greco-Roman context, all on the assumption that the most pertinent background is the original historical. Yet if the locus of biblical authority is not the historically reconstructed sense, but God's address to the church in the present dispensation, other passages from Scripture or even later readings of the text may in fact constitute an equally appropriate context for interpretation. According to my argument, there is no obvious reason to prefer Greco-Roman conceptions of *logos* over the Nicene decrees as a backdrop for interpreting John 1:1-3. This perspective qualifies the importance of historical criticism, but it better resembles the church's practice in earlier times.

The final issue is in some ways the most obvious but may also be the hardest to receive, particularly in the West. The model of Scriptural authority we have witnessed in Hebrews does not present God's Word as an object for our inquiry and control. It is God who addresses us; he addresses us now, and theoretical reflection will not defer his confrontation with humanity. The seriousness of these claims bears consequences for the interpretive task. In *De doctrina Christiana,* Augustine lists seven stages in the interpretation of Scripture: fear of God, holiness, knowledge, for-

Conclusion

titude, resolve of compassion, purification of vision, and wisdom.[3] Augustine draws on Isa. 11:2-3 for this list, roughly and in reverse order, and his aim is not to produce a precise formula for successful reading. But it is no accident that he considers knowledge only one step among six others. Knowledge admittedly enjoys some prominence as the primary focus of Augustine's attention in *De doctrina* 2-3. Augustine will proceed to discuss the importance of studying history, grammar, the meaning of words, and so forth. But fear of God and holiness must come first for knowledge to issue the proper response: love of God and neighbor. For Augustine, the historical and academic task is a secondary element of Scriptural interpretation that utterly fails its purpose if it does not produce virtue. The challenge in Hebrews is to listen for God's voice, which we will hear only through repentance and faith. These are the prerequisites for Scriptural interpretation and the ultimate relation between Scripture and ecclesiology.

3. *Doc. Chr.* 2.7.9-11.

Bibliography

Works by Augustine

c. Adim. = *Contra Adimantum Manichei discipulum.* CSEL 25.1.
  Answer to Adimantus, A Disciple of Mani. Translated by Roland J. Teske. In *The Manichean Debate.* WSA 1.19. Hyde Park, NY: New City, 2006.

c. adv. leg. = *Contra adversarium legis et prophetarum.* CCSL 49.
  Answer to an Enemy of the Law and the Prophets. Translated by Roland J. Teske. In *Arianism and Other Heresies.* WSA 1.18. Hyde Park, NY: New City, 1995.

cat. rud. = *De catechizandis rudibus.* CCSL 46.
  Instructing Beginners in Faith. Translated by Raymond Canning. The Augustine Series 5. Hyde Park, NY: New City, 2006.

civ. Dei = *De civitate Dei.* CCSL 47-48.
  Concerning the City of God against the Pagans. Translated by Henry Bettenson. New York: Penguin, 1972. Primary translation used.
  The City of God against the Pagans. Edited and translated by R. W. Dyson. Cambridge Texts in the History of Political Thought. Cambridge: Cambridge University Press, 1998.
  La Cité de Dieu. Edited by G. Bardy. Translated by Gustave Combès. 5 vols. Œuvres de Saint Augustin: Bibliothèque Augustinienne 33-37. Paris: Desclée de Brower, 1959-60.
  La Cité de Dieu. Translated by Gustave Combès, revised by Goulven Madec. 3 vols. Introduction by Isabelle Bochet. Nouvelle Bibliothèque Augustinienne 3-4. Paris: Institut d'Études Augustiniennes, 1993-95.

conf. = *Confessiones.* CCSL 27.
  The Confessions. Translated by Maria Boulding. New York: Vintage Spiritual Classics, 1997. Primary translation used.
  Confessions. Translated by R. S. Pine-Coffin. New York: Penguin, 1961.

Bibliography

dial. = *De dialectica.* PL 32.

div. qu. = *De diversis quaestionibus octoginta tribus.* CCSL 44A.
 Saint Augustine: Eighty-Three Different Questions. Translated by David L. Mosher. Fathers of the Church 70. Washington, DC: Catholic University of America Press, 1982.

doc. Chr. = *De doctrina Christiana.* CCSL 32.
 On Christian Teaching. Translated by R. P. H. Green. Oxford: Oxford University Press, 1997. Primary translation used.
 On Christian Doctrine. Translated by D. W. Robertson, Jr. Library of Liberal Arts. 1958. Upper Saddle River, NJ: Prentice Hall, 1997.
 *Teaching Christianity (*De doctrina christiana*).* Translated by Edmund Hill. WSA 1.11. Hyde Park, NY: New City, 1996.

en. Ps. = *Enarrationes in Psalmos.* CCSL 38-40.
 Expositions of the Psalms. Translated by Maria Boulding. 6 vols. WSA 3.15-20. Hyde Park, NY: New City, 2000-2004.

ench. = *Enchiridion ad Laurentium de fide spe et caritate.* CCSL 46.
 The Enchiridion on Faith, Hope, and Charity. Translated by Bruce Harbert. In *On Christian Belief.* WSA 1.8. Hyde Park, NY: New City, 2005.

ep. = *Epistula(e).* CSEL 34.1-2, 44, 57, 58, 88.
 Letters. Translated by Roland J. Teske. 4 vols. WSA 2.1-4. Hyde Park, NY: New City, 2001-5.

c. ep. Pel. = *Contra duas epistulas Pelagianorum.* CSEL 60.
 Answer to the Two Letters of the Pelagians. Translated by Roland J. Teske. In *Answer to the Pelagians II.* WSA 1.24. Hyde Park, NY: New City, 1998.

ep. Rm. inch. = *Epistulae ad Romanos inchoata expositio.* CSEL 84.
 Augustine on Romans: Propositions from the Epistle to the Romans; Unfinished Commentary on the Epistle to the Romans. Edited and translated by Paula Fredriksen Landes. SBLTT 23: Early Christian Literature Series 6. Chico, CA: Scholars, 1982.

ex. Gal. = *Expositio Epistulae ad Galatas.* CSEL 84.
 Augustine's Commentary on Galatians. Edited and translated by Eric Plumer. Oxford: Oxford University Press, 2003.

ex. prop. Rm. = *Expositio quarundum propositionum ex epistula Apostoli ad Romanos.* CSEL 84.
 Augustine on Romans: Propositions from the Epistle to the Romans; Unfinished Commentary on the Epistle to the Romans. Edited and translated by Paula Fredriksen Landes. Society of Biblical Literature Text and Translations 23: Early Christian Literature Series 6. Chico, CA: Scholars, 1982.

BIBLIOGRAPHY

c. Faust. = *Contra Faustum Manicheum.* CSEL 25.1.
> *Answer to Faustus the Manichean.* Translated by Roland J. Teske. WSA 1.20. Hyde Park, NY: New City, 2007.

Gn. adv. Man. = *De Genesi adversus Manicheos.* CSEL 91.
> *On Genesis: A Refutation of the Manichees.* Translated by Edmund Hill. In *On Genesis.* WSA 1.13. Hyde Park, NY: New City, 2002.

Gn. litt. = *De Genesi ad litteram.* CSEL 28.1.
> *The Literal Meaning of Genesis.* Translated by Edmund Hill. In *On Genesis.* WSA 1.13. Hyde Park, NY: New City, 2002.

Gn. litt. imp. = *De Genesi ad litteram imperfectus liber.* CSEL 28.1.
> *Unfinished Literal Commentary on Genesis.* Translated by Edmund Hill. In *On Genesis.* WSA 1.13. Hyde Park, NY: New City, 2002.

Jo. ev. tr. = *In Johannis evangelium tractatus.* CCSL 36.
> *Homilies on the Gospel of John 1-40.* Translated by Edmund Hill. WSA 1.12. Hyde Park, NY: New City, 2009.
> *Saint Augustine: Tractates on the Gospel of John.* Translated by John W. Rettig. Fathers of the Church 78, 79, 88, 90, and 92. Washington, DC: Catholic University of America Press, 1988-95.

adv. Jud. = *Adversus Judaeos.* PL 42.
> *In Answer to the Jews.* Translated by Marie Liguori. In *Saint Augustine: Treatises on Marriage and Other Subjects,* edited by Roy J. Deferrari. Fathers of the Church 27. New York: Fathers of the Church, 1955.

mor. = *De moribus ecclesiae catholicae et de moribus Manichaeorum.* CSEL 90.
> *The Catholic Way of Life and the Manichean Way of Life.* Translated by Roland J. Teske. In *The Manichean Debate.* WSA 1.19. Hyde Park, NY: New City, 2006.
> *Political Writings.* Edited by E. M. Atkins and R. J. Dodaro. Cambridge Texts in the History of Political Thought. Cambridge: Cambridge University Press, 2001.

qu. = *Quaestiones in Heptateuchum.* CCSL 33.

retr. = *Retractationes.* CCSL 57.
> *Saint Augustine: The Retractations.* Translated by Mary Inez Bogan. Fathers of the Church 60. Washington, DC: Catholic University of America Press, 1968.

s. = *Sermones.* PL 38-39; PLS 2; CCSL 41, 41Ba.
> *Sermons.* Translated by Edmund Hill. 11 vols. WSA 3.1-11. Hyde Park, NY: New City, 1990-97.

spir. et litt. = *De spiritu et littera.* CSEL 60.
> *The Spirit and the Letter.* Translated by Roland J. Teske. In *Answer to the Pelagians.* WSA 1.23. Hyde Park, NY: New City, 1997.

Bibliography

Trin. = *De Trinitate.* CCSL 50.
The Trinity. Translated by Edmund Hill. WSA 1.5. Hyde Park, NY: New City, 1991.

vera rel. = *De vera religione.* CCSL 32.
True Religion. Translated by Edmund Hill. In *On Christian Belief.* WSA 1.8. Hyde Park, NY: New City, 2005.

Secondary Works Concerning Augustine

Aers, David. *Salvation and Sin: Augustine, Langland, and Fourteenth-Century Theology.* Notre Dame, IN: University of Notre Dame Press, 2009.
Alici, Luigi. "The Violence of Idolatry and Peaceful Coexistence: The Current Relevance of *civ. Dei.*" *AugStud* 41 (2010): 203-18.
Andrews, James A. *Hermeneutics and the Church: In Dialogue with Augustine.* Notre Dame, IN: University of Notre Dame Press, 2012.
Angus, Samuel. "The Sources of the First Ten Books of Augustine's De Civitate Dei." PhD diss., Princeton University, 1906.
Arnold, Duane W. H., and Pamela Bright, eds. De Doctrina Christiana: *A Classic of Western Culture.* Notre Dame, IN: University of Notre Dame Press, 1995.
Ayres, Lewis. *Augustine and the Trinity.* Cambridge: Cambridge University Press, 2010.
Barnes, Michel René. "The Arians of Book V, and the Genre of 'de Trinitate'." *JTS* 44 (1993): 185-95.
———. "Augustine in Contemporary Trinitarian Theology." *TS* 56 (1995): 237-50.
Barrow, R. H. *Introduction to St. Augustine,* The City of God. London: Faber and Faber, 1950.
Baynes, Norman H. "The Political Ideas of St. Augustine's *De Civitate Dei.*" In idem, *Byzantine Studies and Other Essays,* 288-306. London: Athlone, 1955.
Bernard, Robert William. "*In Figura:* Terminology Pertaining to Figurative Exegesis in the Works of Augustine of Hippo." PhD diss., Princeton University, 1984.
———. "The Rhetoric of God in the Figurative Exegesis of Augustine." In *Biblical Hermeneutics in Historical Perspective: Studies in Honor of Karlfried Froehlich on His Sixtieth Birthday,* edited by Mark S. Burrows and Paul Rorem, 88-99. Grand Rapids: Eerdmans, 1991.
Bochet, Isabelle. *"Le firmament de l'Écriture": L'herméneutique augustinienne.* Collection des Études Augustiniennes: Série Antiquité 172. Paris: Institut d'Études Augustiniennes, 2004.
Bonner, Gerald. "Augustine as Biblical Scholar." In *From the Beginnings to Jerome,* edited by P. R. Ackroyd and C. F. Evans, 541-63. Vol. 1 of *The Cambridge History of the Bible.* Cambridge: Cambridge University Press, 1970.
———. "*Quid imperatori cum ecclesia?* St. Augustine on History and Society." *AugStud* 2 (1971): 231-51.
———. *St Augustine of Hippo: Life and Controversies.* 3rd ed. Norwich: Canterbury, 2002.
Bright, Pamela, ed. *Augustine and the Bible.* Translated by Pamela Bright. Notre Dame, IN: University of Notre Dame Press, 1999. Based on Anne-Marie La Bonnardière,

ed., *Saint Augustin et la Bible*. Vol. 3 of *Bible de tous les temps*. Paris: Beauchesne, 1986.

———. "Biblical Ambiguity in African Exegesis." In *De Doctrina Christiana: A Classic of Western Culture*, edited by Duane W. H. Arnold and Pamela Bright, 25-32. Notre Dame, IN: University of Notre Dame Press, 1995.

———. *The Book of Rules of Tyconius: Its Purpose and Inner Logic*. Notre Dame, IN: University of Notre Dame Press, 1988.

———. "'The Preponderating Influence of Augustine': A Study of the Epitomes of the *Book of Rules* of the Donatist Tyconius." In *Augustine and the Bible*, edited and translated by Pamela Bright, 109-28. Notre Dame, IN: University of Notre Dame Press, 1999.

Brown, Peter. *Augustine of Hippo: A Biography*. New ed. Berkeley: University of California Press, 2000.

———. *Religion and Society in the Age of Saint Augustine*. London: Harper and Row, 1972.

Burnaby, John. *Amor Dei: A Study of the Religion of St. Augustine*. London: Canterbury, 1938.

Burnell, Peter J. "The Status of Politics in St. Augustine's *City of God*." *History of Political Thought* 13 (1992): 13-29.

Burt, Donald X. *Friendship and Society: An Introduction to Augustine's Practical Philosophy*. Grand Rapids: Eerdmans, 1999.

Byassee, Jason. *Praise Seeking Understanding: Reading the Psalms with Augustine*. Grand Rapids: Eerdmans, 2007.

Cameron, Michael. "Augustine's Construction of Figurative Exegesis against the Donatists in the *Enarrationes in Psalmos*." PhD diss., University of Chicago, 1996.

———. *Christ Meets Me Everywhere: Augustine's Early Figurative Exegesis*. OSHT. Oxford: Oxford University Press, 2012.

———. "The Christological Substructure of Augustine's Figurative Exegesis." In *Augustine and the Bible*, edited and translated by Pamela Bright, 74-103. Notre Dame, IN: University of Notre Dame Press, 1999.

Canning, Raymond. *The Unity of Love for God and Neighbor in St. Augustine*. Heverlee-Leuven, Belgium: Augustinian Historical Institute, 1993.

Cicero. *De Re Publica*. Edited by J. G. F. Powell. Oxford Classical Texts. Oxford: Oxford University Press, 2006.

———. *On the Commonwealth* and *On the Laws*. Edited by James E. G. Zetzel. Cambridge Texts in the History of Political Thought. Cambridge: Cambridge University Press, 1999.

Clark, Elizabeth A. "Contesting Abraham: The Ascetic Reader and the Politics of Intertextuality." In *The Social World of the First Christians: Essays in Honor of Wayne A. Meeks*, edited by L. Michael White and O. Larry Yarbrough, 353-65. Minneapolis: Fortress, 1995.

———. "Interpretive Fate amid the Church Fathers." In *Hagar, Sarah, and Their Children*, edited by Phyllis Trible and Letty M. Russell, 127-47. Louisville: Westminster John Knox, 2006.

Cochrane, Charles Norris. *Christianity and Classical Culture: A Study of Thought and Action from Augustus to Augustine*. Indianapolis: Amagi, 1940.

Bibliography

Cohen, Jeremy. *Living Letters of the Law: Ideas of the Jew in Medieval Christianity.* Berkeley: University of California Press, 1999.

———. "The Mystery of Israel's Salvation: Romans 11:25-26 in Patristic and Medieval Exegesis." *HTR* 98 (2005): 247-81.

———. "'Slay Them Not': Augustine and the Jews in Modern Scholarship." *ME* 4 (1998): 78-92.

Cranz, F. Edward. "*De Civitate Dei,* XV, 2, and Augustine's Idea of the Christian Society." *Spec* 25 (1950): 215-25. Reprinted in *Augustine: A Collection of Critical Essays,* edited by R. A. Markus, 404-21. Garden City, NY: Anchor Books, 1972.

Curbelié, Philippe. *La justice dans* La Cité de Dieu. Paris: Institut d'Études Augustiniennes, 2004.

Dawson, David. "Sign Theory, Allegorical Reading, and the Motions of the Soul." In De Doctrina Christiana: *A Classic of Western Culture,* edited by Duane W. H. Arnold and Pamela Bright, 123-41. Notre Dame, IN: University of Notre Dame Press, 1995.

Deane, Herbert A. *The Political and Social Ideas of St. Augustine.* New York: Columbia University Press, 1963.

Deferrari, Roy J., and M. Jerome Keeler. "St. Augustine's 'City of God': Its Plan and Development." *AJP* 50 (1929): 109-37.

Dodaro, Robert. "Augustine of Hippo between the Secular City and the City of God." In *Augustinus Afer. Saint Augustin: africanité et universalité. Actes du colloque international, Alger-Annaba, 1-7 avril 2001,* edited by Pierre-Yves Fux, Jean-Michel Roessli, and Otto Wermelinger, 287-305. Fribourg, Switzerland: Éditions Universitaires, 2003.

———. *Christ and the Just Society in the Thought of Augustine.* Cambridge: Cambridge University Press, 2004.

———. "Eloquent Lies, Just Wars and the Politics of Persuasion: Reading Augustine's *City of God* in a 'Postmodern' World." *AugStud* 25 (1994): 77-137.

Dodaro, Robert, and George Lawless, eds. *Augustine and His Critics: Essays in Honour of Gerald Bonner.* London: Routledge, 2000.

Donnelly, Dorothy F. *The City of God: A Collection of Critical Essays.* New York: Peter Lang, 1995.

Donnelly, Dorothy F., and Mark A. Sherman, eds. *Augustine's* De Civitate Dei: *An Annotated Bibliography of Modern Criticism, 1960-1990.* New York: Peter Lang, 1991.

Doody, John, Kevin L. Hughes, and Kim Paffenroth, eds. *Augustine and Politics.* Augustine in Conversation: Tradition and Innovation. Lanham, MD: Lexington, 2005.

Dubois, Marcel. "Jews, Judaism and Israel in the Theology of Saint Augustine: How He Links the Jewish People and the Land of Zion." *Imm* 22/23 (1989): 162-214.

Duchrow, Ulrich. "'Signum' und 'Superbia' beim jungen Augustin (386-390)." *REAug* 7 (1961): 369-72.

Dupont, Anthony. "Using or Enjoying Humans: *Uti* and *Frui* in Augustine." *Augustiniana* 54 (2004): 475-506.

Efroymson, David P. "Whose Jews? Augustine's *Tractatus* on John." In *A Multiform Heritage: Studies on Early Judaism and Christianity in Honor of Robert A. Kraft,* edited by Benjamin G. Wright, 197-211. Homage Series 24. Atlanta: Scholars, 1999.

Elshtain, Jean Bethke. *Augustine and the Limits of Politics.* Notre Dame, IN: University of Notre Dame Press, 1998.

Enos, Richard Leo, and Roger C. Thompson, eds. *The Rhetoric of St. Augustine of Hippo: De Doctrina Christiana and the Search for a Distinctly Christian Rhetoric.* Waco, TX: Baylor University Press, 2008.

Eusebius. *Die Chronik des Hieronymus.* Edited by Rudolf Helm. 3rd ed. Eusebius Werke 7. Berlin: Akademie, 1984.

Figgis, Neville. *The Political Aspects of St. Augustine's "City of God."* London: Longmans, Green, 1921.

Fitzgerald, Allan D., John Cavadini, Marianne Djuth, James J. O'Donnell, and Frederick Van Fleteren, eds. *Augustine through the Ages: An Encyclopedia.* Grand Rapids: Eerdmans, 1999.

Fleteren, Frederick Van, and Joseph C. Schnaubelt, eds. *Augustine: Biblical Exegete.* Collectanea Augustiniana. New York: Peter Lang, 2001.

Fredriksen, Paula. *Augustine and the Jews: A Christian Defense of Jews and Judaism.* New York: Doubleday, 2008.

———. "Augustine's Early Interpretation of Paul." PhD diss., Princeton University, 1979.

———. "*Excaecati Occulta Justitia Dei:* Augustine on Jews and Judaism." *JECS* 3 (1995): 299-324.

Fredriksen, Paula, Sabrina Inowlocki, Phillip Cary, and Elena Procario-Foley. "Reviews of Paula Fredriksen, *Augustine and the Jews: A Christian Defense of Jews and Judaism.*" *AugStud* 40 (2009): 279-99.

Frend, W. H. C. *The Donatist Church: A Movement of Protest in Roman North Africa.* Oxford: Clarendon, 1952.

Gilson, Etienne. "Foreword." In Saint Augustine, *The City of God: Books 1-7,* translated by Demetrius B. Zema and Gerald G. Walsh, xi-xcviii. Fathers of the Church 8. New York: Fathers of the Church, 1950.

Gorday, Peter. *Principles of Patristic Exegesis: Romans 9–11 in Origen, John Chrysostom, and Augustine.* Studies in the Bible and Early Christianity 4. New York: Edwin Mellen, 1983.

Grafton, Anthony, and Megan Williams. *Christianity and the Transformation of the Book: Origen, Eusebius, and the Library of Caesarea.* Cambridge, MA: Belknap, 2006.

Gregory, Eric. *Politics and the Order of Love: An Augustinian Ethic of Democratic Citizenship.* Chicago: University of Chicago Press, 2008.

Guy, Jean-Claude. *Unité et structure logique de la "Cité de Dieu" de saint Augustin.* Paris: Études Augustiniennes, 1961.

Hagendahl, Harald. *Augustine and the Latin Classics.* 2 vols. Studia Graeca et Latina Gothoburgensia 20:1-2. Göteburg: Acta Universitatis Gothoburgensis, 1967.

Harkins, Franklin T. "Nuancing Augustine's Hermeneutical Jew: Allegory and Actual Jews in the Bishop's Sermons." *JSJ* 36 (2005): 41-64.

Harrison, Carol. *Augustine: Christian Truth and Fractured Humanity.* Christian Theology in Context. Oxford: Oxford University Press, 2000.

Heyking, John von. *Augustine and Politics as Longing in the World.* Eric Voegelin Institute Series in Political Philosophy. Columbia: University of Missouri Press, 2001.

Horn, Christoph, ed. *Augustinus, De civitate dei.* Klassiker Auslegen 11. Berlin: Akademie, 1997.

Bibliography

Irwin, T. H. "Splendid Vices? Augustine for and against Pagan Virtues." *Medieval Philosophy and Theology* 8 (1999): 105-27.

Jackson, Belford Darrell. "Semantics and Hermeneutics in Saint Augustine's *De Doctrina Christiana*." PhD diss., Yale University, 1967.

———. "The Theory of Signs in St. Augustine's *De doctrina christiana*." *REAug* 15 (1969): 9-49.

Jordan, Mark D. "Words and Word: Incarnation and Signification in Augustine's *De Doctrina Christiana*." *AugStud* 11 (1980): 177-96.

Kannengiesser, Charles. "Augustine and Tyconius: A Conflict of Christian Hermeneutics in Roman Africa." In *Augustine and the Bible,* edited by Pamela Bright, 149-77. Notre Dame, IN: University of Notre Dame Press, 1999.

———. "Interrupted *De Doctrina Christiana*." In De Doctrina Christiana: *A Classic of Western Culture,* edited by Duane W. H. Arnold and Pamela Bright, 3-13. Notre Dame, IN: University of Notre Dame Press, 1995.

Kirwan, Christopher. *Augustine*. London: Routledge, 1989.

Kugler, Robert A. "Tyconius's Mystic Rules and the Rules of Augustine." In *Augustine and the Bible,* edited by Pamela Bright, 129-48. Notre Dame, IN: University of Notre Dame Press, 1999.

La Bonnardière, Anne-Marie. *Biblia augustiniana: Le livre de Jérémie*. Paris: Études Augustiniennes, 1972.

———. "L'épître aux Hébreux dans l'œuvre de saint Augustin." *REAug* 3 (1957): 137-62.

La Bonnardière, Anne-Marie, ed. *Saint Augustin et la Bible*. Vol. 3 of *Bible de tous les temps.* Paris: Beauchesne, 1986.

Lancel, Serge. *St Augustine*. Translated by Antonia Nevill. London: SCM, 2002.

Lauras, A., and H. Rondet. "Le thème des deux cités dans l'œuvre de saint Augustin." In *Études Augustiniennes,* edited by H. Rondet, M. Le Landais, A. Lauras, and C. Couturier, 97-160. Paris: Aubier, 1953.

Lee, Gregory. "Republics and Their Loves: Rereading *City of God* 19." *Modern Theology* 27 (2011): 553-81.

Margerie, Bertrand de. *Introduction à l'histoire de l'exégèse*. Vol. 3, *Saint Augustin.* Paris: Cerf, 1983.

Markus, R. A., ed. *Augustine: A Collection of Critical Essays*. Garden City, NY: Anchor, 1972.

———. *Christianity and the Secular*. Notre Dame, IN: University of Notre Dame Press, 2006.

———. "*De Ciuitate Dei:* Pride and the Common Good." In *Augustine: "Second Founder of the Faith,"* edited by J. C. Schnaubelt and F. Van Fleteren, 245-59. Collectanea Augustiniana. New York: Peter Lang, 1990. Reprinted in R. A. Markus, *Sacred and Secular: Studies on Augustine and Latin Christianity.* Aldershot, UK: Variorum, 1994.

———. *Sacred and Secular: Studies on Augustine and Latin Christianity.* Aldershot, UK: Variorum, 1994.

———. *Saeculum: History and Society in the Theology of St. Augustine.* Rev. ed. Cambridge: Cambridge University Press, 1988.

———. "St. Augustine on Signs." *Phronesis* 2 (1957): 60-83.

Marrou, Henri-Irénée. "Civitas Dei, civitas terrena: num tertium quid?" In *Studia Pa-*

tristica: Papers presented to the Second International Conference in Patristic Studies held at Christ Church, Oxford, edited by Kurt Aland and F. L. Cross, 2.342-50. Berlin: Akademie, 1957.

———. "La théologie de l'histoire." In *Augustinus Magister: Congrès International Augustinien, Paris, 21-24 Septembre 1954,* 3.193-212. Paris: Études Augustiniennes, 1954.

Mathewes, Charles. *Evil and the Augustinian Tradition.* Cambridge: Cambridge University Press, 2001.

———. *A Theology of Public Life.* Cambridge Studies in Christian Doctrine. Cambridge: Cambridge University Press, 2007.

Mayer, Cornelius, ed. *Augustinus-Lexikon.* 3 vols. Basel, Switzerland: Schwabe, 1986-2008.

Meilaender, Gilbert. *The Way That Leads There: Augustinian Reflections on the Christian Life.* Grand Rapids: Eerdmans, 2006.

Milbank, John. *Theology and Social Theory: Beyond Secular Reason.* 2nd ed. Malden, MA: Blackwell, 2006.

Niebuhr, Reinhold. "Augustine's Political Realism." In *Christian Realism and Political Problems,* 119-46. New York: Charles Scribner's Sons, 1953.

Nygren, Anders. *Agape and Eros.* Translated by Philip S. Watson. Rev. ed. New York: Harper and Row, 1969.

O'Connor, William Riordan. "The *Uti/Frui* Distinction in Augustine's Ethics." *AugStud* 14 (1983): 45-62.

O'Daly, Gerald. *Augustine's* City of God: *A Reader's Guide.* Oxford: Oxford University Press, 1999.

O'Donnell, James J. *Augustine.* Boston: Twayne, 1985.

———. *Augustine: A New Biography.* New York: Ecco, 2005.

———. "Augustine, *City of God.*" Written on commission in 1983, but never published. Accessed April 18, 2010. http://www9.georgetown.edu/faculty/jod/augustine/civ.html.

———. *Augustine:* Confessions. 3 vols. Oxford: Clarendon, 1992.

———. "Augustine's Classical Readings." *Recherches Augustiniennes* 15 (1980): 144-75.

———. "The Inspiration for Augustine's *De Civitate Dei.*" *AugStud* 10 (1979): 75-79.

O'Donovan, Oliver. "Augustine's *City of God* XIX and Western Political Thought." *Dionysius* 11 (1987): 89-110.

———. *Common Objects of Love: Moral Reflection and the Shaping of Community.* Grand Rapids: Eerdmans, 2002.

———. "The Political Thought of *City of God* 19." In *Bonds of Imperfection: Christian Politics, Past and Present,* edited by Oliver O'Donovan and Joan Lockwood O'Donovan, 48-72. Grand Rapids: Eerdmans, 2004.

———. *The Problem of Self-Love in St. Augustine.* New Haven: Yale University Press, 1980.

———. "*Usus* and *Fruitio* in Augustine, *De Doctrina Christiana* I." *JTS* 33 (1982): 361-97.

O'Meara, John. *Charter of Christendom: The Significance of* City of God. New York: Macmillan, 1961.

Oort, Johannes van. *Jerusalem and Babylon: A Study into Augustine's* City of God *and the Sources of His Doctrine of the Two Cities.* Leiden: Brill, 1991.

Bibliography

Pecknold, C. C. "Theo-Semiotics and Augustine's Hermeneutical Jew: Or, 'What's a Little Supersessionism between Friends?'" *AugStud* 37 (2006): 27-42.

Pollmann, Karla. *Doctrina christiana: Untersuchungen zu den Anfängen der christlichen Hermeneutik unter besonderer Berücksichtigung von Augustinus, De doctrina christiana*. Freiburg, Switzerland: Universitätsverlag, 1996.

Polman, A. D. R. *The Word of God according to St. Augustine*. Translated by A. J. Pomerans. Grand Rapids: Eerdmans, 1961.

Pontet, Maurice. *L'éxegèse de S. Augustin prédicateur*. Paris: Aubier, 1944.

Portalié, Eugène. *A Guide to the Thought of Saint Augustine*. Translated by Ralph J. Bastian. Library of Living Catholic Thought. Chicago: Henry Regnery, 1960.

Preus, James Samuel. *From Shadow to Promise: Old Testament Interpretation from Augustine to the Young Luther*. Cambridge, MA: Belknap, 1969.

Quintot, Bernard. "L'influence de l'Epître aux Hébreux dans la notion augustinienne du vrai sacrifice." *REAug* 8 (1962): 129-68.

Ratzinger, Joseph. "Beobachtungen zum Kirchenbegriff des Tyconius im 'Liber regularum'." *REAug* 2 (1956): 173-85.

Rist, John M. *Augustine: Ancient Thought Baptized*. Cambridge: Cambridge University Press, 1994.

Ruokanen, Miikka. *Theology of Social Life in Augustine's* De Civitate Dei. Göttingen: Vandenhoeck & Ruprecht, 1993.

Stump, Eleonore, and Norman Kretzmann, eds. *The Cambridge Companion to Augustine*. Cambridge: Cambridge University Press, 2001.

Tardieu, Michel. "Principes de l'exégèse manichéenne du Nouveau Testament." In *Les règles de l'interprétation*, edited by Michel Tardieu, 123-46. Paris: Cerf, 1987.

TeSelle, Eugene. *Augustine the Theologian*. New York: Herder and Herder, 1970.

———. *Living in Two Cities: Augustinian Trajectories in Political Thought*. Scranton, PA: University of Scranton Press, 1988.

Teske, Roland J. "Criteria for Figurative Interpretation in St. Augustine." In De Doctrina Christiana: *A Classic of Western Culture*, edited by Duane W. H. Arnold and Pamela Bright, 109-22. Notre Dame, IN: University of Notre Dame Press, 1995.

Tyconius. *The Book of Rules*. Translated by William S. Babcock. Atlanta: Scholars, 1989.

———. *Le livre des règles*. Edited by Jean-Marc Vercruysse. Sources chrétiennes 488. Paris: Cerf, 2004.

Unterseher, Lisa A. "The Mark of Cain and the Jews: Augustine's Theology of Jews." *AugStud* 33 (2002): 99-121.

———. *The Mark of Cain and the Jews: Augustine's Theology of Jews and Judaism*. Gorgias Dissertations 39. Piscataway, NJ: Gorgias, 2009.

Vessey, Mark, Karla Pollmann, and Allan D. Fitzgerald, eds. *History, Apocalypse and the Secular Imagination: New Essays on Augustine's* City of God. Bowling Green, OH: Philosophy Documentation Center, 1999.

Walsh, P. G., ed. *Augustine:* De Civitate Dei (The City of God). 6 vols. Oxford: Aris and Phillips Classical Texts, 2005-14.

Wetzel, James. *Augustine and the Limits of Virtue*. Cambridge: Cambridge University Press, 1992.

———. "Splendid Vices and Secular Virtues: Variations on Milbank's Augustine." *JRE* 32 (2004): 271-300.

BIBLIOGRAPHY

Williams, Rowan. "Language, Reality and Desire in Augustine's *De Doctrina.*" *Journal of Literature and Theology* 3 (1989): 138-50.

———. "Politics and the Soul: A Reading of *City of God.*" *MilS* 19/20 (1987): 55-72.

Wills, Garry. *Saint Augustine*. Penguin Lives. New York: Viking, 1999.

Works by Calvin

Comm. Eph. = *In Epistolam Pauli ad Ephesios Iohannis Calvini Commentarius*. OE 16.
: *Commentaries on the Epistle of Paul to the Ephesians*. CTS 21.

Comm. Ev. = *Commentarius in harmoniam evangelicam*. CO 45.
: *Commentary on a Harmony of the Evangelists, Matthew, Mark, and Luke*. CTS 16-17.

Comm. Gal. = *In Epistolam Pauli ad Galatas Iohannis Calvini Commentarius*. OE 16.
: *Commentaries on the Epistle of Paul to the Galatians*. CTS 21.

Comm. Gen. = *Commentariorum in quinque libros Mosis. Pars 1*. CO 23.
: *Commentaries on the First Book of Moses Called Genesis*. CTS 1.

Comm. Heb. = *Commentarius in Epistolam ad Hebraeos*. OE 19.
: *Commentaries on the Epistle of Paul the Apostle to the Hebrews*. CTS 22.

Comm. Jer. = *Praelectionum in Ieremiam prophetam*. CO 37-39.
: *Commentaries on the Prophet Jeremiah*. CTS 9-11.

Comm. Ps. = *Commentarii in librum Psalmorum*. CO 31-32.
: *Commentary on the Book of Psalms*. CTS 4-6.

Comm. Rom. = *Commentarius in Epistolam Pauli ad Romanos*. OE 13.
: *Commentaries on the Epistle of Paul the Apostle to the Romans*. CTS 19.

Comm. 2 Cor. = *Ioannis Commentarii in secundam Pauli Epistolam ad Corinthios*. OE 15.
: *Commentaries on the Second Epistle of Paul the Apostle to the Corinthians*. CTS 20.

Inst. = *Institutio Christianae Religionis* (1559). OS 3-5.
: *Institutes of the Christian Religion*. Edited by John T. McNeill. Translated by Ford Lewis Battles. Library of Christian Classics 20-21. Philadelphia: Westminster, 1960.

Mos. Harm. = *Commentariorum in quinque libros Mosis. Pars 2. Mosis reliqui libri quatuor in formam harmoniae digesti a Ioanne Calvino. Cum eiusdem commentariis*. CO 24-25.
: *Commentaries on the Four Last Books of Moses, Arranged in the Form of a Harmony*. CTS 2-3.

Bibliography

Ad quaestiones et obiecta Iudaei cuiusdam. CO 9.
  Laver, Mary Sweetland. "Calvin, Jews, and Intra-Christian Polemics," 229-61. PhD diss., Temple University, 1987.

Reply to Sadoleto.
  In *Calvin: Theological Treatises.* Edited and translated by J. K. S. Reid. Louisville: Westminster John Knox, 1954.

Secondary Works Concerning Calvin

Armstrong, Brian G. "*Duplex Cognitio Dei,* Or? The Problem and Relation of Structure, Form, and Purpose in Calvin's Theology." In *Probing the Reformed Tradition: Historical Studies in Honor of Edward A. Dowey, Jr.,* edited by Elsie Anne McKee and Brian G. Armstrong, 135-53. Louisville: Westminster John Knox, 1989.

———. "The Nature and Structure of Calvin's Thought according to the *Institutes:* Another Look." In *John Calvin's Institutes: His Opus Magnum,* 55-81. Potchefstroom, South Africa: Potchefstroom University for Christian Higher Education, 1986.

Baron, Salo W. "John Calvin and the Jews." In *Harry Austryn Wolfson Jubilee Volume: On the Occasion of His Seventy-Fifth Birthday,* edited by Saul Lieberman, 1:141-63. Jerusalem: American Academy for Jewish Research, 1965.

Battles, Ford Lewis. *Interpreting John Calvin.* Edited by Robert Benedetto. Grand Rapids: Baker, 1996.

Benedict, Philip. *Christ's Churches Purely Reformed: A Social History of Calvinism.* New Haven: Yale University Press, 2002.

Blacketer, Raymond A. *The School of God: Pedagogy and Rhetoric in Calvin's Interpretation of Deuteronomy.* Studies in Early Modern Religious Reforms 3. Dordrecht: Springer, 2006.

De Klerk, Peter, ed. *Calvin as Exegete: Papers and Responses Presented at the Ninth Colloquium on Calvin and Calvin Studies.* Grand Rapids: Calvin Studies Society, 1995.

Detmers, Achim. "Calvin, the Jews, and Judaism." In *Jews, Judaism and the Reformation in Sixteenth-Century Germany,* edited by Dean Phillip Bell and Stephen G. Burnett, 197-217. Studies in Central European Histories 37. Leiden: Brill, 2006.

Dowey, Edward A., Jr. *The Knowledge of God in Calvin's Theology.* Exp. ed. Grand Rapids: Eerdmans, 1994.

———. "The Structure of Calvin's Theological Thought as Influenced by the Two-Fold Knowledge of God." In *Calvinus Ecclesiae Genevensis Custos,* edited by Wilhelm H. Neuser, 135-48. New York: Peter Lang, 1984.

Edmondson, Stephen. *Calvin's Christology.* Cambridge: Cambridge University Press, 2004.

———. "Christ and History: Hermeneutical Convergence in Calvin and Its Challenge to Biblical Theology." *Modern Theology* 21 (2005): 1-35.

Engel, Mary Potter. "Calvin and the Jews: A Textual Puzzle." *Princeton Seminary Bulletin,* Supp. 1 (1990): 106-23.

Gamble, Richard C. "*Brevitas et Facilitas:* Toward an Understanding of Calvin's Hermeneutic." *WTJ* 47 (1985): 1-17.

———. "Calvin as Theologian and Exegete: Is There Anything New?" *CTJ* 23 (1988): 178-93.
———. "Calvin's Theological Method: Word and Spirit, A Case Study." In *Calviniana: Ideas and Influence of John Calvin,* edited by Robert V. Schnucker, 63-75. Sixteenth Century Essays and Studies 10. Kirksville, MO: Sixteenth Century Journal, 1988.
———. "Exposition and Method in Calvin." *WTJ* 49 (1987): 153-65.
Gamble, Richard C., ed. *Calvin and Hermeneutics.* Vol. 6 of *Articles on Calvin and Calvinism.* New York: Garland, 1992.
Ganoczy, Alexandre, and Stefan Scheld. *Die Hermeneutik Calvins: Geistgeschichtliche Voraussetzungen und Grundzüge.* Wiesbaden: Steiner, 1983.
Gerrish, B. A. *Grace and Gratitude: The Eucharistic Theology of John Calvin.* Minneapolis: Fortress, 1993.
———. *The Old Protestantism and the New: Essays on the Reformation Heritage.* Chicago: University of Chicago Press, 1982.
Greef, Wulfert de. *The Writings of John Calvin: An Introductory Guide.* Translated by Lyle D. Bierma. Exp. ed. Louisville: Westminster John Knox, 2008.
Greene-McCreight, Kathryn. "'We Are Companions of the Patriarchs' or Scripture Absorbs Calvin's World." *Modern Theology* 14 (1998): 213-24.
Harbison, E. Harris. "Calvin's Sense of History." In *Christianity and History: Essays by E. Harris Harbison,* 270-88. Princeton: Princeton University Press, 1964.
Hesselink, I. John. "Calvin and Heilsgeschichte." In *Oikonomia, Heilsgeschichte als Thema der Theologie: Oscar Cullmann zum 65. Geburtstag gewidmet,* edited by Felix Christ, 163-70. Hamburg: Herbert Reich Evangelischer, 1967.
———. *Calvin's Concept of the Law.* Allison Park, PA: Pickwick, 1992.
———. "Calvin's Understanding of the Relation of the Church and Israel Based Largely on His Interpretation of Romans 9–11." *ExAud* 4 (2006): 59-69.
———. "Law and Gospel or Gospel and Law? Calvin's Understanding of the Relationship." In *Calviniana: Ideas and Influences of John Calvin,* edited by Robert V. Schnucker, 13-32. Sixteenth Century Essays and Studies 10. Kirksville, MO: Sixteenth Century Journal, 1988.
Hillerbrand, Hans J. *The Division of Christendom: Christianity in the Sixteenth Century.* Louisville: Westminster John Knox, 2007.
Hoekema, Anthony A. "The Covenant of Grace in Calvin's Teaching." *CTJ* 2 (1967): 133-61.
Holder, R. Ward. *John Calvin and the Grounding of Interpretation: Calvin's First Commentaries.* Studies in the History of Christian Traditions 127. Leiden: Brill, 2006.
Holwerda, David E. "Eschatology and History: A Look at Calvin's Eschatological Vision." In *Calvin's Theology, Theology Proper, and Eschatology,* edited by Richard C. Gamble, 130-59. Vol. 9 of *Articles on Calvin and Calvinism.* New York: Garland, 1992.
Jones, Serene. *Calvin and the Rhetoric of Piety.* Columbia Series in Reformed Theology. Louisville: Westminster John Knox, 1995.
Kraeling, Emil G. *The Old Testament Since the Reformation.* London: Lutterworth, 1955.
Kraus, Hans-Joachim. "Calvin's Exegetical Principles." *Int* 31 (1977): 8-18.
———. "Israel in the Theology of Calvin — Towards a New Approach to the Old Testament and Judaism." *Christian Jewish Relations* 22 (1989): 75-86.

Bibliography

Lane, Anthony N. S. *John Calvin: Student of the Church Fathers*. Grand Rapids: Baker, 1999.

Laver, Mary Sweetland. "Calvin, Jews, and Intra-Christian Polemics." PhD diss., Temple University, 1987.

Lehmann, Paul L. "The Reformers' Use of the Bible." *ThTo* 3 (1946): 328-44.

Lillback, Peter A. *The Binding of God: Calvin's Role in the Development of Covenant Theology*. Texts and Studies in Reformation and Post-Reformation Thought. Grand Rapids: Baker Academic, 2001.

McKee, Elsie Anne. "Exegesis, Theology, and Development in Calvin's *Institutio*: A Methodological Suggestion." In *Probing the Reformed Tradition: Historical Studies in Honor of Edward A. Dowey, Jr.*, edited by Elsie Anne McKee and Brian G. Armstrong, 154-72. Louisville: Westminster John Knox, 1989.

———. "Some Reflections on Relating Calvin's Exegesis and Theology." In *Biblical Hermeneutics in Historical Perspective: Studies in Honor of Karlfried Froehlich on His Sixtieth Birthday*, edited by Mark S. Burrows and Paul Rorem, 215-26. Grand Rapids: Eerdmans, 1991.

McKim, Donald K., ed. *Calvin and the Bible*. Cambridge: Cambridge University Press, 2006.

———, ed. *The Cambridge Companion to John Calvin*. Cambridge Companions to Religion. Cambridge: Cambridge University Press, 2004.

Millet, Olivier. *Calvin et la dynamique de la parole: Étude de rhétorique réformée*. Geneva: Slatkine, 1992.

———. *Readings in Calvin's Theology*. Grand Rapids: Baker, 1984.

Milner, Charles, Jr. *Calvin's Doctrine of the Church*. Studies in the History of Christian Thought. Leiden: Brill, 1970.

Muller, Richard A. "*Fides* and *Cognitio* in Relation to the Problem of the Intellect and Will in the Theology of John Calvin." *CTJ* 25 (1990): 207-24.

———. "The Hermeneutic of Promise and Fulfillment in Calvin's Exegesis of the Old Testament Prophecies of the Kingdom." In *The Bible in the Sixteenth Century*, edited by David C. Steinmetz, 68-82. Duke Monographs in Medieval and Renaissance Studies 11. Durham, NC: Duke University Press, 1990.

———. *Post-Reformation Reformed Dogmatics: The Rise and Development of Reformed Orthodoxy, ca. 1520 to ca. 1725*. Vol. 2: *Holy Scripture: The Cognitive Foundation of Theology*. 2nd ed. Grand Rapids: Baker Academic, 2003.

———. *The Unaccommodated Calvin: Studies in the Foundation of a Theological Tradition*. OSHT. Oxford: Oxford University Press, 2000.

Muller, Richard A., and John L. Thompson, eds. *Biblical Interpretation in the Era of the Reformation: Essays Presented to David C. Steinmetz in Honor of His Sixtieth Birthday*. Grand Rapids: Eerdmans, 1996.

Neuser, Wilhelm H., ed. *Calvinus Sacrae Scripturae Professor: Calvin as Confessor of Holy Scripture*. Die Referate des Internationalen Kongresses für Calvinforschung vom 20. bis 23. August 1990 in Grand Rapids. Grand Rapids: Eerdmans, 1994.

Niesel, Wilhelm. *The Theology of Calvin*. Translated by Harold Knight. Orig. 1938. Repr. Philadelphia: Westminster, 1956.

Oort, Johannes van. "John Calvin and the Church Fathers." In *The Reception of the*

Church Fathers: From the Carolingians to the Maurists, edited by Irena Backus, 2:661-700. Leiden: Brill, 1997.

Opitz, Peter. *Calvins theologische Hermeneutik.* Neukirchener-Vluyn: Neukirchener Verlag, 1994.

Osterhaven, Eugene. "Calvin on the Covenant." In *Readings in Calvin's Theology,* edited by Donald K. McKim, 89-106. Grand Rapids: Baker, 1984.

Pak, G. Sujin. *The Judaizing Calvin.* OSHT. Oxford: Oxford University Press, 2010.

Parker, T. H. L. *Calvin's New Testament Commentaries.* 2nd ed. Louisville: Westminster John Knox, 1993.

―――. *Calvin's Old Testament Commentaries.* Louisville: Westminster John Knox, 1986.

―――. *Calvin's Preaching.* Louisville: Westminster John Knox, 1992.

―――. *John Calvin: A Biography.* Orig. 1992. Repr. Louisville: Westminster John Knox, 2006.

―――. *The Oracles of God: An Introduction to the Preaching of John Calvin.* Library of Ecclesiastical History. Orig. 1947. Repr. Cambridge, UK: James Clark, 2002.

Parker, Thomas D. "The Interpretation of Scripture: A Comparison of Calvin and Luther on Galatians." *Int* 17 (1963): 61-75.

Partee, Charles. *The Theology of John Calvin.* Louisville: Westminster John Knox, 2008.

Pitkin, Barbara. "John Calvin and the Interpretation of the Bible." In *The Medieval through the Reformation Periods,* edited by Alan J. Hauser and Duane F. Watson, 341-71. Vol. 2 of *A History of Biblical Interpretation.* Grand Rapids: Eerdmans, 2009.

―――. *What Pure Eyes Could See: Calvin's Doctrine of Faith in Its Exegetical Context.* Oxford: Oxford University Press, 1999.

Puckett, David L. *John Calvin's Exegesis of the Old Testament.* Columbia Series in Reformed Theology. Louisville: Westminster John Knox, 1995.

Ravenswaay, J. Marius J. Lange van. *Augustinus totus noster: Das Augustinverständnis bei Johannes Calvin.* Göttingen: Vandenhoeck & Ruprecht, 1990.

Robinson, Jack Hughes. *John Calvin and the Jews.* American University Studies, Series 7: Theology and Religion 123. New York: Peter Lang, 1992.

Schreiner, Susan E. *The Theater of His Glory: Nature and the Natural Order in the Thought of John Calvin.* Grand Rapids: Baker Academic, 1991.

―――. *Where Shall Wisdom Be Found? Calvin's Exegesis of Job from Medieval and Modern Perspectives.* Chicago: University of Chicago Press, 1994.

Selderhuis, Herman J., ed. *The Calvin Handbook.* Translated by Henry J. Baron, Judith J. Guder, Randi H. Lundell, and Gerrit W. Sheeres. Grand Rapids: Eerdmans, 2009.

Shute, Dan. "And All Israel Shall Be Saved: Peter Martyr and John Calvin on the Jews according to Romans, Chapters 9, 10 and 11." In *Peter Martyr Vermigli and the European Reformations: Semper Reformanda,* edited by Frank A. James, III, 159-76. Studies in the History of Christian Traditions. Leiden: Brill, 2004.

Smits, Luchesius. *Saint Augustin dans l'œuvre de Jean Calvin.* 2 vols. Assen: Van Gorcum, 1957.

Steinmetz, David C. "Calvin and Patristic Exegesis." In idem, *Calvin in Context,* 122-40. Oxford: Oxford University Press, 1995.

―――. *Calvin in Context.* Oxford: Oxford University Press, 1995.

Bibliography

———. "John Calvin as an Interpreter of the Bible." In *Calvin and the Bible*, edited by Donald K. McKim, 282-91. Cambridge: Cambridge University Press, 2006.

———. "The Judaizing Calvin." In *Die Patristik in der Bibelexegese des 16. Jahrhunderts*, edited by David C. Steinmetz, 135-45. Wolfenbütteler Forschungen 85. Wiesbaden: Harrassowitz, 1999.

Thompson, John Lee. *John Calvin and the Daughters of Sarah: Women in Regular and Exceptional Roles in the Exegesis of Calvin, His Predecessors, and His Contemporaries*. Geneva: Droz, 1992.

Vischer, Wilhelm. "Calvin, exégète de l'Ancien Testament." *RRef* 18 (1967): 1-20.

Wallace, Ronald S. *Calvin's Doctrine of the Word and Sacrament*. Edinburgh: Oliver and Boyd, 1953.

Wendel, François. *Calvin: Origins and Development of His Religious Thought*. Translated by Philip Mairet. Orig. 1950. Repr. Grand Rapids: Baker, 1963.

Wolf, Hans Heinrich. *Die Einheit des Bundes: Das Verhältnis von Altem und Neuem Testament bei Calvin*. Neukirchen: Verlag der Buchhandlung des Erziehungsvereins, 1958.

Yeaton, Kenneth. "Aspects of Calvin's Eschatology, Part 1." *Chm* 100 (1986): 114-28.

———. "Aspects of Calvin's Eschatology, Part 2." *Chm* 100 (1986): 198-209.

Zachman, Randall C. *Image and Word in the Theology of John Calvin*. Notre Dame, IN: University of Notre Dame Press, 2007.

———. *Reconsidering John Calvin*. Current Issues in Theology. Cambridge: Cambridge University Press, 2012.

Works Concerning the Epistle to the Hebrews

Aschim, Anders. "Melchizedek and Jesus: 11QMelchizedek and the Epistle to the Hebrews." In *The Jewish Roots of Christological Monotheism: Papers from the St. Andrews Conference on the Historical Origins of the Worship of Jesus*, edited by Carey C. Newman, James R. Davila, and Gladys S. Lewis, 129-47. Supplements to the JSJ 63. Leiden: Brill, 1999.

Attridge, Harold W. *Hebrews*. Hermeneia. Philadelphia: Augsburg Fortress, 1989.

———. "'Let Us Strive to Enter That Rest': The Logic of Hebrews 4:1-11." *HTR* 73 (1980): 279-88.

———. "New Covenant Christology in an Early Christian Homily." *QR* 8 (1988): 89-108.

———. "The Psalms in Hebrews." In *The Psalms in the New Testament*, edited by Steve Moyise and Maarten J. J. Menken, 197-212. London: T&T Clark, 2004.

Barrett, C. K. "The Eschatology of the Epistle to the Hebrews." In *The Background of the New Testament and Its Eschatology*, edited by W. D. Davies and D. Daube, 369-93. Cambridge: Cambridge University Press, 1956.

Barth, Markus. "The Old Testament in Hebrews: An Essay in Biblical Hermeneutics." In *Current Issues in New Testament Interpretation: Essays in Honor of Otto A. Piper*, edited by William Klassen and Graydon F. Snyder, 53-78. New York: Harper, 1962.

Bateman, Herbert W., IV. *Early Jewish Hermeneutics and Hebrews 1:5-13: The Impact of Early Jewish Exegesis on the Interpretation of a Significant New Testament Passage*.

American University Studies, Series 7: Theology and Religion 193. New York: Peter Lang, 1997.

Bauckham, Richard, Daniel R. Driver, Trevor A. Hart, and Nathan MacDonald, eds. *The Epistle to the Hebrews and Christian Theology.* Grand Rapids: Eerdmans, 2009.

Bauckham, Richard, Trevor Hart, Nathan MacDonald, and Daniel R. Driver, eds. *A Cloud of Witnesses: The Theology of Hebrews in Its Ancient Contexts.* LNTS 387. London: T&T Clark, 2008.

Blackstone, Thomas Ladd. "The Hermeneutics of Recontextualization in the Epistle to the Hebrews." PhD diss., Emory University, 1995.

Blomberg, Craig L. "'But We See Jesus': The Relationship between the Son of Man in Hebrews 2.6 and 2.9 and the Implications for English Translations." In *A Cloud of Witnesses: The Theology of Hebrews in Its Ancient Contexts,* edited by Richard Bauckham, Trevor Hart, Nathan MacDonald, and Daniel R. Driver, 88-99. LNTS 387. London: T&T Clark, 2008.

Brawley, Robert L. "Discursive Structure and the Unseen in Hebrews 2:8 and 11:1: A Neglected Aspect of the Context." *CBQ* 55 (1983): 81-98.

Brock, S. P. "Hebrews 2:9b in Syriac Tradition." *NovT* 27 (1983): 236-44.

Bruce, F. F. *The Epistle to the Hebrews.* Rev. ed. NICNT. Grand Rapids: Eerdmans, 1990.

Burns, Lanier. "Hermeneutical Issues and Principles in Hebrews as Exemplified in the Second Chapter." *JETS* 39 (1996): 587-607.

Caird, George B. "The Exegetical Method of the Epistle to the Hebrews." *CJT* 5 (1959): 44-51.

Childs, Brevard S. "Psalm 8 in the Context of the Christian Canon." *Int* 23 (1969): 20-31.

Chrysostom, John. *Homilies on The Epistle to the Hebrews.* NPNF[2] 14, 1889.

Clements, Ronald E. "The Use of the Old Testament in Hebrews." *SwJT* 28 (1955): 36-45.

Cockerill, Gareth Lee. "The Melchizedek Christology in Heb. 7:1-28." PhD diss., Union Theological Seminary in Virginia, 1976.

———. "Melchizedek without Speculation: Hebrews 7:1-25 and Genesis 14:17-24." In *A Cloud of Witnesses: The Theology of Hebrews in Its Ancient Contexts,* edited by Richard Bauckham, Trevor Hart, Nathan MacDonald, and Daniel R. Driver, 128-44. LNTS 387. London: T&T Clark, 2008.

Combrink, H. J. B. "Some Thoughts on the Old Testament Citations in the Epistle to the Hebrews." *Neot* 5 (1971): 22-36.

Cosby, Michael R. *The Rhetorical Composition and Function of Hebrews 11: In Light of Example Lists in Antiquity.* Macon, GA: Mercer University Press, 1988.

———. "The Rhetorical Composition of Hebrews 11." *JBL* 107 (1988): 257-73.

Delcor, M. "Melchizedek from Genesis to the Qumran Texts and the Epistle to the Hebrews." *JSJ* 2 (1971): 115-35.

Demarest, Bruce. *A History of Interpretation of Hebrews 7, 1-10 from the Reformation to the Present.* BGBE 19. Tübingen: Mohr (Siebeck), 1976.

———. "Hebrews 7:3: A *Crux Interpretum* Historically Considered." *EvQ* 49 (1977): 141-62.

deSilva, David Arthur. *Despising Shame: Honor Discourse and Community Maintenance in the Epistle to the Hebrews.* SBLDS 152. Atlanta: Scholars, 1995.

———. "Entering God's Rest: Eschatology and the Socio-Rhetorical Strategy of Hebrews." *TJ* 21 (2000): 25-43.

———. *Perseverance in Gratitude: A Socio-Rhetorical Commentary on the Epistle "to the Hebrews."* Grand Rapids: Eerdmans, 2000.

Docherty, Susan E. *The Use of the Old Testament in Hebrews: A Case Study in Early Jewish Interpretation.* WUNT 2. Reihe 260. Tübingen: Mohr Siebeck, 2009.

Dunnill, John. *Covenant and Sacrifice in the Letter to the Hebrews.* Cambridge: Cambridge University Press, 1992.

Dunning, Benjamin H. *Aliens and Sojourners: Self as Other in Early Christianity.* Divinations: Rereading Late Ancient Religion. Philadelphia: University of Pennsylvania Press, 2009.

Eisenbaum, Pamela Michelle. *The Jewish Heroes of Christian Antiquity: Hebrews 11 in Literary Context.* SBLDS 156. Atlanta: Scholars, 1997.

———. "Locating Hebrews within the Literary Landscape of Christian Origins." In *Hebrews: Contemporary Methods, New Insights,* edited by Gabriella Gelardini, 213-37. Leiden: Brill, 2005.

Ellingworth, Paul. *The Epistle to the Hebrews: A Commentary on the Greek Text.* NIGTC. Grand Rapids: Eerdmans, 1993.

Enns, Peter. "The Interpretation of Psalm 95 in Hebrews 3.1–4.13." In *Early Christian Interpretation of the Scriptures of Israel,* edited by Craig A. Evans and James A. Sanders, 352-63. JSNTSup 148. Sheffield: Sheffield Academic, 1997.

Fitzmyer, Joseph A. "Further Light on Melchizedek from Qumran Cave 11." *JBL* 86 (1967): 25-41.

———. "Melchizedek in the MT, LXX, and the NT." *Bib* 81 (2000): 63-69.

———. "'Now This Melchizedek . . .' (Heb 7, 1)." *CBQ* 25 (1963): 305-21.

France, R. T. "The Writer of Hebrews as a Biblical Expositor." *TynBul* 47 (1996): 245-76.

Gelardini, Gabriella, ed. *Hebrews: Contemporary Methods — New Insights.* Leiden: Brill, 2005.

Gleason, Randall C. "Angels and the Eschatology of Heb 1–2." *NTS* 49 (2003): 90-107.

———. "The Old Testament Background of Rest." *BSac* 157 (2000): 281-303.

Greer, Rowan A. *The Captain of Our Salvation: A Study of the Patristic Exegesis of Hebrews.* BGBE 15. Tübingen: Mohr (Siebeck), 1973.

Grogan, Geoffrey W. "Christ and His People: An Exegetical and Theological Study of Hebrews 2:5-18." *VE* 6 (1969): 54-71.

Guthrie, George H. "Hebrews." In *Commentary on the New Testament Use of the Old Testament,* edited by G. K. Beale and D. A. Carson, 919-95. Grand Rapids: Baker Academic, 2007.

———. "Hebrews' Use of the Old Testament: Recent Trends in Research." *CurBR* 1 (2003): 271-94.

———. "Old Testament in Hebrews." In *Dictionary of the Later New Testament and Its Developments,* edited by Ralph P. Martin and Peter H. Davids, 841-50. Downers Grove, IL: InterVarsity, 1997.

———. *The Structure of Hebrews: A Text-Linguistic Analysis.* Leiden: Brill, 1994.

Guthrie, George H., and Russell D. Quinn. "A Discourse Analysis of the Use of Psalm 8:4-6 in Hebrews 2:5-9." *JETS* 49 (2006): 235-46.

Hanson, A. T. "Hebrews." In *It Is Written: Scripture Citing Scripture: Essays in Honour of*

Barnabas Lindars, SSF, edited by D. A. Carson and H. G. M. Williamson, 292-302. Cambridge: Cambridge University Press, 1998.
Hay, David M. *Glory at the Right Hand: Psalm 110 in Early Christianity.* SBLMS 18. Atlanta: Society of Biblical Literature, 1973.
Hays, Richard B. "'Here We Have No Lasting City': New Covenantalism in Hebrews." In *The Epistle to the Hebrews and Christian Theology,* edited by Richard Bauckham, Daniel R. Driver, Trevor A. Hart, and Nathan MacDonald, 151-73. Grand Rapids: Eerdmans, 2009.
Heen, Erik M., and Philip D. Krey, eds. *Hebrews.* ACCS 10. Downers Grove, IL: InterVarsity, 2005.
Horton, Fred L. *The Melchizedek Tradition: A Critical Examination of the Sources to the Fifth Century A.D. and in the Epistle to the Hebrews.* Cambridge: Cambridge University Press, 1976.
Howard, George. "Hebrews and the Old Testament Quotations." *NovT* 10 (1968): 208-15.
Hughes, Graham. *Hebrews and Hermeneutics: The Epistle to the Hebrews as a New Testament Example of Biblical Interpretation.* Cambridge: Cambridge University Press, 1979.
Hurst, L. D. "The Christology of Hebrews 1 and 2." In *The Glory of Christ in the New Testament: Studies in Christology in Memory of George Bradford Caird,* edited by L. D. Hurst and N. T. Wright, 151-64. Oxford: Clarendon, 1987.
———. *The Epistle to the Hebrews: Its Background of Thought.* Cambridge: Cambridge University Press, 1990.
Jobes, Karen H. "The Function of Paronomasia in Hebrews 10:5-7." *TJ* 13 (1992): 181-91.
Johnson, Luke Timothy. *Hebrews: A Commentary.* NTL. Louisville: Westminster John Knox, 2006.
———. "The Scriptural World of Hebrews." *Int* 57 (2004): 237-50.
Johnson, Richard W. *Going Outside the Camp: The Sociological Function of the Levitical Critique in the Epistle to the Hebrews.* JSNTSup 209. Sheffield: Sheffield Academic, 2001.
Joslin, Barry C. *Hebrews, Christ, and the Law: The Theology of the Mosaic Law in Hebrews 7:1–10:18.* Pasternoster Biblical Monographs. Eugene, OR: Wipf and Stock, 2008.
Käsemann, Ernst. *The Wandering People of God.* Translated by Roy A. Harrisville and Irving L. Sandberg. Orig. 1939. Minneapolis: Augsburg, 1984.
Kistemaker, Simon. *The Psalm Citations in the Epistle to the Hebrews.* Amsterdam: Soest, 1961.
Koester, Craig R. *Hebrews: A New Translation with Introduction and Commentary.* AB 36. New York: Doubleday, 2001.
Kurianal, James. *Jesus Our High Priest: Ps 110, 4 as the Substructure of Heb 5, 1-7, 28.* Frankfurt am Main: Peter Lang, 2000.
Laansma, Jon C. *"I Will Give You Rest": The Rest Motif in the New Testament with Special Reference to Mt 11 and Heb 3–4.* Tübingen: Mohr Siebeck, 1997.
Laansma, Jon C., and Daniel J. Treier, eds. *Christology, Hermeneutics, and Hebrews: Profiles from the History of Interpretation.* London: T&T Clark, 2012.
Lane, William L. *Hebrews 1–8.* WBC 47a. Dallas: Word, 1991.

Bibliography

———. *Hebrews 9–13*. WBC 47b. Dallas: Word, 1991.
Lefler, Nathan. "The Melchizedek Traditions in the Letter to the Hebrews: Reading through the Eyes of an Inspired Jewish-Christian Author." *ProEccl* 16 (2007): 73-89.
Lehne, Susanne. *The New Covenant in Hebrews*. JSNTSup 44. Sheffield: Sheffield Academic, 1990.
Leschert, Dale F. *Hermeneutical Foundations of Hebrews: A Study in the Validity of the Epistle's Interpretation of Some Core Citations from the Psalms*. National Association of Baptist Professors of Religion Dissertation Series 10. Lewiston, NY: Edwin Mellen, 1995.
Lincoln, A. T. "Sabbath, Rest, and Eschatology in the New Testament." In *From Sabbath to Lord's Day: A Biblical, Historical, and Theological Investigation,* edited by D. A. Carson, 197-220. Grand Rapids: Zondervan, 1982.
Lindars, Barnabas. *The Theology of the Letter to the Hebrews*. New Testament Theology. Cambridge: Cambridge University Press, 1991.
Longenecker, Richard N. "Hebrews and the Old Testament." In idem, *Biblical Exegesis in the Apostolic Period,* 2nd ed., 140-65. Grand Rapids: Eerdmans, 1999.
———. "The Melchizedek Argument of Hebrews: A Study in the Development and Circumstantial Expression of New Testament Thought." In *Unity and Diversity in New Testament Theology: Essays in Honor of George E. Ladd,* edited by Robert A. Geulich, 161-85. Grand Rapids: Eerdmans, 1978.
Mason, Eric F. *"You Are a Priest Forever": Second Temple Jewish Messianism and the Priestly Christology of the Epistle to the Hebrews*. Studies on the Texts of the Desert of Judah 74. Leiden: Brill, 2008.
McCullough, J. C. "The Old Testament Quotations in Hebrews." *NTS* 26 (1980): 363-79.
Miller, James C. "Paul and Hebrews: A Comparison of Narrative Worlds." In *Hebrews: Contemporary Methods, New Insights,* edited by Gabriella Gelardini, 245-64. Leiden: Brill, 2005.
Moffitt, David. *Atonement and the Logic of Resurrection in the Epistle to the Hebrews*. Leiden: Brill, 2011.
———. "'If Another Priest Arises': Jesus' Resurrection and the High Priestly Christology of Hebrews." In *A Cloud of Witnesses: The Theology of Hebrews in Its Ancient Contexts,* edited by Richard Bauckham, Trevor Hart, Nathan MacDonald, and Daniel R. Driver, 68-79. LNTS 387. London: T&T Clark, 2008.
———. "Jesus the High Priest and the Mosaic Law: Reassessing the Appeal to the Heavenly Realm in the Letter 'To the Hebrews.'" In *Problems Translating Texts about Jesus,* edited by John T. Greene and Mishael Caspi. Lewiston, NY: Edwin Mellen, 2010.
Motyer, Stephen. "The Psalm Quotations of Hebrews 1: A Hermeneutic-Free Zone?" *TynBul* 50 (1999): 3-22.
Neyrey, Jerome H. "'Without Beginning of Days or End of Life' (Hebrews 7:3): Topos for a True Deity." *CBQ* 53 (1991): 439-55.
Parsons, Mikael C. "Son and High Priest: A Study in the Christology of Hebrews." *EvQ* 60 (1988): 195-215.
Peterson, David. *Hebrews and Perfection: An Examination of the Concept of Perfection in the "Epistle to the Hebrews."* Cambridge: Cambridge University Press, 1982.

Rad, Gerhard von. "There Remains Still a Rest for the People of God: An Investigation of a Biblical Conception." In *The Problem of the Hexateuch and Other Essays*, translated by E. W. Trueman Dicken, 94-102. New York: McGraw-Hill, 1966.

Rendall, Robert. "The Method of the Writer to the Hebrews in Using Old Testament Quotations." *EvQ* 27 (1955): 214-20.

Rooke, Deborah W. "Jesus as Royal Priest: Reflections on the Interpretation of the Melchizedek Tradition in Heb 7." *Bib* 81 (2000): 81-94.

Salevao, Iutisone. *Legitimization in the Letter to the Hebrews: The Construction and Maintenance of a Symbolic Universe*. JSNTSup 219. Sheffield: Sheffield Academic, 2002.

Schenck, Ken. "God Has Spoken: Hebrews' Theology of the Scriptures." In *The Epistle to the Hebrews and Christian Theology*, edited by Richard Bauckham, Daniel R. Driver, Trevor A. Hart, and Nathan MacDonald, 321-36. Grand Rapids: Eerdmans, 2009.

Scholer, John M. *Proleptic Priests: Priesthood in the Epistle to the Hebrews*. JSNTSup 49. Sheffield: Sheffield Academic, 1991.

Smothers, Thomas G. "A Superior Model: Hebrews 1:1–4:13." *RevExp* 82 (1985): 333-43.

Sowers, Sidney G. *The Hermeneutics of Philo and Hebrews: A Comparison of the Interpretation of the Old Testament in Philo Judaeus and the Epistle to the Hebrews*. Basel Studies of Theology 1. Richmond: John Knox, 1965.

Thiessen, Matthew. "Hebrews 12.5-13, the Wilderness Period, and Israel's Discipline." *NTS* 55 (2009): 366-79.

———. "Hebrews and the End of the Exodus." *NovT* 49 (2007): 353-69.

Thomas, Kenneth J. "The Old Testament Citations in Hebrews." *NTS* 11 (1965): 303-25.

Treier, Daniel J. "Speech Acts, Hearing Hearts, and Other Senses: The Doctrine of Scripture Practiced in Hebrews." In *The Epistle to the Hebrews and Christian Theology*, edited by Richard Bauckham, Daniel R. Driver, Trevor A. Hart, and Nathan MacDonald, 337-50. Grand Rapids: Eerdmans, 2009.

Urassa, Wenceslaus Mkeni. *Psalm 8 and Its Christological Re-Interpretations in the New Testament Context*. European University Studies, Series 23: Theology 577. Frankfurt am Main: Peter Lang, 1998.

Vanhoye, Albert. *Old Testament Priests and the New Priest According to the New Testament*. Translated by J. Bernard Orchard. Orig. 1980. Repr. Petersham, MA: St. Bede's, 1986.

———. *Structure and Message of the Epistle to the Hebrews*. SubBi 12. Rome: Editrice Pontificio Instituto Biblico, 1989.

Wedderburn, A. J. M. "Sawing Off the Branches: Theologizing Dangerously *Ad Hebraeos*." *JTS* 56 (2005): 393-414.

Williamson, Clark M. "Anti-Judaism in Hebrews?" *Int* 57 (2008): 266-79.

Williamson, Ronald. *Philo and the Epistle to the Hebrews*. Leiden: Brill, 1970.

General Works

Ackroyd, P. R., and C. F. Evans, eds. *The Cambridge History of the Bible*. Vol. 1: *From the Beginnings to Jerome*. Cambridge: Cambridge University Press, 1970.

Bibliography

Alexander, T. Desmond, Brian S. Rosner, D. A. Carson, and Graeme Goldsworthy, eds. *New Dictionary of Biblical Theology: Exploring the Unity and Diversity of Scripture.* Downers Grove, IL: InterVarsity, 2000.

Allison, Dale C., Jr. *The Intertextual Jesus: Scripture in Q.* Harrisburg: Trinity, 2000.

Anatolios, Khaled. *Athanasius.* New York: Routledge, 2004.

―――. *Retrieving Nicaea: The Development and Meaning of Trinitarian Doctrine.* Grand Rapids: Baker Academic, 2011.

Aquinas, Thomas. *Summa Theologiae.* Translated by Fathers of the English Dominican Province. 6 vols. Notre Dame, IN: Christian Classics, 1948. Latin text: Cinisello Balsamo, Italy: San Paolo, 1988.

Auerbach, Erich. "Figura." In *Scenes from the Drama of European Literature,* translated by Ralph Manheim, 11-76. Theory and History of European Literature 9. Minneapolis: University of Minnesota Press, 1984. Essay originally published in 1944.

―――. *Mimesis: The Representation of Reality in Western Literature.* Translated by Willard R. Trask. 50th-anniv. ed. Princeton: Princeton University Press, 2003.

Ayres, Lewis. *Nicaea and Its Legacy: An Approach to Fourth-Century Trinitarian Theology.* Oxford: Oxford University Press, 2004.

Baker, David L. *Two Testaments, One Bible: The Theological Relationship between the Old and New Testaments.* 3rd ed. Downers Grove, IL: InterVarsity, 2010.

Barr, James. "The Literal, the Allegorical, and Modern Biblical Scholarship." *JSOT* 44 (1989): 3-17.

―――. *Old and New in Interpretation: A Study of the Two Testaments.* New York: Harper and Row, 1964.

―――. *The Semantics of Biblical Language.* Oxford: Oxford University Press, 1961.

―――. "Wilhelm Vischer and Allegory." In *Understanding the Poets and Prophets: Essays in Honour of George Wishart Anderson,* edited by A. Graeme Auld, 38-60. JSOTSup 152. Sheffield: Sheffield Academic, 1993.

Barrera, Julio Trebolle. *The Jewish Bible and the Christian Bible: An Introduction to the History of the Bible.* Grand Rapids: Eerdmans, 1998.

Barth, Karl. *Church Dogmatics* 1/1. Translated by G. W. Bromiley. 2nd ed. London: T&T Clark, 1975. German text: *Die Kirchliche Dogmatik* 1/1. Munich: Chr. Kaiser, 1932.

―――. *Church Dogmatics* 1/2. Translated by G. T. Thomson and Harold Knight. Orig. 1938. London: T&T Clark, 1956.

―――. *Church Dogmatics* 2/2. Translated by J. C. Campbell, G. W. Bromiley, Iain Wilson, J. Strathearn McNab, Harold Knight, and R. A. Stewart. Orig. 1942. London: T&T Clark, 2004.

―――. *Credo: A Presentation of the Chief Problems of Dogmatics with Reference to the Apostles' Creed.* Translated by J. Strathearn McNab. London: Hodder & Stoughton, 1936.

―――. *The Epistle to the Romans.* Translated by Edwyn C. Hoskyns. 6th ed. Orig. 1918. Oxford: Oxford University Press, 1933.

―――. *The Word of God and the Word of Man.* Translated by Douglas Horton. Orig. 1928. New York: Harper and Row, 1957.

Basil. *On the Holy Spirit.* Translated by Stephen Hildebrand. Popular Patristics Series 42. Yonkers, NY: St. Vladimir's Seminary Press, 2011.

BIBLIOGRAPHY

Bauckham, Richard. *God Crucified: Monotheism and Christology in the New Testament.* Grand Rapids: Eerdmans, 1998.

Beale, G. K., ed. *The Right Doctrine from the Wrong Texts? Essays on the Use of the Old Testament in the New.* Grand Rapids: Baker, 1994.

Beale, G. K., and D. A. Carson, eds. *Commentary on the New Testament Use of the Old Testament.* Grand Rapids: Baker Academic, 2007.

Becker, Adam H., and Annette Yoshiko Reed, eds. *The Ways That Never Parted: Jews and Christians in Late Antiquity and the Early Middle Ages.* Minneapolis: Fortress, 2007.

Behr, John. *Formation of Christian Theology.* 2 vols. Crestwood, NY: St. Vladimir's Seminary Press, 2001.

Bergen, Jeremy M. *Ecclesial Repentance: The Churches Confront Their Sinful Pasts.* London: T&T Clark, 2011.

Billings, J. Todd. *The Word of God for the People of God: An Entryway to the Theological Interpretation of Scripture.* Grand Rapids: Eerdmans, 2010.

Birch, Bruce C. *Let Justice Roll Down: The Old Testament, Ethics, and Christian Life.* Louisville: Westminster John Knox, 1991.

Bockmuehl, Markus. *Jewish Law in Gentile Churches: Halakhah and the Beginning of Christian Public Ethics.* Grand Rapids: Baker Academic, 2000.

———. *Seeing the Word: Refocusing New Testament Study.* STI. Grand Rapids: Baker Academic, 2006.

Bockmuehl, Markus, and Alan J. Torrance, eds. *Scripture's Doctrine and Theology's Bible: How the New Testament Shapes Christian Dogmatics.* Grand Rapids: Baker Academic, 2008.

Boyarin, Daniel. *Border Lines: The Partition of Judaeo-Christianity.* Divinations: Rereading Late Ancient Religion. Philadelphia: University of Pennsylvania Press, 2004.

———. *A Radical Jew: Paul and the Politics of Identity.* Berkeley: University of California Press, 1994.

Braaten, Carl E., and Robert W. Jenson, eds. *Church Unity and the Papal Office: An Ecumenical Dialogue on John Paul II's Encyclical* Ut Unum Sint *(That All May Be One).* Grand Rapids: Eerdmans, 2001.

———, eds. *In One Body through the Cross: The Princeton Proposal for Christian Unity.* Grand Rapids: Eerdmans, 2003.

———, eds. *Marks of the Body of Christ.* Grand Rapids: Eerdmans, 1999.

Brown, Daniel W. *Rethinking Tradition in Modern Islamic Thought.* Cambridge Middle East Studies. Cambridge: Cambridge University Press, 1996.

Bruce, F. F. *The Canon of Scripture.* Downers Grove, IL: InterVarsity, 1988.

Buckley, James J., and David S. Yeago. *Knowing the Triune God: The Work of the Spirit in the Practices of the Church.* Grand Rapids: Eerdmans, 2001.

Bultmann, Rudolf. *The New Testament and Mythology: And Other Basic Writings.* Translated by Schubert M. Ogden. Philadelphia: Fortress, 1984.

———. *Theology of the New Testament.* Translated by Kendrick Grobel. Orig. 1955. Waco, TX: Baylor University Press, 2007.

Buren, Paul M. van. "On Reading Someone Else's Mail: The Church and Israel's Scriptures." In *Die Hebräische Bibel und ihre zweifache Nachgeschichte: Festschrift für*

Bibliography

Rolf Rendtorff zum 65. Geburtstag, edited by Erhard Blum, Christian Macholz, and Ekkehard W. Stegemann, 595-606. Neukirchen-Vluyn: Neukirchener, 1990.

Campbell, Douglas A. "An Evangelical Paul: A Response to Francis Watson's *Paul and the Hermeneutics of Faith.*" *JSNT* 28 (2006): 337-51.

Carson, D. A., Peter T. O'Brien, and Mark A. Seifrid, eds. *Justification and Variegated Nomism.* 2 vols. Grand Rapids: Baker Academic, 2001.

Carson, D. A., and H. G. M. Williamson. *It Is Written: Scripture Citing Scripture: Essays in Honour of Barnabas Lindars, SSF.* Cambridge: Cambridge University Press, 1988.

Childs, Brevard S. *Biblical Theology in Crisis.* Philadelphia: Westminster, 1970.

———. *Biblical Theology of the Old and New Testaments.* Minneapolis: Fortress, 1992.

———. "Critical Reflections on James Barr's Understanding of the Literal and the Allegorical." *JSOT* 46 (1990): 3-9.

———. *Introduction to the Old Testament as Scripture.* Philadelphia: Fortress, 1979.

———. "Old Testament in Germany 1920-1940: The Search for a New Paradigm." In *Altes Testament: Forschung und Wirkung: Festschrift für Henning Graf Reventlow,* 233-46. Frankfurt am Main: Peter Lang, 1994.

———. "The Sensus Literalis of Scripture: An Ancient and Modern Problem." In *Beiträge zur Alttestamentlichen Theologie,* edited by Herbert Donner, Robert Hanhart, and Rudolf Smend, 80-93. Göttingen: Vandenhoeck & Ruprecht, 1977.

Congar, Yves M.-J. *La Tradition et les traditions.* 2 vols. Paris: Librairie Artheme Fayard, 1960. English translation: *Tradition and Traditions: The Biblical, Historical, and Theological Evidence for Catholic Teaching on Tradition.* Translated by Michael Naseby (original vol. 1) and Thomas Rainborough (original vol. 2). San Diego: Basilica, 1966.

Court, John M. *New Testament Writers and the Old Testament.* London: SPCK, 2002.

Cullmann, Oscar. *Christ and Time: The Primitive Christian Conception of Time and History.* Translated by Floyd V. Filson. Philadelphia: Westminster, 1950.

———. *The Early Church.* Translated by A. J. B. Higgins. London: SCM, 1956.

Daniélou, Jean. *From Shadows to Reality: Studies in the Biblical Typology of the Fathers.* Translated by Don Wulstan Hibberd. Orig. 1950. Westminster, MD: Newman, 1960.

Dauphinais, Michael, and Matthew Levering, eds. *Reading John with St. Thomas Aquinas: Theological Exegesis and Speculative Theology.* Washington, DC: Catholic University of America Press, 2005.

Davis, Ellen F., and Richard B. Hays, eds. *The Art of Reading Scripture.* Grand Rapids: Eerdmans, 2003.

Dawson, John David. *Allegorical Readers and Cultural Revision in Ancient Alexandria.* Berkeley: University of California Press, 1992.

———. *Christian Figural Reading and the Fashioning of Identity.* Berkeley: University of California Press, 2002.

DeHart, Paul J. *The Trial of the Witnesses: The Rise and Decline of Postliberal Theology.* Challenges in Contemporary Theology. Malden, MA: Blackwell, 2006.

Dodd, C. H. *According to the Scriptures.* London: Fontana, 1952.

———. *The Parables of the Kingdom.* Rev. ed. Glasgow: Fount, 1961.

Drobner, Hubertus R. *The Fathers of the Church: A Comprehensive Introduction.* Translated by Siegfried S. Schatzmann. Orig. 1994. Peabody, MA: Hendrickson, 2007.
Dulles, Avery. *The Craft of Theology: From Symbol to System.* New exp. ed. New York: Crossroad, 1995.
———. "A Half Century of Ecclesiology." *TS* 50 (1989): 419-42.
———. "Moderate Infallibilism: An Ecumenical Approach." In *A Church to Believe In*, 133-48. New York: Crossroad, 1982. Originally published in *Teaching Authority and Infallibility in the Church*, edited by Paul C. Empie, T. Austin Murphy, and Joseph A. Burgess, 81-100. Lutherans and Catholics in Dialogue 6. Minneapolis: Augsburg, 1978.
———. "Papal Authority in Roman Catholicism." In *A Pope for All Christians: An Inquiry into the Role of Peter in the Modern Church*, edited by Peter J. McCord, 48-70. New York: Paulist, 1976.
———. "Toward a Renewed Papacy." In *The Resilient Church: The Necessity and Limits of Adaptation.* Garden City, NY: Doubleday, 1977.
Dunn, James D. G. *Jesus, Paul, and the Law.* Louisville: Westminster John Knox, 1990.
———. *Romans 1-8.* WBC 38a. Dallas: Word, 1988.
———. *Romans 9-16.* WBC 38b. Dallas: Word, 1988.
———. *The Theology of Paul the Apostle.* Grand Rapids: Eerdmans, 1998.
Dunn, James D. G., ed. *Paul and the Mosaic Law.* Grand Rapids: Eerdmans, 2001.
Ebeling, Gerhard. *Word and Faith.* Translated by James W. Leitch. Orig. 1960. London: SCM, 1963.
Emery, Gilles. *Trinity in Aquinas.* Ypsilanti, MI: Sapientia, 2003.
Empie, Paul C., and T. Austin Murphy, eds. *Papal Primacy and the Universal Church.* Lutherans and Catholics in Dialogue 5. Minneapolis: Augsburg, 1974.
Empie, Paul C., T. Austin Murphy, and Joseph A. Burgess, eds. *Teaching Authority and Infallibility in the Church.* Lutherans and Catholics in Dialogue 6. Minneapolis: Augsburg, 1978.
Ernest, James D. *The Bible in Athanasius of Alexandria.* The Bible in Ancient Christianity. Boston: Brill, 2004.
Evans, Craig A., and James A. Sanders. *Luke and Scripture: The Function of Sacred Tradition in Luke-Acts.* Minneapolis: Fortress, 1993.
Evans, Craig A., and W. Richard Stegner, eds. *The Gospels and the Scriptures of Israel.* JSNTSup 104. SSEJC 3. Sheffield: Sheffield Academic, 1994.
Farrow, Douglas. *Ascension and Ecclesia: On the Significance of the Doctrine of the Ascension for Ecclesiology and Christian Cosmology.* Grand Rapids: Eerdmans, 1999.
Fishbane, Michael. *Biblical Interpretation in Ancient Israel.* Oxford: Clarendon, 1988.
Fowl, Stephen E. *Engaging Scripture: A Model for Theological Interpretation.* Challenges in Contemporary Theology. Malden, MA: Blackwell, 1998.
Fowl, Stephen E., ed. *The Theological Interpretation of Scripture: Classic and Contemporary Readings.* Blackwell Readings in Modern Theology. Oxford: Blackwell, 1997.
Frei, Hans W. *The Eclipse of Biblical Narrative: A Study in Eighteenth and Nineteenth Century Hermeneutics.* New Haven: Yale University Press, 1974.
———. *The Identity of Jesus Christ: The Hermeneutical Bases of Dogmatic Theology.* Philadelphia: Fortress, 1975.
———. "The 'Literal Reading' of Biblical Narrative in the Christian Tradition: Does It

Bibliography

Stretch or Will It Break?" In idem, *Theology and Narrative: Selected Essays,* edited by George Hunsinger and William C. Placher, 117-52. Oxford: Oxford University Press, 1993.

———. *Theology and Narrative: Selected Essays.* Edited by George Hunsinger and William C. Placher. Oxford: Oxford University Press, 1993.

———. *Types of Christian Theology.* Edited by George Hunsinger and William C. Placher. New Haven: Yale University Press, 1992.

Frymer-Kensky, Tikva, David Novak, Peter Ochs, David Fox Sandmel, and Michael A. Signer, eds. *Christianity in Jewish Terms.* Boulder, CO: Westview, 2000.

Gaventa, Beverly Roberts, and Richard B. Hays, eds. *Seeking the Identity of Jesus: A Pilgrimage.* Grand Rapids: Eerdmans, 2008.

Geiselmann, Josef Rupert. *The Meaning of Tradition.* QD 15. Montreal: Palm, 1966.

Gilkey, Langdon B. "Cosmology, Ontology, and the Travail of Biblical Language." *JR* 41 (1961): 194-205.

Goppelt, Leonhard. *Typos: The Typological Intepretation of the Old Testament in the New.* Translated by Donald H. Madvig. Orig. 1939. Grand Rapids: Eerdmans, 1982.

Graham, William A. *Beyond the Written Word: Oral Aspects of Scripture in the History of Religion.* Cambridge: Cambridge University Press, 1987.

Granados, José, Carlos Granados, and Luis Sánchez-Navarro, eds. *Opening Up the Scriptures: Joseph Ratzinger and the Foundations of Biblical Interpretation.* Retrieval and Renewal: Ressourcement in Catholic Thought. Grand Rapids: Eerdmans, 2008.

Grant, Robert M., and David Tracy. *A Short History of Biblical Interpretation.* 2nd ed. Minneapolis: Fortress, 1984.

Green, Garrett, ed. *Scriptural Authority and Narrative Interpretation.* Philadelphia: Fortress, 1987.

Green, Joel B., and Max Turner, eds. *Between Two Horizons: Spanning New Testament Studies and Systematic Theology.* Grand Rapids: Eerdmans, 2000.

Greene-McCreight, K. E. *Ad Litteram: How Augustine, Calvin, and Barth Read the "Plain Sense" of Genesis 1–3.* Issues in Systematic Theology 5. New York: Peter Lang, 1999.

Greenslade, S. L., ed. *The Cambridge History of the Bible.* Vol. 3: *The West from the Reformation to the Present Day.* Cambridge: Cambridge University Press, 1963.

Gregory of Nazianzus. "The Theological Orations." In *Christology of the Later Fathers,* edited by Edward Rochie Hardy and Cyril C. Richardson, translated by Charles Gordon Browne and James Edward Swallow. LCC. Louisville: Westminster John Knox, 1954.

Hanson, R. P. C. *Allegory and Event: A Study of the Sources and the Significance of Origen's Interpretation of Scripture.* Orig. 1959. Repr. Louisville: Westminster John Knox, 2002.

———. *The Search for the Christian Doctrine of God: The Arian Controversy, 318-381.* Edinburgh: T&T Clark, 1988.

Harink, Douglas. *Paul among the Postliberals: Pauline Theology beyond Christendom and Modernity.* Grand Rapids: Brazos, 2003.

Harnack, Adolf von. *What Is Christianity?* Translated by Thomas Bailey Saunders. Fortress Texts in Modern Theology. Orig. 1900. Philadelphia: Fortress, 1986.

Harrisville, Roy A., and Walter Sundberg. *The Bible in Modern Culture: Baruch Spinoza to Brevard Childs.* 2nd ed. Grand Rapids: Eerdmans, 2002.
Hauerwas, Stanley. *Matthew.* Brazos Theological Commentary on the Bible. Grand Rapids: Brazos, 2006.
———. *Unleashing the Scripture: Freeing the Bible from Captivity to America.* Nashville: Abingdon, 1993.
Hauerwas, Stanley, and L. Gregory Jones, eds. *Why Narrative? Readings in Narrative Theology.* Grand Rapids: Eerdmans, 1997.
Hauser, Alan J., and Duane F. Watson, eds. *A History of Biblical Interpretation.* 2 vols. Grand Rapids: Eerdmans, 2003.
Hays, Richard B. *The Conversion of the Imagination: Paul as Interpreter of Israel's Scripture.* Grand Rapids: Eerdmans, 2005.
———. *Echoes of Scripture in the Letters of Paul.* New Haven: Yale University Press, 1989.
———. *The Faith of Jesus Christ: The Narrative Substructure of Galatians 3:1–4:11.* 2nd ed. Biblical Resource Series. Grand Rapids: Eerdmans, 2002.
———. *The Moral Vision of the New Testament: A Contemporary Introduction to New Testament Ethics.* San Francisco: HarperSanFrancisco, 1996.
Heron, Alasdair. "'Logos, Image, Son': Some Models and Paradigms in Early Christology." In *Creation, Christ, and Culture: Studies in Honour of T. F. Torrance,* edited by Richard W. A. McKinney, 43-62. Edinburgh: T&T Clark, 1975.
Heschel, Abraham J. *The Prophets.* Orig. 1962. Repr. New York: HarperPerennial, 2001.
International Theological Commission. *Memory and Reconciliation: The Church and the Faults of the Past,* 1999. http://www.vatican.va/roman_curia/congregations/cfaith/cti_documents/rc_con_cfaith_doc_20000307_memory-reconc-itc_en.html.
Irenaeus. *Against Heresies. ANF* 1, 1885.
Isasi-Díaz, Ada María. "'By the Rivers of Babylon': Exile as a Way of Life." In *Social Location and Biblical Interpretation in the United States,* edited by Fernando F. Segovia and Mary Ann Tolbert, 149-63. Vol. 1 of *Reading from This Place.* Minneapolis: Augsburg Fortress, 1995.
John Paul II. "Day of Pardon." March 12, 2000. http://www.vatican.va/holy_father/john_paul_ii/homilies/documents/hf_jp-ii_hom_20000312_pardon_en.html.
———. *Ut Unum Sint: On Commitment to Ecumenism.* Vatican City: Libreria Editrice Vaticana, 1995.
Juel, Donald. *Messianic Exegesis: Christological Interpretation of the Old Testament in Early Christianity.* Philadelphia: Fortress, 1988.
Justin Martyr. *Dialogue with Trypho.* Edited by Thomas P. Halton and Michael Slusser. Translated by Thomas B. Falls. Washington, DC: Catholic University of America Press, 2003.
———. *The First and Second Apologies.* Translated by Leslie William Barnard. Ancient Christian Writers 56. New York: Paulist, 1997.
Kannengiesser, Charles. *Handbook of Patristic Exegesis: The Bible in Ancient Christianity.* Leiden: Brill, 2006.
Kelly, J. N. D. *Early Christian Doctrines.* 5th ed. New York: Continuum, 1977.

Bibliography

Kelsey, David H. *Proving Doctrine: The Uses of Scripture in Modern Theology*. Harrisburg: Trinity, 1999.
Kerr, Fergus. *Theology after Wittgenstein*. 2nd ed. London: SPCK, 1997.
Kim, Seyoon. *Paul and the New Perspective: Second Thoughts on the Origin of Paul's Gospel*. Grand Rapids: Eerdmans, 2002.
King, J. Christopher. *Origen on the Song of Songs as the Spirit of Scripture: The Bridegroom's Perfect Marriage-Song*. Oxford Theological Monographs. Oxford: Oxford University Press, 2005.
Klausner, Joseph. *Jesus of Nazareth: His Life, Times, and Teaching*. Translated by Herbert Danby. Orig. 1922. New York: Bloch, 1989.
Kraftchick, Steven J., Charles D. Myers, Jr., and Ben C. Ollenburger, eds. *Problems and Perspectives in Biblical Theology: In Honor of J. Christiaan Beker*. Nashville: Abingdon, 1995.
Kuhn, Thomas S. *The Structure of Scientific Revolutions*. 3rd ed. Chicago: University of Chicago Press, 1996.
Lampe, G. W. H., ed. *The Cambridge History of the Bible*. Vol. 2: *The West from the Fathers to the Reformation*. Cambridge: Cambridge University Press, 1969.
Laszlo, Stephen. "Sin in the Holy Church of God." In *Council Speeches of Vatican II*, edited by Hans Küng, Yves M.-J. Congar, and Daniel O'Hanlon, 44-48. Glen Rock, NJ: Paulist, 1964.
Leithart, Peter J. *Athanasius*. Foundations of Theological Exegesis and Christian Spirituality. Grand Rapids: Baker Academic, 2011.
Levenson, Jon D. *Resurrection and the Restoration of Israel: The Ultimate Victory of the God of Life*. New Haven: Yale University Press, 2006.
Levering, Matthew. *Christ's Fulfillment of Torah and Temple: Salvation according to Thomas Aquinas*. Notre Dame, IN: University of Notre Dame Press, 2002.
Levering, Miriam, ed. *Rethinking Scripture: Essays from a Comparative Perspective*. Albany: State University of New York Press, 1989.
Levinson, Sanford. *Constitutional Faith*. Princeton: Princeton University Press, 1988.
Lewis, C. S. "Transposition." In *The Weight of Glory: And Other Addresses*, 91-115. New York: HarperOne, 1976.
Lieu, Judith. *Neither Jew nor Greek? Constructing Early Christianity*. London: T&T Clark, 2002.
Lindars, Barnabas. *New Testament Apologetic*. Philadelphia: Westminster, 1961.
Lindbeck, George A. *The Nature of Doctrine: Religion and Theology in a Postliberal Age*. Louisville: Westminster John Knox, 1984.
———. "Postcritical Canonical Interpretation: Three Modes of Retrieval." In *Theological Exegesis: Essays in Honor of Brevard S. Childs*, edited by Christopher Seitz and Kathryn Greene-McCreight, 26-51. Grand Rapids: Eerdmans, 1999.
———. "The Story-Shaped Church: Critical Exegesis and Theological Interpretation." In *Scriptural Authority and Narrative Interpretation*, edited by Garrett Green, 161-78. Philadelphia: Fortress, 1987.
Longenecker, Richard N. *Biblical Exegesis in the Apostolic Period*. 2nd ed. Grand Rapids: Eerdmans, 1999.
Louth, Andrew. *Discerning the Mystery: An Essay on the Nature of Theology*. Oxford: Clarendon, 1983.

Lubac, Henri de. *Catholicism: Christ and the Common Destiny of Man.* Translated by Lancelot C. Sheppard and Elizabeth Englund. Orig. 1947. San Francisco: Ignatius, 1988.

———. *Exégèse médiévale: Les quatre sens de l'écriture.* 4 vols. Paris: Aubier, 1959. English translation: *Medieval Exegesis: The Four Senses of Scripture.* Retrieval and Renewal: Ressourcement in Catholic Thought. Vol. 1, translated by Mark Sebanc, 1998. Vols. 2-3, translated by E. M. Macierowski, 2000 and 2009. Grand Rapids: Eerdmans.

———. *History and the Spirit: The Understanding of Scripture according to Origen.* Translated by Anne Englund Nash and Juvenal Merriell. Orig. 1950. San Francisco: Ignatius, 2007.

———. *Scripture in the Tradition.* Translated by Luke O'Neill. Orig. 1967. New York: Herder and Herder, 2000.

MacIntyre, Alasdair. *After Virtue: A Study in Moral Theory.* 2nd ed. Notre Dame, IN: University of Notre Dame Press, 1984.

———. *Whose Justice? Which Rationality?* Notre Dame, IN: University of Notre Dame Press, 1988.

Madigan, Daniel A. *The Qur'ân's Self-Image: Writing and Authority in Islam's Scripture.* Princeton: Princeton University Press, 2001.

Madigan, Kevin J., and Jon D. Levenson. *Resurrection: The Power of God for Christians and Jews.* New Haven: Yale University Press, 2008.

Marshall, Bruce D. "Absorbing the World: Christianity and the Universe of Truths." In *Theology and Dialogue: Essays in Conversation with George Lindbeck,* edited by Bruce D. Marshall, 69-102. Notre Dame, IN: University of Notre Dame Press, 1990.

Marshall, Bruce D., ed. *Theology and Dialogue: Essays in Conversation with George Lindbeck.* Notre Dame, IN: University of Notre Dame Press, 1990.

Martens, Peter W. *Origen and Scripture: The Contours of the Exegetical Life.* OECS. Oxford: Oxford University Press, 2012.

———. "Revisiting the Allegory/Typology Distinction: The Case of Origen." *JECS* 16 (2008): 283-317.

McDonald, Lee Martin. *The Biblical Canon: Its Origin, Transmission, and Authority.* Peabody, MA: Hendrickson, 2007.

McDonald, Lee Martin, and James A. Sanders, eds. *The Canon Debate.* Peabody, MA: Hendrickson, 2002.

McKim, Donald K., ed. *Dictionary of Major Biblical Interpreters.* Downers Grove, IL: IVP Academic, 2007.

McLeod, Frederick C., ed. *Theodore of Mopsuestia.* London: Routledge, 2009.

Menken, Maarten J. J. *Old Testament Quotations in the Fourth Gospel: Studies in Textual Form.* CBET 15. Kampen: Kok Pharos, 1996.

Moore, George Foot. "Christian Writers on Judaism." *HTR* 14 (1921): 197-254.

Morgan, Robert, ed. *The Nature of New Testament Theology: The Contribution of William Wrede and Adolf Schlatter.* Translated by Robert Morgan. Studies in Biblical Theology, Second Series 25. Naperville, IL: Allenson, 1973.

Morgan, Robert, and John Barton. *Biblical Interpretation.* Oxford Bible Series. Oxford: Oxford University Press, 1988.

Bibliography

Moyise, Steve. "Intertextuality and the Study of the Old Testament in the New Testament." In *The Old Testament in the New Testament: Essays in Honour of J. L. North,* 14-41. JSNTSup 189. Sheffield: Sheffield Academic, 2000.

Mulder, Martin Jan, and Harry Sysling, eds. *Mikra: Text, Translation, Reading, and Interpretation of the Hebrew Bible in Ancient Judaism and Early Christianity.* Peabody, MA: Hendrickson, 2004.

Neuhaus, Richard John. *Biblical Interpretation in Crisis: The Ratzinger Conference on the Bible and Church.* Grand Rapids: Eerdmans, 1989.

Newman, John Henry. *An Essay on the Development of Christian Doctrine.* 6th ed. Notre Dame, IN: University of Notre Dame Press, 1989.

Niebuhr, Reinhold. *An Interpretation of Christian Ethics.* Orig. 1935. Repr. San Francisco: Harper and Row, 1963.

Obermann, Heiko A. *Forerunners of the Reformation: The Shape of Late Medieval Thought.* New York: Holt, Rinehart and Winston, 1966.

O'Keefe, John J., and R. R. Reno. *Sanctified Vision: An Introduction to Early Christian Interpretation of the Bible.* Baltimore: Johns Hopkins University Press, 2005.

Origen. *Commentary on the Gospel according to John: Books 1-10.* Translated by Ronald E. Heine. Fathers of the Church 80. Washington, DC: Catholic University of America Press, 1989.

———. *Contra Celsum.* Translated by Henry Chadwick. Cambridge: Cambridge University Press, 1953.

———. *Homilies on Genesis and Exodus.* Translated by Ronald E. Heine. Fathers of the Church 71. Washington, DC: Catholic University of America Press, 1981.

———. *On First Principles.* Translated by G. W. Butterworth. Gloucester, MA: Peter Smith, 1973.

Pao, David W. *Acts and the Isaianic New Exodus.* Biblical Studies Library. Grand Rapids: Baker Academic, 2000.

Pontifical Biblical Commission. *The Interpretation of the Bible in the Church.* Vatican City: Libreria Editrice Vaticana, 1993.

———. *The Jewish People and Their Sacred Scriptures in the Christian Bible.* Vatican City: Libreria Editrice Vaticana, 2002.

Preus, James Samuel. *From Shadow to Promise: Old Testament Interpretation from Augustine to the Young Luther.* Cambridge, MA: Belknap, 1969.

Prügl, Thomas. "Thomas Aquinas as Interpreter of Scripture." In *The Theology of Thomas Aquinas,* edited by Rik Van Nieuwenhove and Joseph Wawrykow, 386-415. Notre Dame, IN: University of Notre Dame Press, 2005.

Radner, Ephraim. *A Brutal Unity: The Spiritual Politics of the Christian Church.* Waco: Baylor University Press, 2012.

———. *The End of the Church: A Pneumatology of Christian Division in the West.* Grand Rapids: Eerdmans, 1998.

Räisänen, Heikki. *Beyond New Testament Theology.* 2nd ed. London: SCM, 2000.

Ratzinger, Joseph. "Biblical Interpretation in Crisis: On the Question of the Foundations and Approaches of Exegesis Today." In *Biblical Interpretation in Crisis: The Ratzinger Conference on Bible and Church,* edited by Richard John Neuhaus, 1-23. Encounter. Grand Rapids: Eerdmans, 1989.

Ratzinger, Joseph/Pope Benedict XVI. *Jesus of Nazareth: From the Baptism in the Jor-*

dan to the Transfiguration. Translated by Adrian J. Walker. New York: Doubleday, 2007.

Reid, J. K. S., ed. *Calvin: Theological Treatises*. LCC 22. Louisville: Westminster John Knox, 1956.

Reumann, John, ed. *The Promise and Practice of Biblical Theology*. Minneapolis: Fortress, 1991.

Ricoeur, Paul. *Oneself as Another*. Translated by Kathleen Blamey. Orig. 1990. Chicago: University of Chicago Press, 1992.

Ridderbos, Herman. *Paul: An Outline of His Theology*. Translated by John Richard de Witt. Orig. 1966. Grand Rapids: Eerdmans, 1975.

Rogers, Eugene F. "How the Virtues of an Interpreter Presuppose and Perfect Hermeneutics: The Case of Thomas Aquinas." *JR* 76 (1996): 64-81.

Rowe, C. Kavin. "Biblical Pressure and Trinitarian Hermeneutics." *ProEccl* 11 (2002): 295-312.

———. *Early Narrative Christology: The Lord in the Gospel of Luke*. Grand Rapids: Baker Academic, 2009.

———. *World Upside Down: Reading Acts in the Graeco-Roman Age*. Oxford: Oxford University Press, 2009.

Rowe, C. Kavin, and Richard B. Hays. "What Is a Theological Commentary?" *ProEccl* 16 (2007): 26-32.

Sanders, E. P. *The Historical Figure of Jesus*. London: Penguin, 1993.

———. *Jesus and Judaism*. Minneapolis: Fortress, 1985.

———. *Paul and Palestinian Judaism: A Comparison of Patterns of Religion*. Minneapolis: Fortress, 1977.

———. *Paul, the Law, and the Jewish People*. Minneapolis: Fortress, 1983.

———. *Paul: A Very Short Introduction*. Oxford: Oxford University Press, 1991.

Sanneh, Lamin. *Translating the Message: The Missionary Impact on Culture*. American Society of Missiology Series 13. Maryknoll, NY: Orbis, 1989.

Sarisky, Darren. *Scriptural Interpretation: A Theological Account*. Challenges in Contemporary Theology. Oxford: Wiley-Blackwell, 2013.

Scalia, Antonin. *A Matter of Interpretation: Federal Courts and the Law*. University Center for Human Values Series. Princeton: Princeton University Press, 1997.

Schlabach, Gerald W. *Unlearning Protestantism: Sustaining Christian Community in an Unstable Age*. Grand Rapids: Brazos, 2010.

Schüssler Fiorenza, Elisabeth. *In Memory of Her: A Feminist Theological Reconstruction of Christian Origins*. 10th anniv. ed. New York: Crossroad, 1994.

Schweitzer, Albert. *The Mysticism of Paul the Apostle*. Translated by William Montgomery. Orig. 1931. Baltimore: Johns Hopkins University Press, 1998.

———. *Paul and His Interpreters: A Critical History*. Translated by William Montgomery. Orig. New York: Macmillan, 1912. Repr. Eugene, OR: Wipf and Stock, 2004.

———. *The Quest of the Historical Jesus*. Edited by John Bowden. Translated by William Montgomery, J. R. Coates, Susan Cupitt, and John Bowden. 1st complete ed. 1906. Minneapolis: Fortress, 2001.

Seitz, Christopher R. "Old Testament or Hebrew Bible? Some Theological Considerations." *ProEccl* 5 (1996): 292-303.

Bibliography

———. *Prophecy and Hermeneutics: Toward a New Introduction to the Prophets.* STI. Grand Rapids: Baker Academic, 2007.
———. *Word without End: The Old Testament as Abiding Theological Witness.* Grand Rapids: Eerdmans, 1998.
Seitz, Christopher R., and Kathryn Greene-McCreight, eds. *Theological Exegesis: Essays in Honor of Brevard S. Childs.* Grand Rapids: Eerdmans, 1999.
Smalley, Beryl. *The Study of the Bible in the Middle Ages.* Notre Dame, IN: University of Notre Dame Press, 1964.
Smith, Christian. *How to Go from Being a Good Evangelical to a Committed Catholic in Ninety-Five Difficult Steps.* Eugene, OR: Cascade, 2011.
Smith, Wilfred Cantwell. *What Is Scripture? A Comparative Approach.* Minneapolis: Fortress, 1993.
Soskice, Janet Martin. *Metaphor and Religious Language.* Oxford: Clarendon, 1985.
Sparks, Kenton L. *God's Word in Human Words: An Evangelical Appropriation of Critical Biblical Scholarship.* Grand Rapids: Baker Academic, 2008.
Spinoza, Benedict de. *Theological-Political Treatise.* Edited by Jonathan Israel. Translated by Michael Silverthorne and Jonathan Israel. Cambridge: Cambridge University Press, 2007. Latin text: *Œuvres III, Tractatus Theologico-Politicus, Traité théologico-politique.* Edited by Fokke Akkerman. Paris: Presses Universitaires de France, 1999.
Steinmetz, David C. *Luther in Context.* 2nd ed. Grand Rapids: Baker Academic, 2002.
———. "The Superiority of Pre-Critical Exegesis." *ThTo* 37 (1980): 27-38.
———. "Uncovering a Second Narrative: Detective Fiction and the Construction of the Historical Method." In *The Art of Reading Scripture,* edited by Ellen F. Davis and Richard B. Hays, 54-65. Grand Rapids: Eerdmans, 2003.
Stendahl, Krister. "Biblical Theology, Contemporary." Edited by George Buttrick. *The Interpreter's Dictionary of the Bible: An Illustrated Encyclopedia.* Nashville: Abingdon, 1962.
———. *Paul among Jews and Gentiles.* Philadelphia: Fortress, 1976.
Stout, Jeffrey. "What Is the Meaning of a Text?" *New Literary History* 13 (1982): 1-12.
Sullivan, Francis A. "The Papal Apology." *America,* April 8, 2000. http://www.americamagazine.org/content/article.cfm?article_id=657.
Tanner, Kathryn E. "Theology and the Plain Sense." In *Scriptural Authority and Narrative Interpretation,* edited by Garrett Green, 59-78. Philadelphia: Fortress, 1987.
Tanner, Norman P. *Decrees of the Ecumenical Councils.* 2 vols. Washington, DC: Georgetown University Press, 1990.
Tavard, George H. *Holy Writ or Holy Church: The Crisis of the Protestant Reformation.* London: Burns and Oates, 1959.
Tertullian. *Adversus Marcionem.* Edited and translated by Ernest Evans. 2 vols. Oxford: Oxford University Press, 1972.
———. *Tertullian's Treatise Against Praxeas.* Edited by Ernest Evans. London: SPCK, 1948.
Thompson, John L. *Reading the Bible with the Dead: What You Can Learn from the History of Exegesis That You Can't Learn from Exegesis Alone.* Grand Rapids: Eerdmans, 2007.

BIBLIOGRAPHY

Troeltsch, Ernst. *Religion in History*. Translated by James Luther Adams and Walter F. Bense. Edinburgh: T&T Clark, 1991.

Udoh, Fabian E., Susannah Heschel, Mark Chancey, and Gregory Tatum, eds. *Redefining First-Century Jewish and Christian Identities: Essays in Honor of Ed Parish Sanders*. Christianity and Judaism in Antiquity 16. Notre Dame, IN: University of Notre Dame Press, 2008.

Vanhoozer, Kevin J. *The Drama of Doctrine: A Canonical-Linguistic Approach to Christian Theology*. Louisville: Westminster John Knox, 2005.

———. *First Theology: God, Scripture, and Hermeneutics*. Downers Grove, IL: IVP Academic, 2002.

———. *Is There a Meaning in This Text? The Bible, the Reader, and the Morality of Literary Knowledge*. Grand Rapids: Zondervan, 1998.

———. "A Person of the Book? Barth on Biblical Authority and Interpretation." In *Karl Barth and Evangelical Theology: Convergences and Divergences*, edited by Sung Wook Chung, 26-59. Grand Rapids: Baker Academic, 2006.

Vanhoozer, Kevin J., Craig G. Bartholomew, Daniel J. Treier, and N. T. Wright, eds. *Dictionary for Theological Interpretation of the Bible*. Grand Rapids: Baker Academic, 2005.

Verhey, Allen. *Remembering Jesus: Christian Community, Scripture, and the Moral Life*. Grand Rapids: Eerdmans, 2002.

Vischer, Wilhelm. *The Witness of the Old Testament to Christ*. Vol. 1: *The Pentateuch*. Translated by A. B. Crabtree. Orig. 1936. London: Lutterworth, 1949.

Wagner, J. Ross. "Psalm 118 in Luke-Acts: Tracing a Narrative Thread." In *Early Christian Interpretation of the Scriptures of Israel*, edited by Craig A. Evans and James A. Sanders, 154-78. JSNTSup 148. Sheffield: Sheffield Academic, 1997.

Wagner, J. Ross, C. Kavin Rowe, and A. Katherine Grieb, eds. *The Word Leaps the Gap: Essays on Scripture and Theology in Honor of Richard B. Hays*. Grand Rapids: Eerdmans, 2008.

Wainwright, Geoffrey. *Doxology: The Praise of God in Worship, Doctrine and Life: A Systematic Theology*. Oxford: Oxford University Press, 1980.

———. "Gospel Hermeneutics in Joseph Ratzinger's *Jesus of Nazareth*." *NV* 7 (2009): 7-17.

———. "Psalm 33 Interpreted of the Triune God." *ExAud* 16 (2000): 101-20.

———. "Reading Scripture Together." In *Embracing Purpose: Essays on God, the World and the Church*, 85-104. Peterborough, UK: Epworth, 2007.

———. "Towards an Ecumenical Hermeneutic: How Can All Christians Read the Scriptures Together?" *Greg* 76 (1995): 639-62.

Watson, Francis. *Paul and the Hermeneutics of Faith*. London: T&T Clark, 2004.

———. *Paul, Judaism, and the Gentiles: Beyond the New Perspective*. Rev. and exp. ed. Grand Rapids: Eerdmans, 2007.

———. *Text and Truth: Redefining Biblical Theology*. Grand Rapids: Eerdmans, 1997.

———. *Text, Church, and World: Biblical Interpretation in Theological Perspective*. London: T&T Clark, 1994.

Webster, John. *Holy Scripture: A Dogmatic Sketch*. Current Issues in Theology. Cambridge: Cambridge University Press, 2003.

Bibliography

———. "Purity and Plenitude: Evangelical Reflections on Congar's *Tradition and Traditions.*" *International Journal of Systematic Theology* 7 (2005): 399-413.
———. *Word and Church: Essays in Christian Dogmatics.* Edinburgh: T&T Clark, 2001.
Weinandy, Thomas G., Daniel A. Keating, and John P. Yocum, eds. *Aquinas on Scripture: An Introduction to His Biblical Commentaries.* London: T&T Clark, 2005.
Wells, Samuel. *Improvisation: The Drama of Christian Ethics.* Grand Rapids: Brazos, 2004.
Westermann, Klaus, ed. *Essays on Old Testament Hermeneutics.* Translated by James Luther Mays. Orig. 1960. Richmond: John Knox, 1963.
Wilken, Robert Louis. "In Defense of Allegory." *Modern Theology* 14 (1998): 197-212.
———. *The Spirit of Early Christian Thought: Seeking the Face of God.* New Haven: Yale University Press, 2003.
Williams, Rowan. *Arius: Heresy and Tradition.* Rev. ed. Grand Rapids: Eerdmans, 2001.
———. "The Literal Sense of Scripture." *Modern Theology* 7 (1991): 121-34.
———. *A Ray of Darkness: Sermons and Reflections.* Cambridge, MA: Cowley, 1995.
Wolterstorff, Nicholas. *Divine Discourse: Philosophical Reflections on the Claim That God Speaks.* Cambridge: Cambridge University Press, 1995.
———. "Resuscitating the Author." In *Hermeneutics at the Crossroads,* edited by Kevin J. Vanhoozer, James K. A. Smith, and Bruce Ellis Benson, 35-50. Bloomington, IN: Indiana University Press, 2006.
Work, Telford. *Living and Active: Scripture in the Economy of Salvation.* Sacra Doctrina. Grand Rapids: Eerdmans, 2002.
Wright, N. T. *The Climax of the Covenant: Christ and the Law in Pauline Theology.* Minneapolis: Fortress, 1991.
———. "How Can the Bible Be Authoritative?" *VE* 21 (1991): 7-32.
———. *What Saint Paul Really Said: Was Paul of Tarsus the Real Founder of Christianity?* Grand Rapids: Eerdmans, 1997.
Yeago, David. "The New Testament and Nicene Dogma: A Contribution to the Recovery of Theological Exegesis." In *The Theological Interpretation of Scripture: Classic and Contemporary Readings,* edited by Stephen E. Fowl, 87-100. Blackwell Readings in Modern Theology. Oxford: Blackwell, 1997.
Yetzer, Bernard E. "Holiness and Sin in the Church: An Examination of *Lumen Gentium* and *Unitatis Redintegratio* of the Second Vatican Council." STD diss., Catholic University of America, 1988.
Young, Frances M. *Biblical Exegesis and the Formation of Christian Culture.* Peabody, MA: Hendrickson, 1997.
Young, Frances M., Lewis Ayres, and Andrew Louth, eds. *The Cambridge History of Early Christian Literature.* Cambridge: Cambridge University Press, 2004.
Zizioulas, John D. *Being and Communion: Studies in Personhood and the Church.* Crestwood, NY: St. Vladimir's Seminary Press, 2002.

Author Index

Anatolios, Khaled, 233n50, 234nn57-58, 236nn62-63
Anders, Aschim, 163n78, 164n83
Andrews, James A., 20n9, 47n139, 48n146
Armstrong, Brian G., 93n178, 98n199
Athanasius, 234-38, 240
Attridge, Harold W., 115n1, 117n5, 140n52, 144n1, 145n6, 152n39, 153n43, 155n49, 156n50, 162n73, 164n84, 165n87, 173n102, 208-9
Ayres, Lewis, 219n1, 233n50, 234nn55-56, 237

Barrett, C. K., 140-41
Barth, Karl, 98n196, 182, 200-203, 216, 240, 243, 255
Basil of Caesarea, 235
Baynes, Norman H., 32n70, 35n88
Behr, John, 233n50, 234n55, 236n62, 236nn64-65
Bergen, Jeremy M., 258
Blacketer, Raymond A., 62n6, 67n43
Boyarin, Daniel, 4n4, 5n5, 189-94
Braaten, Carl E., 15n28, 254n118, 261n139
Brawley, Robert L., 128n27, 173n103
Bright, Pamela, 20n9, 48n146, 54nn172-73, 54n175

Caird, George B., 125-26, 134n39, 145, 175-76
Cameron, Michael, 19n5, 19n9, 20n9, 23n32, 23n34, 28n62, 28n64, 47, 55n181, 147n8
Cappadocian Fathers, 240
Childs, Brevard S., 2n2, 173n103, 211n94, 233, 251-52
Cockerill, Gareth Lee, 162n78, 163n81, 165n87
Cohen, Jeremy, 36n89, 40n109, 42
Congar, Yves M.-J., 222-31, 240-41, 253-56, 257n125, 263
Cosby, Michael R., 126n23, 144n3

Dawson, John David, 2n2, 49n150, 192-96
deSilva, David Arthur, 115n1, 140n52, 152n39
Docherty, Susan E., 144n1, 152-56, 162n74
Dodaro, Robert, 32n70, 33n74, 34n79
Dowey, Edward A., Jr., 73n82, 94n179, 95n181, 98n196, 98n196, 98n198, 99n207, 101n217
Dulles, Avery, 257n125, 260

Edmondson, Stephen, 59n1, 62n6, 103n224, 105

Author Index

Eisenbaum, Pamela Michelle, 126-29, 131, 143-45, 267-68
Engel, Mary Potter, 81n117, 86n139
Enns, Peter, 152n39, 153n43

Fitzmyer, Joseph A., 162n78, 164n83
Fowl, Stephen E., 13n25, 251
France, R. T., 122n13, 145n7
Fredriksen, Paula, 19n9, 30, 36n89, 40n109, 41-45
Frei, Hans W., 2n2, 12, 194-96, 241-43, 246-47, 249

Gamble, Richard C., 93n178, 98n197, 103n223
Gerrish, B. A., 97n187
Greene-McCreight, Kathryn, 13n25, 20n9, 94n178, 243
Gregory of Nazianzus, 236, 248
Guthrie, George H., 122n14, 143n1, 144n2, 173n103, 174n104

Hauerwas, Stanley, 250-51
Hay, David M., 4n3, 162n76, 162n78
Hays, Richard B., 14-15, 123n15, 129-30, 224n21, 250-51
Hesselink, I. John, 6n6, 67n44, 73n82, 74n87, 78-79, 81n117
Hoekema, Anthony A., 6n6, 73n81
Hugh of St. Victor, 248
Hurst, L. D., 173n103, 175

Irenaeus of Lyons, 1, 2n1, 106, 228,

Jackson, Belford Darrell, 48n146, 51n160
Jenson, Robert W., 15n28, 254n118, 261n139
Jobes, Karen H., 143n1, 144n3
John Paul II, 228, 254, 257, 261
Justin Martyr, 1, 2n1, 42, 234

Kannengiesser, Charles, 6n7, 20n9, 54nn172-73, 54n175
Koester, Craig R., 4n3, 115n1, 162n77
Kraus, Hans-Joachim, 6n6, 81n117, 103

Lane, William L., 115n1, 174n105, 176
Laver, Mary Sweetland, 81nn116-17
Lehne, Susanne, 123-24
Levenson, Jon D., 137-38n45
Lillback, Peter A., 62n6, 79n107
Lincoln, A. T., 152n39, 154n47
Lindbeck, George A., 242n86, 258-59, 262n140
Longenecker, Richard N., 14n27, 145n7, 163n78, 164n82, 165n86
Lubac, Henri de, 186-89, 191, 198-99, 248

Markus, R. A., 31n70, 48n146
Marshall, Bruce D., 245, 249-50
Melito of Sardis, 42
Moffitt, David M., 117-21, 174, 175n110
Muller, Richard A., 6n6, 100n209, 103-5

O'Donnell, James J., 31n69, 35n87, 169n90, 203n75, 205n82
Opitz, Peter, 6n6, 74n87, 79n109
Origen, 1, 2n1, 7, 193-94, 196, 234

Parker, T. H. L., 59n1, 6n16, 64n23, 67n44, 73n82, 76n93, 77n102, 81n117, 149n21
Philo, 141, 163
Pitkin, Barbara, 94n178, 98n196, 100n209, 101n217
Pollmann, Karla, 48n146, 51n162, 54n173
Puckett, David L., 62n6, 103-4

Quinn, Russell D., 173n103, 174n104

Radner, Ephraim, 262-63
Ratzinger, Joseph/Benedict XVI, 12, 13nn23-24, 55n176, 56n182, 246n98
Rogers, Eugene F., 243-47
Rooke, Deborah W., 124n18, 163n78, 164n85
Rowe, C. Kavin, 15n27, 23n39, 96n186, 232-33

AUTHOR INDEX

Sarisky, Darren, 235nn60-61
Schenck, Ken, 144n1, 184-85
Spinoza, Benedict de, 207-8
Steinmetz, David C., 6n7, 9n17, 94n178, 105n229, 107n232, 141-42
Stendahl, Krister, 5n5, 180

Tanner, Kathryn E., 243, 245-46, 249
Tertullian, 1, 2n1, 42, 106, 188, 228, 234
Teske, Roland J., 19n5, 51n157
Thiessen, Matthew, 130-32, 153n39
Thomas Aquinas, 197-98, 215-16, 244-45
Treier, Daniel J., 14n25, 144n1, 184-85, 210n91

Vanhoozer, Kevin J., 12, 14n25, 182-84, 203n73, 209n91, 223-27, 241
Vanhoye, Albert, 116n4

Wainwright, Geoffrey, 2n2, 253n112
Watson, Francis, 5n5, 13n25, 15n27, 251-52
Webster, John, 12, 180-82, 202-3
Wheaton Center for Early Christian Studies, The, 15n29
Williams, Rowan, 32n70, 50n152, 57n187, 234n55, 237-39, 258n131
Williamson, Ronald, 163n79
Wolf, Hans Heinrich, 60n5, 61n6
Wolterstorff, Nicholas, 12n20, 203n74, 207, 209-14

Yeago, David S., 232-33

Zachman, Randall C., 73n82, 108n233
Zizioulas, John D., 256

Subject Index

Aaronic priesthood, 39, 158-59, 161, 165
Abraham, Abrahamic, 20n9, 27-30,
  37-38, 63-64, 70, 73, 76, 81-86, 88n151,
  90-92, 95-96, 108-11, 120-21, 126-128,
  131, 148n18, 149-50, 155, 161, 164-66,
  175, 191
Adam, 36n90, 63, 94-95, 172
adoption, 25, 59, 70, 83, 86, 96, 256, 267
Anabaptists, 92
angel(s), 7, 30, 33, 36n90, 119-21, 132,
  139, 160-61, 163-64, 167-70, 172-77,
  203, 211, 214, 220
apostolic age, 2, 4, 14n27, 145n7, 179,
  200, 218-19, 221-22, 225, 256
Arius, Arian, 219, 233n50, 234-38
Assyrian Empire, 34, 38, 262
  Ninus, King, 34-35
atonement, 96, 117, 119nn8-9, 120n10,
  141, 175n110
Augustine
  and divine address, 203-6
  and Faustus the Manichee, 18-24,
    42-46
  and Tyconius's rules, 53-57
  on authorial intent, 214-15
  on the earthly city, 30-35
  on Israel, 35-41, 109-12, 136-37
  on Jews and Judaism, 42-46
  on Old Testament saints, 27-29, 109
  on Ps. 8, 167-69
  on Ps. 95, 147-49
  on Ps. 110, 156-59
  on the relationship between the covenants, 18-29, 107-8, 133-34
  on senses of Scripture: allegory, 6-7;
    signs and realities, 46-53, 112-13,
    197-98
  on the Trinity, 219-20, 236
authorial intent, 206-17
awareness of divinity, 97

baptism, 58, 62, 91-93, 147, 203-5, 220,
  246n98, 256
Bishop of Rome, 250, 254

Canaan, 38, 62, 85, 125, 127, 131, 136-37,
  150-51, 154-55, 178, 196, 198, 214
Cain, 35, 36n89, 43-45
Calvin
  on eschatology, 139-42
  on fear and bondage of Old Testament, 74-80
  on grace and merit, 71-74
  on Israel, 80-93, 109-12, 137-38
  on knowledge of God, 93-102
  on law, 64-71
  on Old Testament saints, 75-80, 81-85, 109-10
  on promise of immortality, 61-64
  on Ps. 8, 169-73

SUBJECT INDEX

on Ps. 95, 149-52
on Ps. 110, 159-61
on the relationship between the covenants, 58-93, 107-8, 134-35
on sacraments, 90-93
on Scripture, 96-102
on senses of Scripture, 102-6, 112-13; allegory, 7-8
on the Trinity, 220-21
Catholic(s), Catholicism, 237n71
in distinction from Donatist(s), Donatism, 17, 20, 42-43, 45, 107
Roman, 10, 13, 15, 186n20, 188n29, 218, 222, 225-31, 239n77, 241, 248n100, 250, 252-58, 260-63
ceremonies, 3, 26-27, 42, 45, 52-53, 66-69, 74-75, 90-91, 111, 134-36, 188, 191
church, 250-64; and individual Christian, 253-56; errors and sins of, 256-61; unity of, 261-64
City of God. *See* heavenly city
corporal goods. *See* temporal goods
corpus permixtum, 169
Council of Trent, 227-28

David, 6-7, 27, 28n62, 38, 63, 96, 100n208, 139, 145n5, 150-52, 155-60, 166, 168, 170-73, 185, 213-14, 263
Day of Pardon, 257-58
Decalogue. *See* Ten Commandments
development of doctrine, 225, 241, 246
devil, 7, 55, 121, 148, 234
Donatist(s), Donatism, 20n9, 53-55

earthly goods. *See* temporal goods
elect, election, 64n22, 82, 84-86, 98, 149, 163, 190, 263
Eli, 38-39
Elijah, 40, 41n114, 127
Esau, 38, 86
eschaton, eschatology, 30-32, 35, 104, 112, 128-29, 133, 139-41, 152n39, 154-55, 164, 174n103, 177, 184, 200, 208, 258
eternal goods, 9, 21-22, 29, 31, 33, 46, 49, 60, 62-65, 71, 78-79, 82-83, 85, 90-92, 108, 110, 118-21, 127, 132, 136-41, 151, 155-56, 165, 167, 172, 177, 185, 187, 193-94, 196, 198, 227
exile, 44, 150, 213n99, 262
expiation, 77, 118, 121, 136

food laws, 43, 129, 191
form analysis, 152-54

gospel, 5n5, 27, 51, 61n6, 62, 65, 71-80, 89, 94n179, 139-40, 150, 184, 190, 201, 223-24, 227, 238, 258-59, 261
grace, 6, 8-9, 14, 23, 25, 27-29, 38, 40, 44, 47n143, 56, 58-59, 61n6, 70-71, 73, 74n87, 75-79, 86-88, 90-91, 96, 97n187, 107-10, 138, 155, 161, 172-73, 176, 191, 206, 253, 258

Hagar, 7, 20n9, 36n90, 103
Hannah, 38, 96
heavenly city, 31-33, 35-38, 41, 45-46, 57
heavenly goods. *See* eternal goods
Hebrews, Epistle to the, 4-5
and use of Old Testament, 143-45, 177-78, 198-200
on Christ's high priesthood, 116-22
on eschatology, 139-42
on Israel, 136-38
on Old Testament saints, 126-32
on Ps. 8, 173-77
on Ps. 95, 152-56
on Ps. 110, 162-66
on the relationship between the covenants, 122-26, 133-36
perfection, 117-121, 123, 131-32, 134, 136, 138, 165
history of interpretation, 7, 14
historical method, 206-17, 245-46
hope, 1, 9, 21-22, 30-31, 45, 59-60, 63-64, 69n64, 79, 85-86, 88, 92-93, 96, 107-9, 112, 114, 120-21, 128, 131-32, 136-38, 142, 150, 152, 155-56, 177-78, 189, 191, 263, 265

idol(s), idolatry, 29, 31, 33-36, 38, 52, 82, 97
inheritance, 9, 59-60, 64, 83, 102, 120-

Subject Index

21, 127, 131-32, 136-37, 142, 151, 155-56, 185, 192, 196, 198
Isaac, 28, 38, 63, 86, 105, 120
Ishmael, 38, 83, 86
Islam, 239n77

Jacob, 8, 28n64, 38, 86, 89
Joseph, 38, 127, 131
Joshua, 38n98, 130-32, 151, 191, 198
Judaism and Christianity, 4-5, 189-92
  adversus Iudaeos tradition, 42-43
  supersessionism, 3, 4, 15, 30, 36n89, 41, 110-11, 129, 188n29, 189-192, 194, 216, 251, 265
Judas Iscariot, 90

land, 36n89, 38, 56, 64, 83, 85, 110, 126-27, 130-32, 136, 138, 150-51, 154-55, 178, 196, 198
law(s), 1, 3, 4n4, 5n5, 14, 18, 20-29, 36n89, 40, 42-43, 45-46, 50, 52, 55, 58-59, 61-62, 64-80, 83, 87, 92n177, 94n179, 96, 98, 101, 106-9, 111, 117, 122-24, 129, 133-34, 139-40, 149-51, 155, 161, 164-66, 184, 187-93, 207, 247
Levites, 104, 116, 161
Levitical priesthood, 4, 37, 116-17, 123-26, 128-29, 133-34, 159-61, 164-66, 178, 191
love commandment (twofold), 50-51, 147
lust for glory, 34

magisterium, 227, 230-31, 253-54, 256
Mariology, 228-31
Melchizedek, 4n3, 116, 118, 119n7, 124n18, 125, 156, 158-166, 177, 198
Moses, Mosaic, 1, 5n5, 23n32, 27-30, 38n98, 64-67, 70-71, 73, 75, 79, 108-9, 111, 120, 124, 127-29, 131, 135-36, 141, 145n5, 148, 152, 161, 163, 171-72, 188, 191, 198, 214-16, 260

papal infallibility, 230-31, 254n118, 260
Paul, 1-3, 5, 266-67
pilgrim(s), pilgrimage, 33n73, 49

Platonic, 141, 209
pneumatology, 219, 222, 262n140
pope(s), 254, 257, 260
promise(s), 1, 2n2, 3, 18, 19n9, 21, 23, 25, 28, 33, 38, 41, 55-56, 60-64, 67, 70-74, 79, 82-88, 90-92, 96, 99-102, 103n224, 104n226, 105, 107-12, 120, 122, 126-28, 130-32, 135-38, 148, 150-51, 154-57, 160, 174, 176, 178-79, 185-86, 188-89, 191-92, 199, 210, 216, 219-22, 253, 259-60, 265, 267

Qumran, 124, 163-64

reality, realities (of New Testament), 1, 2n2, 4, 17, 20-22, 29, 36, 39, 46, 47n143, 48, 50n152, 51, 53, 57, 60, 79, 107, 111, 113, 117, 120-21, 125, 134-35, 154, 157, 177, 183, 186-87, 191, 194-95, 198, 201-2, 221-22, 227, 229, 233, 250, 253, 259, 263
redemptive history, 3, 6, 8-10, 18, 29, 56-59, 63, 65, 74, 93, 95, 102, 106, 112-16, 126, 135, 137-42, 145, 156, 166, 178, 181-82, 185-86, 188, 191-96, 198, 200, 206, 213, 216-18, 220-23, 226, 239, 266
rest, 21-22, 125, 130-32, 137, 140n52, 144n4, 146, 148-55, 177-78, 185, 191-92, 196, 198, 214, 260
resurrection, 8, 29, 117, 119-21, 137n45, 138n45, 148, 157, 170-71, 173, 175n110, 224
righteousness, 3, 25-29, 60, 62, 64-66, 70, 72, 74-75, 82, 87, 108, 129, 155, 161, 163-64, 167, 198, 263
Rome, Roman, 30, 31n69, 32-36, 44, 46, 54n173, 129, 204, 268

Sabbath, 20-21, 27, 43-44, 52-53, 66n34, 151, 152n39, 154n47, 155, 191
sacrament, 20-21, 61n6, 62, 63n11, 81, 90-91, 109, 222
salvation history. *See* redemptive history
Samuel, 38
Sarah, 7, 20n9, 36n90, 93n178, 103, 120

309

SUBJECT INDEX

Satan. *See* devil
Saul, King, 38-39
Scripture
  and divine address, 180-86
  and the doctrine of the Trinity, 218-25, 232-41
  and revelation, 180-82
  and theology, 12-15, 268
  and tradition, 15, 222-31, 248-64
  and virtue, 243-45, 247-48, 268-69
  canon, canonical, 1, 4, 10, 12, 15, 137n45, 173n103, 181, 182, 184, 194, 201-2, 203n73, 206, 211-12, 214, 216, 219, 222-26, 233, 236-37, 240n79, 241, 251-52, 256, 259, 264-68
  Christological interpretation of, 14n27, 16, 23, 58, 82, 99, 101-2, 104-5, 113, 116, 163, 167, 173-77, 196, 200, 213, 236n63, 266
  improvisation, 183-84, 224
  interpretive diversity, 241-43, 246-47
  meaning potential, 184, 226, 246
  relationship between Old and New Testaments, 1-3, 186-92
  Rule of Faith, 230, 242-43
  sanctification of, 181-182
  senses of, 186-89; figural reading, 192-200; literal sense, 241-50
  sola scriptura, 225-26, 230, 255
  Word and Spirit, 93n178, 98-99, 221, 230, 266
  Word of God, 7, 14n25, 19n9, 49, 83, 90, 102, 143, 150, 170, 199-203, 216, 221, 223, 228, 240-41, 247
shadow(s) (of Old Testament), 2n2, 4, 19n9, 36-37, 45, 60, 73-74, 77, 83, 91, 107, 110, 117, 124-25, 133-35, 185-86, 188, 191, 209, 259
sojourner(s), 38, 44, 127, 131, 134n39
speech-act theory, 182-86, 209-17
spiritual goods. *See* eternal goods

temporal goods, 21, 28, 30-31, 33-35, 45-46, 49, 63-65, 82-83, 85, 92, 108, 136-37, 168, 193
Ten Commandments, 26, 65, 67-69
Totus Christus, 55

unity of identity, 8-9, 106-7, 266
unity of reference, 8-9, 57, 107, 266

wilderness, 130-32, 146, 149, 154-55, 260

Scripture Index

OLD TESTAMENT

Genesis
1	214
1–3	243
2	155
2:2	144n4, 154
4:12	44
4:15	44
5	82
5:24	144n4
10	82
12:3	82
12:7	82
13:14	84
14	165, 166
14:18-20	163, 164
15:1	64
15:6	82
17:7	82, 90
22	105

Exodus
1–19	66
17	130n35
20	66
25:40	141

Leviticus
26:12	63

Numbers
13:2-3	131
14	130
16:1-3	131
25:1-5	131

Deuteronomy
6:16	130n35
9:22	130n35
10:12-13	66
12:32	65
30:12	171
33:8	130n35

Joshua
21:44	130

1 Samuel
15:29	39

2 Samuel
7:14	175

1 Kings
8:56	130

2 Chronicles
26:21	160

Psalms
2:5-9	173n103
2:7	118, 154, 175
8	9, 120, 125, 145, 166-77
8:3	169
8:4	167
8:4-6	120
8:5	174
8:6	174
8:6a	173
8:7b	176
22:22	145n6
26:13 (27:13)	56
40:6-8	145n6
45:6-7	175
59	43, 44
59:11	42, 44
67:18	171
78:55	127n24
95	9, 125, 145, 146-56, 177, 196
95:5	155
95:6	149
95:7	147, 147n12
95:7-11	130
95:9	155
102:25-27	175
105:42-44	126
110	9, 119n7, 125,

SCRIPTURE INDEX

	145, 156-66, 177, 178
110:1	119n7, 158, 162, 162n74, 166, 174
110:4	116, 118, 158, 162, 162n77, 163, 164, 165, 166
135:10-12	127
136:18-22	127n24
137	212, 213

Proverbs
3:11-12	144
8:22	235

Song of Songs
4:2	147
4:15	7
6:5	147

Isaiah
8:17-18	145
11:2-3	269
29:11-12	263
45:21-24	232
51:4-5	188
59:20	89

Jeremiah
31	110, 123, 125, 129, 133, 145, 177
31:31-32	188
31:31-34	25, 76, 77, 122
31:33	77

Ezekiel
11:14-21	263
16	259
18:23	23n37
23	259
33:11	23n37
36:17-19	56
36:23-29	56

Daniel
12:1-3	137n45

Hosea
2:23	86
3:5	40

Haggai
2:7	7

Zechariah
12:9-10	40

Malachi
4:5-6	40

APOCRYPHA

1 Maccabees
2:51-60	127

NEW TESTAMENT

Matthew
5:17	25, 92n177
13:16-17	73
20:30	157n54
22:41-46	162n76
22:43-45	157n53

Mark
12:35-37	162n76

Luke
10:23-24	73
16:16	80n113
20:41-44	162n76

John
1:1	239
1:1-3	268
1:17	23n32
1:18	73
4:13-14	7
5:46	73
8:56	73
14:26	222

16:12-14	223
16:13	183
17:21	261

Acts
2:34-35	162
7	4
15	1

Romans
1:2-3	62
1:3	157
1:21-22	203n75
3:3-4	267
3:19	62
3:21	25, 62
3:21-24	24
4	155
4:17	203n75
5:5	24, 24n44, 108, 220
7	26
7:7-11	24
7:16-17	203n75
7:17	203n75
7:20	203n75
7:22-25	203n75
8:9	224
8:15	26, 71
8:34	162
9	83, 85, 86
9–11	85, 89n158, 92
9:4-5	267
9:7	86
10:6	152, 171, 172
11	87, 111, 147, 190, 193
11:11	88
11:16	83, 88n151
11:18	267
11:21	259
11:22	267
11:24	267
11:25	41
11:26	89
11:29	267

Scripture Index

13:10	50
13:13	203n75, 206
14:1	203n75, 206
15:8	83

1 Corinthians

9:9	51
10	21, 62
10:5-11	259
10:6	21
10:11	21, 22
15:25	162n75, 174

2 Corinthians

1:20	101
3	74, 110
3:3	25
3:6	24, 52, 98, 133
3:7	26
3:10-11	75
11:2	23n36
11:14	7

Galatians

3	133, 155
3-4	189
3:16	56
3:21-23	25
3:28	189
4	28, 37, 74, 110
4:1-2	64
4:21–5:1	37
4:24	27
5:6	192

Ephesians

1:13-14	62
1:20	162n75
1:20-22	174
4:8	171

Philippians

2:6-7	236
2:9	232
2:10-11	232

Colossians

1:4-5	62
3:1	162n75

2 Thessalonians

2:14	62

1 Timothy

1:5	50

2 Timothy

2:8	157n54

Hebrews

1	120, 164, 174, 175
1:1	184
1:1-2	139, 141, 145
1:2	176, 184
1:3	118n7, 119n7
1:3-13	175
1:5	175
1:5-13	174
1:5-14	176
1:5a	154
1:6	119, 164, 174
1:7	119
1:8	119
1:8-9	175
1:10-12	175
1:12-13	119
1:13	119n7, 174
1:14	119
1:16	119
2	174, 176
2:1-4	141, 260n135
2:2	184
2:3	184
2:5	119, 173, 174
2:5-9	16, 119, 128, 166, 208
2:6-8	120
2:6-8a	176
2:6a	173
2:6b-8	173
2:7	119, 174
2:8	128, 141
2:8b	176
2:8b-9	176
2:9	173, 175, 176
2:10	118, 131, 175
2:10-18	117, 118, 119n7, 120
2:11	175
2:12-13	145n6
2:14	118, 175
2:14-15	118
2:16	175
2:17	175
2:17-18	118
3-4	150, 154
3:7	145n6
3:7-11	130
3:7–4:11	130, 137, 139, 146, 153
3:9	155
3:12-15	130
3:13	139, 154
3:15	139
3:16–4:1	260
4:3	151
4:4	144n4
4:7	145n5
4:7-8	155
4:8	127, 131, 154
4:12	143
5:5-6	118
5:5-10	118, 119n7, 121
5:6	116n3, 162
5:7	118, 121
5:7-10	118
5:8	176
5:8-9	118
5:9	121, 176
5:9-10	118
5:10	116n3, 162
6:4-6	141
6:13	148n18
6:20	116n3, 162
7	162, 164, 165
7-10	116
7:3	165
7:7	164

SCRIPTURE INDEX

7:8	117	9:12	117	11:16	120, 127		
7:11	116n3, 123, 161, 165	9:12-20	145n5	11:17-19	121		
		9:14	117	11:19	120		
7:11-19	123	9:15-22	122	11:24-25	136		
7:12	123	9:19-20	145n5	11:26	120		
7:16	121, 165	9:23-24	124	11:32	116n2, 136		
7:17	116n3, 162	9:23-28	141	11:32-38	131		
7:18	123	9:24	117	11:35	120		
7:18-19	124	9:25-28	117, 124	11:39	127, 131		
7:19	123	9:28	140	11:39-40	138		
7:20-21	164	10:1	108n233, 117, 209	11:40	120		
7:21	116n3, 162	10:1-4	124, 134	12	131		
7:22	122	10:2	117	12:1	131n37, 137		
7:23	124	10:3	117	12:1-2	121		
7:23-25	117	10:5-7	145n6	12:1-3	131		
7:24-28	124	10:9	123	12:2	118, 119, 120		
7:25	165	10:10	209	12:5-6	144		
7:26	117	10:11	117, 124	12:5-13	131		
7:27	117, 124	10:12	119n7, 141	12:18-29	131, 260n135		
7:28	117, 165	10:14	117	12:18-22	71		
8	129	10:15	145n6	12:18-24	132, 139, 140		
8:1	118n7, 119n7	10:16	123	12:22-24	141		
8:1-2	117	10:17-18	123	12:24	122		
8:1-6	133	10:18	123	12:27	140		
8:5	124	10:25	139, 140	12:29	140		
8:6	122, 134	10:26-31	260n135	13:9	129		
8:7-13	122, 134	10:27	140	13:10	129		
8:8	123	10:31	140	13:20	122		
8:8-12	122	10:39	140				
8:8-13	77	11	63, 121, 126, 127, 128, 131, 136, 137n44, 156, 267n2	**1 John**			
8:9	123			2:16	169, 169n90		
8:10	123			2:20	256		
8:12	123			2:27	256		
8:13	123	11:1–12:2	120				
9	117	11:1	128	**Revelation**			
9:1-10	117, 134	11:4	120	5:5	7		
9:9	117	11:5	120, 144n4	21:1	56		
9:10	117, 129	11:7	120				
9:11	117	11:10-12	120				

www.ingramcontent.com/pod-product-compliance
Lightning Source LLC
Chambersburg PA
CBHW021136230426
43667CB00005B/133